Contents

1 **Introduction** 1
Pınar Gözen Ercan

2 **Sovereignty Redefined: The Promise and Practice of R2P** 13
Alex J. Bellamy

3 **Darfur: R2P and Dilemmas of Implementation** 33
Rahel Kessete Afewerky

4 **Kenya and Guinea: Preventive Strategies in R2P** 55
Ezgi Nur Koç

5 **Boko Haram in Nigeria: R2P and Non-State Armed Groups** 81
Çağlar Açıkyıldız

6 **Côte D'Ivoire: A Timely and Decisive R2P Action?** 107
Menent Savaş-Cazala

7 **Libya and Syria: The Protection of Refugees and R2P** 133
Selin Kul

8 **Gaza: R2P and Selective Implementation** 153
Özgecan Eskiduman

9 The Forsaken War in Yemen: R2P as Mere Rhetoric? 171
Haseenah Huurieyah Wan Rosli

10 Afghanistan: An R2P Concern 197
Sevgi Balkan-Şahin

11 The Rohingya of Myanmar: R2P, International Justice and Accountability 221
Vildan Taştemel Kapucu

12 'Three Evils' of Xinjiang: Suppression, Violent Separatism and R2P 245
İrem Karamık

13 Venezuela: An R2P Impasse? 271
Hazal Arslan

14 R2P at Twenty: A Shared Responsibility? 289
Pınar Gözen Ercan

Index 303

Notes on Contributors

Çağlar Açıkyıldız is a Ph.D. candidate at Pompeu Fabra University (UPF) and a Predoctoral Researcher FI at Institut Barcelona d'Estudis Internacionals (IBEI). He holds an M.A. in International Relations from Hacettepe University. He wrote his M.A. thesis on R2P and continues his research in this field.

Rahel Kessete Afewerky is a Ph.D. candidate at the Department of International Relations of Hacettepe University, Turkey. She researches on R2P and is a project assistant at the 2R2Ps for Sustainable Peace Research Group of Hacettepe University.

Hazal Arslan is a research assistant and a Ph.D. candidate at the Department of International Relations of Hacettepe University, Turkey. She also contributes as a research assistant in the 2R2Ps for Sustainable Peace Research Group of Hacettepe University.

Sevgi Balkan-Şahin is Associate Professor of International Relations at Çağ University, Turkey. Her research interests include international political economy and counter-hegemonic movements. She has published articles in journals such as *Cooperation and Conflict*, *Environment and Planning C: Politics and Space*, and *Journal of Balkans* and *Near Eastern Studies*.

Alex J. Bellamy is Professor of Peace and Conflict Studies and Director of the Asia Pacific Centre for the Responsibility to Protect at the University of Queensland, Australia. His most recent book is *Syria Betrayed: War, Atrocities, and the Failure of International Diplomacy* (Columbia, 2022).

Menent Savaş Cazala is Associate Professor of International Relations at Galatasaray University. She holds a Ph.D. from Paris II Panthéon-Assas University. Her research areas are humanitarian interventions, International Relations theories and peace and conflict studies.

Özgecan Eskiduman is a Ph.D. candidate at the University of Hacettepe, Turkey. She contributes to the 2R2Ps for Sustainable Peace Research Group of Hacettepe University as a research assistant.

Pınar Gözen Ercan is Associate Professor of International Relations. She is a Faculty Member at the Department of International Relations of Hacettepe University, Turkey. She is Director of the 2R2Ps for Sustainable Peace Research Group. She researches and publishes intensively on R2P.

Vildan Taştemel Kapucu is a Ph.D. candidate at the Department of International Relations of Hacettepe University, Turkey. She contributes to the 2R2Ps for Sustainable Peace Research Group of Hacettepe University as a project assistant.

İrem Karamık is a Ph.D. candidate at Hacettepe University, the Department of International Relations. She also is a Lecturer in Mardin Artuklu University and contributes as a research assistant in the 2R2Ps for Sustainable Peace Research Group. She was awarded Jean Monnet Scholarship and received her Master's degree from the University of Birmingham, UK.

Ezgi Nur Koç holds an M.A. from Hacettepe University. She researches on R2P and is a project assistant at the 2R2Ps for Sustainable Peace Research Group of Hacettepe University.

Selin Kul is a research assistant and a Ph.D. candidate at the Department of International Relations of Hacettepe University, Turkey. She researches on R2P and is a project assistant in the 2R2Ps for Sustainable Peace Research Group of Hacettepe University.

Haseenah Huurieyah Wan Rosli obtained her law degree from IIUM, Malaysia and thereafter completed her M.A. in Peace and Conflict Studies at Hacettepe University, Turkey with the thesis entitled 'Intervention by Invitation within the Responsibility to Protect Framework'. She is currently pursuing research in the same field.

Abbreviations

ACHPR	African Commission on Human and Peoples' Rights
ACLED	Armed Conflict Location and Event Data Project
ADB	Asian Development Bank
ALBA	*Alianza Bolivariana para los Pueblos de Nuestra América*
AMIS	African Union Mission in Sudan
ANDS	Afghanistan National Development Strategy
ARSA	Arakan Rohingya Salvation Army
ARTF	Afghanistan Reconstruction Trust Fund
ASEAN	Association of Southeast Asian Nations
AU	African Union
CCP	Concerned Citizens for Peace
CERD	United Nations Committee on the Elimination of Racial Discrimination
CIA	Central Intelligence Agency
CIPEV	Commission of Inquiry into Post-Election Violence
CJTF	Civilian Joint Task Force
COE	Council of Elders
COG	Commonwealth Observer Group
CPA	Comprehensive Peace Agreement
CTV	*Confederación de Trabajadores de Venezuela*
DDR	Disarmament, Demobilisation and Reintegration
DLF	Darfur Liberation Front
ECK	Electoral Commission of Kenya
ECOFORCE	ECOWAS Force for Côte d'Ivoire
ECOWARN	ECOWAS Warning and Response Network
ECOWAS	Economic Community of West African States

ETIM	East Turkestan Islamic Movement
ETR	East Turkistan Republic
EU	European Union
EUNAVFOR MED	European Union Naval Force Mediterranean
EUOM	European Observation Mission
EUPOL	EU Police Mission to Afghanistan
FAAC	Framework of Analysis for Atrocity Crimes
FANCI	National Armed Forces of Côte d'Ivoire (*Forces armées nationales de Côte d'Ivoire*)
FPI	Ivorian Popular Front (*Front Populaire Ivoirien*)
GCC	Gulf Cooperation Council
GCR2P	Global Centre for the Responsibility to Protect
GDP	Gross Domestic Product
GoF	The Group of Friends of the Responsibility to Protect
HRW	Human Rights Watch
ICC	International Criminal Court
ICG-G	International Contact Group on Guinea
ICISS	International Commission on Intervention and State Sovereignty
ICJ	International Court of Justice
ICRtoP	International Coalition for the Responsibility to Protect
IDA	International Development Association
IDF	Israeli Defence Forces
IDPs	Internally Displaced Persons
IGAD	Intergovernmental Authority on Development
IHL	International Humanitarian Law
IHRL	International Human Rights Law
IMF	International Monetary Fund
INA	Ili National Army
IOM	International Organization for Migration
IREC	Independent Review Commission
ISAF	International Security Assistance Force
ISIL	The Islamic State of Iraq and the Levant
ISIS	Islamic State of Iraq and Syria
ISKP	Islamic State-Khurasan Province
ISWAP	Islamic State West Africa Province
IvI	Intervention by Invitation
JEM	Justice and Equality Movement
KNDR	Kenyan National Dialogue and Reconciliation
KPTJ	Kenyans for Peace with Truth and Justice
LCBC	Lake Chad Basin Commission
LTTE	Tamil Tigers
MINUCI	United Nations Mission in Côte d'Ivoire

MNJTF	Multinational Joint Task
MPIGO	Ivorian Popular Movement of the Great West (*Mouvement Populaire Ivoirien du Grand Ouest*)
MPJ	Movement for Justice and Peace (*Mouvement pour la Paix et la Justice*)
NATO	North Atlantic Treaty Organization
NGOs	Non-Governmental Organizations
NIAC	Non-International Armed Conflict
NSAGs	Non-State Armed Groups
NSF	Nigerian Security Forces
OAS	Organization of American States
OAU	Organization of African Unity
OCHA	Office for the Coordination of Humanitarian Affairs
ODM	Orange Democratic Movement
OECD	Organization for Economic Cooperation and Development
OHCHR	Office of the High Commissioner for Human Rights
OTP	Office of the Prosecutor
P3	The United States, the United Kingdom and France
P5	Permanent Five Members of the United Nations Security Council
PA	Palestinian Authority
PDCI	Democratic Party of Côte d'Ivoire (*Parti Démocratique de Côte d'Ivoire*)
PDRY	People's Democratic Republic of Yemen
PDVSA	*Petróleos de Venezuela, S.A.*
PLO	Palestinian Liberation Organization
PNPA	Peace and National Partnership Agreement
PNU	Party of National Unity
PRC	People's Republic of China
PRTs	Provincial Reconstruction Teams
R2P	Responsibility to Protect
RDR	Rally of the Republicans (*Rassemblement des Républicains*)
RFIC	Republican Forces of Côte d'Ivoire
RHDR	Rally of Houphouëtists for Democracy and Peace Party
RRM	European Rapid Reaction Mechanism
SLM/A	Sudanese Liberation Movement/Army
TIP	Turkestan Islamic Party
TIRET	Turkish Islamic Republic of Eastern Turkistan
TJRC	Truth, Justice and Reconciliation Commission
TSJ	*Tribunal Supremo de Justicia*
UAE	United Arab Emirates
UK	United Kingdom

UKGFCO	United Kingdom Government Foreign & Commonwealth Office
UN	United Nations
UNAMA	United Nations Mission in Afghanistan
UNAMID	United Nations–African Union Mission in Darfur
UNASUR	*Unión de Naciones Suramericanas*
UNDP	United Nations Development Program
UNGA	United Nations General Assembly
UNHRC	United Nations Human Rights Council
UNMCPR	United Nations Media Coverage and Press Releases
UNOAU	United Nations Office to the African Union
UNOC	United Nations Operation in Congo
UNOCA	United Nations Regional Office for Central Africa
UNOCI	United Nations Operation in Côte d'Ivoire
UNOWAS	United Nations Office for West Africa and the Sahel
UNSC	United Nations Security Council
UNSG	United Nations Secretary-General
UPR	United Nations Universal Periodic Review
US	United States
USDS	United States Department of State
WSOD	World Summit Outcome Document
WWII	World War II
XUAR	Xinjiang Uyghur Autonomous Region
YAR	Yemen Arab Republic

CHAPTER 1

Introduction

Pınar Gözen Ercan

It has already been fifteen years since the Member States of the United Nations (UN) adopted the Responsibility to Protect (R2P) at the 2005 World Summit, where they made a commitment to protect populations from four mass atrocity crimes—namely genocide, war crimes, ethnic cleansing and crimes against humanity. December 2021 marked the twentieth anniversary of R2P, and this is an important milestone to reflect on the question of the norm's implementation and query whether or not R2P has turned into a shared responsibility since the International Commission on Intervention and State Sovereignty (ICISS) introduced it.

Over the last two decades, R2P has been the subject matter of numerous academic and political debates. Especially after the UN Secretary-General presented the first extensive report on the norm in 2009, a vast body of literature has emerged addressing R2P's normative evolution as well as different aspects of practice in the face of the humanitarian crises taking place on a large geographical scale. Nevertheless, most accounts of R2P have been focused only on specific aspects/pillars of the

P. Gözen Ercan (✉)
Department of International Relations, Hacettepe University, Ankara, Turkey

P. Gözen Ercan (ed.), *The Responsibility to Protect Twenty Years On*,
https://doi.org/10.1007/978-3-030-90731-0_1

norm, especially Pillar Three, or certain popular cases (such as Darfur and Libya).

Rich in its geographical scope, this edited volume provides a critical analysis of R2P practice over the last two decades by focusing on representative cases from different regions. Accordingly, it analyses not only recent and/or underexplored cases but also focuses on widely studied cases from a fresh and alternative perspective to shed light on the depth and scope of the norm as well as the variety of actors involved in the R2P processes and how they impact R2P practice. While doing so, it focuses on measures pertaining to the three-pillar implementation strategy of R2P and examines how and to what extent the three pillars have been practised. In this regard, diverging from a vast majority of previous accounts on R2P, this edited volume does not approach the cases as a success or failure of the R2P norm itself. By studying the background to the conflicts and making assessments on a pillar-by-pillar basis, each chapter addresses the root causes, traces the process of implementation, investigates the actions of the actors involved, identifies elements of success and failure and finally questions the sustainability of the protection provided to date. Accordingly, the two conceptual chapters of the book—Chapters 2 and 14—complement the analyses of the case chapters by providing an overall evaluation of R2P's first two decades as well as the progress achieved so far with the aim to draw lessons for future implementations of R2P.

Structure of the Book

In Chapter 2, Alex Bellamy provides an overview of R2P's first two decades as a normative standard. In this introductory piece, he reflects on the progress made and identifies the remaining challenges and limitations. After addressing difficult questions such as the recognition of R2P as a 'right' or 'duty', and shared expectations on the UN Security Council (UNSC)'s responsibility, Bellamy continues with a discussion on R2P's influence and norm compliance vis-à-vis the challenges posed by world politics. Establishing that politics both enables and constrains R2P's implementation, he continues with an evaluation of R2P's performance over the last twenty years. Hinting at the gap between expectations and practice, he reminds 'that because R2P is a practical norm—a principle embedded in world politics itself, not university textbooks—its use, framing and effectiveness are all buffeted by and contingent upon broader geopolitical forces', and hence, R2P's practice is constrained by the political context. Observing that R2P's track record has been mixed, as to the assessments of R2P he suggests to pursue 'a more differentiated account—comprising intent, practices and outcomes'. Following from this, the subsequent chapters focus on R2P's implementation—or lack thereof—in various humanitarian crises that have been taking place in different parts of the world with the aim to identify components of success and failure in R2P practices.

In Chapter 3, Rahel Kessete Afewerky focuses on the case of Darfur, which has been studied extensively in the R2P literature but still has a lot to offer in reflecting on the first two decades of R2P practice. In this chapter, Afewerky first focuses on the root causes of the genocide and how it unfolded and then analyses the international response to understand how and why the international community failed to prevent mass atrocities as well as to decisively react to the escalating humanitarian crisis despite the manifest failure of the State authorities. She suggests that although upholding the responsibility to protect was indeed a concern in the case of Darfur, in the early years of the crisis the conceptual ambiguities and lack of an agreed implementation strategy constituted the deficiencies that curtailed a timely and effective response. Then, she reflects on the consequences of the delayed response as well as the failure to take on the responsibility to rebuild to eradicate persisting tension in the region. Turning to the question of sustainable protection, Afewerky also touches upon the current situation and asks what is still missing in terms of the R2P approach to the continuing imminent threat of mass atrocity crimes in the region? She observes that the modicum of peace the hybrid peacekeeping forces achieved has fallen short with the untimely downsizing of the forces and complete withdrawal planned for June 2021. Accordingly, she posits that even a decade after the genocide, there is still no sustainable protection for the Darfuris, and a prominent reason for this is the lack of international engagement to rebuild.

In Chapter 4, Ezgi Nur Koç focuses on the cases of Kenya and Guinea, which are widely recognised as two successful cases of early implementation in R2P's history. To date, Kenya has found wide coverage in the R2P literature whereas the case of Guinea has rather been overlooked. Nevertheless, both cases still need to be further explored as to understand how and why early R2P action was possible in Kenya and Guinea, especially considering that lack of political will on the part of States has arguably been the main impediment to the protection of populations from mass atrocity crimes. Accordingly, aiming to take previous works one step further, Koç analyses these two successful prevention examples by focusing specifically on structural and direct prevention mechanisms employed by different agents of the international community. After setting the background as to why the two cases are deemed as successful efforts of prevention by studying the preventive mechanisms adopted in each case, she comparatively studies the situations in Kenya and Guinea by investigating the specific context of the two crises, the perpetrators and victims of the mass atrocity crimes, the agents/actors involved in the R2P processes as well as the structural and direct preventive measures employed. With her focus on situations of peacetime atrocities, Koç seeks for key drives and components for successful prevention. Accordingly, in the penultimate section, she studies what sorts of measures are likely to lead to successful prevention. Finally, she underlines the importance of a tailored approach that is applied in harmony by various actors, the role played by regional organisations in atrocity prevention, as well as root cause prevention for achieving sustainable protection.

In Chapter 5, Çağlar Açıkyıldız focuses on the ongoing case of Nigeria wherein escalating intercommunal violence due to Boko Haram insurgency remains a major R2P concern. Drawing attention to the limitations imposed by the state-centric focus on R2P implementation, he aims to understand the place of non-state armed groups (NSAGs) vis-à-vis the responsibility to protect populations from mass atrocity crimes. After addressing the root causes of the conflict and Boko Haram's influence in the region, he conducts a pillar-by-pillar analysis to demonstrate to what extent and how R2P has been implemented in the case of Nigeria. Under Pillar One, he studies the failure of the Nigerian authorities to uphold their responsibility and finds that such failure stemmed not only from incapability of the national authorities but also from the way they conduct their war against Boko Haram terror, which also resulted in atrocity crimes. Establishing the failure of the State to protect its population, he then focuses on the efforts of the international community under Pillar Two and discusses the effectiveness of the measures adopted. Afterwards, he moves on to discuss the potential impact of coercive measures under Pillar Three. Açıkyıldız concludes that the involvement of NSAGs complicates the implementation of R2P measures and that we need to step away from the state-centric perception of the responsibility to protect populations at the national and international levels. As the Nigerian case shows, the national and international measures have been constrained by traditional security concerns. Hence, Açıkyıldız posits that it is not the absence of a response or lack of political will per se, but rather responses that are not tailored to tackle mass atrocity crimes that have culminated in a failure to protect the Nigerian population.

In Chapter 6, Menent Savaş Cazala focuses on the case of Côte d'Ivoire, which is one of the exceptional cases in R2P history wherein the use of force was authorised by the UNSC, and explores the 2011 post-electoral crisis. Different from the case of Libya which marked the first instance of a UNSC-sanctioned military intervention under Pillar Three, in the case of Côte d'Ivoire, we see each pillar of R2P in action. Savaş Cazala argues that despite the failures to prevent the escalation of the conflict and provide protection for the Ivorian population at an earlier stage, R2P was successfully implemented under Pillar Three. Putting this assumption to test, she first provides a historical overview of the root causes of the humanitarian crisis. Then, she studies the case in the light of the measures implemented under each pillar of R2P and identifies the reasons why the national authorities and the international community failed to prevent the escalation of the situation. Afterwards, she analyses the election process that brought the country to the brink of civil war and scrutinises issues such as the impartiality of the UNSC as well as State consent in peace operations to paint us the big picture for a better understanding of the use of force under R2P. While she concludes that the UNSC's dismissal of its impartiality may be considered as the Council's readiness to act in cases of mass atrocity crimes, she also observes that not pursuing a rebuilding process and not addressing the root causes have resulted in the failure to achieve sustainable protection of the Ivorian population.

In Chapter 7, Selin Kul brings a fresh perspective to two widely studied cases, namely Libya and Syria which remain a primary R2P concern after a decade of internal unrest and international involvement of various sorts in both States. Most often, Libya and Syria are discussed in relation to each other as the military intervention in the former was used as a pretext to block a UNSC decision on the latter. While both humanitarian crises have been at the centre of debates regarding coercive measures of Pillar Three, an important aspect common to both has been neglected in the growing literature. Hence, approaching the issue from an underexplored aspect, Kul studies R2P's implementation in Libya and Syria focusing on the protection of refugees. Providing a background on the events and the international response that have culminated in an unprecedented refugee protection crisis, she then establishes the link between R2P and refugee protection. Through a pillar-by-pillar analysis, she examines the responses to the refugee protection crises that emerged with the civil wars in Libya and Syria. She first studies how the host States have carried out their responsibility towards refugees coming from both countries. Moreover, she sheds light on the problems the host States have been facing in protecting the refugees they have received, and links them with the responsibility of the international community. Accordingly, she scrutinises the international response delivered primarily under Pillar Two and then discusses alternative proposals such as resettlement under Pillar Three. Kul concludes by arguing that in cases of threat of and/or actual mass atrocity crimes, the protection of refugees constitutes an inherent part of the R2P framework, which if internalised as a mindset would contribute to sustainable and responsible protection under R2P.

In Chapter 8, Özgecan Eskiduman focuses on a highly politicised case, Gaza, which has received little R2P attention to date. This case presents a challenge in terms of how we should understand the notion of sovereignty as responsibility, as it is possible to connect three different sovereign authorities to the protection of the Gazan population. In this regard, Eskiduman specifically focuses on the devastating impact of two major Israeli military operations, namely Operation Cast Lead and Operation Protective Edge, in relation to R2P. For both operations, serious human rights violations amounting to mass atrocity crimes were reported by independent UN bodies. Nevertheless, due to the politicised nature of the Israeli-Palestinian conflict, and deeming the issue an interstate crisis, the international community has been selective in terms of applying R2P measures. Eskiduman argues that Gaza presents a test case for R2P's implementation, and it allows us to shed light on the practical implications of a complicated distribution of political power on fulfilling the responsibility to protect populations. After providing a general background on the Israeli-Palestinian conflict, Eskiduman first focuses on Pillar One and discusses whose responsibility it is to protect the population of Gaza. She demonstrates that Hamas, the Palestinian Authority and Israel, due to the control they assume over the territory, have a Pillar One responsibility. Given their manifest failure to protect the Gazan population, Eskiduman continues with an analysis of the international community's responsibilities under Pillars Two and Three and demonstrates how political constraints and neo-colonial drives have led to the failure of the international community to protect the Gazan population. Finally, she argues that R2P is not inherently a neo-colonial tool of interference but can be used as such. She concludes that R2P's selective implementation stemming from the structural limitations of the UNSC, and specifically the policies Permanent Members (P5) pursue constrain the attempts of various agents of the international community in fulfilling their responsibility to protect, and block any sort of R2P action even in most obvious R2P situations.

In Chapter 9, Haseenah Huurieyah Wan Rosli focuses on the case of Yemen, which is another underexplored R2P crisis in the literature. As Wan Rosli shows, this case helps a critical overview of R2P's scope of implementation in two distinctive ways. The first is the involvement of non-state actors since it is primarily the Houthi armed rebels who are allegedly the perpetrators of the war crimes and crimes against humanity committed in Yemen. The second is that Yemen constitutes an exceptional example of Intervention by Invitation (IvI) in the two-decades-long history of R2P. Considering the rapidly increasing number of fatalities as proof of the failure to protect the Yemeni population, she studies the national and international responses step-by-step through the lens of the three-pillar implementation strategy of R2P. After she critically assesses the attempts to prevent the outbreak of mass atrocity crimes, she focuses on the use of force by the Saudi-led coalition forces upon the invitation of President Hadi. Wan Rosli demonstrates that while the R2P language has been instrumentalised in justifying calls for and carrying out the Saudi-led military operation, the true motivation was reinstating President Hadi. Accordingly, in the penultimate section of the chapter, she scrutinises the (mis)use of force by international agents on the basis of the guidelines laid down in Secretary-General's 2004 Report of the High-level Panel on Threats, Challenges and Change. Following from this, she concludes that the Yemeni case brings to the fore the question of accountability not only for the States but also for the international community and suggests that the 'five basic criteria of legitimacy' should be considered for inclusion in R2P's implementation strategy to ensure responsible uses of force.

In Chapter 10, Sevgi Balkan-Şahin studies the case of Afghanistan, which has been the scene of relentless conflict with various sorts of international involvement for decades. While the measures adopted in Afghanistan have not been intended as an R2P response, and R2P has not been invoked in this specific situation, Balkan-Şahin demonstrates that they very much relate to R2P, specifically Pillars One and Two. After providing a general background on the case, she studies in detail the measures undertaken by the Afghan governments to build national resilience. Given the complexity of the situation as well as the mass atrocities perpetrated both by government and non-government forces, she turns to the Pillar Two responsibilities of the international community. Dwelling into the efforts of the international community in the form of military assistance, political support and development aid to help the Afghan State to ensure peace and stability, Balkan-Şahin evaluates to what extent the international community has achieved the goal of the protection of the Afghan population. She observes that the international efforts and measures centred on counterterrorism has undermined R2P objectives and resulted in a failure to provide a sustainable solution to the Afghan population's aggravated suffering. She concludes that no matter what the level of involvement is and how abundant resources are, when humanitarian objectives are undermined by competing security-oriented agendas such as counterterrorism, and measures are carried out in the absence of the R2P mindset, it is possible to achieve neither sustainable protection nor development.

In Chapter 11, Vildan Taştemel Kapucu addresses the ongoing crisis in Myanmar wherein the concerned population itself has been calling for R2P action in rallies. She first provides a background on this prolonged crisis, which has drawn increasing interest in the international community's agenda only as of the 2010s. Afterwards, she conducts a pillar-by-pillar analysis to reveal the responsibility of national authorities and the responses of the international community. Acknowledging the uniqueness of this case due to the de facto stateless status of the Rohingya, she first establishes that statelessness is not an impediment to the application of R2P, and thus, the State of Myanmar has full responsibility over the Rohingya population. Demonstrating the unwillingness on the part of the state authorities to protect the Rohingya from mass atrocities, she continues with a discussion within the framework of Pillar Two as to why assistance and capacity-building efforts have also failed both at the regional and international levels. Subsequently, with a focus on Pillar Three, and specifically the method of judicial settlement as a peaceful measure, Kapucu discusses the actions taken through the international justice system—namely the International Criminal Court, the International Court of Justice and universal jurisdiction. She suggests that efforts pertaining to the search for justice by utilising the international justice system have helped to raise awareness about the case and let the voice of the victims heard by the international community raising hopes for accountability and justice for the Rohingya. Accordingly, she concludes that the international justice system plays an instrumental and complementary role in the realisation of R2P and helps to cope with the issue of impunity by holding the perpetrators accountable for the mass atrocity crimes they committed, which in the mid- to long-term may contribute to sustainable protection.

In Chapter 12, İrem Karamık addresses an overlooked and a highly politicised case among R2P crises, namely the human rights conditions of the Turkic-originated Uyghur minorities in Xinjiang Uyghur Autonomous Region, China. To understand the nature of this humanitarian crisis, she first traces the historical roots of the Uyghur case vis-à-vis the policies pursued by China in the region. Tracing the geographical shift followed by a population resettlement and Uyghurs' nation-building venture trapped in China's 'new dominion', Karamık introduces the case of the Uyghurs, which is interwoven with certain-times-violent self-determination attempts and their harsh backlash to the extent of cultural suppression, religious inhibition and mass detention. Accordingly, she places China's policies under an R2P focus and pursues a pillar-by-pillar analysis to unfold how and to what extent an R2P approach has been present in tackling this humanitarian crisis. With her Pillar One analysis, she reveals the Chinese authorities' failure to fulfil their responsibility towards the Uyghur population. She then continues with a discussion of the roles that the international community can play to end or help ease the Uyghurs' suffering under Pillars Two and Three. Subsequently, she discusses the consequences of the deadlock caused by China as one of the P5 wielding the veto power. In conclusion, drawing attention to the blind spots in the R2P practice, Karamık argues that re-thinking the implementation strategy of R2P as to the positions of the P5 and the UNSC are vital for effective protection of populations. She further suggests that the link between acts of self determination of peoples and R2P should be explored for purposes of root cause prevention.

In Chapter 13, Hazal Arslan studies a current crisis from the Latin American region, namely the case of Venezuela, which has been a situation of concern since 2014. While there is a mounting literature on the Venezuelan crisis addressing the political and economic aspects of the situation, this case remains underexplored from an R2P point of view despite evidence of State-sanctioned persecution that may amount to mass atrocity crimes. Arslan begins her R2P analysis by providing background information on the current political and economic crisis Venezuela is in. Following from this, she conducts a pillar-by-pillar analysis to identify components of national and international action relating to R2P's implementation in the ongoing crisis. After she demonstrates the failure of the State authorities to protect the Venezuelan population, Arslan continues with an evaluation of the measures undertaken by the international community and their impact from a Pillar Two lens. Subsequently, she discusses the effectiveness as well as the consequences of the coercive measures adopted with respect to Pillar Three and reflects on the negative impact of the sanctions imposed vis-à-vis the humanitarian aspects of the crisis. Arslan concludes that the humanitarian crisis in Venezuela has been ignored and underestimated by the international community for too long for any preventive measure to be undertaken in a timely and effective manner. She considers this not as a failure of the R2P norm itself but as the failure of the international community and the national authorities. Finally, she asserts that in the absence of an R2P mindset in the policies pursued towards Venezuela and the persisting crisis, the self-interested motives of the involved internal and external actors have resulted in the failure to protect the Venezuelan population.

Following the comprehensive case analyses of the preceding chapters that cover the first two decades of R2P, in lieu of conclusion, I ask in Chapter 14 whether or not R2P has become a shared responsibility? Countering the common assumption of the critics that 'R2P is a failed norm', I scrutinise the primary reasons for the failure of States and the international community to protect populations in different parts of the world. To this end, reflecting on the gap between growing verbal support for R2P among the Member States of the UN and actual practices in R2P related crises, I aim to assess components of success and failure in R2P implementation based on the case analyses of this edited volume. Following from this, I conclude with a discussion on what is required for sustainable protection of populations in a dynamic global governance structure and to turn R2P into a shared responsibility, and argue for the value and viability of R2P despite all its imperfections.

References

United Nations General Assembly (UNGA). (2005, October 24). *Resolution adopted by the General Assembly on 16 September 2005, 60/1.* 2005 World Summit Outcome, A/Res/60/1.

United Nations General Assembly (UNGA). (2009, January 12). *Implementing the responsibility to protect*. Report of the Secretary-General, A/63/677.

CHAPTER 2

Sovereignty Redefined: The Promise and Practice of R2P

Alex J. Bellamy

In a 1999 opinion piece written for *The Economist* shortly after North Atlantic Treaty Organization's (NATO) humanitarian intervention in Kosovo, United Nations (UN) Secretary-General Kofi Annan presented the case for a seemingly new conception of sovereignty: 'sovereignty as responsibility'. Sovereignty was being redefined, Annan (1999a) argued:

> States are now widely understood to be instruments at the service of their peoples, and not vice-versa. At the same time individual sovereignty—by which I mean the fundamental freedom of each individual, enshrined in the Charter of the UN and subsequent international treaties—has been enhanced by a renewed and spreading consciousness of individual rights. When we read the Charter today, we are more than ever conscious that its aim is to protect individual human beings, not to protect those who abuse them.

A. J. Bellamy (✉)
University of Queensland, St Lucia, QLD, Australia

P. Gözen Ercan (ed.), *The Responsibility to Protect Twenty Years On*,
https://doi.org/10.1007/978-3-030-90731-0_2

The intervention in Kosovo was an imperfect expression of this duty to protect, imperfect because NATO had acted without the authorisation of the UN Security Council (UNSC) since Russia and China, two of the Council's permanent members, had refused to grant their consent. Yet there was another country seared into Annan's mind, whose horrors five years earlier had been so much more extensive than Kosovo's: Rwanda. For all its imperfections, a clumsy intervention in Kosovo was far preferable to callous non-intervention in Rwanda. The comparative scale of the mass graves in those two countries spoke for themselves.

Two days after this article was published, Annan addressed the plenary session of the UN General Assembly (UNGA). He wanted Member States to figure out a way of harnessing the humanitarian activism that had helped deliver Kosovo out of war and mass atrocities without disrupting the essential rules that made peaceful co-existence in world politics possible. So, Annan challenged the organisation's Member States to embrace this new conception of sovereignty and realise an accommodation between the humanitarian responsibilities of sovereignty and the traditional rules of non-interference so important to maintaining a basic degree of order in world politics. He expressed the challenge thus:

> To those for whom the greatest threat to the future of international order is the use of force in the absence of a Security Council mandate, one might ask…in the context of Rwanda: If, in those dark days and hours leading up to the genocide, a coalition of States had been prepared to act in defence of the Tutsi population but did not receive prompt Council authorization, should such a coalition have stood aside and allowed the horror to unfold?
>
> To those for whom the Kosovo action heralded a new era when States and groups of States can take military action outside the established mechanisms for enforcing international law, one might ask: Is there not a danger of such interventions undermining the imperfect, yet resilient, security system created after the Second World War, and of setting dangerous precedents for future interventions without a clear criterion to decide who might invoke these precedents, and in what circumstances? (Annan, 1999b)

Annan insisted that the state was the servant of the people and that state sovereignty therefore implied a responsibility to protect. In fact, this idea was not new at all—sovereignty has always entailed responsibilities as well as rights (Glanville, 2009). As he saw it, the UN's role should be to assist States in the fulfilment of their responsibilities and achievement of their sovereignty. This much was clearly set out in the UN Charter, Annan explained. The question, however, was one of how to determine what the responsibility to protect entailed and how it should be implemented.

The UNGA's response to Annan's challenge came in the form of the Responsibility to Protect (R2P) principle, unanimously agreed in 2005 and reaffirmed many times since by the UNSC and the UN Human Rights Council. In a remarkably short space of time, R2P was transformed from a loose concept proposed by the International Commission on Intervention and State Sovereignty (ICISS) in 2001, into an international norm endorsed by the world's governments and usefully employed in more than a dozen situations. It is a principle that has come to frame how large sections of the world's governments think about the prevention of atrocity crimes and responses to them. Translating that principle into consistent practice has proven difficult, however, and the practical record is mixed. That is primarily because R2P does not sit apart from world politics, but is a part of world politics. Even when actors agree on the substance of R2P as a principle, they may still disagree radically on the best way of achieving its ambitions or on whether doing so is more, or less, important than achieving other goals, such as protecting allies, maintaining international stability and order and pursuing geopolitical ambitions. Justin Morris (2015) coined the apt phrase 'dual responsibility' to highlight that the great powers have not just a responsibility to protect but also a responsibility to maintain international peace and security and emphasised that there are times in which the two imperatives might not correspond. Most proponents of R2P—including Annan himself—believed that agreement on the principle would be the start, not the endpoint, of a struggle to redefine sovereignty to make it better suited to protecting peoples from genocide and mass atrocities and less suited to protecting their tormentors. Others, though, seemed to think that the principle itself should carry agency and that R2P's evident inability to change *everything* about the politics of protection in the space of its first two decades meant there was no possibility of changing *anything*.

Taking Kofi Annan's ambition as a starting point, this chapter examines the past two decades of thought and practice on R2P. It demonstrates that whilst there have been significant ideational, political and operational shifts during that time, significant challenges remain, and it offers a reminder that because R2P is a practical norm—a principle embedded in world politics itself, not university textbooks—its use, framing and effectiveness are all buffeted by and contingent upon broader geopolitical forces.

A Normative Standard

Since its adoption in 2005, R2P has become part of the diplomatic language used, albeit unevenly and with patchy results, by international society to prevent and respond to atrocity crimes. Described as an 'emerging norm' by the ICISS in 2001, R2P became established as an international norm over the following two decades. That is because there are now 'shared expectations', arising out of R2P, within international society, that (1) States should protect their own populations from genocide, war crimes, ethnic cleansing and crimes against humanity, (2) that States ought to encourage and assist one another to that end and (3) that international society should act to protect populations when States are manifestly failing to protect their own. Since R2P is a norm, failure to exercise this responsibility should attract criticism—if it did not, we would be unable to describe R2P thus. The combination of practice, in which measures have been adopted in the hope of fulfilling R2P, and the ongoing consideration of the norm in the UNGA and UNSC have been central to its emergence by helping establish precedents and shared expectations which limit the decisions that can be legitimately taken in response to genocide and mass atrocities, making it more difficult (but by no means impossible) for those institutions charged with protection responsibilities, most notably the UNSC, to avoid acting upon them altogether. In that context, R2P constitutes moral progress in terms of its capacity to balance the competing demands of justice and order, serving as both a limited license for intervention (properly authorised and conducted) and a leash against unfettered interventionism (Doyle, 2015).

To what extent do States recognise a 'right' or a 'duty' to act on R2P? The question of 'rights' is the more straightforward of these issues. In contrast to earlier times, when the UNSC's authority over domestic matters was challenged as being contrary to the principle of non-interference (see Wheeler, 2000), no state now disputes the right of the UNSC to adopt measures in respect to R2P or the right of individual States and regional organisations to provide encouragement and assistance to States on a consensual basis. Moreover, not even the more conservative UNSC members, such as China and Russia, now openly question the appropriateness of including R2P matters on the Council's agenda. When justifying their first UNSC vetoes on the crisis in Syria in October 2011, Russia argued that it undertook 'intensive, constructive efforts to develop an effective response on the part of the Council' whilst China called for the Council to do more to encourage domestic reform and indicated its support for an alternative draft resolution focused on political dialogue. Neither questioned whether it was legitimate for the UNSC to involve itself in Syria, despite the fact that the situation was then still a largely domestic affair.

The associated question of whether there exists a 'duty' to protect populations in other countries from atrocity crimes is altogether more difficult to untangle. It is also an issue that has vexed and divided moral philosophers (compare Glanville, 2021; Pattison, 2010; Roff, 2013). Whilst the 2005 agreement on R2P did not extend international society's legal rights with respect to intervention and interference in the domestic affairs of States, it did award special responsibilities to the UNSC. These agreements have made it more difficult—though certainly not impossible—for the UNSC to justify complete inaction in the face of atrocity crimes. In Paragraph 139 of the World Summit Outcome Document, which endorsed R2P, States acknowledged an international responsibility to 'use appropriate diplomatic, humanitarian and other peaceful means, in accordance with Chapters VI and VIII of the Charter of the United Nations, to help protect populations from genocide, war crimes, ethnic cleansing and crimes against humanity'. This responsibility should be exercised 'through the United Nations' and specifically through Chapters VI (peaceful measures), VII (enforcement measures) and VIII (regional arrangements) of the UN Charter, awarding a special role to the UNSC. Since 2005, most UN Member States have at some time acknowledged these responsibilities in their statements to the UNGA or UNSC. For example, even China has recognised that international community ought to take steps to prevent genocide and mass atrocities, arguing that 'the international community *should* use dialogue, good offices and mediation, among other tools, to promote the settlement of disputes and differences and contain the escalation of conflict and halt genocide and other crimes against humanity at source' (UNSC, 2014, p. 12, emphasis added).

Another key normative test is the extent to which clear compliance failures—in this case failures to exercise the international responsibility to protect—attract criticism. Because norms set expectations of appropriate behaviour, it is somewhat easier to see them at work when they are violated than when they are complied with. If clear failures to comply with a norm do not elicit criticism from within the relevant society, this is an obvious sign that the shared expectations related to it are non-existent, weak or else easily trumped by competing norms. Conversely, criticism is a clear indication that a society judges a course of action to be inappropriate because it does not comply with its norms.

The most obvious failure to comply with international expectations associated with R2P has been in Syria, where the UNSC has been too divided to lead a timely and decisive response. The UNGA responded to this ineffectualness by signalling its strong disapproval of the Council's actions and endorsing a more resolute approach. Large majorities in the Assembly voted to recommend many of the measures vetoed in the UNSC. On 26 February 2012, the Assembly voted by 137 to 12 (with 17 abstentions) to condemn 'widespread and systematic human rights violations by the Syrian authorities', to call on all armed groups to end the violence, and to support the Arab League peace initiative (UNGA, 2012). Among the supporters of that resolution were many States from the global south, including Brazil, India, South Africa and Pakistan. In addition, the UNGA, including States such as Brazil and South Africa, has expressly criticised the UNSC's handling of the crisis in Syria. The UN Human Rights Council's Commission of Inquiry on Syria, led by Paulo Pinheiro, argued that the UNSC 'bears responsibility' for allowing the continuation of war crimes and crimes against humanity by all sides (see Bellamy, 2021). All this is clear evidence of shared expectations within international society about the UNSC's responsibility to do what it can to protect populations from atrocity crimes and evince a shared sense that in the case of Syria the Council has failed. That widely shared sense of failure is explicable in part because R2P has become a shared normative standard.

When Norms Meet World Politics

There are practical limits to what norms—any norms—can achieve. Some of these limits are inherent to norms themselves: they can influence behaviour and shape social reactions to different types of behaviour, but they cannot determine behaviour. Some actors may be willing to pay the social, political and material costs of non-compliance, perhaps judging that those costs are likely to be lesser than the costs of compliance. Moreover, R2P does not exist in a normative vacuum—it cohabits with other norms, interests and cherished values which sometimes collide, forcing political leaders to choose between different sets of norms or prioritise perceived interests at their expense. It is also important to bear in mind that even with the best will, there are some basic practical limitations to what outsiders can do to protect populations from harm at a reasonable cost and risk. Thus, to write—as I have done—that R2P has begun to change the world, is not to say that it has changed *everything*, that it has solved all the problems of mass atrocity crimes in perpetuity, no norm could ever do that. But it is to say that by establishing shared normative standards, R2P has created change. The world of mass atrocity prevention and response does not look today as it did in 2000.

A norm's capacity to shape behaviour is in part influenced by its specificity. In general, the more precisely a norm indicates the behaviour it expects in a given situation, the stronger its 'compliance-pull' (Franck, 1990, p. 52). That is part of the reason why R2P's first pillar (States should protect their own populations) has emerged as a somewhat stronger norm than the third pillar (the international community should respond to atrocities in a timely and decisive fashion): the first pillar is very clear about who is responsible for what and violations are relatively obvious; the third pillar is less clear on who has responsibility (though the UNSC clearly has a special responsibility) and more ambiguous still on what precisely is required in any given situation.

Beyond that, much like the law itself, norms cannot by themselves *compel* people or States to take particular actions or physically *prevent* them from doing so. Norms, like law, depend upon physical institutions, such as a police force, judiciary and prisons system, to achieve these effects and neither has ever been able to do so perfectly. Moreover, because we inhabit a system of sovereign States rather than a single world government, the international community has few of the institutions usually associated with law enforcement—the closest we have to such an institution is the UNSC. Instead, therefore, international laws and norms influence behaviour indirectly by shaping governments' own judgements about appropriate and inappropriate behaviour and influencing the way in which other governments will respond to that behaviour. Behaviour compliant with shared norms is likely to be welcomed and praised; non-compliance is likely to be met with criticism, punishment and social exclusion. Just as some people can cope better with ostracism than others, so some States are more able than others to withstand these costs and might calculate that what they can secure by breaking the norms is more valuable to them than what they expect to lose. But there are limits to the costs that even the most powerful actors can withstand—as the terrible price the US paid for its invasion of Iraq, widely seen as illegitimate, shows only too well. To further complicate matters, what counts as a breach of a norm, and the consequences that flow from that, are not decided objectively or in mechanistic fashion. Instead, judgements are contingent on their context and are highly political—usually influenced by situations themselves.

There are at least four particularly relevant factors that shape judgements about norm compliance and violation (Bellamy, 2012). First, how a situation is perceived at the time, which is based on usually imperfect contemporaneous knowledge. Second, the nature of the relationships involved. *Who* is presenting an argument about norm compliance/violation may sometimes matter more than what is being argued. We are more likely to be persuaded by those we think are good and legitimate than those who we do not hold in such high esteem. Third, decision-making sovereignty remains important, so how the issue relates to the interests and priorities of relevant States matters. The importance attached to the issue or the norm relative to other concerns might dictate whether someone is prepared to turn a blind eye to norm violations or react more strongly to them. Fourth, another nod to decision-making sovereignty, the relative power of the various groups involved. The powerful are less likely to be punished or socially excluded because doing so is often more expensive to other members of the society costs on other society. What is more, the powerful are often able to protect their friends and allies.

That international community is comprised of States that jealously guard their own sovereignty, pursue their own interests (however defined), privilege domestic over foreign concerns creates structural obstacles for atrocity prevention. The UN's activities are overseen by *political* (as opposed to judicial) organs comprised of sovereignty-wielding Member States whose ideologies, interests, allegiances and preferences influence their positions. Most significantly, these States are often unwilling to commit more than very limited resources to the prevention of atrocities in foreign countries. The central issues here are often labelled 'political will', though that term can be used to obscure as much as to illuminate. At stake is the state's determination to cling on to its prerogative to decide for itself how to respond to atrocities, unconstrained by international norms and other considerations. One facet of the problem is that States sometimes judge that their own interests are best served by not preventing atrocity crimes. For example, the link between Russia's obstinate support for the Assad regime in Syria and its political, strategic and economic interests in the region are well known. The UN's position on

Sri Lanka in 2008–2009 was made particularly difficult by the collusion of the world's major powers in shielding the Sri Lankan government from blame. This collusion derived from a shared interest in the elimination of the Tamil Tigers (LTTE). Indeed, historically, the UN has struggled to assert its primacy in situations where the interests of powerful States, especially Permanent Members of the UNSC, are engaged (e.g. US on Iraq; Russia on Chechnya).

Norms, then, are therefore understandings of appropriate behaviour shared by members of a group. They influence behaviour indirectly through social pressures that promote compliance and threats of punishment and exclusion. As a result, they do not determine or compel behaviour and their role in any given situation is influenced by a range of other contextual factors. As self-interested actors prioritise their own interests or those of their governing elites. As such, they are generally reluctant to commit extensive resources to prevent atrocity crimes in other countries. The issue here is not whether governments support atrocity prevention as a goal, but the depth of their support relative to their other goals—including cherished domestic objectives such as health care and social welfare. Political and diplomatic capital is also a finite resource. Sometimes, States may judge that trade-offs have to be made to achieve the greatest good or least harm overall. For example, one of the reasons States adopted an initially cautious response to Syria's crisis was their fear that instability there might provoke a rise of jihadism. As it transpired, the emergence of extremists was aided and abetted by international society's failure to properly support Syria's mainstream opposition and peaceful protestors at the outset. It is not surprising, therefore, that the application and role of a norm such as R2P in actual crises are shaped in profound ways by the political context at hand. It is the responsibility of those charged with implementing R2P to think creatively about how better to utilise these contextual factors to support implementation of the norm.

These different political considerations have such a significant effect on the implementation of R2P because not only do the UN's principal organs play a critical role in determining the mandates and policies, the effectiveness of the UN's resolutions and the work of its Secretariat, missions and country-teams depend to a great extent on their capacity to *persuade* Member States to implement their decisions. Although the UN's Secretariat, agencies, funds and programs can operate without specific mandates from the political organs, the UN has limited material resources at its direct disposal for atrocity prevention and therefore relies almost entirely on the goodwill of Member States to provide the (sometimes extensive) resources required. As a result of all this, even the implementation of UNSC decisions has historically been patchy at best. Such unevenness is an inevitable consequence of practical implementation. The only way to avoid it is to leave the status quo intact. That was not what Annan hoped to achieve.

Yet even when the normative and political context allows for it, the effective protection of populations from atrocity crimes confronts significant practical challenges. It is important to be upfront about what these challenges are—since some advocates and many critics of R2P alike tend to underestimate the practical scale and immense difficulty of the task of preventing atrocities and protecting vulnerable populations. Preventing and ending atrocities is difficult and demanding. Even if there were abundant enthusiasm, consensus and resources available for protection and atrocity prevention, it would likely still prove impossible to prevent every atrocity and protect every individual—absent some fundamental reforms to the human condition. To understand the operational practice of R2P, we need to appreciate the significant limitations imposed by the global context.

Many internal conflicts are not readily susceptible to outside mediation whether (as in the case of Rwanda or Iraq [Islamic State]) because one or more of the parties have embarked implacably on a course of action leading to atrocities or (as in the case of Syria and South Sudan) because a situation is so complex and fraught with danger as to defy easy resolution. International efforts can facilitate protection and prevention either through massive and costly interventions or where there is local will and capacity, and the levels and types of resilience can be different in different parts of a country producing different patterns of violence, but the so-called structural or 'root' causes of atrocities are often not easily influenced by external actors. While outsiders can play important enabling and facilitative roles, foreign assistance cannot by itself achieve structural change except through massive intervention and even then, there are inherent limits and high risks. As Scott Straus (2015, p. 326) observed, '[i]n the long-run … domestic actors are likely to be more effective than international ones at prevention'. Well-targeted operations can sometimes protect populations or prevent atrocity crimes (e.g. as in Côte d'Ivoire and Kenya).

Structural reforms to better manage global forces such as economic inequality or the arms trade may have some positive effect, but they are not a panacea. That is because the primary determinants of violence or peace typically rest within individual countries. Countries confronted by very similar systematic challenges (such as poverty, inequality and the accessibility of arms) can produce very dissimilar outcomes when it comes to the prevention of mass atrocities. Compare, for example, the very different trajectories of Rwanda and Malawi in the 1990s and consider that measured in terms of GDP per capita, at the turn of the decade, Rwanda was the more prosperous of the two. Or compare Yugoslavia and Vietnam in 1989. Both were awash with arms and legacies of past violence (Vietnam's much more recent), but Yugoslavia's economic position was much stronger than Vietnam's, its GDP per capita some 400 times greater. Yet it was Yugoslavia that experienced mass atrocities in the 1990s, not Vietnam. Critics point to World Bank structural adjustments as principal causes of bloodshed in both Rwanda and Yugoslavia. As ill-advised as this policy was, many other countries including Mexico, the Philippines, Zimbabwe and even Malawi, underwent similar reforms—with similarly disastrous short-term effects—without, however, succumbing to mass violence and atrocities. In short, it is largely what happens at the national level that determines whether or not global systemic conditions contribute to mass atrocity onset. If the connection between the global systemic level and the onset of atrocity crimes were causal, we would expect to see much less variation than we do in the experiences of similarly situated places.

From the UN's perspective, the problem of external influence is compounded by the fact that the global organisation tends to be confronted only by the world's most difficult cases. Situations usually reach the UNSC only when others have tried, and failed, to resolve them. As a rule of thumb, where conflicts have an easy remedy, solutions tend to be found at the local, national or regional level and without the need for major international involvement or the UN. The world body tends to assume the lead only on those crises for which others have found no solution. In such circumstances, a modest success rate might partly reflect the sheer difficulty of the cases presented to the UN system.

Another limiting factor is that R2P operates in a world of finite global capacity and competes with other cherished norms and values for resources. The problem of limited resources is compounded by the ongoing climate of financial scarcity caused by the COVID-19 pandemic, though it precedes that crisis too. It is a truism that case-for-case, preventing atrocities is cheaper than responding and rebuilding societies afterwards. But things are not so simple in practice. According to some critics (e.g. Valentino, 2011), a fully comprehensive approach to atrocity prevention, comprising efforts to reduce the underlying structural and systemic sources of risk as well to respond to imminent emergencies, could be judged to require determined action to raise living standards, improve governance institutions and resolve disputes in every country thought to be harbouring factors associated with risk, rather than in only those countries where risks are imminent or violence present. Pursued holistically, the costs of implementing this agenda on a global scale could be substantial. Of course, these concerns need to be set against substantial evidence pointing to the massive costs associated with violent conflict. What is more, the mathematics are further complicated by the fact that in most situations 'preventive' and 'responsive' action are not easily distinguished from one another. Most often, international engagement with specific crises includes elements of both prevention and response, sliding up and down a continuum of mindsets and measures rather than being easily distinguishable as one or the other. Yet the critique does point to the fact that governments confront multiple calls on their resources and that rationing in some form or other is both inevitable and necessary.

All this means that the implementation of R2P is political, and controversial, all the way down. Indeed, it could not be anything but. The practice of R2P is both enabled and constrained by politics and can generate acute controversies and disputes by, for instance, requiring that some States be identified as being at risk of atrocities and demanding actions that some governments might object to (see Sharma & Welsh, 2016). Even long-term preventive measures entail a significant degree of intrusion into the domestic affairs of States, which is not likely to be always welcome because it could, among other things, empower and legitimise a government's domestic opponents (Purdekova, 2019). In this context, it is important to recognise that 'in the nation-state era there will be limits to both the practicality and the wisdom of formally breaching the proper boundaries of sovereignty' (Luck, 2009, pp. 20–21). Typically, States jealously guard their sovereign prerogatives and are sensitive about perceived incursions on their rights or criticisms of their conduct or domestic conditions. As such, they rarely invite assistance or look kindly upon external efforts to prevent atrocities within their jurisdiction. As a result, it is false to assume that preventive action will always be less contentious than intervention once atrocities have erupted. The general unwillingness of States to recognise atrocity risks at home and cooperate with international actors constitutes a significant barrier to effective early prevention, much of which must be done with the support and consent of the state. This, of course, can make prevention just as politically sensitive and highly contentious as armed intervention itself.

In practice, the field is plagued by the problem of uncertainty since the precise consequences of an action or inaction are unknowable in advance. This dilemma stems from the fact that despite significant advances in conflict forecasting, early warning models remain insufficiently accurate to provide a firm foundation for confident action and there is never any way of knowing—precisely—the overall effect of a course of action. What is more, since cause and effect in the social world is so contingent upon agency, structure and context which interact in ways that are always unique and never repeated in exactly the same way, it is always difficult to know with any precision what the effects of a course of action—or inaction—are likely to be. This is a problem that exacerbates governments' predisposition to risk averseness arising from concerns about their capacity to influence events on the ground at a reasonable price, opportunity costs and the political dangers associated with preventive action. As a result, although early action is imperative, there is seldom a sufficiently strong evidentiary basis on which to marshal international action in advance of the actual commission of atrocities. Moreover, since any type of action entails risks, the cards are stacked firmly in support of inaction: better to stand aside and minimise risk to oneself than to act and incur potential costs. Often, the best that can be achieved is an early response to atrocities that might prevent further escalation, as in Kenya 2007–2008 and Burundi after 2015.

The role of that confidence can play in enabling preventive action in particular was shown by the fact that lessons learned from Kenya in 2008 spurred a genuinely preventive approach to that country's 2013 elections that made that exercise a largely peaceful affair despite the presence of the same centrifugal forces that had caused violence five years earlier. It is that sort of precision about the triggers and timing of potential atrocities that is needed to give leaders sufficient confidence to act. Sometimes, circumstance and past experience provide such clarity, as with South Sudan's 2011 referendum, Gaddafi's imminent attack on Benghazi in 2011, and Kenya's 2013 election. In those situations, preventive action may be more likely. In most cases, however, there is a much greater degree of uncertainty about whether, when, and where atrocity risks might be actualised, and this is a significant obstacle to decisive preventive action.

Judging R2P

How, then, should we go about judging R2P's performance in its first two decades? One of the principal problems with the debate thus far is the use of different metrics to determine whether the principle is having an effect and whether or not that effect is beneficial. Keenly aware of the arduous diplomatic struggles that lay beneath international acceptance of R2P, advocates have sometimes rushed with undue haste to describe some actions, such as the NATO-led intervention in Libya, as 'textbook examples' of R2P in practice (Evans, 2011). Critics, meanwhile, have sometimes gone to equally great lengths to suggest that those same actions had little to do with the principle, despite clear references to it (e.g. Morris, 2013). More often, though, they have pointed to signs of international inaction or ineffectual engagement in crises such as Darfur, Sri Lanka, Bahrain and Syria as indicative of R2P's 'failure' or 'irrelevance'. The problem with ascertaining R2P's influence, of course, is that understanding an actor's motivation is a notoriously difficult business, especially when that actor is a state or an international organisation. Meanwhile, the problem with focusing on outcomes is that it radically simplifies the interplay of decisions, factors and forces that give rise to them.

Perhaps the first thing that should be said is that R2P has helped to raise global expectations about prevention and protection. Norms, as we mentioned earlier, are all about establishing shared expectations. Notwithstanding the difficulties of the situation, the lamentations of the UNGA and the popular media about the UNSC's failure to protect Syrians evinces a deep sense of shared expectation that the Council *ought* to protect Syrians from their own government. It was not always the case that the UNSC was thought to have this protection role, yet today its legitimacy—indeed that of the whole UN system—rests largely on judgements about its performance in the field of protection. This elevation of expectations makes it possible to see 'failure' everywhere, for even with the best of intentions the international community will seldom have the wherewithal to prevent every atrocity. R2P has always had an aspirational quality. Annan meant it as a challenge to governments, groups and individuals to do better and to aim higher. Without some level of discomfort and dissatisfaction with current practice, international society would never get better at prevention and protection.

Wherever we set the expectations associated with R2P, clear international failures to protect, by which is commonly meant failures to forcibly intervene to halt atrocities as in, for example, Darfur and Syria, are commonly taken as evidence of limited commitment and the norm's fragility. As Jennifer Welsh (2011, p. 126) explains, however, whether or not armed intervention occurs is an inappropriate measure of R2P's effectiveness for at least two reasons. First, because the norm is indeterminate with respect to which courses of action the international community should adopt and there are often genuine disagreements over the most prudential courses of action. Second, as Morris (2015) shows, in determining a course of action States have to weigh up multiple considerations, not only the potential effects on the crisis at hand.

What, though, does it mean to say an actor is fulfilling its R2P and how do we ascribe value to the norm's contribution? Common definitions of humanitarian intervention tended to emphasise the humanitarian *motivations* of the interveners. Wil Verwey (1992, p. 114) famously defined humanitarian intervention as 'the threat or use of force … *for the sole purpose* of preventing or putting a halt to a serious violation of human rights'. Writing in the early 1990s, Verwey argued that there had not yet been any genuine humanitarian interventions because in practice interventions had always been motivated by a mix of different concerns. But there are at least three reasons to doubt this approach and think that a more differentiated account—comprising intent, practices and outcomes—might be a better way of evaluating R2P.

First, organisations—be they States or non-state actors—always have mixed motives. States, for instance, are not black boxes guided by singular interests or motivations. They are composites of multiple bureaucracies guided by governments themselves comprised of multiple individuals. What is more, the issues States confront are never monocausal and neither does state action produce only singular effects. Atrocity crimes are complex, multicausal phenomena and actions directed at stemming them have multiple effects not limited to atrocity crimes themselves. In practice, States have to weigh up competing practical considerations and make normative judgments about the relative weight of different ethically sound norms which may sometimes pull in different directions.

For instance, should States risk the lives of their own citizens to potentially save populations in other countries? If so, how much risk should they expose their own to? Less dramatically, should States pursue policies aimed at preventing atrocities in third countries when those policies impose economic costs—for instance by diverting funds from national social policies to foreign aid, or by enforcing sanctions regimes that have a deleterious effect on national incomes and employment? The reality is that national policy—and the policies of other types of organisations—is always a product of a combination of different motives, interests and normative impulses. We should not, therefore, expect to see R2P cited as an exclusive motive for action, but instead look for instances where it forms part of the rationale.

Second, motives are subjective, difficult to discern and easily disguised by clever political leaders. A better approach is to focus on an actor's intentions—i.e. what does the actor hope to achieve—rather than its' motivations—i.e. why does it want to achieve it—since the former necessarily gives rise to public manifestations whereas the latter may not. How, though, are we to judge a state's intentions, and the place of R2P considerations within it, when it comes to relations with other States? We can look at the *explanations* offered to justify a particular course of action, paying particular attention not to normative framework it evinces (since this can be mendacious) but to the outcomes it wants to achieve. If preventing or halting atrocity crimes is among the desired outcomes, then the intent is at least consistent with R2P. Intentions can also be inferred from acts themselves. As Michael Walzer (1977, pp. 155–156) argued in a different context, soldiers that truly intend not to kill non-combatants will take measures to ensure, as far as possible, that they do not. Thus, practice allows us to make inferences about intentions. For instance, was practice calibrated to prevent atrocities or protect vulnerable populations, or was it driven by other considerations? We can infer from the deployment of French forces during the Rwandan genocide in 1994, for example, that their primary intention was not to stem the genocide. France deployed its forces in areas predominantly populated by Hutus, including the *genocidaires* responsible for the genocide and in a posture that appeared to deter incursions by the Tutsi Rwandan Patriotic Front. Similarly, we can infer from the actual targets of Russian bombing in Syria that the primary purpose of intervention there was to support the regime of Bashar al-Assad and not to protect populations from ISIS. Although evaluating intentions is a far from exact science, it is possible to achieve at least a proximate view by looking at what actors say they want to achieve and the strategies they employ.

Third, focusing on what motivates an action distracts us from its consequences. There are good prudential grounds for thinking that what ultimately matters is whether atrocities are prevented and populations protected, irrespective of *why*. In domestic life, little time is dedicated to worrying about why a person did not commit a murder on any given day: fidelity to the anti-murder norm, fear of retribution, lack of interest or need and psychological disposition are all potential explanations. Self-conscious adherence to the norm is only one potential explanation, though of course in the background the anti-murder norm also works to shape the likelihood of retribution, the balance of interests and sub-conscious dispositions. The same might be said of the more complex set of norms that comprise R2P. From this perspective, it is the outcome of an action rather than its motivation that is most crucial. This is not to say that motives are unimportant, only that they are not of singular importance to evaluating norms such as R2P. In the final calculation, it is most important that actors try to fulfil their responsibilities. *Why* they do so, and how they articulate and justify their actions is of secondary importance. In the context of R2P, it is more important that States and other actors do what is necessary to support protection than that they ascribe their actions to this particular norm, so that as the actions do not themselves undermine the norm (Wheeler, 2000, pp. 38–39). Of course, it is impossible to fully know the outcomes of an action beforehand. By itself, therefore, this approach cannot offer a way of evaluating efficacy because of the wide range of external variables that impact on whether a policy succeeds or fails. That said, if we are to preserve R2P's critical edge, it is important that we keep in mind the question of whether, or not, populations are in fact being better protected from atrocity crimes.

What we should look for, therefore, in evaluating R2P is evidence of intent to fulfil its requirements (protecting populations from atrocity crimes), practices directed towards the achievement of this goal, and the practical outcomes—bearing in mind the limitations described earlier as well as the wide range of other considerations and factors that impact on decision-making and its results. This is a 'responsibility to try'. As Welsh (2011, p. 126) explains, 'the norm of R2P is primarily a responsibility to *consider* a real or imminent crisis involving atrocity crimes…; whether international action actually occurs depends on a series of other factors, such as agreement on the facts (and what they signify) and the likelihood that ... [the] tools will have a positive effect'. This, she calls a 'duty of conduct' borne by the international community, which comprise duties to identify when atrocity crimes are being committed, or are imminently apprehended, and deliberate on how the three-pillar framework might apply (Welsh, 2011, p. 136).

Conclusion

R2P does not outside world politics. It is a product of world politics and, to the extent that it is impactful, achieves things by operating through world politics. As such, it is subjected to all the forces—power, interest, sovereignty and other competing norms and conflict—of world politics. But although R2P is limited by politics and practicality, it can and does influence behaviour and can shape judgments about right and wrong, costs and benefits, in such a way as to make affirmative action on prevention and protection more likely, and idleness in the face of atrocity threats and crimes less likely. Because each case of mass atrocity has its own exigencies, which can push the international community to greater or lesser activism, it is to overall trends and patterns of behaviour that we must look in order to evaluate the wider impact of R2P. Doing that, we can see clear shifts towards greater international proactivity on atrocity crimes and greater prioritisation of protection that are associated with the emergence of R2P. In that context, R2P is best understood as a responsibility to try—a responsibility for actors to do what they reasonably can. Obvious limits to decisive action remain, but R2P must retain its critical edge by shaping expectations about how the world ought to act in order to expose the failings of how it does act and galvanise remedial action.

Although significant diplomatic and practical progress has been made, it is important to recognise the limits, challenges and continuing areas of contestation. The precise role that R2P can play in a given situation, like that of any norm or regime, is influenced by the political context. As such, variation from case to case is to be expected as is a degree of selectivity and a patchy overall record. We need to do a better job of managing expectations, for when international principles meet global practicalities the outcomes are seldom consistent and linear (Gallagher, 2015).

Although normative consensus on R2P has progressed apace, there remains profound contestation about its implementation in really existing situations. It is one thing for States to agree on a standard of behaviour and another thing entirely for them to agree on how best to achieve those aspirations both in general and in the face of specific crises. The most obvious challenge relates to the fact that the use of coercive measures remains controversial and continues to pose questions about the relationship between rights and order. R2P attempted to manoeuvre around this problem—the issue at the heart of Annan's challenge to the UNGA—by bestowing special responsibilities upon the UNSC which, by virtue of the UN Charter, already had the legal right to intervene in a state's domestic affairs should it judge that to be necessary for the maintenance of international peace and security. But R2P now finds itself confronted with a crisis of trust arising from criticism of the 2011 NATO-led intervention in Libya and a growing view that the UNSC and States acting on its mandates need to be held more accountable for their actions. The NATO-led intervention drew sharp criticism from Brazil, China, India, Russia and South Africa, among others, who complained that the mission overstepped its mandate by pursuing regime change, employing disproportionate force, ignoring or outright rejecting opportunities for political dialogue and violating the arms embargo mandated by Resolution 1970. If international society is to become more proactive in its pursuit of R2P, it is inevitable that demands for political accountability will become more significant. Future agreement about everything from long-term prevention to the appropriateness of coercive military force against States as a tool of R2P will likely depend upon how these questions of accountability are addressed. That, after all, was Annan's vision—that the UN become the fulcrum of a new global system capable of both better protecting people from mass atrocities and maintaining international peace and security.

References

Annan, K. (1999a, September 18). Two concepts of sovereignty. *The Economist*.

Annan, K. (1999b, September 20). Annual report of the Secretary-General to the General Assembly.

Bellamy, A. J. (2012). *Massacres and morality: Mass atrocities in an age of civilian immunity*. Oxford University Press.

Bellamy, A. J. (2021). *The betrayal of Syria: War, atrocities, and the failure of international diplomacy*. Columbia University Press.

Doyle, M. W. (2015). *The question of intervention: John Stuart mill and the responsibility to protect*. Yale University Press.

Evans, G. (2011, April 15). Interview with Nayan Chanda. *Yale Global Online*.

Franck, T. (1990). *The power of legitimacy among nations*. Oxford University Press.
Gallagher, A. (2015). The responsibility to protect ten years on from the world summit: A call to manage expectations. *Global Responsibility to Protect, 7*(3–4), 254–274.
Glanville, L. (2009). *Sovereignty and the responsibility to protect*. University of Chicago Press.
Glanville, L. (2021). *Sharing responsibility: The history and future of protection from atrocities*. Princeton University Press.
Luck, E. C. (2009). Sovereignty, choice and the responsibility to protect. *Global Responsibility to Protect, 1*(1), 10–21.
Morris, J. (2013). Libya and Syria: R2P and the specter of the swinging pendulum. *International Affairs, 89*(5), 1265–1283.
Morris, J. (2015). The responsibility to protect and the great powers: The tensions of dual responsibility. *Global Responsibility to Protect, 7*(3–4), 401–424.
Pattison, J. (2010). *Humanitarian intervention and the responsibility to protect: Who should intervene?* Oxford University Press.
Purdekova, A. (2019). #StopthisMovie and the pitfalls of mass atrocity prevention: Framing of violence and anticipation of escalation in Burundi's crisis (2015–2017). *Genocide Studies and Prevention, 13*(2), 22–37.
Roff, H. M. (2013). *Global justice, kant, and the responsibility to protect*. Routledge.
Sharma, S. K., & Welsh, J. M. (Eds.). (2016). *The responsibility to prevent: Overcoming the challenges to atrocity prevention*. Oxford University Press.
Straus, S. (2015). *Making and unmaking nations: War, leadership and genocide in Modern Africa*. Cornell University Press.
United Nations General Assembly (UNGA). (2012, February 16). *The situation in the Syrian Arab Republic*, A.66/L.36.
United Nations Security Council (UNSC). (2014, April 16). 7155th meeting, S.PV.7155.
Valentino, B. (2011). The true costs of humanitarian intervention. *Foreign Affairs, 90*(6), 60–73.
Verwey, W. (1992). Legality of Humanitarian Intervention after the Cold War. In E. Ferris (Ed.), *The challenge to intervene: A new role for the United Nations?* Uppsala: Life & Peace Institute.
Walzer, M. (1977). *Just and unjust wars: A moral argument with historical illustrations*. Basic Books.
Welsh, J. (2011). Implementing the responsibility to protect: Where expectations meet reality. *Ethics and International Affairs, 24*(4), 415–430.
Wheeler, N. J. (2000). *Saving strangers: Humanitarian intervention in international society*. Oxford University Press.

CHAPTER 3

Darfur: R2P and Dilemmas of Implementation

Rahel Kessete Afewerky

The Darfur genocide stems from years of systematic marginalisation of the minority non-Arab citizens (Badescu & Bergholm, 2009; Flint & De Waal, 2008). However, the mass carnage escalated with the failure of the international community to intervene in a timely and effective manner. Since 2003, the genocide has claimed the lives of over 300,000 people and displaced 2.7 million people rendering the calls for 'Genocide No More – Save Darfur' mere rhetoric (UN, 2020a).

Despite a trove of evidence piling up, the international community failed to deter the series of events that led to the genocide. The relief that came much later with the deployment of the African Union Mission in Sudan (AMIS) peacekeeping forces in 2004 could not curtail the spiralling events engrossing the country into tumultuous cycles of conflicts (Bellamy, 2005; Kreps, 2007; Spandler, 2020). Darfur was the first case that challenged the international community in terms of its responsibility to protect (R2P), but the norm was in its infancy when

R. K. Afewerky (✉)
Department of International Relations, Hacettepe University, Ankara, Turkey

P. Gözen Ercan (ed.), *The Responsibility to Protect Twenty Years On*,
https://doi.org/10.1007/978-3-030-90731-0_3

the crisis escalated, and the 2005 consensus of the United Nations (UN) Member States was not there yet. On 31 August 2006, the UN Security Council (UNSC) reached an agreement to implement R2P in Darfur, but it took the massacre of hundreds of thousands and the influx of millions of refugees into the neighbouring countries (UNSC, 2006b).

Though South Sudan claimed independence in 2011 following a referendum, today the peril persists with the international community's failure to prevent growing tensions, which hold the potential of reigniting the genocide. This chapter focuses on the case of Darfur, which offers important lessons as to the implementation of R2P in its 20-year history. R2P was newly introduced when the genocide unfolded, yet it also was the first case where the UNSC for the first time referred to Paragraphs 138 and 139 of the World Summit Outcome Document (WSOD) in a country-specific resolution. Most accounts of Darfur take it as a failed test case of R2P, wherein the concentration has rather been on military intervention (Badescu & Bergholm, 2009; Thakur, 2004). Nevertheless, undermining R2P's toolkit solely to the use of force is misleading as it overlooks aspects of prevention as well as measures short of use of force under the responsibility to react (and Pillar Three). Moreover, the literature that has been compiled so far disregards R2P's stage of evolution when the genocide unfolded. As Gifkins (2016) argues, 'Darfur does not make a good "test case" of R2P as the escalation and height of the Darfur conflict occurred prior to the international agreement on R2P in 2005'. Nevertheless, it makes a good case overall as it helps us to shed light on the dilemmas of the international community as to R2P and state sovereignty. It also allows us to seek what is needed for sustainable prevention and protection and to question the significance of the responsibility to rebuild in achieving the purposes of R2P.

Accordingly, this chapter addresses the predicaments present in the initiatives that curtailed a prompt and effective intervention in Darfur. It explicates how the crisis unfolded and examines fundamental aspects that could have helped to prevent the genocide earlier. It continues to discuss the harm instigated by the delayed response vis-à-vis the failure to eradicate existing tension, and questions the non-implementation of the responsibility to rebuild—that is the third element of R2P originally suggested in the 2001 Report of the International Commission on Intervention and State Sovereignty (ICISS) but was left out of the norm's scope in the 2005 consensus. This chapter asserts that the absence of a conflict transformation period to combat resurgent threats and strong rebuilding initiatives makes previous interventions futile. The wave-like features of the mass atrocities that surface with the deteriorating security situation in the region (IRRI, 2016) have not been thoroughly addressed in the literature. They endure rolling bases in the absence of the responsibility to rebuild. Hence, the chapter concludes that the non-involvement of the international community to ascertain a transformation period that would aid to eradicate tension among different ethnic groups is a question that needs to be addressed along with the reconsideration of the responsibility to rebuild as part of the R2P framework.

Background

As in most other dominant conflicts in Sudan, the Darfur genocide has its origins in the cultural and economic tensions inherent in the politics of the country. The roots of the genocide stretch to several atrocities that pitied ethnic groups against one another (Flint & De Waal, 2008; Gifkins, 2016). The genocide has had a long gestation period where the tension between ethnic groups compounded into a long violent conflict.

The forty post-independence years were smeared with the legacy of colonialism that left Sudan with an intricate economic, political and social crisis (Bøås et al., 2020). A series of droughts and desertification aggravated the tension between nomadic Arabs and agrarian Fur, Zaghawa and Masalit Darfuri tribes. 'The basic pattern of grievances is shared by all the marginalised peoples: they were denied their share in political power and national wealth, and the government used divide-and-rule tactics to allow local militias to run amok and destroy their modest livelihoods' (De Waal, 2007, p. 2). The Sudanese government promoted the tension between nomadic Arabs and agrarian tribes. The lure of land and livestock resources became primary incentives to the conflicts, and Darfuris had to contend with Khartoums' relentless manipulation of resources (Hagan & Rymond-Richmond, 2008). Consequently, an 'us' and 'them' division flared into a full-blown conflict with growing land and resource competition between settled agrarian tribes and the predominantly nomadic Arab herders. In early 2003, different insurgent groups started to emerge (Tanner et al., 2007). They waged war against the government targetting public facilities and civilians (Salih, 2005).

The second catalyst that laid the foundation of the genocide was the armament of Arab Janjaweed militias. The Sudanese government had been equipping the Arab groups since the mid-1980s (Bellamy,

2005; Flint & De Waal, 2008). Khartoum augmented the distribution of weapons as a retaliation to the Darfur Liberation Front (DLF) attack in April 2003 on the Sudanese air force in Al Fashir (HRW, 2004a). This enabled the continuation of the bombings of the villages, while the government-backed Janjaweed looted and burnt them. Nomad Arab militias launched attacks against the factions of the DLF—such as the Sudanese Liberation Movement/Army (SLM/A), the Justice and Equality Movement (JEM) and other emerging opposition factions.

The nomadic Arab tribes were promised land in return for their military allegiance to the government in its fight against rising insurgence in Darfur (HRW, 2004a). Moreover, Sudan's National Security Act grants full immunity to members of its defence and security forces against any criminal prosecution (FIDH/ACJPS, 2019). Considered as members of the Sudanese defence and security forces, the nomadic Arab tribes held immediate functional immunity from criminal prosecution (REDRESS, 2014). The government's full support has enabled them to wreak havoc unchecked: they kidnapped, raped and killed Darfuris (HRW, 2008).

The Failure to Prevent the Genocide

Given its role in the mass atrocity crimes being committed, the Sudanese government's failure to protect the Darfuri population was quite obvious. Nevertheless, when the UNSC convened to address the case, Algeria, China, Pakistan and Russia abstained from the vote. They argued that imposing sanctions on Sudan would be counterproductive since they believed that Khartoum had taken positive steps and progress was made (UNSC, 2004b).

It is noteworthy that the Darfur genocide was occurring at a time when the intentions behind the Iraq invasion were being questioned. The intricacies of the questionable military intervention overshadowed the delicate situation in Darfur and protracted a prompt response from the international community. The justifications of 'humanitarian' intervention employed to invade Iraq brought the United States (US) and other Western countries under international scrutiny (Thakur, 2016; Williams & Bellamy, 2005). This made countries reluctant to react to the Darfur genocide as R2P continued to be equated to a 'Trojan Horse' of the West allowing them to pursue their national interests. The status quo made gathering the necessary resources to intervene in Darfur unfeasible with great powers stating that they have already overstretched their military capacity in the Middle East conflicts (Badescu & Bergholm, 2009). Thus, timing became an obstacle that restrained the reaction of States and sealed the fate of Darfuris.

The North–South War was another element that constrained a prompt reaction. The genocide unfolded in parallel to an ongoing negotiation to end the war. Although the Office for the Coordination of Humanitarian Affairs (OCHA) continuously lobbied for the inclusion of Darfur in the then-ongoing North–South talks, there was active resistance to the inclusion of the Darfur case in the UNSC's agenda (Gifkins, 2016). The Troika—namely the US, the United Kingdom (UK) and Norway—refused to include Darfur in the negotiations. They considered a sequential approach more viable than the inclusion of the case in the North–South negotiations or for that matter prioritising Darfur's stability. There were arguably two reasons behind the Troika's reluctance. One was the fact that the North–South War, which accompanied two long-running civil wars, posed a far more devastating threat to Sudan than the unfolding genocide in Darfur (Natsios, 2012). Nearly 2 million people lost their lives because of the war and war-related famine and diseases, while around 4 million people were forcibly displaced from their homes (USCfR, 2004). The other was the perception that the talks were nearing an end. As such, bringing Darfur to the negotiation table would jeopardise hard-won progress (Totten & Markusen, 2013). It took two more years before the Sudanese government and the South Sudan opposition came to an agreement. On 9 January 2005, they signed the Comprehensive Peace Agreement (CPA) that officially ended the war. Thus, the international community's reluctance to include Darfur in an ongoing talk in order not to hamper the resolution of another conflict in the country became one of the reasons for the belated response and the failure to prevent further mass atrocities.

The South Sudan Independence War had already exhausted the diplomatic and financial investments of Member States (Rossi, 2016). As such, the international community was reluctant to invest in yet another conflict in the country. Major regional and international actors such as the Intergovernmental Authority on Development (IGAD) wanted to conclude the Machakos-Naivasha peace agreements before they moved on to solve the conflict in Darfur. The initiatives regarding the Darfur genocide became an appendage to the resolution inceptions of the North–South conflict in Sudan.

Moreover, geostrategic interests of the US, Russia, China and others in Sudan undermined the international community's responsibility to protect the Darfuri population (Williams & Bellamy, 2005). Lucrative oil and other trade interests made countries, intergovernmental and non-governmental organisations reluctant to sever their ties with Khartoum in response to what was going on in Darfur (Badescu & Bergholm, 2009). Using its favourable position, the Sudanese government manipulated international actors to champion its sovereign rights and curtail interventions in Darfur. The backing of these countries encouraged Sudanese officials to state that the Darfur conflict was an internal matter, and any interference would be a breach of Sudan's national sovereignty (Benjamin, 2010). The preference of these States to keep on the good side of the Sudanese government compelled them to turn a blind eye to the genocide and heed Khartoum's right to refuse interference. As such, the situation in Darfur deteriorated with the reluctance of Member States to take immediate action to deter the genocide. 'Later the problem ranged from the conflicts of interest on the UN Security Council to sustaining public interest in Darfur as the crisis wore on year after year' (Grzyb, 2009, p. 18). Hence, step-by-step the international community failed on its initial responsibility to prevent the unfolding mass atrocities in Darfur.

The Failure to React in a Timely and Effective Manner

The first UNSC resolution concerning Darfur was adopted a year into the genocide. Resolution 1556 dated 30 July 2004 cited the situation as a 'threat to international peace and security'. The UN International Commission of Inquiry that was sent on 18 September 2004 reported back on 25 January 2005 that the Sudanese government together with the Janjaweed was accountable for the genocide (ICoIoD, 2005). The Janjaweed had already been committing alleged mass atrocities: kidnapping, raping and killing Darfuris. By the end of 2004, more than 70,000 Darfuris have been killed and hundreds of thousands were under dire risk (HRW, 2005; Refugees International, 2004). However, instead of adopting enforcement mechanisms accompanying a coherent action plan, ensuing measures were followed by a series of sporadic initiations that did not steer a timely and effective reaction (Bøås et al., 2020).

The absence of a consolidated political will encumbered these initiations to achieve the protection of the Darfuri population. Member States' national interests preceded the necessity to take measures to protect the Darfuris. When the UNSC convened in Nairobi on 19 November 2004, calls to sanction Sudan were watered down by two of the Permanent Members. China—the largest share owner of Sudan's oil production—and Russia—the main arms supplier to Khartoum—used their stronghold to pressure other countries against pushing for sanctions on the Sudanese government (Clough, 2005). The UN Member States were unable to consent to a unified action plan to stop the genocide. Thus, aside from a general agreement that the situation in Darfur posed an international threat, there was no consent on how to proceed with implementation or for that matter how to apply R2P.

These political challenges engendered inadequate negotiation mechanisms. From the Ndjamena Agreement of 8 April 2004 to the Darfur Peace Agreement of 5 May 2006, on six different occasions the UNSC called on the Sudanese government to disarm the Janjaweed. These ultimatums were backed by empty threats to sanction Khartoum, which negatively impacted future negotiation incentives (Thakur, 2016). The measures taken proved to be quick-fix solutions that failed to address vital features that sustained the mass atrocities. The Sudanese government encouraged the perpetrators to intensify their violence, rejected peace negotiation initiations and effectively worked to cripple international initiatives to intervene in Darfur.

> Khartoum continued to arm militias responsible for mass death, destruction, and displacement and reneged on its numerous promises to disarm them; it expelled the Special Representative of the Secretary-General Jan Pronk from Sudan in October 2006; it has violated the UN-Sudan Status of Forces Agreement (SOFA), especially relating to the freedom of movement of UN Mission in Sudan (UNMIS) personnel; and it repeatedly lied about the capacity of its justice system to deal with war crimes while rejecting the Security Council's referral of the Darfur crisis to the International Criminal Court. (Human Rights Briefs, 2007, p. 28)

Nonetheless, the UNSC did not pursue its threats to impose sanctions on the country's oil and responsible government officials (ICG, 2006). Such failure to follow through encouraged the Sudanese government's intransigence. Despite the 2005 consensus that led to the adoption of R2P by Member States, Khartoum put forth its sovereign rights and the non-intervention principle as a shield against international intervention in Darfur. In the absence of consensus in the UNSC, the international community did not have the mandate to intervene in Darfur without the consent of the Sudanese government under R2P. Hence, with manipulation sovereignty and norms of non-intervention happened to hinder potential measures to protect the Darfuris. When talks on deploying forces to protect civilian monitors who have been positioned in Al Fashir began, Khartoum objected to the presence of any international force in Darfur and threatened to use force against the peacekeepers who were to be deployed in the region (UNMIS, 2004).

The UNSC championed subtle measures that delegated the responsibility to the African Union (AU). The Council unanimously supported the AU initiatives under 'African solutions to African conflicts' and promptly devolved the responsibility to the Union (Bellamy, 2005; Beswick, 2010; Keith, 2007). The AU sent AMIS to protect civilian ceasefire monitors on what it hoped would be a cornerstone to ensuing diplomatic negotiations.

However, the AU was constrained from the beginning by the challenges presented by the Sudanese government, Member States, international actors and donors. These interferences proved to be major predicaments that disrupted the Mission's success potential (Guicherd, 2007). The restricted mandate only allowed the AMIS to protect the civilian ceasefire monitors present in the region (Guicherd, 2007). 'Although an armed humanitarian intervention was possible under the AU Constitutive Act, the Council did not consider any options beyond those stipulated in the Ndjamena Agreement—traditional ceasefire monitoring—and the troops were not mandated to protect civilians' (Flint & De Waal, 2008, p. 174). Hence, despite the presence of peacekeepers, the Darfuris were left vulnerable, and the number of internally displaced persons (IDPs), as well as refugees in neighbouring countries, continued to rise.

Later, a disagreement erupted among African countries contributing troops to the AMIS deployment. The mandate that failed to authorise the AMIS to protect civilians evolved to be another predicament that ensued to prolong a timely and effective intervention. When Rwanda sent 155 troops to Darfur, President Kagame insisted that 'Rwandan troops would intervene if civilians are threatened' (HRW, 2004b). Other AU members had reservations and remarked that such action would compromise the mission. For instance, President Obasanjo voiced his disagreement and affirmed that the Nigerian forces would operate under the Sudanese government's accord (HRW, 2004b). These disagreements were later mildly resolved when the AU decided to revaluate the mandate. Nonetheless, also considering the appeals of Member States regarding protection of civilians, the AU had to acknowledge the wishes of various actors in Darfur. 'The AU's leadership redrafted the mandate of AMIS in a way that responded to humanitarian appeals but at the same time satisfied the Sudanese host state, the AU membership, and the foreign donors' (Badescu & Bergholm, 2009, p. 297). The AU Peace and Security Council gave further mandate on 20 October 2004, to 'Protect civilians whom it encounters under imminent threat and in the immediate vicinity, within resources and capability, it being understood that the protection of the civilian population is the responsibility of the Government of Sudan' (AU, 2004, p. 2).

Another challenge that set limitations to AMIS operations in Darfur was the lack of resources. AMIS did not have the necessary resources to monitor the ceasefire and conform to the expectations of the mission, based on the Ndjamena agreement. The mission's expectations, as such, exceeded AMIS mandated authority (Williams & Bellamy, 2005). Intergovernmental organisations and international donors did not deliver on their promise to provide the resources to support the mission (De Waal, 2007). Neither did the AU's Member States contribute to the mission as they promised (Bellamy, 2005). The Sudanese government's unyielding commitment restrained the AMIS operations (Müller, 2020). Khartoum imposed restrictions on AMIS movements with a curfew and by limiting access to resources such as petroleum. These restrictions, in turn, hampered AMIS movements. These shortages restrained the potential of AMIS and made the peacekeepers vulnerable to armed militia attacks. On 29 September 2007, twelve AMIS soldiers were killed and another eight were severely wounded (ICC, 2010). The militia allegedly looted, destroyed and appropriated AMIS's property. The mission not only lacked logistics and finances but also the experience that could expedite it to success (Guicherd, 2007). Thus, the peacekeeping forces were neither able to decimate the sporadic escalation of conflicts nor the deteriorating humanitarian conditions in Darfur (Bellamy, 2005; Deen, 2005).

Consequently, Resolution 1706 was adopted on 31 August 2006 authorising a UN force takeover. The Sudanese government did not consent to a UN deployment but agreed to the deployment of a UN-AU hybrid force. A gradual transition process was agreed upon so as not to provoke tension among the militias. Resolution 1769 was adopted on 31

July 2007, authorising United Nations–African Union Mission in Darfur (UNAMID) takeover. The hybrid mission that was tasked to implement the 2006 Darfur Peace Agreement became operational on 31 December 2007.

The UNAMID mandate—which was completed on 31 December 2020—encompassed the protection of civilians including the IDPs scattered throughout different refugee camps in the region (UNAMID, 2020). Despite the objective of the mission to protect the population of Darfur, disagreements rose on whether UNAMID was responsible for disarming the perpetrators of the genocide (UNAMID, 2008). Diverse interpretations of UNAMID's mandate by the States contributing to the force provoked misunderstandings. The lack of a consolidated strategy and false assumptions precluded a comprehensive operation (Keith, 2007; Müller, 2020). One of these challenges arose from the failure of UNAMID to engage in a coherent assessment of various armed militias present (De Waal, 2007). Overall, the diverging interpretations attached to the mandate by the participants hindered the realisation of the mission promises to uphold Chapter VII of the UN Charter.

Moreover, the UNAMID forces were not authorised to stop combat between the SLM/A, JEM, the Janjaweed or any other splinters. As a result, the role of UNAMID troops evolved into that of a silent observer. Their designated role was not to fight a war but to keep peace with their presence (Badescu & Bergholm, 2009). As such, their mandated stand continuously made them vulnerable against the Janjaweed. The convoy was caught in crossfires several times. On 08 July 2008, the Janjaweed attack killed seven UNAMID soldiers and wounded 19 others (UNAMID, 2008). Eventually, UNAMID faced the same fate as AMIS. The convoy was neither capable of protecting the Darfuri population nor itself. Thus, the mission became engrossed in predicaments that rendered its operations unsuccessful.

The UNAMID forces were limited in their movements owing not only to the Sudanese government but also to insufficient resources and personnel capacity. The promised 26,000 troops were never deployed (UNAMID, 2008). Furthermore, differences of understanding among the soldiers from different countries as to what the mission entailed further complicated the operation. There was a need to expand the capabilities of the soldiers and train them on how to efficiently intervene to stop the genocide. Consequently, despite the deployment of AMIS and UNAMID, the international community delivered an inadequate response to deter the genocide of hundreds of thousands and the displacement of millions.

The Failure to Deter Recurrent Threats and Initiate a Sustainable Resolution

Although the intensity of the atrocities has abated in Darfur, there is no sign that the threat has been completely eradicated since there are only meagre initiations to aid rebuilding the region. The post-genocide period emulates the same features that led to the genocide. Given the wave-like features of the genocide and the already present early warning signs, the international community is prone, yet again, to fail to mitigate growing tension between nomad Arabs and Darfur tribes. This begs the question what role would the responsibility to rebuild play if it were still operational under the three-pillar implementation strategy of R2P. In the absence of an international effort to initiate a sustainable resolution to the conflict, the security situation in Sudan is in decline with continuous acts of looting, raping, killing and burning (FIDH/ACJPS, 2019), and new challenges hindering resolution and transformation of the conflicts continue to arise.

In the current state of affairs, the modicum of peace the hybrid peace-keeping forces were able to bring falls short with the untimely downsizing and a complete withdrawal planned in 2021 (UN, 2020b). A national plan to replace UNAMID soldiers with national troops is underway (OCHA, 2020). However, even with the new government in office, the legacy of the genocide hinders trust among Darfuris and government institutions. As Executive Director of Human Rights Watch, Kenneth Roth reminds: 'Past and ongoing violence there means civilians can't trust Sudanese security forces alone and still look to peacekeepers for protection' (HRW, 2020). In the light of the increasing tension among the tribes, the planned withdrawal of UNAMID aggravates the threat of armed violence.

As Thakur (2018) observes, the resurgence of violence becomes less likely with the presence of peacekeeping forces. Hence, a more gradual drawdown period of the peacekeeping forces is fundamental to deter recurrent conflicts and improve dire humanitarian conditions in Darfur. Peacekeeping forces' long-term presence can help to lay a foundation for a secure environment and support rebuilding Darfur. Contrary to the existing determination for full withdrawal, the escalating situation begs for an augmented operational capacity for UNAMID. Hybrid features of the peacekeeping forces restrain cooperation strategies that can efficiently consolidate the mission (Müller, 2020; Spandler, 2020), whereas the efficiency of UNAMID depends on consistent diplomatic and material assistance. Thus, there is a need to mould the force's capacity to commensurate its expansion and install contingency planning.

Moreover, the consolidation of various fractions to deter recurrence of armed violence among tribes is of prominence. There is a dire need to initiate conflict resolution and transformation strategies that would enable stabilisation in Darfur by adding reconstruction and re-establishment of governance institutions. The international community has failed to bring together various factions of opposition groups present in the region. There are allegedly more than half a dozen opposition factions (Berridge, 2020; Totten, 2008) and most of them are not included in the peace talks. The acrimony among these factions bears internecine strife that precludes conflict transformation and resolution in the region.

Intra-power struggles within these factions have escalated to the level of sporadic violence and continue to stall peace talks. The disarmament of these factions is a prerequisite for initiating successful peace talks, while peaceful disarmament is crucial to smooth demobilisation and is a path for reintegrating these factions into the community. Moreover, the rehabilitation of the faction members has to ensure an inclusive policy to engage them in the reconstruction process. Such path has the potential of saving Darfur from being trapped in a vicious conflict cycle.

Another element that feeds the conflict is the continuing land dispute between the predominantly nomadic Arabs and agrarian African tribes. Post-genocide, as nomad Arabs have settled on the abandoned lands of the agrarian Darfuris, grievances over land surface as a persistent threat. 'Former Janjaweed militiamen still occupy the lands of members of the Fur, Massalit and Zaghawa ethnic groups who have been chased from their homeland over the past 16 years, and persecute those who have remained or return[ed], including by perpetrating sexual violence' (FIDH/ACJPS, 2019, p. 5).

Moreover, growing banditry sets another challenge to the repatriation of the IDPs and refugees. Nomad Arabs have fanned out across Darfur ceasing abandoned properties (HRW, 2006). Concomitantly, the desertification of lands and recurring droughts aggravate economic tensions among the tribes and impede conflict transformation initiatives (Flint & De Waal, 2008; Totten, 2008). These accumulated situations have grown to be precarious predicaments to the repatriation of Darfuris. Hence, there is a need for immediate and efficacious efforts to resolve the land conflict before it spirals into armed violence.

The absence of strategies and policies to preclude potential threats and transform the conflicts leaves the IDPs and refugees vulnerable and makes their return a challenge. As Toten observes, 'most are destitute and will be destitute when they return to their villages' (Totten, 2008, p. 105). Despite the ceasefire talks and the deployment of peacekeeping forces alleged attacks on civilians make it difficult for the IDPs and refugees to return to their lands (HRW, 2018; OCHA, 2019). This is why the international community and the Sudanese government need to step in and assist them to return, rebuild their homes and get their properties back.

A related concern is the continuous 'genocide by attrition' committed against fleeing Darfuris. The severity of the massacre has overshadowed the threat fleeing victims continue to face on the road and in refugee camps (Reeves, 2005; Totten, 2015). Many Darfuris who fled have died from drinking poisoned water. It is alleged that the Janjaweed and the Sudanese government have poisoned wells and filled them with the bodies of the villagers (Flint & De Waal, 2008, p. 190). While on the route and living in refugee camps many Darfuris continue to lose their lives due to malnutrition, lack of medical attention, dehydration, unsanitary conditions and trauma, which feeds into the slow-motion genocide (Müller, 2020; OCHA, 2007; Rasmussen & Annan, 2010).

Moreover, the impunity of the perpetrators of the genocide carries the potential of instigating resentment among the survivors of the massacre. Following the UNSC's referral of the case, the International Criminal Court (ICC) issued an arrest warrant against former President Omar Al Bashir along with two ministers and a Janjaweed militia commander (ICC, 2009). That said, as these people are still at large and the ICC does not try individuals in their absence, the cases are stuck at the pre-trial stage (Charity, 2011; FIDH/ACJPS, 2019). Although in 2005 the Special Criminal Court on the Events in Darfur was established, no convictions have been brought against the perpetrators at the national level. This largely owes to the absence of an independent judiciary system in the country and the lack of political will to hold the perpetrators accountable. Besides, the laws of the country provide full immunity to its defence and security forces (REDRESS, 2014), and as the Janjaweed have long been integrated into the national forces, they cannot be held legally accountable for their actions under national law.

Consequently, more than a decade later, it still has not been possible to end impunity and send a message to potential future perpetrators that they will be accountable for their actions. While delayed justice has emboldened perpetrators to continue committing heinous crimes, it also ignites the sense of revenge for victimised Darfuris (O'Neill & Cassis, 2005). As the ICISS (2001, p. 40) notes, the absence of impunity poses a threat of 'revenge killings and even reverse ethnic cleansing', and thus, holds potential for setting a cycle of revenge and violence, which consequently hinders cooperation and slows down the rebuilding process. This also reminds us of the importance of a constitutionally mandated system, which can guide and nurture the tribes to negotiate, bargain and resolve their issues, and live together peacefully. This suggests the urgency to restore the national justice system and to bring the perpetrators to justice through either national courts or the ICC. Holding the perpetrators accountable also requires a transformation of the compromised national armed and police forces of the State. As such, 'the disarmament, demobilisation and reintegration of local security forces' is of crucial importance to set a platform for a secure administration (ICISS, 2001, p. 41).

Aside from the lack of trust in the government (HRW, 2020) due to the abovementioned reasons, the ongoing political transition in Sudan impedes the country from overseeing a peaceful transformation of the conflicts in Darfur. The Sudanese transition government that took office on 05 July 2019 falls short of carrying out the responsibility to rebuild on its own. Whether considered as part of the rebuilding process or as prevention of future atrocities, Darfur needs the international community's support to overcome the profound challenges of the post-genocide legacy. Durable prosperity needs to be embedded with a sustainable support capacity. This would ensure resource availability as well as logistical planning supported with consistent financial backing, which in return increases the level of compliance of all factions.

Each of these obstacles presents a dilemma standing before the successful implementation of R2P and sustainable protection in Darfur. They have become a predicament to effective conflict resolution and transformation. As such, the Darfur genocide demonstrates the importance of endorsing the responsibility to rebuild as an integral part of R2P. The existent loopholes in R2P's implementation strategy and lack of measures to ensure sustainable protection manifest themselves in the case of Darfur as the deteriorating situation in the region signals the threat of mass atrocity crimes. The eradication of these threats heavily depends on expedited conflict resolution and transformation mechanisms.

Conclusion

In reflecting over the last two decades of R2P, the case of Darfur offers a lot to think about. While this was the first case wherein the UNSC referred to R2P in a country-specific resolution, the response came too late, too weak. The prolonged response of the international community despite the manifest failure of Khartoum constrained the commitment to prevent the spiralling genocide. Despite a long period of escalating tension between ethnic groups and evidence of mass atrocities piling up, the international community failed to deter the series of events that led to the genocide. Although the deployment of the AMIS peacekeeping forces and then the UN-AU Hybrid Operation brought some relief, they could not prevent the spiralling events that killed and displaced Darfuris. This is why the R2P literature focusing on Darfur considers this specific case as a failure of the norm. Nevertheless, considering the timeline of events, arguably an immediate R2P response to the escalating situation was not possible as the 2005 consensus was not there yet. About eight months after the WSOD, as evinced by UNSC Resolution 1706, we see that upholding the responsibility to protect was indeed a concern in the case of Darfur. This, however, does not mean that the international community carried out its responsibility successfully.

The mass atrocities in Darfur, like other major conflicts in Sudan, stemmed from cultural and economic tensions inherent in the politics of the country. These root causes are still existent, and hence, the population is still facing imminent risk of mass atrocities. This chapter argues that the persistence of such risk owes to the absence of an international commitment to ensure a peaceful transformation in the region as well as to a lack of initiatives that would follow the mentality put forth under responsibility to rebuild. Though the responsibility to rebuild is no longer considered to be part of the R2P framework as adopted under the WSOD (which was later strategised with the 2009 Report of the Secretary-General), the Darfuri case allows us to highlight its relevance in post-conflict peacebuilding. While the ICISS (2001, p. xi) suggests that the responsibility to rebuild is to follow international intervention for purposes of 'full assistance with recovery, reconstruction, and reconciliation, addressing the causes of the harm the intervention was designed to halt or avert', rebuilding can also be seen as a crucial process for sustainable protection of populations. The responsibility to rebuild rests under three fundamental elements: security, justice and economic development. It holds the potential to lead a path to prosperous peace and sustainable economic development, and thus, it should be considered as an integral part of R2P without a strict limitation to the circumstance of a military intervention taking place under the responsibility to react.

As we have seen in Darfur, the modicum of peace the hybrid peacekeeping forces achieved so far has fallen short with the untimely downsizing of the forces and complete withdrawal planned for 2021. Following from this, the absence of a rebuilding initiative has arguably made prior responses futile. In this vein, with its long history of mass atrocities, the case of Darfur allows us to see what has been missing in achieving sustainable protection. Lack of political will and national interests of the UN Member States, on the one hand, and the politically driven concerns as to not to hamper continuing peace negotiations between Khartoum and South Sudan, on the other hand, were major obstacles in delivering a timely and decisive response. The measures adopted were quick fixes to muffle the anger of the masses, which proved ineffectual in deterring the genocide. Meanwhile, disengagement hindered the moral ambition to react in an effective manner. As it was observed, sticking to the traditional definition of state sovereignty in the absence of Khartoum's consent and just denouncing the massacre did not yield to the aspired resolutions. This hints that we also need to build congruence through clear and persistent strategies and policies, as well as a process of rebuilding. As Badescu and Bergholm (2009, p. 291) suggest, 'R2P was framed in a sufficiently flexible and broad language to temporarily "veil" the important differences in opinion among states over when and how to respond to mass atrocities'. All in all, the reaction of the international community to the Darfur genocide demonstrates R2P's vague legal significance that renders the commitment to be inundated with the dilemmas of when and how to carry out the responsibility responsibly and successfully.

References

African Union (AU). (2004, October 20). *Communiqué of the seventeenth meeting of the Peace and Security Council*. The Report of the High-Level Mission in Darfur. PSC/PR/Comm. (XVII). Addis Ababa, Ethiopia.

Badescu, C. G., & Bergholm, L. (2009). The responsibility to protect and the conflict in Darfur: The big let-down. *Security Dialogue, 40*(3), 287–309.

Bellamy, A. J. (2005). Responsibility to protect or Trojan horse? The crisis in Darfur and humanitarian intervention after Iraq. *Ethics and International Affairs, 19*(2), 31–54.

Benjamin, D. (2010). Sudan and the resort to regional arrangements: Putting effect to the responsibility to protect? *The International Journal of Human Rights, 14*(2), 233–245.

Beswick, D. (2010). Peacekeeping, regime security, and 'African solutions to African problems': Exploring motivations for Rwanda's involvement in Darfur. *Third World Quarterly, 31*(5), 739–754.

Berridge, W. J. (2020). Briefing: The uprising in Sudan. *African Affairs, 119*(474), 164–176.

Bøås, M., & Bliesemann de Guevara, B. (Eds.). (2020). *Doing fieldwork in areas of international intervention: A guide to research in violent and closed contexts*. Bristol University Press.

Charity, M. H. (2011). The criminalized state: The international criminal court, the responsibility to protect, and Darfur, Republic of Sudan. *Ohio NUL Rev, 37*, 67–110.

Deen, T. (2005). New UN Force for Sudan will Skirt Darfur crisis. *Global Policy Forum*. New York, USA.

De Waal, A. (2007). Darfur and the failure of the responsibility to protect. *International Affairs, 83*(6), 1039–1054.

Flint, J., & De Waal, A. (2008). *Darfur: A new history of a long war*. Zed Books Ltd.

Gifkins, J. (2016). Darfur. In A. J. Bellamy & T. Dunne (Eds.), *The Oxford handbook of the responsibility to protect*. Oxford University Press.

Grzyb, A. (Ed.). (2009). *The world and Darfur: International response to crimes against humanity in Western Sudan* (Vol. 5). McGill-Queen's University Press.

Guicherd, C. (2007). *The AU in Sudan: Lessons for the African standby force*. International Peace Academy.

Hagan, J., & Rymond Richmond, W. (2008). *Darfur and the crime of genocide*. Cambridge University Press.

Human Rights Briefs. (2007). *Ensuring a responsibility to protect: Lessons from Darfur*. https://digitalcommons.wcl.american.edu/cgi/viewcontent.cgi?article=1210andcontext=hrbrief. Accessed 12 March 2020.

Human Rights Watch (HRW). (2004a, August 3). *Sudan: New Darfur documents. Ties between government, and Janjaweed Militias confirmed*. https://web.archive.org/web/20060810094616/http://www.humanrightswatch.org/english/docs/2004/07/20/darfur9095.htm. Accessed 22 April 2020.

Human Rights Watch (HRW). (2004b, August 17). *Darfur: Rwandan troops to protect civilians, Sudanese Government should accept African Union Plan for civilian protection*. https://www.hrw.org/news/2004/08/17/darfur-rwandan-troops-protect-civilians. Accessed 22 April 2020.

Human Rights Watch (HRW). (2005). *Darfur: Whose responsibility to protect*. Michael Clough. https://www.hrw.org/legacy/wr2k5/darfur/darfur.pdf. Accessed 21 February 2020.

Human Rights Watch (HRW). (2006). *Imperatives for immediate change the African Union Mission in Sudan*. 18,(1(A)). https://www.hrw.org/reports/2006/sudan0106/sudan0106web.pdf. Accessed 4 May 2020.

Human Rights Watch (HRW). (2008, April 25). *Q and A: Crisis in Darfur*. https://www.hrw.org/news/2008/04/25/q-crisis-darfur. Accessed 24 March 2020.

Human Rights Watch (HRW). (2020, March 16). *Sudan: UN/AU plan for Darfur falls short*. https://www.hrw.org/news/2020/03/16/sudan-un/au-plan-darfur-falls-short. Accessed 12 May 2020.

International Commission of Inquiry on Darfur (ICoIoD). (2005, January 25). *Report of the International Commission of Inquiry on Darfur to the United Nations Secretary-General, Geneva*. https://www.un.org/ruleoflaw/files/com_inq_darfur.pdf. Accessed 20 March 2020.

International Commission on Intervention and State Sovereignty (ICISS). (2001, December). *The responsibility to protect*. http://responsibilitytoprotect.org/ICISS%20Report.pdf. Accessed 12 May 2020.

International Criminal Court (ICC). (2009, March 4). *ICC issues a warrant of arrest for Omar Al Bashir, President of Sudan*. ICC-CPI-20090304-PR394. https://www.icc-cpi.int/pages/item.aspx?name=icc+issues+a+warrant+of+arrest+for+omar+al+bashir_+president+of+sudan. Accessed 12 May 2020.

International Criminal Court (ICC). (2010, June 16). *Trying individuals for genocide, war crimes, crimes against humanity, and aggression: New suspects in the situation in Darfur, Sudan arrive voluntarily at the ICC: First appearance scheduled for tomorrow*. ICC-CPI- 20100616-PR547. https://www.icc-cpi.int/Pages/item.aspx?name=pr547. Accessed 12 May 2020.

International Crisis Group (ICG). (2006, October 12). *Getting the UN into Darfur* (Africa Briefing No. 43). https://www.crisisgroup.org/africa/horn-africa/sudan/getting-un-darfur. Accessed 20 May 2020.

International Federation for Human Rights/African Center for Justice and Peace Studies (FIDH/ACJPS). (2019). *Will there be justice for Darfur? Persisting impunity in the face of political change* (Fact-finding mission report, No. 745a). https://www.fidh.org/IMG/pdf/sudan_darfur._pdf.pdf. Accessed on 23 May 2020.

International Refugee Rights Initiative (IRRI). (2016, June). *'No one on the earth cares if we survive except God and sometimes UNAMID': The challenges of peacekeeping in Darfur*. http://refugee-rights.org/wp-content/uploads/2017/11/UNAMID20FINAL.pdf. Accessed 20 May 2020.

Keith, A. (2007). The African Union in Darfur: An African solution to a global problem? *Journal of Public and International Affairs, 18*, 149–164.

Kreps, S. E. (2007). The United Nations-African Union Mission in Darfur: Implications and prospects for success. *African Security Studies, 16*(4), 65–79.

Müller, T. R. (2020). Protection of civilians mandates and 'collateral damage' of UN peacekeeping missions: Histories of refugees from Darfur. *International Peacekeeping, 27*(5), 760–784.

Natsios, A. S. (2012). *Sudan, South Sudan, and Darfur: What everyone needs to know*. Oxford University Press.

Office for the Coordination of Humanitarian Affairs (OCHA). (2007, August 24). *Genocide in slow motion: How Darfur's refugees are dying a protracted death*. https://reliefweb.int/report/sudan/genocide-slow-motion-how-darfurs-refugees-are-dying-protracted-death. Accessed 20 May 2020.

Office for the Coordination of Humanitarian Affairs (OCHA). (2019, March 13). *Humanitarian needs overview*. https://reliefweb.int/sites/reliefweb.int/files/resources/DRAFT_Sudan_2019_HNO_13Mar20.pdf. Accessed 20 March 2020.

Office for the Coordination of Humanitarian Affairs (OCHA). (2020, October 25). *Sudan has begun to replace UNAMID by national troops: official*. https://reliefweb.int/report/sudan/sudan-has-begun-replace-unamid-national-troops-official. Accessed 31 October 2020.

O'Neill, W. G., & Cassis, V. (2005). *Protecting two million internally displaced: The successes and shortcomings of the African Union in Darfur*. Brookings Institution.

Rasmussen, A., & Annan, J. (2010). Predicting stress related to basic needs and safety in Darfur refugee camps: A structural and social ecological analysis. *Journal of Refugee Studies, 23*(1), 23–40.

REDRESS. (2014, February). *Human Rights concerns and barriers to justice in Sudan: National, regional and international perspectives - A compilation of Sudan Law Reform Advocacy Briefings*. https://www.refworld.org/docid/5331852e4.html. Accessed 22 March 2020.

Reeves, E. (2005). Genocide by attrition: Agony in Darfur. *Dissent, 52*(1), 21–25.

Refugees International. (2004, September 02). *Sudan: Hiding death in Darfur*. https://reliefweb.int/report/sudan/sudan-hiding-death-darfur. Accessed 22 March 2020.

Rossi, C. R. (2016). The international community, South Sudan, and the responsibility to protect. *NYU Journal of International Law and Politics, 49*(129), 129–180.

Salih, M. (2005). *Understanding the conflict in Darfur*. Centre of African Studies (Occasional papers).

Spandler, K. (2020). UNAMID and the legitimation of global-regional peacekeeping cooperation: Partnership and friction in UN-AU relations. *Journal of Intervention and Statebuilding, 14*(2), 187–203.

Tanner, V., Tubiana, J., & Griffin, M. (2007). *Divided they fall: The fragmentation of Darfur's rebel groups*. Geneva, Switzerland: Small Arms Survey.

Thakur, R. (2004). Developing countries and the intervention—Sovereignty debate. *The United Nations and Global Security* (pp. 193–208). Palgrave Macmillan.

Thakur, R. (2016). *The United Nations, peace and security: From collective security to the responsibility to protect*. Cambridge University Press.

Thakur, R. (2018). Peacebuilding and the responsibility to rebuild. *Asian International Studies Review, 19*(2), 1–12.

Totten, S. (2008). Darfur: After the Genocide comes to an end, then what? *Journal of African Conflicts and Peace Studies, 1*(1), 89–110.

Totten, S. (2015). *Genocide by attrition: The Nuba Mountains of Sudan* (Vol. 1). Routledge.

Totten, S., & Markusen, E. (Eds.). (2013). *Genocide in Darfur: Investigating the atrocities in the Sudan*. Routledge.

United Nations (UN). (2020a, January 7). *Sudan: Intercommunal clashes displace tens of thousands in volatile Darfur region*. https://news.un.org/en/story/2020/01/1054911. Accessed 15 March 2020.

United Nations (UN). (2020b, December 30). *UN confirms closure of Darfur peacekeeping mission*. https://news.un.org/en/story/2020/12/1081122#:~:text=The%20process%20should%20result%20in,administrative%20closure%20of%20the%20mission. Accessed 12 February 2020.

United Nations–African Union Mission in Darfur (UNAMID). (2008, July 14). *UNAMID stresses peacekeeping operations will continue throughout Darfur*. El Fasher (Press release). https://unamid.unmissions.org/12-july-2008-unamid-stresses-peacekeeping-operations-will-continue-throughout-darfur. Accessed 20 April 2020.

United Nations–African Union Mission in Darfur (UNAMID). (2020). *Closure of UNAMID*. https://unamid.unmissions.org/about-unamid-0. Accessed 20 April 2020.

United Nations General Assembly (UNGA). (2005, October 24). *Resolution adopted by the General Assembly on 16 September 2005*. '60/1. 2005 World Summit Outcome', A/Res/60/1.

United Nations General Assembly (UNGA). (2009, January 12). *Implementing the responsibility to protect*. Report of the Secretary-General, A/63/677.

United Nations Security Council (UNSC). (2004a, July 30). Resolution 1556, S/RES/1556.

United Nations Security Council (UNSC). (2004b, September 18). Resolution 1564, S/RES/1564.

United Nations Security Council (UNSC). (2004c, September 18). *Sudan—Political conditions*. Report of the Secretary-General on the Sudan. S/PV.5040.

United Nations Security Council (UNSC). (2006a, April 28). Resolution 1674. S/RES/1674.

United Nations Security Council (UNSC). (2006b, August 31). Resolution 1706. S/RES/1706.

United Nations Security Council. (UNSC). (2007, July 31). Resolution 1769. S/RES/1769.

United Nations Mission in the Sudan (UNMIS). (2004). *UNMIS background*. https://peacekeeping.un.org/en/mission/past/unmis/background.shtml. Accessed 3 March 2020.

United States Committee for Refugees (USCfR). (2004, 10 December). *Crisis in Sudan*. https://web.archive.org/web/20041210024759/http://www.refugees.org/news/crisis/sudan.htm. Accessed 12 April 2020.

Williams, P. D., & Bellamy, A. J. (2005). The responsibility to protect and the crisis in Darfur. *Security Dialogue, 36*(1), 27–47.

CHAPTER 4

Kenya and Guinea: Preventive Strategies in R2P

Ezgi Nur Koç

Over the last twenty years, the debates on the Responsibility to Protect (R2P) have mainly been focused on the responsibility to react aspect of the norm, and particularly its third pillar, as the goal of prevention could not be achieved in most cases. Nevertheless, in terms of R2P's normative evolution under the roof of the United Nations (UN), prevention has been put forth as a priority. Following his predecessor Kofi Annan (2004) who argued that prevention is where R2P's nobility resides, former UN Secretary-General Ban Ki-moon has put great effort on instrumentalising prevention strategies and placed the emphasis on prevention as a priority (UNGA, 2009; UNGA–SC, 2011, 2013, 2014). After assuming office, current Secretary-General António Guterres too has placed prevention at the core of R2P and focused on the significant contributions of regional and sub-regional organisations to atrocity prevention and protection (UNGA–SC, 2017, 2021; UNSG, 2018). Diverging from the critical R2P literature discussing cases of humanitarian crises from a responsibility

E. N. Koç (✉)
Department of International Relations, Hacettepe University, Ankara, Turkey

P. Gözen Ercan (ed.), *The Responsibility to Protect Twenty Years On*,
https://doi.org/10.1007/978-3-030-90731-0_4

to react perspective (see, for instance, Cunliffe, 2011; De Waal, 2007; Hehir, 2010; Morris, 2016; Newman, 2013; O'Connell, 2010; Reinold, 2010; Williams & Pearlman, 2019), this chapter focuses on the cases of Kenya (2007) and Guinea (2009–2010), which are cited as successful examples of R2P implementation. A point of significance for these two cases is that while they are regarded mostly as examples of preventive action (Babbitt, 2014; Halakhe, 2013; Weiss, 2010; Welsh, 2016), they are also considered as responses through peaceful measures under Pillar Three of R2P (Bellamy, 2015; Negrón-Gonzales & Contarino, 2014).

As Woocher (2012) suggests, there is no definitive answer to the question 'whether international responses to post-electoral violence in Kenya and violent attacks in Guinea in September 2009 represent prevention or reaction efforts'. In this regard, the main goal of this chapter is to seek what is needed to achieve successful prevention of mass atrocity crimes under R2P by comparing the cases of Kenya and Guinea following the categorisation of structural and operational[1] prevention as put forth by Ban Ki-moon (UNGA–SC, 2011). Ban suggests that the 'three pillars are not sequential' and international assistance under Pillar Two could be implemented in 'a state under-stress, before crises and conflicts break out' (UNGA, 2009). He also reminds that the lines between prevention and response are not always clear because early action also aims for preventing the escalation of the crisis (UNGA–SC, 2012, p. 4), while a Pillar Three response is likely to result in reoccurrence prevention (UNGA–SC, 2012, p. 5). That is why in practice it is not always easy and necessary to determine under which pillar the action is carried out (UNGA–SC, 2012, p. 4).

Following from this, the chapter conducts a twofold analysis. First, it examines on what grounds the cases of Kenya and Guinea can be considered as examples of successful prevention of mass atrocities. To this end, it focuses on direct and structural prevention mechanisms and questions to what extent, and under which circumstances these strategies were successful. Second, by comparing the contexts of and responses to the Kenyan and Guinean cases, it aims to provide a better understanding of the similarities and differences between the two cases. In the light of these

[1] Ban notes that operational prevention may also be considered as a Pillar Three response because it is implemented to stop imminent atrocities and is about conflict prevention (UNGA–SC, 2011).

findings, we can identify the necessary circumstances and actions that may lead to successful prevention.

Implementation of R2P in Kenya and Guinea

Kenya and Guinea have witnessed smaller-scale atrocities compared to other R2P crises such as in Darfur, Libya and Myanmar. Kenya faced communal violence after the 2007 presidential elections, while Guinean junta intervened in a peaceful protest against the government, which resulted in a massacre of civilians in 2009 (UNSC, 2009b; Weiss, 2010). Both in Kenya and Guinea, the mass atrocities were committed not during an armed conflict but in peacetime.[2] That is why, as Bellamy (2011) suggests, we need to use an 'atrocity lens' and think outside the context of armed conflict in order to understand the preventive actions undertaken.

Atrocity prevention measures, in general, are carried out to decrease the likelihood of recurrence as well as the risk of both armed conflict and peacetime atrocities; to stop imminent conflict or peacetime atrocities; and to prevent atrocities in armed conflict (Bellamy, 2011). While structural/root cause prevention is to mitigate the general risk of mass atrocities for a longer-term, direct/operational prevention should be implemented in the case of imminent threat of atrocities and serious political and social unrest (Bellamy, 2011; Stamnes, 2009; Woocher, 2012). Accordingly, this section first provides an overview of the emergence of the atrocities, and then the measures adopted in Kenya and Guinea within the framework of the responsibility to prevent. Rather than limiting the analysis to a strict division between Pillars Two and Three, the international response is analysed from the perspective of structural and operational prevention efforts. Such approach allows us to also assess in which ways and to what extent success was achieved in terms of mass atrocity prevention.

Kenya

To examine the post-election violence in Kenya, first we should understand the political and ethnic circumstances that paved the way for the unrest throughout the country. Communal violence after the 27

[2] Peacetime atrocities may appear in cases of State-directed suppression, communal violence and post-war retribution (Bellamy, 2011, p. 3).

December 2007 elections was not only due to a general political fraction in the society, but also the reasons behind it were also socio-economic realities and growing ethnic tension since Kenya's independence (Weiss, 2010). In Kenya, ethnic identity is highly politicised because of the uneven distribution of resources among primary ethnic communities. Nepotism and unequal allocation of lands have fed the grievances between different communities. Forty-two different ethnic groups reside in Kenya's lands (Crossley, 2013). The largest groups—namely Kikuyu, Lou and Kalenjin—have been competing to seize the power. In diverse societies as such, power means access to economic facilities and resources, and hence the elections are of great importance (Deng, 2008, as cited in Weiss, 2010). Furthermore, land management institutions are not independent of political administration, and this leads to lack of trust in State institutions (Kagwanja & Southall, 2009). Therefore, in Kenya, the politicised ethnic grievances and inherited socio-economic inequalities have arguably resulted in the post-election violence which appeared as an imminent threat of crimes against humanity.

On 27 December 2007, Mwai Kibaki of the Party of National Unity (PNU) and Raila Odinga of the Orange Democratic Movement (ODM) competed in presidential elections (Lindenmayer & Kaye, 2009). Kibaki—who was from Kikuyu origin—was elected as president in 2002. However, during his term his government could not address historical injustices and failed to keep several promises he made in 2002. Hence, Odinga—who was of Lou political/ethnic origin—challenged Kibaki to end the Kikuyu's domination and the poverty that seriously affected certain ethnic communities during Kibaki's term (Kanyinga et al., 2010, p. 10). While the electoral campaigns were relatively peaceful, problems arose during the vote counting. Electoral Commission of Kenya (ECK)'s delayed announcement of the election results ignited tension (KHRC, 2008, p. 53). Three days after the elections, the ECK Chair declared Kibaki as the winner although Odinga's party ODM held the majority of the seats in the parliament. The European Union (EU) and other local and international monitoring groups, European Observation Mission (EUOM), the Commonwealth Observer Group (COG) and Kenyans for Peace with Truth and Justice (KPTJ), expressed concerns about the credibility of the election results (KHRC, 2008). Right after the ECK's announcement, protests started in Nairobi (in Kibera and Kisumu) and violence erupted wherein Kikuyu lands and properties especially in Rift

Valley were targeted (OHCHR, 2008, p. 8). Within a few days, the situation escalated to the level of ethnic conflict which was driven by poverty and injustice. While majority of the victims were Kikuyus, at least four different ethnic community members gave causalities (Lindenmayer & Kaye, 2009, p. 3).

Human Rights Watch (HRW) (2008) reported the police's use of excessive force against the protestors. Meanwhile, some of the protestors took advantage of the lack of rule of law to 'loot, rape, and riot' (HRW, 2008). The Fact-Finding Team of the OHCHR (2008) found that violence not only occurred spontaneously, but also there were organised and retaliatory acts. It was reported that organised crimes were committed mostly by the Kalenjin ethnic group (ICG, 2008). The violence resulted in over 1,300 deaths and with 600,000 Kenyans displaced (TJRC, 2008). The threat of mass atrocities was imminent; the police were using indiscriminate force; sexual and gender-based violence not connected to ethnic tension was also reported; and forced displacement was accelerated due to ethnic-based violence (OHCHR, 2008). According to Lindenmayer and Kaye (2009), ethnic cleansing was a risk in Kenya under the current circumstances.

While tension was about to escalate, international efforts to prevent imminent atrocity crimes came rapidly. However, initial attempts failed due to redundancy and discord (Sharma, 2016). The first visit was carried out by Bishop Desmond Tutu and followed by the Forum of Former African Heads of States, Jendayi Frazer—United States (US) Secretary of State for African Affairs—and Ugandan President Museveni—Chairman of the Heads of State Summit of the East African Community (Mwagiru, 2008). Initial efforts were echoed by the UN Secretary-General Ban Ki-moon, who reminded Kenyan authorities of their responsibility to protect their people (UNMCPR, 2008). Moreover, the UN Special Adviser on the Prevention of Genocide, Francis Deng, urged the Kenyan government to end the violence while placing special emphasis on R2P (UNNC, 2008a).

The escalation prevention began with a strong mediation request on 10 January 2008 when former UN Secretary-General Kofi Annan, Tanzanian President Benjamin Mkapa and Mozambican politician Graça Machel formed an African Union (AU) Panel of Eminent African Personalities owing to the efforts of Ghanaian president John Kufuor (Babbitt, 2014). At the time, the Panel arrived in Kenya, Kibaki was not willing to share his power with the opposition and wanted to form a national unity government without the ODM to stop the crisis, whereas Odinga refused Kibaki's proposition as he believed that only an international mediation would bring an end to the crisis (Wallis & Moody, 2008). Although they were blaming each other for vote-rigging and the escalation of the crisis, Kufuor announced that 'both sides agreed there should be an end to the violence, and they also agreed there should be dialogue' (Gettleman, 2008). On 22 January, the AU Panel of Eminent African Personalities commenced with Annan leading the mediation. Two days later, the first handshake was accomplished.

Nevertheless, as the parties continued to accuse each other, the tension started to escalate again. This time the situation was controlled with the agreement on a 'Road Map'. The process of Kenyan National Dialogue and Reconciliation (KNDR) began with the four agenda items set. The first two were directly related with prevention of mass atrocities and the humanitarian crisis. The third concerned the settling of the political crisis while the fourth envisaged finding long-term solutions to the root causes of the crisis (Weiss, 2010). Accordingly, both operational and structural prevention were planned to be implemented through mediation.

Nonstop mediation took 41 days and adopted measures under operational prevention. The first two agenda items were accomplished rapidly with both parties making statements to 'promote peace, ensure freedom of expression and the right to peaceful assembly' on 4 February (Lindenmayer & Kaye, 2009, p. 11). They also pledged to provide safe relocation of internally displaced persons. According to Bellamy (2011), governance measures (such as strengthening democracy and power-sharing) can be used for structural prevention. The political agenda of the Kenyan Road Map implemented direct prevention measures to stop the escalation of the tension, but it also had structural effects. To settle the public, it was necessary to show people that an agreement between the opposing sides was achievable. Thanks to the UN Member States (especially the US and the EU) as well as the new AU Chair President Kikwete joining the mediation efforts, Kibaki and Odinga agreed on the establishment of a coalition government under 'Acting together for Kenya' (Weiss, 2010, p. 23). Respectively, a constitutional change was envisioned. Accordingly, 'the National Accord and Reconciliation Act', establishing a powerful prime minister position for Odinga with two deputy prime ministers, and presidency for Kibaki, would be adopted (UNP, 2008).

The fourth agenda item was to eliminate the root causes of the ethnic conflict. After the mediation succeeded in operational terms, the focus was shifted to the long-term progress for purposes of recurrence prevention. For effective regional assistance, former Nigerian Foreign Minister Adeniji was appointed by the AU panel. With his efforts, parties agreed to establish the Independent Review Commission (IREC) of 2007; the Truth, Justice and Reconciliation Commission (TJRC); the Commission of Inquiry into Post-Election Violence (CIPEV); as well as two constitutional arrangements (Security Council Report, 2008). In terms of the structural issues, the new government also bore a responsibility under Pillar One. CIPEV determined the root causes as 'land grievances and the centralization of power in presidency' (ICTJ, 2008). It recommended the creation of a Special Tribunal to break the culture of impunity. The government accepted the Commission's proposal for the submission to the International Criminal Court (ICC) of those who are responsible for crimes against humanity in the case of inaction through domestic courts (TJRC, 2008). However, when the parliament rejected twice the proposals for establishing a court, in 2009, Annan gave the sealed envelope including the names responsible for mass atrocity crimes to the ICC Prosecutor (Annan, 2013). The Prosecutor commenced the investigations against powerful names like Uhuru Kenyetta and William Ruto. Thus, both direct and structural measures had been used for prevention of recurrence. It is noteworthy that while the ongoing ICC investigation against Kenyatta and Ruto damaged their accountability for standing in elections, it did not prevent them from claiming the power. In the 2013 elections, Kenyatta was elected as president, and Ruto was elected as prime minister (Annan, 2013).

That said, the measures undertaken by the government to prevent the resurgence of tension in the forthcoming elections should not be underestimated. These efforts too can be considered as part of both structural and direct prevention efforts. While the ICC prosecution constituted a sort of direct prevention, it was followed by structural prevention efforts. Kenya adopted a new constitution in 2010 which included land reforms, bill of rights, local government empowerment, creation of mandatory seats for Kenyan women in parliament and the formation of an Independent Electoral and Boundaries Commission (ICRtoP, n.d.). Police and Security reform was also implemented by the government to train the police on human rights matters.

Despite all, due to lack of a sustainable solution for tackling the root causes, tension resurged in the 2013 and 2017 elections (GCR2P, 2017; HRW, 2013). As the Kenyan Commission of Inquiry stated in 2008, fundamental issues, such as police reform, corruption, criminal groups, displaced people persisted (HRW, 2013; ICRtoP, n.d.). As Annan (2013) remarks, 'the first aim of the mediation was to stop the violence, which it did'. Moreover, it set up several ad hoc bodies to end discrimination. Yet, it did not fully address the underlying grievances within the society (Babbitt, 2014). Hence, the risk of recurrence persisted even though the 2013 elections were relatively more peaceful owing to the international assistance and capacity-building measures that intergovernmental organisations and civil society carried out before and after the elections (ICRtoP, n.d.).

Guinea

In December 2008, the junta seized power and its head Captain Dadis Camara became the president. Although Camara promised free elections to establish a civilian government soon, he instead banned the parliament and suspended the constitution. Regional and international organisations collaboratively condemned his actions. Meanwhile, a peaceful protest started when Camara broke his promise to not to rally for upcoming elections (GCR2P, 2019). On 28 December 2009, in the infamous Stadium Massacre, gendarmerie and police forces used excessive force against civilian protestors. Raising the international community's concern as to whether mass atrocities were committed, the widespread and systemic attack resulted in 109 women raped, 67 people killed and 89 disappeared (UNSC, 2009b, p. 47). The situation was regarded as a failure of the Guinean government to protect its population (ICRtoP, 2010) and followed by a rapid response by first regional and then international actors to halt the atrocities and prevent escalation.

Immediate measures were imposed by regional organisations. The AU and ECOWAS called on the UN to form an International Commission of Inquiry (AU–ECOWAS, 2009). On 7 October 2009, ECOWAS appointed a mediation team to settle the issues between the opposition and the junta, as well as to determine what should be done to prevent the escalation of the situation (ICRtoP, 2010). Moreover, ECOWAS imposed an arms embargo while the AU imposed a travel ban and assets freeze on the junta members (HRW, 2009). Early regional response was followed by international efforts. France and the US condemned the junta. French Foreign Minister Bernard Kouchner challenged the Guinean government with the possibility of an international intervention (France24, 2009).

The EU and the US imposed an arms embargo, as well as assets freeze, and travel ban on the members of the junta (EU, 2009; HRW, 2009).

Besides the targeted sanctions, the establishment of the UN Commission of Inquiry in Guinea by the UN Secretary-General and the ICC's preliminary examination can be considered as direct prevention measures adopted in the face of mass atrocity crimes. The Commission of Inquiry found that the violence did not spontaneously occur, and that this was an organised act by the government and security forces wherein they committed crimes against humanity (UNSC, 2009b). The Commission also stated that the use of force was selective and directed against a particular ethnic origin, namely the Peul (UNSC, 2009b, pp. 28, 40). Likewise, upon preliminary examination ICC Prosecutor Fatou Bensouda stated that crimes against humanity had taken place (ICRtoP, 2010).

With the efforts of the envoy of ECOWAS President of Burkina Faso Blaise Compaore, Declaration of Ouagadougou was signed to form a national unity government led by interim Prime Minister Jean-Marie Doré (Ouagadougou Joint Declaration, 2010). Hence, in a way, direct prevention measures to deter violence recurrence were implemented simultaneously with rapid reaction and they were followed by mediation. The declaration scheduled a free and democratic election for 27 June, and both the government and the UN called for the international community to support the monitoring and financing of the elections (UNGA, 2010a). The Human Rights Council (HRC), the AU, ECOWAS and UN Humanitarian Air Services expressly welcomed free elections (ICRtoP, 2010). While the election took place peacefully, the opposition challenged the results with claims of rigging. As the Supreme Court delayed the second round thrice due to technical difficulties, politicised ethnic tension began to unfold, with reported incidents of excessive use of force on Diallo's supporters (ICG, 2010). While Cellou Dalein Diallo's party mainly represented the Peul ethnic group, Condé was associated with Malinke. According to the data of the International Committee of the Red Cross, until the election took place, 2,800 people were displaced (Penney, 2010). After the Supreme Court announced the opposition leader Alpha Conde as the first democratically elected president, violence accelerated, and a state of emergency was declared (VOA, 2010).

ECOWAS assumed the responsibility to prevent the escalation of the situation, and hence recurrence of atrocity crimes, and worked to achieve progress by organising meetings between parties (Clottey, 2010b). The AU warned groups attempting to delay peaceful elections (AU–AHSG,

2010, Para. 24). After the second round, UN Secretary-General Ban Ki-moon called the international community to assist the election process and urged the Guineans to accept the results (UNNC). Then, the UN Security Council (UNSC) urged political leaders to ease the tension and recalled the responsibility of the State and security forces to protect the population (UNNC, 2010b). The US called for respect to democratic transition, while the International Crisis Group and Amnesty International made statements to draw the international community's attention to escalation prevention (ICRtoP, 2010).

The violence continued with the subsequent elections in Guinea due to lack of accountability for past crimes. The State did not hold trials for the violence committed by the security forces in the 2018 protests, as it was previously the case for the 2015 presidential elections and 2013 parliamentary elections (HRW, 2020a). Although the government collaborated with the HRC and reported on its progress regarding several reforms on human rights, Guinea still needed to establish capacity-building institutions (UNGA, 2014, 2019). In 2014, due to the 2013 elections and the threat of the resurgence of tension, the HRC recalled 'primary responsibility of the Government of Guinea to protect its population' (UNGA, 2014, p. 1). At the same time, it emphasised the ongoing rebuilding efforts made by the AU, ECOWAS and the Guinean government to establish democratic institutions under structural prevention. However, the lack of rule of law allowed for violent treatment in the 2019 protests that were organised against the constitutional amendment and lasted until the end of 2020 presidential elections (HRW, 2020b, 2021). The African Commission on Human and Peoples' Rights (ACHPR), the Special Representative of the UN Office for West Africa and the Sahel (UNOWAS), ECOWAS, the EU, France and the US condemned the use of force (HRW, 2020a, 2020b). While the Secretary-General pursued preventive diplomacy, the AU, ECOWAS and the UN sent representatives to act as mediators (GCR2P, 2020).

In the case of Guinea, the efforts to prevent the recurrence of violence can be categorised under both direct and structural prevention. Although the risk of tension has not disappeared, there are no new atrocity crimes reported. Moreover, while the government has established democratic institutions, security sector reforms still fall short. The violence had mostly been committed by the security forces of the government due to the culture of impunity. While the ICC played a positive role in the investigation of the crimes committed in 2009, the Guinean people are still waiting for the persecution of those who were responsible for the Stadium Massacre (HRW, 2020b; ICC, 2020).

Towards Successful Prevention

As Serrano and Weiss (2014) observe, both in Kenya (2008, 2013) and Guinea (2010), regional and international efforts achieved credible success in preventing violence from rekindling and mass atrocities from recurring. As studied in the previous section, direct prevention efforts such as mediation, economic sanctions, threats and inducements, condemnations, ICC prosecution and other international assistance efforts were effective in achieving such success. Nevertheless, structural prevention efforts and related reforms that aimed to eliminate the root causes of the conflicts—i.e. long-term prevention efforts—were not as successful as the direct prevention measures. It is noteworthy that resurging tension was common to the cases of both Kenya and Guinea. While the cleavages in the society remained below the surface in peacetime, during the elections they erupted into violence—for example, in Kenya in 2013 and 2017, and in Guinea in 2010, 2013, 2015, 2018, 2019 and 2020 (GCR2P, 2017, 2019, 2020). Based on the recurrence frequency, arguably Kenya has been more stable than Guinea because the Kenyan prevention strategy was implemented in a more systemic manner wherein the short-term and long-term measures were utilised sustainably. Moreover, while the Kenyan government actively established institutions and implemented some of the structural prevention measures itself, the Guinean government was less involved in the process of development and could not fully implement the measures due to technical problems (HRW, 2021).

Despite their shortfalls, both cases proved to be examples of successful prevention to a considerable extent. In this regard, a further comparison allows us to identify additional necessities and factors for achieving success in prevention. In both crises, rapid action was one of the steering factors that internationalised the cases and led to a timely R2P response. As Ban argues, early engagement leaves no need to use force (UNGA, 2009, p. 9). Early resolution of crises may prevent further escalation of atrocity crimes and also prevent crises from turning into mass atrocities. Moreover, as enshrined in Paragraph 139 of the World Summit Outcome Document (WSOD), the international community can adopt peaceful measures under Chapters VI and VIII of the UN Charter. Collective efforts would be successful when 'undertaken at an early point and are carefully targeted and calibrated' (UNGA, 2010b, Para. 3). Considering that both Kenya and Guinea come from the same region and have cultural similarities, the engagement of a regional organisation that is proximate to the territories in crisis and has an understanding of the countries' background was much more preferable and likely to be efficient in response. In this regard, it was one day after the Kibaki swore in Parliament on 30 December that regional mediation efforts were commenced by the AU Chairman Kufuor and followed by other African Heads of States (Halakhe, 2013, p. 8). Although the initial attempts failed, they were able to steer a more planned action through the mediation led by Eminent African Personalities on 22 January. Furthermore, in Guinea, immediately after the massacre, the AU and ECOWAS drew the international community's attention to the issue and prompted an international response (ICRtoP, 2010).

It is also important to underline the variety of measures that were adopted in Kenya and Guinea. While the two cases were distinct from each other, they also shared certain similarities. Both situations had occurred in peacetime. In Kenya right after the elections, and in Guinea during a peaceful protest the mass atrocities became imminent. While in Kenya communal violence occurred mostly spontaneously but was followed by semi-organised use of force, in Guinea, the Commission of Inquiry determined that the government was not only informed about the use of force but also responsible for it (TJRC, 2008, pp. 66–77, 102–105; UNSC, 2009b, pp. 46–55). Moreover, the fact-finding commissions in both cases have traced the root causes of the violence to ethnic divisions, especially in Kenya. They also pointed at the lack of rule of law and trustable democratic institutions fuelled with poverty and a culture of impunity (TJRC, 2008, p. 23; UNSC, 2009b, Paras. 176, 254–275).

Nevertheless, as the perpetrators and the way the violence unfolded were different, the response to each case had to be tailored accordingly. For example, in Guinea the international community imposed more coercive measures such as economic sanctions and arms embargoes, whereas there was only the threat of coercive measures in Kenya (Sharma, 2016; WPF, 2017). As the perpetrators were apparent in Guinea, it was an obvious choice to block the junta's access to weapons to prevent the escalation and resurgence of the tension. The sanctions followed the mediation between the opposition and the government. However, in the case of Kenya the crisis arose due to communal violence between politicised ethnic factions, and thus, the parties needed to be mediated immediately.

In his 2010 report on R2P, Ban suggests that there is need for 'carefully targeted and calibrated' peaceful and preventive measures, and 'differentiated assessment of each case' (UNGA, 2010b). Likewise, he argues that 'what is needed is an early and flexible response tailored to the circumstances of each case, rather than any generalized or prescriptive set of policy options' (UNGA–SC, 2011). We see such approach manifesting itself in the cases of Kenya and Guinea, wherein different measures were adopted in accordance with the unique qualities of each situation.

Furthermore, there is also need for a tailored approach in structural prevention to avert the root causes of violence and to achieve sustainable prevention. For example, in both cases the culture of impunity was one of the main causes of the conflict and the human rights violations were likely to turn into mass atrocities. That is why reforms on the security sector and the rule of law were enacted (ICRtoP, n.d.; WPF, 2017, p. 2). Also, the ICC's involvement has been of significance in the attempts to break the cycle of impunity in both cases as the Court has been assisting the pursuit of justice (ICC, 2020). Moreover, in Guinea rape and gender-based violence were among the qualifiers of the crimes against humanity. Hence, international assistance and capacity-building and also the government's efforts have been focused on establishing the institutions working on gender and human rights (UNGA, 2019). In the case of Kenya, the government established the National Cohesion and Integration Commission in 2008 to prevent the marginalisation of communities and to promote the peaceful coexistence of ethnic groups (UNGPRtoP, 2017, p. 5). Since both crises occurred in peacetime, we see that the measures were adopted with the aim of mass atrocity prevention rather than simply focusing on conflict prevention.

Both in Kenya and Guinea, the prevention efforts were consistently implemented. In Kenya, prevention began in 2008 and lasted until the subsequent elections that took place in 2013 but had to be implemented again in 2017. Thanks to such consistent strategy, despite the escalated tension, the 2013 elections were regarded as legitimate by a joint statement of election monitors from the EU, AU, Carter Center and other regional observation groups (Reliefweb, 2013). The reforms that were implemented by the government showed its success in the judicial settlements. Although Odinga contested the results in 2013, seeking a judicial settlement he took the issue to the Supreme Court. Expressing his commitment to constitutionalism he abided by the decision of the Court (BBC, 2013). Considering the mistrust to State institutions, this was visible progress.

Arguably, the consistent application of preventive measures was accomplished by performing the three pillars of R2P in harmony. When structural and direct prevention measures are simultaneously and successfully applied, they can lead to sustainable prevention, and if the three-pillar implementation strategy is followed while employing these measures, it becomes more likely to achieve successful prevention. Eventually, the main goal common to the three pillars is to help the State authorities to uphold their Pillar One responsibilities. Therefore, short and long-term approaches should follow each other in harmony so that assistance can be provided to States to protect their populations (UNGA–SC, 2012). In Kenya and Guinea, preventive diplomacy was carried out as a response under Pillar Three but it also prevented the escalation of violence. On the other hand, the establishment of a commission of inquiry can be considered as part of international assistance falling under Pillar Two. Yet, it was a timely and decisive response to find the facts and perpetrators in Guinea, which according to Ban, also prevented possible crimes (UNGA–SC, 2012, Para. 12). After the direct preventive response under Pillar Three, the international community continued with international assistance and capacity-building under Pillar Two. Regional and international actors supported structural reforms adopted by the government of Kenya under Pillar One. The Kenyan government revised the constitution to make it more democratic and also made reforms in the security sector, media and state institutions (Halakhe, 2013, p. 18). In line with Pillars One and Two, the government and the UN worked for ending hate speech. Accordingly, before the 2013 elections the UN Special Adviser on the Prevention of Genocide Adama Dieng convened workshops and campaigns on hate speech (Sharma, 2016, p. 11). Furthermore, the international community, especially the AU and ECOWAS worked closely with the transitional government of Guinea to promote democratic transition and upcoming elections in 2010 and 2013 (AU–AHSG, 2010; UNGA, 2014). Also, the UN Peacebuilding Commission, the EU and ECOWAS started to work together on the security sector reform in Guinea after the 2010 presidential elections (WPF, 2017).

Triggering action and overcoming the lack of political will on the part of the international community is perhaps the most important point that needs to be highlighted in terms of the international responsibility to protect. Since R2P is not a legal norm but is grounded on international law, invocation of collective action rests on the willingness of the international actors to respond. To date, most of the time when action was needed the UN mostly faced with unwilling Member States and/or UNSC deadlocks (Gözen Ercan, 2016; Wheeler & Egerton, 2009), but not in the cases of Kenya and Guinea. A primary reason behind this success lies in the early response of regional and sub-regional organisations. As established under Article 52(2) of Chapter VIII of the UN Charter, for carrying out prevention and/or the peaceful measures enshrined under Chapter VI of the UN Charter, regional arrangements do not need 'the explicit authorization of the Security Council or the General Assembly' (UNGA–SC, 2012, Para. 22). Therefore, without facing a UNSC deadlock, in Kenya the AU and in Guinea ECOWAS started prevention. In general terms, it is most likely that a regional organisation would be more willing to act because a crisis in the region could pose a risk for everyone in the region. That said, the vision of the organisation is also significant for having the desire and the right mechanisms to deal with atrocities.[3] In this regard, the AU and ECOWAS stand out as two important regional and sub-regional arrangements that aim to protect their people from violence.

For instance, the AU has not only adopted R2P in the Ezulwini Consensus, but also the African Peace and Security Architecture embodies important mechanisms relating to R2P (AU, 2005, 2012). In this regard, in Kenya the AU mediation started thanks to Chairman Mkapa and the power-sharing agreement enforced by Tanzanian President Kikwete who helped the solution keep in the line with 'African solution for African problems' (Weiss, 2010, p. 28). Moreover, the AU suspended Guinea from membership after the coup, then imposed targeted sanctions (WPF, 2017).

[3] When the AU replaced the Organization of African Unity (OAU), it also shifted its principles from non-interference to non-indifference (Aning & Atuobi, 2009, p. 108). Accordingly, Article 4(h) of the AU's Constitutive Act allows the organisation to intervene in a Member State in the case of grave circumstances (such as war crimes, genocide and crimes against humanity) (AU, 2001). Also, the Peace and Security Council of the AU has a duty to 'prevent disputes and conflict which may lead to genocide and crimes against humanity' and 'undertake ... peacebuilding functions' (AU, 2002).

Furthermore, as a sub-regional organisation ECOWAS has valuable mechanisms to prevent grave circumstances throughout West Africa.[4] For the operationalisation of R2P, it can play an important role in the region as it did in Guinea. Besides the AU, ECOWAS suspended Guinea from organisational meetings due to the junta's violation of Supplementary Protocol on Democracy and Good Governance (Aning & Atuobi, 2012). After its successful mediation, ECOWAS sustained its prevention support by providing financial and technical assistance. For instance, ECOWAS Political Director Abdel-Fatau Musah stated that the Organisation 'had advanced an amount of half a million dollars ... in aid of the Independent Electoral Commission of Guinea in the preparation for the election' (Clottey, 2010a).

While regional organisations were the vanguard of triggering the political will to act and boosting the early response, another reason for both successful and sustained support was the unity of different local and international actors. While action tailored to the specificities of each case is critical, the actors involved in the process need to act in harmony. The efforts of appropriate actors should be instrumentalised in the right place at the right time. For instance, in Kenya internationally respected persons contributed to the mediation and attracted the attention of the international community. Kofi Annan, with years of experience on R2P and conflict resolution, played a vital role in the mediations. He conditioned that there was going to be one channel for the mediation, which was himself and the Panel, and that third parties would support the process when a carrot and stick approach was to be pursued (Lindenmayer & Kaye, 2009, pp. 4–6). Accordingly, the EU Member States and the US successfully used economic and diplomatic incentives and restraints to support the process. The US and the EU informed the Kenyan authorities that they would not return to friendly relations until the crisis was resolved, and when the conflicting parties reached an agreement, the US aided $30 million (Lindenmayer & Kaye, 2009; Sharma, 2016). Canada

[4] Although it was mainly established for economic and technical assistance, ECOWAS realised that stable regional security is needed for long-term regional economic stability (Sampson, 2011, p. 513). Accordingly, it developed ECOWAS Peace and Security Mechanisms and Conflict Prevention Framework for timely prevention and resolution of crises within and between states (ECOWAS, 1999, 2008). Specifically, for atrocity prevention it established the Council of Elders (COE) and the Early Warning System (ECOWARN).

and the US also threatened the parties with sanctions on specific individuals (Sharma, 2016, p. 6). Bernard Kouchner, Desmond Tutu, Francis Deng and Ban Ki-moon invoked R2P in the case of Kenya (Tutu, 2008; UNNC, 2008b). The EU was also engaged in civil society-led projects as well as developing early warning systems, and it provided assistance for long-term rebuilding projects (Babaud & Ndung'u, 2012).

When we look at the big picture, we see that religious communities, eminent individuals, the UN Member States and regional mechanisms became one voice to prevent the escalation of atrocities. Furthermore, assistance by civil society was substantial during mediation and the way forward to the 2013 elections. The Annan-led mediation worked in tandem with both media and local non-governmental organisations to keep the process transparent and reach the Kenyan society (Lindenmayer & Kaye, 2009; Weiss, 2010). For example, PeaceNet was part of a fact-finding commission led by the AMANI Forum—which consists of regional politicians—and it also engaged in activities to promote tolerance among the members of the community (Babaud & Ndung'u, 2012, p. 24; UNGPRtoP, 2017). PeaceNet Kenya also established the 'Uwiano platform for peace' that is financed by Sweden, the UK and UN Women to develop early warning capabilities and technologies (Halakhe, 2013, p. 19). Likewise, 'the Concerned Citizens for Peace (CCP) began forming as soon as the violence began. Even before the AU panel arrived, the CCP reached out to schools, churches, businesses, and the media to forestall the incitement to violence'. They were also active during mediation and helped to 'convey the public's support for a peaceful solution to the leadership and to reassure the public that its leaders were listening' (Babbitt, 2014).

In Guinea, the regional and international actors got engaged in the situation right after the junta's take over. They were acting in harmony before the massacre occurred. Besides individual efforts that were implemented by ECOWAS, the US, the AU and the EU; the UN also formed a group of friends against increasing suppression by the junta. 'The Friends' are called as the International Contact Group on Guinea (ICG-G)—consisting of 'the UN, the AU, the EU, the World Bank, ECOWAS, International Organization of la Francophonie (OIF), the El, the Mano River Union, other regional organizations and partner countries, including France, Morocco, Burkina Faso, the UK, and the United States'—worked for the return to constitutional order in Guinea since early 2009 (UNSC, 2009a). Moreover, the ICG-G was one of the first actors that condemned the Stadium Massacre. It called for ICC prosecution to end impunity and international assistance for socio-economic reconstruction (AU–ECOWAS, 2009, 2010; Reliefweb, 2009). Despite the tension followed by demonstrations in 2013 legislative elections, the vote count was completed peacefully and legitimately thanks to the mediation by UNOWAS and the EU observers (WPF, 2017).

Conclusion

In the post-WSOD period, Kenya and Guinea remain as important examples of R2P in action wherein escalation and recurrence prevention were successfully practised. It is noteworthy that small-scale tensions have been occurring from time to time because the root causes have not been fully addressed. Since recurrence is mostly related to structural prevention, compared to Guinea the risk of recurrence has been less in Kenya as various actors (such as civil society, eminent individuals and regional organisations) were involved in the process, and long-term measures were implemented systematically thanks to the road map. This indicates that a sustainable prevention can yield to successful prevention of mass atrocity crimes.

As the Secretary-General noted in 2011, there is need for comparative studies to improve the tools of R2P (UNGA–SC, 2011, Para. 16). In this vein, an analysis of the Kenyan and Guinean cases offers us valuable lessons on successful prevention. First of all, prevention should be sustainable: in addition to direct measures against imminent risks and escalation, root causes should be determined and addressed in the long-term. To achieve sustainable prevention, structural prevention has to be pursued before mass atrocity crimes become imminent. In cases where atrocities have occurred, structural prevention should be carried out to prevent recurrence.

Second, the response should be delivered as early as possible. Regional organisations, in this regard, have an advantageous position due their proximity and knowledge of the region, and they should be engaged in the process of prevention at this early stage. Even in cases of a UNSC deadlock or failure to act, regional organisations may effectively carry out peaceful measures.

Third, the UN and the international community in general should work together in unison. The examples of Kenya and Guinea evince that the harmony between local civil society, regional organisations, international organisations and individual States could be more effective in responding to R2P crises. In this regard, a subject matter to further explore can be the division of labour among different actors.

Fourth, the individual responsibility to protect should not be undermined in the pursuit of successful prevention. When we talk about Pillar One responsibilities, a fully State-centric approach leads us to ignore individuals' responsibility. Yet, besides their main responsibility to not to take part in atrocities, individuals are also responsible for bringing cases before higher authorities and public attention. Moreover, for purposes of atrocity prevention, prominent international figures can be highly influential in mobilising the international community and invoking action.

Fifth, the case-by-case approach is key for a tailored and flexible action. Under a flexible response, all pillars may be used in tandem when necessary. The three pillars can be implemented simultaneously, and they can reinforce each other. As prevention should be the priority, all the measures under the three pillars can be taken in accordance with the context, perpetrators and the victims of the crimes.

Lastly, the culture of impunity must be broken. For this, we need to start from within the society and while doing so, the international community should assist States to develop the necessary mechanisms as well as to establish the rule of law. However, in the case of States that are not able to do so, the ICC may assist them to take up on that responsibility.

All in all, sustainable prevention should be the primary focus of R2P if we truly wish to turn the words into deeds. Hence, for successful prevention, actors from all levels—individual, local, national, regional, sub-regional and international—must carry out the responsibility to prevent in harmony and in a timely and sustainable manner.

References

African Union (AU). (2001). *Constitutive Act of the African Union*. https://au.int/en/treaties/constitutive-act-african-union. Accessed 2 June 2021.

African Union (AU). (2002). The protocol relating to the establishment of the Peace and Security Council. http://www.peaceau.org/uploads/psc-protocol-en.pdf. Accessed 2 June 2021.

African Union (AU). (2005). *Executive Council 7th extraordinary session*. The common African position on the proposed reform of the United Nations: The Ezulwini Consensus, Addis Ababa, Ethiopia.

African Union (AU). (2012). *African Peace and Security Architecture (APSA)*. http://www.peaceau.org/en/topic/the-african-peace-and-security-architecture-apsa. Accessed 20 October 2020.

African Union & Economic Community of West African States (AU–ECOWAS). (2009). *Eighth session of the International Contact Group on Guinea (ICG-G)—Final communique*. https://reliefweb.int/report/guinea/eighth-session-international-contact-group-guinea-icg-g-final-communique. Accessed 2 June 2021.

African Union Assembly of Heads of State and Government (AU–AHSG). (2010). *Decision on the report of the Peace and Security Council on its activities and the state of peace and security in Africa, Assembly/Au/6(XV), Assembly/AU/Dec.294(XV)*.

African Union & Economic Community of West African States (AU–ECOWAS). (2010). *10th meeting of the International Contact Group on Guinea (ICG-G): Final communique*.

Aning, K., & Atuobi, S. (2009). Responsibility to protect in Africa: An analysis of the African Union's Peace and Security Architecture. *Global Responsibility to Protect, 1*, 90–113.

Aning, K., & Atuobi, S. (2012). The economic community of West African states and the responsibility to protect. In A. Knight & F. Egerton (Eds.), *The Routledge handbook on the responsibility to protect* (pp. 216–231). Routledge.

Annan, K. (2004). *A more secure world: Our shared responsibility*. Report of the Secretary General's Report High-level Panel on Threats, Challenges and Change. http://www.un.org/secureworld/report2.pdf. Accessed 2 June 2021.

Annan, K. (2013). Justice for Kenya. *The New York Times*. https://www.nytimes.com/2013/09/09/opinion/justice-for-kenya.html?_r=0. Accessed 18 June 2020.

Babaud, S., & Ndung'u, J. (2012). Early warning and conflict prevention by the EU: Learning lessons from the 2008 post-election violence in Kenya. *Saferworld*, 1–31.

Babbitt, E. F. (2014). Mediation and the prevention of mass atrocities. In M. Serrano & T. G. Weiss (Eds.), *The international politics of human rights, rallying to the R2P cause?* (pp. 29–47). Routledge.

BBC. (2013, March 30). *Kenya Supreme Court upholds Uhuru Kenyatta election win*. https://www.bbc.com/news/world-africa-21979298. Accessed 2 June 2021.

Bellamy, A. J. (2011). Mass atrocities and armed conflict: Links, distinctions, and implications for the Responsibility to Prevent. *Stanley Foundation*, 1–20.

Bellamy, A. J. (2015). The first response: Peaceful means in the third pillar of the responsibility to protect. *Stanley Foundation*, 1–90.
Clottey, P. (2010a, January). ECOWAS will help Guinea organize credible elections, says official. *VOA News*. https://www.voanews.com/africa/ecowas-will-help-guinea-organize-credible-elections-says-official. Accessed 2 June 2021.
Clottey, P. (2010b, November). ECOWAS calls for peace in Guinea. *VOA News*. https://www.voanews.com/africa/ecowas-calls-peace-guinea. Accessed 2 June 2021.
Crossley, N. (2013). A model case of R2P prevention? Mediation in aftermath of Kenya's 2007 presidential elections. *Global Responsibility to Protect, 5*(2), 192–214.
Cunliffe, P. (Ed.). (2011). *Critical perspectives on the responsibility to protect*. Routledge.
Deng, F. M. (2008). *Identity, diversity, and constitutionalism in Africa*. U.S. Institute of Peace.
De Waal, A. (2007). Darfur and the failure of the responsibility to protect. *International Affairs, 83*(6), 1039–1054.
Economic Community of West African State (ECOWAS). (1999). *Protocol relating to the mechanism for conflict prevention, management, resolution, peace-keeping and security*.
Economic Community of West African State (ECOWAS). (2008). *ECOWAS Conflict Prevention Framework*, MSC/REG.1/01/08.
European Union (EU). (2009, October 27). *Restrictive measures against the Republic of Guinea*, 2009/788/CFSP.
France24. (2009, October). *Paris calls for 'international intervention' against junta*. https://www.france24.com/en/20091004-paris-calls-international-intervention-against-junta-. Accessed 30 February 2021.
Gettleman, J. (2008). Annan to help in Kenya, group says. *The New York Times*. https://www.nytimes.com/2008/01/11/world/africa/11kenya.html. Accessed 2 June 2021.
Global Centre for the Responsibility to Protect (GCR2P). (2017). *Atrocity Alert No. 78: Myanmar (Burma), Kenya, Syria and Central African Republic*. https://www.globalr2p.org/publications/atrocity-alert-no-78-myanmar-burma-kenya-syria-and-central-african-republic/. Accessed 2 June 2021.
Global Centre for the Responsibility to Protect (GCR2P). (2019). *Guinea: Political and ethnic tensions in Guinea have previously left populations at risk of mass atrocity crimes*. https://www.globalr2p.org/countries/guinea/. Accessed 11 July 2020.
Global Centre for the Responsibility to Protect (GCR2P). (2020, October 28). *Atrocity Alert No. 226: Cameroon, Afghanistan and Guinea*. https://www.

globalr2p.org/publications/atrocity-alert-no-226-cameroon-afghanistan-and-guinea/. Accessed 2 June 2021.

Gözen Ercan, P. (2016). *Debating the future of the responsibility to protect: The evolution of a moral norm*. Palgrave Macmillan.

Halakhe, A. B. (2013). *R2P in practice: Ethnic violence, elections and atrocity prevention in Kenya* (Occasional Paper Series 4). Global Centre for the Responsibility to Protect.

Hehir, A. (2010). The responsibility to protect: 'Sound and fury signifying nothing'? *International Relations, 24*(2), 218–239.

Human Rights Watch (HRW). (2008, March). *Ballots to bullets: Organized political violence and Kenya's crisis of governance, 20*(1). https://www.hrw.org/reports/2008/kenya0308/. Accessed 2 June 2021.

Human Rights Watch (HRW). (2009). *Bloody Monday report*. https://www.hrw.org/report/2009/12/17/bloody-monday/september-28-massacre-and-rapes-security-forces-guinea. Accessed 2 June 2021.

Human Rights Watch (HRW). (2013). *High stakes: Political violence and the 2013 election in Kenya*. https://www.hrw.org/report/2013/02/07/high-stakes/political-violence-and-2013-elections-kenya. Accessed 2 June 2021.

Human Rights Watch (HRW). (2020a). *Guinea: Events of 2019*. https://www.hrw.org/world-report/2020/country-chapters/guinea. Accessed 2 June 2021.

Human Rights Watch (HRW). (2020b, April 20). *Guinea: Violence during referendum*. https://www.hrw.org/news/2020/04/10/guinea-violence-during-referendum. Accessed 23 October 2020.

Human Rights Watch (HRW). (2021). *Guinea: Events of 2020*. https://www.hrw.org/world-report/2021/country-chapters/guinea. Accessed 25 April 2021.

International Criminal Court (ICC). (2020). *Statement of ICC prosecutor, Fatou Bensouda, on pre-election violence and growing ethnic tensions: "Guinea can and must demonstrate its will and ability both to combat impunity and to prevent renewed cycles of violence"*. https://www.icc-cpi.int/Pages/item.aspx?name=201009-otp-statement-guinea. Accessed 25 April 2021.

International Center for Transitional Justice (ICTJ). (2008). *The Kenyan Commission of inquiry into post-election violence*. https://www.ictj.org/publication/kenyan-commission-inquiry-post-election-violence. Accessed 25 April 2021.

International Coalition for the Responsibility to Protect (ICRtoP). (n.d.). *The crisis in Kenya*. http://www.responsibilitytoprotect.org/index.php/crises/crisis-in-kenya#2. Accessed 25 April 2021.

International Cooperation for the Responsibility to Protect (ICRtoP). (2010). *Crisis in Guinea*. http://www.responsibilitytoprotect.org/index.php/crises/crisis-in-guinea. Accessed 25 April 2021.

International Crisis Group (ICG). (2008, February). *Kenya in Crisis* (Africa Report, No. 137).

International Crisis Group (ICG). (2010). *Guinea conflict alert*. https://www.crisisgroup.org/africa/west-africa/guinea/guinea-conflict-alert. Accessed 25 April 2021.

Kagwanja, P., & Southall, R. (2009). Introduction: Kenya—A democracy in retreat? *Journal of Contemporary African Studies, 27*(3), 259–277.

Kanyinga, K., Okello, D., & Akech, A. (2010). Contradictions of transition to democracy in fragmented societies: The Kenya 2007 general elections in perspective. In K. Kanyinga & D. Okello (Eds.), *Tensions and reversals in democratic transitions: The Kenya 2007 general elections* (pp. 1–28). Society for International Development.

Kenya Human Rights Commission (KHRC). (2008, September 15). *Violating the vote: A report of the 2007 general elections*. https://www.khrc.or.ke/mobile-publications/civil-political-rights/37-violating-the-vote/file.html. Accessed 20 April 2021.

Lindenmayer, E., & Kaye, J. L. (2009). *A choice for peace: The story of forty-one days of mediation in Kenya*. International Peace Institute.

Morris, J. (2016). The responsibility to protect and the use of force: Remaking the procrustean bed? *Cooperation and Conflict, 51*(2), 200–215.

Mwagiru, M. (2008). *The Water's Edge: Mediation of violent electoral conflict in Kenya*. Nairobi: Institute of Diplomacy and International Studies.

Negrón-Gonzales, M., & Contarino, M. (2014). Local norms matter: Understanding national responses to the responsibility to protect. *Global Governance: A Review of Multilateralism and International Organizations, 20*(2), 255–276.

Newman, E. (2013). R2P: Implications for world order. *Global Responsibility to Protect, 5*(3), 235–259.

O'Connell, M. E. (2010). Responsibility to peace: A critique of R2P. *Journal of Intervention and Statebuilding, 4*(1), 39–52.

Ouagadougou Joint Declaration. (2010, January). https://peacemaker.un.org/guinea-ouagadougou-declaration2010. Accessed 25 April 2021.

Penney, J. (2010, November 4). Guinea violence, intimidation displaces thousands, officials say. *CNN*. https://edition.cnn.com/2010/WORLD/africa/11/02/guinea.violence/index.html?iref=allsearch. Accessed 25 April 2021.

Reinold, T. (2010). The responsibility to protect—Much ado about nothing? *Review of International Studies, 36*(S1), 55–78.

Reliefweb. (2009, December). *OIC participates in the 9th meeting of the International Contact Group on Guinea*. https://reliefweb.int/report/guinea/oic-participates-9th-meeting-international-contact-group-guinea. Accessed 25 April 2021.

Reliefweb. (2013, March). *Post-election joint statement of observer mission*. https://reliefweb.int/report/kenya/post-election-joint-statement-observer-mission. Accessed 25 April 2021.

Sampson, T. I. (2011). The responsibility to protect and ECOWAS mechanisms on peace and security: Assessing their convergence and divergence on intervention. *Journal of Conflict & Security Law, 16*(3), 507–540.

Security Council Report. (2008, May 29). *Update Report No. 6: Kenya*. https://www.securitycouncilreport.org/update-report/lookup_c_glKWLeMTIsG_b_4172957.php?print=true. Accessed 25 April 2021.

Serrano, M., & Weiss, T. G. (2014). Introduction: Is R2P "cascading"? In M. Serrano & T. G. Weiss (Eds.), *The international politics of human rights, rallying to the R2P cause?* (pp. 1–25). Routledge.

Sharma, S. (2016). Kenya. In A. J. Bellamy & T. Dunne (Eds.), *The Oxford handbook of the responsibility to protect* (pp. 750–767). Oxford University Press.

Stamnes, E. (2009). Speaking R2P and the prevention of mass atrocities. *Global Responsibility to Protect, 1*(1), 70–89.

Truth, Justice, and Reconciliation Commission (TJRC). (2008). *Commissions of Inquiry—CIPEV Report* (Waki Report). IX. Government Documents and Regulations, 5. https://digitalcommons.law.seattleu.edu/tjrc-gov/5. Accessed 12 April 2021.

Tutu, D. (2008). Taking the responsibility to protect. *The New York Times*. https://www.nytimes.com/2008/02/19/opinion/19iht-edtutu.1.10186157.html. Accessed 25 April 2021.

United Nations General Assembly (UNGA). (2009, January 12). *Implementing the responsibility to protect* (Report of the Secretary-General, A/63/677).

United Nations General Assembly (UNGA). (2010a, April 15). *Strengthening of technical cooperation and consultative services in the Republic of Guinea*. Resolution adopted by the Human Rights Council, A/HRC/RES/13/21.

United Nations General Assembly (UNGA). (2010b, July 14). *Early warning, assessment and the responsibility to protect*. Report of the Secretary-General, A/64/864.

United Nations General Assembly (UNGA). (2014). *Strengthening of technical cooperation and consultative services in Guinea*. Resolution adopted by the Human Rights Council, A/HRC/RES/25/35.

United Nations General Assembly (UNGA). (2019). *Guinea*. National report submitted in accordance with paragraph 5 of the annex to Human Rights Council Resolution 16/21, A/HRC/WG.6/35/GIN/1.

United Nations General Assembly–Security Council (UNGA–SC). (2011, June 27). *The role of regional and subregional arrangements in implementing the responsibility to protect*. Report of the Secretary-General, A/65/877–S/2011/393.

United Nations General Assembly–Security Council (UNGA–SC). (2012, July 25). *Responsibility to protect: Timely and decisive response.* Report of the Secretary-General, A/66/874–S/2012/578.

United Nations General Assembly–Security Council (UNGA–SC). (2013, July 9). *Responsibility to protect: State responsibility and prevention.* Report of the Secretary-General, A/67/929–S/2013/399.

United Nations General Assembly–Security Council (UNGA–SC). (2014, July 11). *Fulfilling our collective responsibility: International assistance and the responsibility to protect.* Report of the Secretary-General, A/68/947–S/2014/449.

United Nations General Assembly–Security Council (UNGA–SC). (2017, August 10). *Implementing the responsibility to protect: Accountability for prevention.* Report of the Secretary-General, A/71/1016–S/2017/556.

United Nations General Assembly–Security Council (UNGA–SC). (2021, May 3). *Advancing atrocity prevention: Work of the office on genocide prevention and the responsibility to protect.* Report of the Secretary-General, A/75/863-S/2021/424.

United Nations High Commissioner for Human Rights (OHCHR). (2008). *Report from OHCHR fact-finding mission to Kenya, 6–28 February 2008.* http://responsibilitytoprotect.org/OHCHR%20Kenya%20Report.pdf. Accessed 25 April 2021.

United Nations Meetings Coverage and Press Releases (UNMCPR). (2008, January). *Secretary-general troubled by escalating Kenyan tensions, violence.* SG/SM/11356–AFR/1641.

United Nations News Centre (UNNC). (2008a, January). *UN genocide adviser urges end to violence in Kenya, sends staffer there.* https://news.un.org/en/story/2008/01/247072-un-genocide-adviser-urges-end-violence-kenya-sends-staffer-there. Accessed 25 April 2021.

United Nations News Centre (UNNC). (2008b). *Ban Ki-moon calls on Kenyans to 'wake up' and halt violence.* https://news.un.org/en/story/2008/02/247592-ban-ki-moon-calls-kenyans-wake-and-halt-violence. Accessed 21 July 2021.

United Nations News Centre (UNNC). (2010a, November 15). *Ban urges people of Guinea to accept presidential poll results.* https://news.un.org/en/story/2010/11/359072-ban-urges-people-guinea-accept-presidential-poll-results. Accessed 25 April 2021.

United Nations News Centre (UNNC). (2010b, November 18). *Security Council urges leaders in Guinea to end poll differences peacefully.* https://news.un.org/en/story/2010/11/359422. Accessed 25 April 2021.

United Nations Office on Genocide Prevention and the Responsibility to Protect (UNGPRtoP). (2017). *Compendium of practice: Implementation of responsibility to protect 2005–2016.* https://www.un.org/en/genocidep

revention/documents/RtoP%20Compendium%20of%20Practice%20(Provisional%20Pre-Publication%20Version)%20FINAL%2020%20March%202017.pdf. Accessed 25 April 2021.

United Nations Peacemaker (UNP). (2008). *Acting together for Kenya: Agreement on the principles of partnership of the coalition government*. https://peacemaker.un.org/kenya-coalitiongovernmentpartnership2008. Accessed 25 April 2021.

United Nations Secretary-General (UNSG). (2018, June 25). *Remarks to General Assembly debate on the responsibility to protect*. https://www.un.org/sg/en/content/sg/speeches/2018-06-25/responsibility-protect-remarks-general-assembly. Accessed 25 April 2021.

United Nations Security Council (UNSC). (2009a, March 12). Letter dated 11 March 2009 from the permanent representative of Burkina Faso to the United Nations addressed to the President of the Security Council, S/2009/140.

United Nations Security Council (UNSC). (2009b, December 18). Letter dated 18 December 2009 addressed to the President of the Security Council by the Secretary-General, S/2009/693.

Voice of America (VOA). (2010, November). *Guinea army declares state of emergency*. https://www.voanews.com/africa/guinea-army-declares-state-emergency. Accessed 15 April 202.

Wallis, D., & Moody, B. (2008, January). Kufuor to go to Kenya for crisis talks. *Reuters*. https://www.reuters.com/article/us-kenya-violence/kufuor-to-go-to-kenya-for-crisis-talks-idUSL0269316120080105. Accessed 25 April 2021.

Williams, P. R., & Pearlman, S. (2019). Use of force in humanitarian crises: Addressing the limitations of U.N. Security Council authorization. *Case Western Reserve Journal of International Law, 51*, 211–222.

Weiss, T. G. (2010). Halting atrocities in Kenya. *Great Decisions, 2*, 17–30.

Welsh, J. (2016). The responsibility to prevent: Assessing the gap between rhetoric and reality. *Cooperation and Conflict, 51*(2), 216–232.

Wheeler, N. J., & Egerton, F. (2009). The responsibility to protect: 'Precious commitment' or a promise unfulfilled? *Global Responsibility to Protect, 1*, 114–132.

Woocher, L. (2012). The responsibility to prevent: Towards a strategy. In A. Knight & F. Egerton (Eds.), *The Routledge handbook on the responsibility to protect* (pp. 22–35). Routledge.

World Peace Foundation (WPF). (2017). Guinea Short Brief. *African Politics, African Peace*. https://sites.tufts.edu/wpf/files/2017/07/Guinea-brief.pdf. Accessed 3 May 2021.

CHAPTER 5

Boko Haram in Nigeria: R2P and Non-State Armed Groups

Çağlar Açıkyıldız

Over the last two decades—especially since it was unanimously adopted at the 2005 United Nations (UN) World Summit—the 'Responsibility to Protect' (R2P) has challenged the traditional notion of state sovereignty by bringing to the fore the question of the protection of populations as a core objective. Nevertheless, in this twenty-year period the development of R2P as an international norm has vastly remained within the framework of state-led crimes, and hence, been state-centric (Welsh, 2018, p. 361). Although most often the focus has been on state authorities as the main perpetrators of mass atrocity crimes, we have been observing the rise of non-state armed groups (NSAGs) as perpetrators as well.

The consequences of the existence of a variety of actors in mass atrocity crimes manifest themselves in the case of Nigeria and specifically the actions of Boko Haram. This terrorist group has been active for almost twenty years. It acts as an independent state since it has claimed certain territories and imposes its own laws and regulations (Elden, 2014;

Ç. Açıkyıldız (✉)
Pompeu Fabra University, Barcelona, Spain

P. Gözen Ercan (ed.), *The Responsibility to Protect Twenty Years On*,
https://doi.org/10.1007/978-3-030-90731-0_5

Oyewole, 2013). So far, its actions have resulted in the death of more than 35,000 people (GlobalR2P, 2020). According to the Humanitarian Response Plan for Nigeria, an estimated 7.7 million people depend on humanitarian assistance in the three most affected states—namely Borno, Adamawa and Yobe (OCHA, 2018). Overall, more than 21 million people have been impacted by the conflict in Lake Chad Basin Region. Two million of these people constitute the seventh largest internally displaced population in the world. They have been present in north-east Nigeria but since January 2019, due to the escalation of the conflict 134,000 people have been forced to flee (Ekumaoko & Ezemenaka, 2020).

Although several studies discuss the Boko Haram uprising and related human rights abuses in Nigeria (see, for instance, Adesoji, 2010; Aghedo & Osumah, 2012; Aka, 2016; Elden, 2014; Oko et al., 2018; Oyewole, 2013), only a few studies establish a link between Boko Haram and R2P (see, Ajigboye, 2014; Ekumaoko & Ezemenaka, 2020; Welsh, 2018). Yet, in order to better understand the NSAGs' place in R2P and the standing issues before R2P's implementation, there is need for further studies. Hence, focusing on the case of Nigeria, in order to understand what has been missing in terms of the protection of the Nigerian population and the role the NSAGs play, this chapter asks to what extent and how R2P has been implemented in response to the Boko Haram insurgency in Nigeria?

To this end, the chapter proceeds in three sections. First, it provides a brief background on the roots of the conflict in the country and the scope of Boko Haram's influence in the region. The subsequent section explores R2P's implementation in the case of Nigeria through a pillar-by-pillar analysis. It first studies the national response with the aim to understand the extent and nature of the Nigerian State's failure to protect its population with respect to Pillar One. This is followed by an overview of the international responses to the ongoing humanitarian crisis in Nigeria in relation to Pillar Two, and a discussion on Pillar Three including the possibility of forceful measures. The final section reflects on the lessons that can be drawn from the case of Nigeria for future implementations of R2P.

The Roots of the Conflict in Nigeria

Despite declaring independence in 1960, Nigeria continued to experience conflicts stemming from its colonial roots. The country is mainly divided between a Muslim population concentrated in the northern part and a Christian population mostly inhabiting the southern part. Reportedly, there have been serious socio-economic differences between the northern and southern parts of the country due to corruption and varying levels of welfare (Elden, 2014, p. 419). Emanating from social inequality, poverty, low levels of education and disregard to core human security priorities, civilians in Nigeria have been threatened for many years by recurring violence in the 'middle belt' and Niger Delta regions, as well as Boko Haram's extremist actions (Adesoji, 2010; Aghedo & Osumah, 2012, p. 856).

Regarding Nigeria's 'middle belt' and Niger Delta regions, the primary causes of the clash are identified as land disputes, burglary and blocked grazing routes (Bagu & Smith, 2017). Between January 2016 and October 2018, the conflict between nomadic cattle herders of Muslim faith and Christian settled farming populations has resulted in the death of 3,641 people along with 406 injured, as well as 5,000 houses razed down to the ground, and 182,530 people displaced (Amnesty International, 2018a). As of 2021 the conflict has escalated, and both parties have been complaining about dominance of insecurity and lack of accountability for the crimes committed (Tom Lantos Human Rights Commission, 2017). Nevertheless, to date, neither the Nigerian government nor the international community has been able to remedy the situation. The death toll continues to increase and the failure of the authorities to find a permanent solution puts more civilians at risk.

Notwithstanding, arguably terrorism constitutes by far the most serious threat to Nigeria's stability and its population (Popovski & Maiangwa, 2016, p. 159). Boko Haram—which means 'western education is forbidden' and was founded in 2002—is at the core of this threat. This terrorist group originated from the Shabaab Muslim Youth Organization, which was founded in 1995 under the leadership of Abubakar Lawal who was replaced by Mohammed Yusuf in 1999 (Anugwom, 2019, p. 46). The group's main intention is to overthrow the existing State structure, and to function as an Islamist sect under Sharia law. In 2015, Boko Haram was ranked first in the Global Terrorism Index as 'the world's deadliest terrorist group' (The Institute for Economics & Peace, 2015). Since its establishment, it has shaken Nigeria as a whole even though the group is mainly concentrated in the north-east part of the country.

In the secular and independent Nigerian society the idea of religious revivalism has previously been present as manifested in the actions of *Yan Tatsine*—the followers of Nigerian Islamic leader Maitatsine. Nonetheless, different from before, Boko Haram has been able to maintain its large-scale attempts to prompt Islamic revivalism by means of well-planned attacks and strong chain of command (Adesoji, 2010, p. 97). To obtain larger recognition and heighten the fear in the Middle East and North Africa (MENA) region through media, and to showcase the inadequacy of the Nigerian government, Boko Haram has been conducting strategic attacks against civilians, especially minors (Popovski & Maiangwa, 2016, p. 163). While the main motivation of Boko Haram is centred on religious factors, as Adesoji (2010, p. 98) notes, other underlying issues such as youth unemployment, deprivation, inequality, poor political leadership and poverty have contributed to the group's consolidation and ever-increasing terrorist attacks.

All things considered, Nigeria remains a prominent R2P concern. Therefore, it is important to explore to what extent and how R2P has been implemented by national authorities and the international community. This subsequent section seeks an answer through a pillar-by-pillar analysis, following the three-pillar implementation strategy devised in the 2009 report of the United Nations (UN) Secretary-General, which was based on the 2005 consensus on R2P. Hence, it first studies the response of the national authorities.

Pillar One: Protection Responsibilities of the State

Different from a vast majority of the cases analysed in this edited volume, in the case of Nigeria the failure to fulfil Pillar One responsibilities under R2P mainly stems from the inability of the national authorities rather than sheer unwillingness. Over the years, the Nigerian government has declared multiple states of emergency and conducted military operations to combat Boko Haram insurgency. Yet the group has remained functional and active with attacks targeting civilians.

From 2002 to 2009, the early crimes of Boko Haram included physical assault on women, burning down police stations, attacking Christian villages and murdering those who oppose them (Oyewole, 2013, p. 256).

It was in 2009 that after their leader Mohammed Yusuf killed Boko Haram almost went silent for more than a year without committing any major crimes (Oyewole, 2013, p. 257). As can be inferred from the change of approach under their new leader Abubakar Shekau, it is believed that they spent this quiet time training and planning long-term actions (Walker, 2012, p. 4). After 2010, Boko Haram became active again. It conducted assassinations, carried out suicide bomb attacks during Christian holidays and bombed the UN headquarters in the Nigerian capital, Abuja. These led to increasing concern over the Nigerian government's ability and capacity to fight against Boko Haram. Nevertheless, in the Regional Policy Seminar on R2P organised by the Economic Community of West African States (ECOWAS), the Nigerian Minister for External Affairs, Ambassador Olugbenga Ashiru argued that the situation was yet to yield to the international community's responsibility to protect since the government has not forsaken its Pillar One responsibilities (Ojeme, 2012). Meanwhile, upon receiving numerous communications pertaining to Article 15 of the Rome Statute, on 18 November 2010 the Office of the Prosecutor (OTP) of the International Criminal Court (ICC) started a preliminary examination in relation to the alleged crimes committed by Boko Haram in Nigeria (ICC, 2011).

While such development seems rather related to the international community's efforts, it is noteworthy that the alleged crimes committed by the Nigerian Security Forces (NSF) since June 2011 were also included within the scope of the examination (ICC, 2011). Hence, it has implications regarding the compliance of the national authorities with their Pillar One responsibilities. In responding to increasing Boko Haram insurgency, the Nigerian government employed counterterrorism measures including the use of military force. Indeed, major military operations made the problem worse instead of solving it (Oyewole, 2013, p. 258). Nigerian government forces were accused of using excessive force against terrorists. For instance, the video footage that the Amnesty International released on 5 August 2014 not only provided evidence of alleged war crimes committed by Boko Haram but also revealed that Boko Haram militias were being subjected to violent repression by members of the Nigerian military and the Civilian Joint Task Force (CJTF)—i.e. the State-sponsored militias (Amnesty International, 2015a). Such measures included the killing of the members of the terrorist organisation as well as many civilians who were simply in the wrong place at the wrong time. Moreover, coercive measures, especially the use of military force, have considerably restricted the rights of those Nigerian citizens who were living in Boko Haram-controlled areas. Oyewole (2013, p. 258) argues that Nigerians have been uneasy about the strict mode of 'war on terror' because they believe that the government has been using excessive power not only in its fight against terrorism but also in protests, elections and other public matters.

Able to continue its attacks despite the government's extreme measures, in 2014 Boko Haram committed its infamous act of kidnapping 276 schoolgirls from Chibok (BBC News, 2017). This incident promoted a heightened international awareness of the notorious crimes of Boko Haram. Eventually, prominent figures—such as the first lady of the United States (US) Michell Obama—urged the international community for action (McVeigh, 2014). While the current president of Nigeria Muhammadu Buhari and his predecessor Goodluck Jonathan have expressed in separate interviews that they would welcome international help in their fight against terrorism (Al Jazeera, 2014; Reuters, 2016), they also claimed that they have defeated Boko Haram in other platforms (BBC News, 2015a, 2015b; France24, 2015). That said, the Nigerian government has been failing to pursue an effective policy to permanently resolve the situation, and such failure has been accompanied by related outstanding issues. For instance, Amnesty International (2015b) reported that 'more than 7,000 civilians have died, and more than 1,200 people were unlawfully killed in military custody between 2011 and 2015 [and] prompt[ed] calls for senior members of Nigerian military to be investigated for war crimes'.

Poor Nigerian leadership on the one hand and Boko Haram's resilience on the other have fuelled the protection crisis. Given its expansionist structure, various branches and headquarters with changing names, Boko Haram has become a hard to exterminate organisation. Moreover, in 2015, Boko Haram pledged allegiance to the Islamic State of Iraq and the Levant (ISIS) and changed its official name to *Wilayat Gharb Afriqiya*, which translates into Islamic State West Africa Province (ISWAP). However, in a short time, the group fractured as its leader Shekau failed to adhere ISIS guidance (Onuoha, 2016, p. 3). In August 2016, ISIS appointed Abu Musab al-Barnawi as its new leader and this further intensified the clashes within the group. Al-Barnawi accused Shekau of harming their jihadist campaign by targeting Muslims and living in luxury while their fighters were coping with starvation (Onuoha, 2016, p. 4). Consequently, ISIS-West Africa split into two factions as al-Barnawi's faction

ISWAP and Shekau's faction, Boko Haram (UNSC, 2020). It is estimated that ISWAP has around 3,500 to 5,000 fighters, who have carried out several terrorist attacks and committed identity-based violence in Nigeria including a midnight attack against Nigerian troops in the village of Kamuya in January 2017; abduction of 110 schoolgirls in February 2018; abduction of three humanitarian aid workers in March 2018; killing of 18 people and leaving 84 wounded in the outskirts of Maiduguri in April 2018; attacking an army base in the village Metele that killed over 100 Nigerian soldiers in November 2018; and taking over the commercial town of Baga in December 2018 (UNMCPR, 2020). Yet again, the Nigerian government failed to prevent/stop these violent attacks. Taking stock of the overall situation, the 2018 Amnesty International (2018b) in its report titled 'Willingly Unable' reiterated the need for the ICC Prosecutor to open a full investigation given the absence of any significant measures by the Nigerian authorities to investigate and/or prosecute either the crimes of Boko Haram or the NSF.

In the light of the recent developments, while presenting her country's statement during the formal UN General Assembly (UNGA) debate on R2P, Nigerian representative Ninikanwa Olachi Okey-Uche called for 'full implementation of the three pillars of R2P including reviewing and strengthening existing preventive capacities' (UNGA, 2018, p. 27). Condemning the attacks on civilians, humanitarian workers, journalists and peacekeepers, she noted Nigeria's appointment of a national R2P focal point (UNGA, 2018, p. 28). She also highlighted that the proliferation of small arms and light weapons help terrorist activities of Boko Haram, so that the government set up a presidential committee to tackle this issue (UNGA, 2018, p. 28). Moreover, Catherine Imaji Udida of the Nigerian Permanent Mission to the UN in the 96th plenary meeting at the UNGA reaffirmed Nigeria's commitment to R2P and urged the international community to support regional and subregional endeavours in protecting populations from atrocious crimes (UNGA, 2019, p. 8). Although these efforts and statements may be evaluated as signs of willingness on the part of the Nigerian government to fulfil its responsibility to protect and prevent further casualties, their words did not turn into successful practice as terrorist attacks continued in the country.

In May and June 2019, respectively, al-Barnawi's ISWAP conducted an attack on a military base in the town of Gubio resulting with the death of three Nigerian soldiers, and on two military bases in the towns of Marte and Kirenowa (UNMCPR, 2020). More recently, on 9 February

2020, at least 30 people were killed by Shekau's Boko Haram in Auno, Borno State (BBC News, 2020). After this attack, President Buhari has felt the pressure more than ever. Many citizens along with some members of the Parliament as well as the Borno State Governor Babagana Zulum requested Buhari to replace his security chiefs as well as a change of strategy to fight Boko Haram (BBC News, 2020). This implies the dissatisfaction with the government's way of handling the insurgency, and arguably the inadequacy of the government. Meanwhile, the NSF has continued to violate human rights in the country. Amnesty International (2020a) highlights how excessive use of force by the Nigerian military leads to the destruction of entire villages and civilian homes. Furthermore, in its December 2020 report, it documents the atrocities committed by both Boko Haram and the Nigerian military forces against older people in the form of abuse, repression, unlawful military detention and obstruction of humanitarian aid (Amnesty International, 2020b). Such observations not only reveal the gravity of the situation, but also hint at the failure of the Nigerian government to protect its population.

While several efforts to establish a dialogue between the conflicting parties proved unsuccessful—due to reasons such as Boko Haram's unreasonable demands, killing of Boko Haram's negotiating team and the government's premature releases of information to the media—(Olojo, 2019), politically speaking, it is now argued that Nigeria is very close to being a 'failed state' because Boko Haram fully controls certain territories in the country, which results in substantial insecurity for the people living in the region (*Financial Times*, 2020; Oko et al., 2018).

Ekumaoko and Ezemenaka (2020) explain how security has become a bargaining chip for huge budgetary allocations in Nigeria and argue that the end of Boko Haram would also mean the end of the allocations, which mostly have been turned into politicians' personal gains. The UN Development Programme (UNDP) data reveals that the money allocated to the fight against Boko Haram has been increasing since 2009 while Boko Haram instigated deaths have also been increasing each year (UNDP, 2018, p. 34).

On the one hand, Nigerian officials seem no longer to deny the situation. In an international interview, President Buhari acknowledged the security problems[1] in the country, considering it 'very, very disturbing'.

[1] Campbell and Rotberg (2021) report that President Buhari, in a meeting with the US Secretary of State Antony Blinken, requested the headquarters of the US Africa Command

Furthermore, addressing the military, the police and other law enforcement agencies, he stated that 'they could do much better' (*The Guardian*, 2020). Moreover, (now former) Chief of Army Staff, Lieutenant General Tukur Buratai, on his verified Facebook account, posted that 'there is likelihood of terrorism persisting in Nigeria for another 20 years' (AllAfrica, 2020). As Walker (2012, p. 3) puts it, Boko Haram has established a 'state within a state'. Besides tactical disadvantages, the lack of adequate transportation infrastructures makes troop deployment difficult in the north-east Nigeria while members of Boko Haram can easily cross borders and flee to the neighbouring countries, namely to Chad, Niger and Cameroon wherein they are deployed to a large extent (Popovski & Maiangwa, 2016, p. 159). Besides the dismal security situation, Popovski and Maiangwa (2016, p. 165) observe that the Nigerian government not only failed to protect its people from mass atrocities but also from other anticipated dangers such as economic misery, natural disasters and health threats.

On the other hand, on 11 December 2020 Prosecutor Fatou Bensouda of the ICC announced the conclusion of the decade-long preliminary examination of the situation in Nigeria. It was found that

> members of the Nigerian Security Forces have committed the following acts constituting crimes against humanity and war crimes: murder, rape, torture, and cruel treatment; enforced disappearance; forcible transfer of population; outrages upon personal dignity; intentionally directing attacks against the civilian population as such and against individual civilians not taking direct part in hostilities; unlawful imprisonment; conscripting and enlisting children under the age of fifteen years into armed forces and using them to participate actively in hostilities; persecution on gender and political grounds; and other inhumane acts. (ICC, 2020)

Following from this, it can be established that besides its inability to protect its population from the atrocities committed by Boko Haram, with the crimes against humanity and war crimes that they have committed during their fight against terrorism the national authorities

to be moved from Germany to Nigeria to get the US more involved in the fight against jihadist groups. It is unclear, however, whether or not the US would like to be drawn into such a conflict and if the President Buhari is inclined to address the allegations of corruption and economic mismanagement in the country.

have also failed to protect some part of the population. Given the manifest failure of the State as to its Pillar One responsibilities, it is important to understand to what extent and how the international community has been engaged in this humanitarian crisis in relation to Pillars Two and Three.

Pillars Two and Three: The International Community's Response

Since the earlier stages of the situation, the international community's responsibility to protect could have been invoked in Nigeria, even at times that the Nigerian authorities were claiming to have control over the situation. Considering that there is a prevailing situation of inability rather than unwillingness on the part of the national authorities, within the R2P framework international assistance and capacity-building seems like the primary path to follow to support the Nigerian State. Nevertheless, as the Secretary-General reminds, the three pillars are not sequential, and there is not always a clear division between the mechanisms that can be adopted under Pillars Two and Three (UNGA, 2009). While the adoption of a specific peaceful measure may qualify as a preventive measure pertaining to Pillar Two, under different circumstances and with regard to the timing it may be considered as an action under Pillar Three. Accordingly, this section scrutinises several efforts and/or decisions by various international actors in relation to Boko Haram in order to understand the level and scope of international involvement in terms of prevention and reaction.

We see that the first responses have been in the form of defining the status of Boko Haram. In 2011, the US House of Representatives Subcommittee on Counterterrorism and Intelligence Committee on Homeland Security described Boko Haram as 'an emerging threat to U.S. interests and the U.S. homeland' (US–GPO, 2011, p. 4). Later in 2012, the US named Abubakar Shekau, Khalid al-Barnawi and Abubakar Adam Kambar as 'Specially Designated Global Terrorists' (US–DoS, 2012). Similarly, in 2013 the United Kingdom (UK) added Boko Haram to its list of 'proscribed terrorist groups or organisations' (UK–HO, 2013). In 2014, the EU formally recognised the Boko Haram and Al-Qaeda association (European Commission, 2014). Moreover, the same year the Heads of State of Nigeria, Benin, Cameroon, Niger and Chad agreed to wage 'war' against Boko Haram in the Paris Summit (BBC News, 2014a).

While these individual developments do not seem to be directly related to R2P, the recognition of Boko Haram as a terrorist organisation arguably strengthens the position of the Nigerian authorities in their fight against terrorism.

At the level of the UN, in 2014, the UNSC decided for sanctions against Boko Haram. Moreover, the Al-Qaeda Sanctions Committee—which is tasked with determining the entities and individuals to be subjected to an arms embargo and/or financial sanctions in relation to Al-Qaeda—added Boko Haram and its leader Abubakar Shekau to its list of 'Al-Qaeda-linked organisations'. While this can be considered as a supportive step for Nigeria's fight against Boko Haram, it is noteworthy that these sanctions do not have much practical or decisive impact since the members of Boko Haram neither travel with passports nor officially own personal assets (BBC News, 2014b).

On 19 January 2015, the UNSC released a statement that made specific references to the situation in Nigeria. The statement noted the following:

> The Security Council strongly condemns and deplores all abuses of human rights and, where applicable, violations of international humanitarian law by the terrorist group Boko Haram, since 2009, including those involving violence against civilian populations, notably women and children, kidnappings, killings, hostage-taking, pillaging, rape, sexual slavery and other sexual violence, recruitment of children and destruction of civilian property. The Security Council expresses serious concern over the reported violations and abuses of human rights and large-scale displacements of civilian population, including into Nigeria's neighbouring countries. (UNMCPR, 2015)

Furthermore, the human rights abuses and violations of International Humanitarian Law (IHL) and International Human Rights Law (IHRL) by Boko Haram in the Lake Chad Basin region were condemned by the UNSC with a statement on 13 May 2016 (UNMCPR, 2016). In March 2017, the UNSC (2017a) with Resolution 2349 pledged the UN's full support for populations suffering from violence by terrorist groups and acknowledged that Boko Haram attacks caused large-scale displacement and the risk of famine in north-east Nigeria. With this resolution, the UNSC (2017a) condemned the terrorist group's activities and underlined the threat posed by Boko Haram to international peace and security. Although it does not make any explicit reference to the norm, from an

R2P point of view, the resolution is of significance in many respects. For instance, it expresses concern about the civilians who are affected by the actions of Boko Haram and 'reiterates the primary responsibility of Member States to protect civilian populations on their territories, in accordance with their obligations under international law' (UNSC, 2017a). It calls UN entities such as the UN Regional Office for Central Africa (UNOCA), the UN Office for West Africa and the Sahel (UNOWAS) and the UN Office to the African Union (UNOAU) to support the region's governments as well organisations to counter acts of violence by Boko Haram and ISIL (UNSC, 2017a). These aspects are of importance in terms of reminding Member States and related entities of their protection responsibilities under Pillars Two and Three.

Meanwhile, the UN Secretary-General has closely followed the situation in Nigeria and reported to the UNSC regarding specific instances and/or issues. His 'Report on Children and Armed Conflict in Nigeria' dated 10 April 2017, documented the conflict's impact on children. In the period reported, out of the 17,073 persons killed in a total of 1,156 incidents in north-east Nigeria, 3,909 were children while of the 28,788 others who were wounded 7,333 were children (UNSC, 2017b, p. 9). Later in September, with his report the Secretary-General reminded that 'some 10.7 million people across the Lake Chad Basin Region currently need humanitarian assistance, including 8.5 million in Nigeria. Some 5.6 million children also need life-saving assistance, and 2.7 million children need psychosocial support' (UNSC, 2017c, p. 2).

In parallel, on 6 July 2017, the UN Committee on the Rights of the Child called Boko Haram out for the abduction of children and their appalling use of children, especially girls as suicide bombers (OHCHR, 2017). In addition, the UN Committee on the Elimination of Discrimination against Women in the concluding observations on the combined seventh and eighth periodic reports on Nigeria observed that Boko Haram is a big obstacle to the development of women's rights in the country since the terrorist group has committed crimes such as rape, sexual slavery, forced marriage, impregnation and denying children their right to education (OHCHR, 2018). That said, other than presenting fatality numbers these reports on their own cannot trigger change unless the international community has the political will to deliver a satisfactory and decisive response. Also, there is no way to fairly put into statistics the psychological trauma stemming from grave violations against children, discrimination, suicide attacks, abduction, violent killings, rape and other forms of sexual violence.

At the regional level, the African Union Peace and Security Council (AUPSC) has also condemned Boko Haram attacks on innocent civilians and urged the international community to be more involved in this issue in the 'Communique of the 639th PSC meeting on Boko Haram Terrorist Group', dated 29 November 2016 (AU, 2016). The meeting on Peace and Security in Africa held by the UNSC on 22 March 2018 addressed the root causes of the Boko Haram crisis, and drew attention to prominent factors such as youth unemployment, water scarcity, chronic drought, desertification, land degradation, extreme poverty, food insecurity, exclusion and inequality. The outcome of the meeting was the affirmation of the UN's support for the African Union (AU) and the Lake Chad Basin Commission (LCBC) in the fight against Boko Haram (UNSC, 2018). Initially designed as an intergovernmental organisation to regulate and control the natural resources in the basin, LCBC became a political forum that is responsible for the coordination of regional security matters due to the economic instability created by terrorism (Galeazzi et al., 2017, p. 3). Moreover, on 20 August 2018, UN Secretary-General António Guterres, condemning the killing of dozens of people in violence in Borno State, called the international community for increased support to regional actors in the fight against Boko Haram (UNMCPR, 2018a). The UNSC released two press statements following the abduction of schoolgirls from the Government Girls Science and Technical Secondary School in Dapchi, Yobe State on 19 February 2018, and the terrorist attack on 16 June 2019 at Konduga village resulting in at least 30 killed. Both statements condemned the terrorist attacks while the former specifically recognised the threat posed by Boko Haram in the region (UNMCPR, 2018b; UNSG, 2019). On 1 April 2020, the UNSC reiterated its commitment to fight against terrorism in a press statement released after the terrorist acts in the Lake Chad Basin Region (UNMCPR, 2020).

Previously, in September 2019, after visiting Nigeria, UN Special Rapporteur Agnes Callamard had highlighted increasing violence across the country and lack of accountability for perpetrators such as Boko Haram (OHCHR, 2019). Such observation was of significance in terms of the ongoing ICC processes. As mentioned in the previous section, the OTP initiated its preliminary examination of the situation in Nigeria in 2010. This was followed by several progress reports published, which reaffirmed the crimes that Boko Haram committed amounted to crimes against humanity such as murder and persecution, which are, respectively, defined under Article 7 Paragraphs 1(a) and 1(h) of the Rome Statute (ICC, 2012, 2013, 2014). In addition, several non-governmental organisations (NGOs) took the initiative to increase awareness and invited the international community to help the victims of this conflict such as the letter of the Global Justice Centre (2015) to the ICC indicating that the actions of Boko Haram should be considered as genocide.

A milestone was reached on 11 December 2020 as Fatou Bensouda announced that the ICC has found enough evidence of crimes against humanity and war crimes in Nigeria (ICC, 2020), which could lead to a comprehensive investigation (Amnesty International, 2020c). Accordingly, the OTP determined that

> members of Boko Haram and its splinter groups have committed the following acts constituting crimes against humanity and war crimes: murder; rape, sexual slavery, including forced pregnancy and forced marriage; enslavement; torture; cruel treatment; outrages upon personal dignity; taking of hostages; intentionally directing attacks against the civilian population or against individual civilians not taking direct part in hostilities; intentionally directing attacks against personnel, installations, material, units or vehicles involved in a humanitarian assistance; intentionally directing attacks against buildings dedicated to education and to places of worship and similar institutions; conscripting and enlisting children under the age of fifteen years into armed groups and using them to participate actively in hostilities; persecution on gender and religious grounds; and other inhumane acts. (ICC, 2020)

In the light of these developments, it can be argued that the situation in Nigeria remains an imminent R2P concern, and that the international community's endeavours so far to find a permanent solution to the problem in Nigeria have proven insufficient.

Although influential State actors such as the US do not hesitate to draw attention to the gravity of the situation and often remind regional powers to assist Nigeria, they prefer not to get directly involved in the conflict. We also observe that the UNSC has not invoked R2P and has failed to trigger timely and decisive international action that would take effect under Paragraph 139 of the WSOD.

From an R2P point of view, the ongoing ICC processes are of vital importance in terms of ending impunity and holding the perpetrators accountable for their actions, and hence for long-term prevention.

Nevertheless, to achieve immediate protection for the civilian population there is need for continued and simultaneous implementation of Pillars Two and Three measures. In assisting the Nigerian authorities to meet their protection responsibilities, the international community may utilise measures including 'confidential or public suasion, dialogue, education, and training on human rights and humanitarian standards and norms, and military assistance to deal with armed non-state actors threatening both the state and its population' (UNGA, 2009). Meanwhile, considering that there is the manifest failure of the state authorities as well as the international failure to prevent the atrocities, coercive measures under Pillar Three may also be considered. The fact that the main perpetrator of the mass atrocity crimes is an NSAG that operates on different territories complicates the process of devising an appropriate response. As discussed previously, sanctions have not proved to be very effective, and the ICC process is open-ended while international assistance and capacity-building is not enough to stop the actions of Boko Haram. In this regard, there remains the question, can the use of force be a remedy to the ongoing humanitarian crisis?

As former UN Secretary-General Ban Ki-moon underlines, when persuasive measures and positive incentives are insufficient, international military assistance, in compliance with all three pillars, can be a part of the solution to support States (UNGA, 2009) in addressing the challenge posed by NSAGs. In the case of Nigeria, a legally sanctioned international military response against Boko Haram can be undertaken with the consent of the Nigerian government. An external intervention conducted with the invitation of the Nigerian government would also be a consistent measure since the consent of the host State would eliminate the reservations about the legality of the use of force and concerns as to the violation of State sovereignty. Ekumaoko and Ezemenaka (2020) point out that the local population in north-east Nigeria has been increasingly vocal about the necessity of external military intervention. Yet, as Campbell (2014, p. 3) notes, there is a possibility of the Muslim majority perceiving any interference of the international community—especially by the States of the global north—in the region as an attack on Muslim values, regardless of the fact that Boko Haram has been primarily targeting the Christian community of Nigeria and forcing people to convert to Islam in contravention to fundamental human rights and freedoms (Campbell, 2014, p. 3). More significantly, the alleged human rights violations committed by the NSF constitutes an obstacle before the international community to help the government to counterterrorism in the country, as any external involvement is prone to be interpreted as becoming an accomplice in human rights violations (Welsh, 2018, p. 371).

Furthermore, it is observed that regional efforts carried out by the Multinational Joint Task Force (MNJTF)—founded by Benin, Cameroon, Chad, Niger and Nigeria to prevent criminal activities in the border areas—have not yielded the desired outcome. The MNJTF has been conducting military operations with the authorisation of the AU since 2015 (European Commission, 2019), yet Boko Haram still holds under control a significant portion of territory and poses a considerable threat to civilian populations in Nigeria and neighbouring countries. In this regard, if an international military operation is to be carried out, it needs to be well-planned taking into consideration the potential harm it may cause and should have reasonable prospects for success in order not to cause more suffering to the population.

In the current state of affairs, since there is no visible prospect for or willingness in the UNSC to consider the last resort of the use of force, the attention can be focused on the ongoing ICC proceedings. State Parties to the ICC as well as non-party States must ensure that they provide all the resources that ICC needs to conduct its investigations and arrest the perpetrators (Amnesty International, 2020c). Respectively, in an environment where the government is unable to protect its people and the international community's efforts are insufficient, initiating a formal inquiry for the war crimes and crimes against humanity in Nigeria would mean an encouraging step forward to bring justice for victims of the atrocious crimes committed, and deterring the perpetrators from committing further crimes.

Conclusion

This chapter has shown that the ongoing situation in Nigeria is a significant R2P concern, and the current implementation is not enough to end the suffering of the Nigerian population. The conflict between herders and farming communities in the 'Middle Belt' as well as the terrorist activities of Boko Haram have been at the heart of the humanitarian crisis in Nigeria. Indeed, the crimes committed by Boko Haram have destabilised Africa's most populous country. Meanwhile, its extremist violence has become a threat to international peace and security with the attacks it has been carrying out in neighbouring countries, as well as the consequent refugee flows and internal displacement (Welsh, 2018, p. 375).

Although Boko Haram being an NSAG may have placed it under the focus mainly as a national and international security issue, the presence of mass atrocity crimes as established by the OTP undoubtedly makes the case of Nigeria an R2P concern requiring utmost attention. In the light of the above analysis, it can be argued that Nigerian authorities as well as the international community have been failing to provide the necessary protection for the Nigerian population despite clear efforts to tackle the issue. While it remains a question if the international community has consciously attempted to implement R2P but without expressly stating so, various reactions studied in the previous section that nonetheless can be linked to the norm still imply that national and international security concerns were the main drive. In this vein, one important implication of this case is the complexity created by the involvement of the NSAGs in the picture and the state-centric approach leading the international R2P response.

Taking stock of the two decades of R2P implementation, especially since the 2009 Report of the Secretary-General which laid out the three-pillar implementation strategy, there is still need to challenge States and policy-makers to acknowledge the fact that States are not the only actors committing atrocity crimes and R2P's focus in not limited to States. As the first advisor to the UN Secretary-General on R2P Edward Luck notes (2015), such concern has been raised in different UN platforms, as in the occasion of the Arria formula meeting of the UNSC that took place in December 2015, wherein officials from Spain and Chile raised concerns about R2P being too state-centric, hence failing to address other perpetrators of atrocity crimes. Moreover, Ban Ki-moon has drawn attention to this issue in his 2015 Report arguing for the presence of two new challenges to R2P's present state: the terrorist activities of non-state armed groups and the impact of technology (UNGA, 2015). In his 2016 Report, Ban mentions 'non-state actors' in six different paragraphs, urges the international community to acknowledge that they are a factor in R2P, and remarks: 'Today we face a more challenging context, in which some states and non-state actors routinely threaten populations and make calculated decisions to disregard their legal obligations and protection responsibilities' (UNGA, 2016, p. 2). While there is a common understanding that NSAGs enjoy impunity because attributing responsibilities may imply their legitimation, international criminal law establishes the responsibility of individual members of NSAGs for their crimes in order to provide more robust protection to populations (Welsh, 2018, p. 365). Moreover, as part of customary international law, common Article 3 to the Geneva Conventions of 1949, along with the Additional Protocol II (1977), requires all parties to Non-International Armed Conflict (NIAC), including NSAGs, to respect and protect civilian populations.

In today's world, the impact of NSAGs cannot be overlooked. With globalisation and advancements in technology, such groups have become more and more powerful, omnipresent and visible in the international system. Whiteside (2015, p. 232) contends that the rise of non-state actors and the growing number of weak states introduced to us a new phenomenon: 'terrorism as genocide'. As Ban indicates, mass murders take different forms and they are committed by different types of perpetrators, hence, it cannot be ignored that certain terrorist activities of NSAGs make it necessary to adopt R2P implementation strategy to better respond to human rights violations for the sake of people in urgent need (UNGA, 2015).

Eventually, a possible R2P mandate must follow the three-pillar implementation strategy. It is no secret that the Nigerian government has failed to protect its population from the atrocities of Boko Haram. This requires the international community to act under Pillar Two and where relevant under Pillar Three considering that the three pillars may also be implemented simultaneously in a way to complement efforts under each pillar. Accordingly, the international community has a duty to support the government of Nigeria for its counterterrorism measures, while keeping it accountable for its actions as well. The fact remains that the UNSC Member States repeatedly determined the threat posed by Boko Haram to international peace and security and imposed sanctions. However, ineffective responses failed to ensure sustainable protection for the people affected by this threat and resulted in more misery, rendering the international community in a state of failure to uphold its protection responsibilities. Overall, when we look at the big picture, we see that neither the Nigerian State nor the international community has internalised the R2P norm. While it has been relentlessly striving to deal with Boko Haram to end the suffering of the population, the lack of an R2P mindset at the core of the measures adopted resulted in mass atrocity crimes by the State forces. As for the international community, the UN and its Member States have been too much focused on classical notions of national and international security rather than human security, and thus, failed to utilise available tools in the R2P toolkit to provide the necessary protection to the Nigerian population.

References

Adesoji, A. (2010). The Boko Haram uprising and Islamic revivalism in Nigeria. *Africa Spectrum, 45*(2), 95–108.

African Union (AU). (2016). Communique of the 639th PSC meeting on Boko Haram Terrorist Group. 29 November.

Aghedo, I., & Osumah, O. (2012). The Boko Haram uprising: How should Nigeria respond? *Third World Quarterly, 33*(5), 853–869.

Ajigboye, O. (2014). International law and the responsibility to protect: Legal and theoretical basis for international intervention in Nigeria. *Journal of Sustainable Development Law and Policy, 3*(1), 87–98.

Aka, P. (2016). *Human rights in Nigeria's external relations: Building the record of a moral superpower*. Lexington Books.

AllAfrica. (2020). *Nigeria: Terrorism may persist for another 20 years in Nigeria—Buratai.* https://allafrica.com/stories/202012030084.html. Accessed 13 March 2021.

Al Jazeera. (2014). *Nigeria leader seeks help over missing girls.* https://www.aljazeera.com/news/2014/5/5/nigeria-leader-seeks-help-over-missing-girls. Accessed 24 December 2020.

Amnesty International. (2015a). *Boko Haram video details.* https://adam.amnesty.org/asset-bank/action/viewAsset?id=197700&index=49&total=65&view=viewSearchItem. Accessed 23 December 2020.

Amnesty International. (2015b). *Nigeria: Horror in numbers.* https://www.amnesty.org/en/latest/news/2015/06/nigeria-horror-in-numbers/. Accessed 28 December 2020.

Amnesty International. (2018a). *Harvest of death three years of bloody clashes between farmers and herders in Nigeria.* https://www.amnesty.org/en/documents/afr44/9503/2018/en/. Accessed 28 July 2021.

Amnesty International. (2018b). *Willingly unable.* https://www.amnesty.org/en/documents/afr44/9481/2018/en/. Accessed 28 July 2021.

Amnesty International. (2020a). *Nigeria: Military razes villages as Boko Haram attacks escalate.* https://www.amnesty.org/en/latest/news/2020/02/nigeria-military-razes-villages-as-boko-haram-attacks-escalate/. Accessed 23 December 2020.

Amnesty International. (2020b). *Nigeria: Older people often an invisible casualty in conflict with Boko Haram.* https://www.amnesty.org/en/documents/afr44/3376/2020/en/. Accessed 28 July 2021.

Amnesty International. (2020c). *Milestone decision paves the way for full investigation into atrocities in Nigeria.* https://www.amnesty.org/en/latest/news/

2020/12/icc-milestone-decision-paves-the-way-for-full-investigation-into-atrocities-in-nigeria/. Accessed 23 December 2020.

Anugwom, E. E. (2019). *The Boko Haram insurgence in Nigeria: Perspectives from within*. Palgrave Macmillan.

Bagu, C., & Smith, K. (2017). Past is Prologue: Criminality & reprisal attacks in Nigeria's Middle Belt. *Search for Common Ground*. https://www.sfcg.org/wp-content/uploads/2017/04/Criminality-Reprisal-Attack_FINAL.pdf. Accessed 22 June 2021.

BBC News. (2014a). *Africa leaders declare "war" on Nigeria Boko Haram*. https://www.bbc.com/news/world-africa-27451966. Accessed 11 December 2020.

BBC News. (2014b). *UN committee imposes sanctions on Nigeria's Boko Haram*. https://www.bbc.com/news/world-africa-27529566. Accessed 11 December 2020.

BBC News. (2015a). *Nigeria's Goodluck Jonathan: Tide turned against Boko Haram*. https://www.bbc.com/news/world-africa-31620989. Accessed 11 December 2020.

BBC News. (2015b). *Nigeria Boko Haram: Militants "technically defeated"—Buhari*. https://www.bbc.com/news/world-africa-35173618. Accessed 11 December 2020.

BBC News. (2017). *Nigeria Chibok abductions: What we know*. https://www.bbc.com/news/world-africa-32299943. Accessed 10 March 2021.

BBC News. (2020). *Buhari under pressure over Boko Haram attacks*. https://www.bbc.com/news/live/world-africa-47639452?ns_mchannel=social&ns_source=twitter&ns_campaign=bbc_live&ns_linkname=5e456e68a94d06065fba2be3%26Buhari%20under%20pressure%20over%20Boko%20Haram%20attacks%262020-02-13T16%3A59%3A50%2B00%3A00&ns_fee=0&pinned_post_locator=urn:asset:b1731b24-88a7-4699-b738-9e4c47006941&pinned_post_asset_id=5e456e68a94d06065fba2be3&pinned_post_type=share. Accessed 10 March 2021.

Campbell, J. (2014). *U.S. policy to counter Nigeria's Boko Haram* (Special Report No. 70). Council on Foreign Relations. https://www.cfr.org/sites/default/files/pdf/2014/11/Nigeria_CSR70.pdf. Accessed 29 December 2020.

Campbell, J., & Rotberg, R. I. (2021). The giant of Africa is failing. *Foreign Affairs*. https://www.foreignaffairs.com/articles/africa/2021-05-31/giant-africa-failing. Accessed 10 June 2021.

Ekumaoko, C. E., & Ezemenaka, K. E. (2020). Responsibility to protect: External intervention on Boko Haram terrorism in Nigeria. *Security Journal, 33*, 493–513.

Elden, S. (2014). The geopolitics of Boko Haram and Nigeria's "war on terror." *Geographical Journal, 180*(4), 414–425. https://doi.org/10.1111/geoj.12120

European Commission. (2014). Implementing regulation (EU) No. 583/2014 of 28 May 2014. https://eur-lex.europa.eu/legal-content/EN/TXT/PDF/?uri=CELEX:32014R0583&from=en. Accessed 28 July 2021.

European Commission. (2019). *Multinational joint task force (MNJTF) against Boko Haram*. https://knowledge4policy.ec.europa.eu/projects-activities/multinational-joint-task-force-mnjtf-against-boko-haram_en. Accessed 11 November 2020.

Financial Times. (2020). Nigeria is at risk of becoming a failed state. https://www.ft.com/content/9abc218d-3881-4bfd-8951-e76336cde94f. Accessed 30 December 2020.

France24. (2015). *Nigeria's president expects Boko Haram defeat within a month*. https://www.france24.com/en/20150320-boko-haram-defeat-less-month-nigeria-president-jonathan. Accessed 29 November 2020.

Galeazzi, G., Medinilla, A., Ebiede, T., & Desmidt, S. (2017). *Political economy dynamics of regional organisations in Africa: The Lake Chad Basin Commission*. ECDPM. https://ecdpm.org/wp-content/uploads/LCBC-Policy-Brief-PEDRO-Political-Economy-Dynamics-Regional-Organisations-Africa-ECDPM-2017.pdf. Accessed 17 December 2020.

Global Centre for the Responsibility to Protect (GlobalR2P). (2020). *Populations at risk: Nigeria*. https://www.globalr2p.org/countries/nigeria/. Accessed 15 December 2020.

Global Justice Center. (2015). *Letter to the Honourable Fatou Bensouda, Chief Prosecutor, 'Re: The imperative to prosecute the abduction of the schoolgirls in Nigeria as genocide'*. https://globaljusticecenter.net/blog/21-publications/letters/211-letter-to-the-honourable-fatou-bensouda-chief-prosecutor-re-the-imperative-to-prosecute-the-abduction-of-the-schoolgirls-in-nigeria-as-genocide. Accessed 27 November 2020.

International Criminal Court (ICC). (2011). *Report on preliminary examination activities (2011). December*. https://www.icc-cpi.int/NR/rdonlyres/63682F4E-49C8-445D-8C13-F310A4F3AEC2/284116/OTPReportonPreliminaryExaminations13December2011.pdf. Accessed 10 March 2021.

International Criminal Court (ICC). (2012). *Report on preliminary examination activities*. http://www.icc-cpi.int/NR/rdonlyres/C433C462-7C4E-4358-8A72-8D99FD00E8CD/285209/OTP2012ReportonPreliminaryExaminations22Nov2012.pdf. Accessed 29 December 2020.

International Criminal Court (ICC). (2013). *Situation in Nigeria*. https://www.icc-cpi.int/iccdocs/pids/docs/sas%20-%20nga%20-%20public%20version%20article%205%20report%20-%2005%20august%202013.pdf. Accessed 10 March 2021.

International Criminal Court (ICC). (2014). *Report on preliminary examination activities*. http://www.icc-cpi.int/iccdocs/otp/OTP-Pre-Exam-2014.pdf. Accessed 29 December 2020.

International Criminal Court (ICC). (2020). *Statement of the prosecutor, Fatou Bensouda, on the conclusion of the preliminary examination of the situation in Nigeria*. https://www.icc-cpi.int/Pages/item.aspx?name=201211-prosecutor-statement. Accessed 29 December 2020.

Luck, E. (2015). *Statement by Dr. Edward Luck on behalf of the Global Centre at the UN Security Council Arria formula meeting on the Responsibility to Protect and Non-State Actors*. Global Centre for the Responsibility to Protect. https://www.globalr2p.org/publications/statement-by-dr-edward-luck-on-behalf-of-the-global-centre-at-the-un-security-council-arria-formula-meeting-on-the-responsibility-to-protect-and-non-state-actors/. Accessed 30 July 2021.

McVeigh, T. (2014). Michelle Obama raises pressure over kidnapped schoolgirls. *The Guardian*. https://www.theguardian.com/world/2014/may/10/michelle-obama-nigeria-presidential-address. Accessed 29 July 2021.

Office of the United Nations High Commissioner for Human Rights (OHCHR). (2017, July 6). *Concluding observations on the combined third to fifth periodic reports of Cameroon*. CRC/C/CMR/CO/3-5.

Office of the United Nations High Commissioner for Human Rights (OHCHR). (2018, March 29). *Report of the committee on the elimination of discrimination against women*. A/73/38. https://tbinternet.ohchr.org/_layouts/15/treatybodyexternal/Download.aspx?symbolno=A%2f73%2f38&Lang=en. Accessed 29 July 2021.

Office of the United Nations High Commissioner for Human Rights (OHCHR). (2019, September 2). *End of visit statement of the Special Rapporteur on extrajudicial, summary or arbitrary executions on her visit to Nigeria*. https://reliefweb.int/report/nigeria/end-visit-statement-special-rapporteur-extrajudicial-summary-or-arbitrary-executions. Accessed 29 July 2021.

Ojeme, V. (2012). Boko Haram: FG faults calls for foreign intervention. *Vanguard News*. https://www.vanguardngr.com/2012/06/boko-haram-fg-faults-calls-for-foreign-intervention/. Accessed 11 December 2020.

Oko, E., Ufomba, H., & Benjamin, W. (2018). Is Nigeria a failed state? A commentary on the Boko Haram insurgency. *Global Journal of Human Social Science, 18*(5), 34–38.

Olojo, A. (2019). *Dialogue with Boko Haram: Back on the agenda? ISS Africa*. https://issafrica.org/iss-today/dialogue-with-boko-haram-back-on-the-agenda. Accessed 21 November 2020.

Onuoha, F. C. (2016). Split in ISIS-aligned Boko Haram group. *Al Jazeera Centre for Studies*. https://studies.aljazeera.net/en/reports/2016/10/split-isis-aligned-boko-haram-group-161027113247008.html. Accessed 29 November 2020.

Oyewole, S. (2013). Boko Haram and the challenges of Nigeria's war on terror. *Defense and Security Analysis, 29*(3), 253–262.

Popovski, V., & Maiangwa, B. (2016). Boko Haram's attacks and the people's response: A 'fourth pillar' of the responsibility to protect? *African Security Review, 25*(2), 159–175.

Reuters. (2016). *Nigeria says would welcome U.N. help in negotiating schoolgirls' release*. https://www.reuters.com/article/us-nigeria-security-idUSKCN11S0LM. Accessed 27 November 2020.

The Guardian. (2020). Buhari says security problems 'very, very disturbing'. https://guardian.ng/news/buhari-says-security-problems-very-very-disturbing/. Accessed 13 March 2021.

The Institute for Economics and Peace. (2015). *Measuring and understanding the impact of terrorism*. Global Terrorism Index. https://reliefweb.int/report/world/global-terrorism-index-2015-measuring-and-understanding-impact-terrorism. Accessed 17 November 2020.

Tom Lantos Human Rights Commission. (2017). *Nigeria: Conflict in the Middle Belt*. United States Congress. https://humanrightscommission.house.gov/events/hearings/nigeria-conflict-middle-belt. Accessed 17 November 2020.

United Kingdom Home Office (UK–HO). (2013). *Proscribed terrorist organisations*. https://www.gov.uk/government/publications/proscribed-terror-groups-or-organisations--2/proscribed-terrorist-groups-or-organisations-accessible-version. Accessed 17 November 2020.

United Nations Development Program (UNDP). (2018). *National human development report: Achieving human development in North East Nigeria*. http://hdr.undp.org/sites/default/files/hdr_2018_nigeria_finalfinalx3.pdf. Accessed 27 November 2020.

United Nations General Assembly (UNGA). (2009, January 12). *Implementing the responsibility to protect*. Report of the Secretary-General, A/63/677.

United Nations General Assembly (UNGA). (2015, July 13). *A vital and enduring commitment: Implementing the responsibility to protect*. Report of the Secretary-General, A/69/981—S/2015/500.

United Nations General Assembly (UNGA). (2016, July 22). *Mobilizing collective action: The next decade of the responsibility to protect*. Report of the Secretary-General, A/70/999—S/2016/620.

United Nations General Assembly (UNGA). (2018, June 25). *The responsibility to protect and the prevention of genocide, war crimes, ethnic cleansing and crimes against humanity*. A/72/PV.100.

United Nations General Assembly (UNGA). (2019, June 28). *The responsibility to protect and the prevention of genocide, war crimes, ethnic cleansing and crimes against humanity*. A/73/PV.96.

United Nations Meetings Coverage and Press Releases (UNMCPR). (2015). *Security Council presidential statement demands cessation of hostilities by Boko Haram in Nigeria, release of hostages, including 276 girls abducted in*

April. https://www.un.org/press/en/2015/sc11742.doc.htm. Accessed 29 July 2021.

United Nations Meetings Coverage and Press Releases (UNMCPR). (2016). *Security Council presidential statement condemns Boko Haram terrorist attacks in Lake Chad Basin, demanding immediate halt to violence, human rights abuses*. https://www.un.org/press/en/2016/sc12363.doc.htm. Accessed 2 January 2021.

United Nations Meetings Coverage and Press Releases (UNMCPR). (2018a). *Secretary-General condemns killings in Nigeria, while expressing deep concern over persisting violence in Lake Chad Basin region*. https://www.un.org/press/en/2018/sgsm19175.doc.htm. Accessed 2 January 2021.

United Nations Meetings Coverage and Press Releases (UNMCPR). (2018b). *Security Council press statement on 19 February abduction of schoolgirls in Dapchi, 1 March Attack in Rann, Nigeria*. https://www.un.org/press/en/2018/sc13233.doc.htm. Accessed 2 January 2021.

United Nations Meetings Coverage and Press Releases (UNMCPR). (2020). *Security Council press statement on acts of terrorism in Lake Chad Basin region*. https://www.un.org/press/en/2020/sc14155.doc.htm. Accessed 2 January 2021.

United Nations Office for the Coordination of Humanitarian Affairs (OCHA). (2018). *Humanitarian response plan: Nigeria*. https://reliefweb.int/sites/reliefweb.int/files/resources/2018_hrp_v5.4.pdf. Accessed 21 July 2021.

United Nations Security Council (UNSC). (2017a, March 31). Resolution 2349, S/RES/2349. https://digitallibrary.un.org/record/863830?ln=en. Accessed 29 July 2021.

United Nations Security Council (UNSC). (2017b, April 10). *Report of the Secretary-General on children and armed conflict in Nigeria*. https://digitallibrary.un.org/record/1298536?ln=en. Accessed 29 July 2021.

United Nations Security Council (UNSC). (2017c, September 7). *Report of the Secretary-General on the situation in the Lake Chad Basin region*. https://digitallibrary.un.org/record/1303877?ln=en. Accessed 29 July 2021.

United Nations Security Council (UNSC). (2018, March 22). *Peace and security in Africa*. 8212th meeting, S/PV.8212.

United Nations Security Council (UNSC). (2020). *Islamic State West Africa Province (ISWAP)*. https://www.un.org/securitycouncil/content/islamic-state-west-africa-province-iswap-0. Accessed 10 December 2020.

United Nations Secretary-General (UNSG). (2019). *Statement attributable to the Spokesman for the Secretary-General on Nigeria*. https://www.un.org/sg/en/content/sg/statement/2019-06-17/statement-attributable-the-spokesman-for-the-secretary-general-nigeria. Accessed 10 December 2020.

United States Department of State (US–DoS). (2012). *Terrorist designations of Boko Haram Commander Abubakar Shekau, Khalid al-Barnawi and Abubakar Adam Kambar*. https://2009-2017.state.gov/r/pa/prs/ps/2012/06/193574.htm. Accessed 27 November 2020.

United States Government Publishing Office (US–GPO). (2011). *Boko Haram: Emerging threat to the U.S. homeland*. https://www.govinfo.gov/content/pkg/CPRT-112HPRT71725/pdf/CPRT-112HPRT71725.pdf. Accessed 28 November 2020.

Walker, A. (2012). *What is Boko Haram? In United States Institute of Peace*. http://www.usip.org/sites/default/files/SR308.pdf. Accessed 28 December 2020.

Welsh, J. M. (2018). The responsibility to protect and non-state armed groups. In M. Lattimer & P. Sands (Eds.), *The grey zone: Civilian protection between human rights and the laws of war* (pp. 357–376). Hart Publishing.

Whiteside, C. (2015). A case for terrorism as genocide in an era of weakened states. *Dynamics of Asymmetric Conflict, 8*(3), 232–250.

CHAPTER 6

Côte D'Ivoire: A Timely and Decisive R2P Action?

Menent Savaş-Cazala

This chapter explores the 2011 post-electoral crisis in Côte d'Ivoire, which, for the Responsibility to Protect (R2P), is the second exceptional case wherein the UNSC authorised forceful action under Chapter VII of the Charter of the United Nations (UN) in a manner consistent with Pillar Three. Just thirteen days after it decided for the use of all necessary measures in Libya, the UN Security Council (UNSC) unanimously adopted Resolution 1975 on Côte d'Ivoire. While the consecutive decisions to adopt the use of force was a point of convergence for the two cases, their backgrounds, timelines and root causes were not much alike. The apparent reason for the humanitarian crisis in Côte d'Ivoire was the then President Laurent Gbagbo's refusal to accept the election results and step down peacefully. Moreover, since 2004 a UN peacekeeping force backed by the French forces has been operational on the Ivorian territory based on the State's consent. Arguably, when a timely and decisive action was required, the UNSC showed resilience to reinforce the mandate of

M. Savaş-Cazala (✉)
Galatasaray University, Istanbul, Turkey

P. Gözen Ercan (ed.), *The Responsibility to Protect Twenty Years On*,
https://doi.org/10.1007/978-3-030-90731-0_6

the UN Operation in Côte d'Ivoire (UNOCI) and authorised the use of force to ensure the protection of civilians.

Considering that at a time when the credibility of the UNSC was at stake the decisive action in Côte d'Ivoire helped to renew confidence for peace operations and set a positive example for R2P practice unlike the much-debated intervention in Libya, it is quite surprising that the Ivorian case has received little attention in the R2P literature. As Hunt (2016) argues, the example of Côte d'Ivoire could be used more frequently to show how far R2P has come. Besides, this case provides us with various insights into R2P practice thanks to its unique characteristics and offers invaluable lessons as to sustainable protection.

The chapter starts with a background on the crisis and provides a general overview of Côte d'Ivoire's troubled history of mass atrocity crimes. It then analyses the election process which brought the country to the brink of civil war with the aim to understand where and how the State has failed to uphold its responsibility and how the international community responded to the escalating situation vis-à-vis R2P's three-pillar implementation strategy. In this section, the chapter also brings to the fore the question of the UNSC's stance and discusses whether the dismissal of impartiality and State consent can be considered as the Council's readiness to act in cases of mass atrocity crimes. Finally, the chapter concludes with an assessment of R2P's implementation in Côte d'Ivoire. It asks whether it should be considered as a success or a failure, and if it is possible to speak of sustainable protection especially in the light of the 2020 elections.

Root Causes of the Conflict and Prevention Efforts

The hostile environment which brought the country to the brink of civil war in 2011 was not a unique phenomenon but a moment of crisis in a conflict that has a long past in the history of Côte d'Ivoire. Became independent in 1960, the first president of Côte d'Ivoire was Félix Houphouët-Boigny and the Democratic Party of Côte d'Ivoire (*Parti Démocratique de Côte d'Ivoire*, PDCI) was the only political party until 1990 (Bah, 2010). Although Houphouët-Boigny was not concerned much about democratisation, as the first president he managed to keep the country united and transformed it to the biggest exporter of cocoa in the 1960s and 1970s—which as a period is known as the '*miracle ivoirien'* (Mitchell, 2018). For a multi-ethnic country with approximately 60 different ethnic groups, there was political stability and a relative socio-economic prosperity in Houphouët-Boigny's term (UNSC, 2003a). Nevertheless, during his thirty-three-year presidency, wealth was not distributed equally, and the poor Muslim-dominated north was isolated while the Christian-dominated south benefited from development. The relative prosperity of the country was the cause of a long process of immigration mostly from neighbouring countries motivated by economic and religious drives. One of the main problems of Houphouët-Boigny's administration was his ambiguous citizenship policies that allowed immigrant workers from neighbouring countries to be involved in Ivorian politics, which consequently complicated the identification of Ivorian and non-Ivorian (Langer, 2005). In the period following the first multi-party elections held in 1993, such ambiguity manifested itself as a problem with the construction of the doctrine of *Ivoirité*, which is intended to determine who is Ivorian and therefore can elect and be elected in Côte d'Ivoire. This was the main source of antagonism between the political rivals who became belligerents afterwards.

In the first multi-party elections, the opposition led by the formerly exiled union activist Laurent Gbagbo's party Ivorian Popular Front (*Front Populaire Ivoirien*) (FPI) was defeated by PDCI (Bah, 2010). After Houphouët-Boigny's death, Henri Konan Bédié replaced him but he could not reunite PDCI. As of 1993, the country was trapped in the vacuum of a protracted power struggle which caused severe political instability (S/2003/374). Like his predecessor, Bédié was against any democratic reform process. Also, economic disparities between the regions continued to deepen. In 1994, former Prime Minister Alassane Ouattara was proposed as the new leader of the Rally of the Republicans (*Rassemblement des Républicains*, RDR), which was a political party formed by a group that detached from PDCI (Langer, 2005). Ouattara—who previously served as the head of the Africa Department of the International Monetary Fund (IMF) and as the Governor of the Central Bank of West African States—proposed a reform programme and received technocrats' support (Crook, 1997).

The 1995 presidential election was marked by Bédié's anti-democratic policies. Bédié constructed the *Ivoirité* doctrine that defines the Ivorian identity based on a distinction between 'indigenous Ivorians' and 'Ivorians of immigrant ancestry' (Crook, 1997). This conflict-ridden tactic based on the controversies over nationality laws and eligibility conditions for national and presidential elections was targeting northerners[1] to banish them from the elections (Mitchell, 2018). To consolidate his power, Bédié did not hesitate to deny citizenship rights of northerners by adopting new laws. He forced presidential candidates to prove that they and their parents were Ivorians by origin (Bah, 2010). These divisive ethnic policies made it impossible for Ouattara to become a presidential candidate given that his father was from Burkina Faso (Babo, 2012). Finally, this hostile environment led to a military coup organised by General Robert Guéï who overthrew President Bédié in 1999. Nevertheless, the coup did not make a change in terms of ensuring good governance (Toungara, 2001).

In 2000, with the endorsement of the law on the doctrine of *Ivoirité* in the Constitution, the marginalisation of the northerners became more blatant. They were forced into a clear discrimination policy in their daily lives wherein even requesting an identity document became problematic since they had to prove their nationality by obtaining a statement of origin. The same year, presidential elections led to serious street protests organised by FPI, and violent clashes occurred between the supporters of General Guëi and Gbagbo. It was after the Supreme Court's decision that Gbagbo was declared winner. After claiming victory Gbagbo unsurprisingly sustained the doctrine of *Ivoirité* to disqualify Ouattara and the RDR.

After the victory of the RDR in municipal elections in March 2001, President Gbagbo shifted to a policy of national reconciliation to ease the tensions in what had become a highly polarised Ivorian society (Toungara, 2001). In July 2002, Gbagbo, Ouattara and Bédié gathered to adopt a 'broad-based government' in which all political parties of opposition would have their part (UNSC, 2003a). Meanwhile, Ouattara obtained his nationality certificate from the Court, so that his origins were no longer disputed.

Countering the efforts for national reconciliation, the rebels of the northern regions organised simultaneous attacks on military installations on 19 September 2002 and retained control of some northern and western regions of the country. In 2002, soon after the clash with the national army which seized the control of the capital Abidjan, the Ivorian

[1] The Muslim north was inhabited mainly by the descendants of poor immigrant workers from Mali and Burkina Faso working on coffee and cocoa plantations.

Popular Movement of the Great West (*Mouvement Populaire Ivoirien du Grand Ouest*, MPIGO) and the Movement for Justice and Peace (*Mouvement pour la Paix et la Justice*, MPJ) were united with the MPCI. They aimed to centralise power, built *Forces Nouvelles*—a group of ex-northern rebels—and organised an armed insurrection for ending the *Ivoirité* doctrine. *Forces Nouvelles* demanded for a clear definition of who a citizen is, voting rights, transparent elections, right to a just representation in central government, as well as the resignation of President Gbagbo. In response, Gbagbo organised militia groups and hired foreign combatants to fight his fight. As the report of Human Rights Watch (2010) clearly demonstrates, the involvement of foreign fighters resulted in a series of war crimes and crimes against humanity. The Ivorian armed forces—few in number, undisciplined and poorly endowed with material resources—were incapable of playing a role in the fight, because for decades instead of strengthening its armed forces Côte d'Ivoire had relied on its defence agreement with France to ensure its national security.[2]

The Defence Agreement with France

During the decolonisation process, France concluded defence agreements (*accords de défense*) with its ex-colonies in Africa, which allowed it to intervene militarily to provide security in cases of internal and external threats. The first general defence agreement between Paris and Abidjan was signed in April 1961 for maintaining order in the country. This was followed by five other technical agreements concluded between 1965 and 1998 (Livre blanc, 2008a). Permanent presence of the French military forces in Port Bouët provided technical assistance in terms of materials and training. Hence, it served as a security umbrella for Côte d'Ivoire until 1990 (Banga, 2020). That year, facing street protests, President Houphouët-Boigny asked for a French military intervention on grounds of their defence agreement. Nevertheless, French President François Mitterand (1994) had adopted a new doctrine that allowed France to intervene in its ex-colonies only in cases of external aggression, or when French citizens were in danger. Consequently, France refused to intervene and left Houphouët-Boigny alone in dealing with internal security issues.

[2] It is essentially after 2003 that National Army—i.e. the loyalists—were formed and equipped.

A second appeal came in December 1999, that is on the first day of the coup. This time it was President Bédié who received a negative response from France (Marshall, 2005). In January 2001, President Gbagbo made the third request for a massive military intervention, and changing its stance, France decided to provide a limited military cooperation. Owing to its past relations with authoritarian governments of Zaire and Chad as well as the allegations of the international community regarding its role in the Rwandan genocide (because of their support to the Hutu government), France preferred to restrain its unilateral actions (Gautier, 2011). Accordingly, in September 2002, when loyalist security forces failed to remove the rebel forces and take control of the occupied regions, considering the ongoing crisis an internal issue France only agreed to deliver logistical aid to Ivorian authorities. Despite France's reluctance to get involved in Ivorian domestic issues, starting from September 2002 its armed forces were heavily engaged with more than 4,000 soldiers in what is called Côte d'Ivoire's 'first civil war'.

During Operation Licorne that aimed to create a buffer zone between the belligerents, the French forces were drawn into a cooperation with the troops of the Economic Community of West African States (ECOWAS) under ambiguous conditions (Piccolino, 2017). ECOWAS was a dynamic actor seeking for a solution to the crisis, and it promoted dialogue between the rebels and the Government. After the Summit held in Accra on 29 September 2002, the circumstances forced ECOWAS to deploy troops to Côte d'Ivoire with the aim of ending this humanitarian crisis. Concerned about the prospect of a civil war, France mobilised its diplomatic means to convince ECOWAS to deploy a peacekeeping mission. The plan was to pull back approximately 3,900 personnel for something more of a supporting mandate and progressively hand over responsibility to the ECOWAS force along the ceasefire line. Although France encouraged ECOWAS Member States to deploy a multilateral force in Côte d'Ivoire, President Gbagbo consented only to French troops' presence on the soil of his country. He wanted to delay to the extent possible the deployment of the ECOWAS force and asked France to strengthen its presence in Côte d'Ivoire. Ultimately, with the efforts of external actors, a ceasefire agreement was concluded between MPCI and President Gbagbo on 17 October 2002. The agreement anticipated peace talks between the belligerents and the two sides met in Lomé on 24 October 2002. Among various subjects of negotiation, the two parties agreed to respect and preserve the territorial integrity of Côte d'Ivoire. Unfortunately, the

Lomé Talks ended in a deadlock 'as MPCI insisted on the resignation of President Gbagbo, a review of the Constitution and the holding of fresh elections, while the Government demanded that the rebels disarm and honour their commitment to preserve the territorial integrity of the country' (UNSC, 2003a).

Given the circumstances, the ECOWAS force for Côte d'Ivoire, namely ECOFORCE, was deployed with the mandate of 'monitoring a proposed ceasefire, ensuring the disengagement of the insurgents from the areas that had fallen under their control, and disarming the rebel groups' (UNSC, 2003a). However, ECOFORCE suffered from serious shortfalls. Consequently, the handing over of responsibility from the French forces to ECOFORCE was delayed, making the former vulnerable to deliberate attacks of rebels (Olonisakin, 2004). It is under such imprecise and perilous conditions that France tried to gather all the belligerents in a roundtable for adopting the Linas-Marcoussis Agreement, which was signed on 26 January 2003 in France.[3] This comprehensive agreement created a Government of National Reconciliation which would be 'in charge of preparing a timetable for holding credible and transparent national elections, rebuilding the security forces and organizing the disarmament of all armed groups' (UNSC, 2003b). The government of reconciliation was also responsible for organising the national elections that were scheduled for 2005 (Olonisakin, 2004). The annex of the agreement revealed a list of fundamental and problematic issues such as 'the question of citizenship, the status of foreign nationals, the electoral system, the eligibility to run for the presidency of the country, land tenure, media, disarmament and demobilization and economic recovery' (UNSC, 2003b).

From Linas-Marcoussis Agreement to the 2010 Elections

In February 2003, seizing the matter, the UNSC determined in Resolution 1464 that the situation in Côte d'Ivoire constitutes a threat to international peace and security in the region. Acting under Chapter

[3] The roundtable organised by the invitation of the President of the French Republic 'brought together the following parties: FPI, MFA, MJP, MPCI, MPIGO, PDCI-RDA, PIT, RDR, UDCY and UDPCI. The conference was chaired by Mr. Pierre MAZEAUD, assisted by Judge Keba Mbaye, former Prime Minister Seydou Diarra and facilitators appointed by the UN, the African Union and ECOWAS' (UNSC, 2003b, p. 2).

VII, the Council authorised ECOWAS and French forces 'to take the necessary steps to guarantee the security and freedom of movement of their personnel and to ensure [...] the protection of civilians immediately threatened with physical violence within their zone of operation, using the means available to them, for a period of six months' (UNSC, 2003c).

On 26 March 2003, the UN Secretary-General submitted a report on the origins and evolution of the crisis in Côte d'Ivoire (UNSC, 2003a). The report determined the existence of challenges to the stability of the country and provided a list of recommendations on the role of the UN for the implementation of the Linas-Marcoussis Agreement. On 3 May 2003, a complete ceasefire has been decided between *Forces Armées Nationales de Côte d'Ivoire* (FANCI) and *Forces Nouvelles*. ECOWAS and French forces supported and supervised the implementation of this ceasefire. On 13 May 2003, the UNSC established the UN Mission in Côte d'Ivoire (MINUCI) with Resolution 1479. This was a political mission with a mandate to facilitate the implementation of the Linas-Marcoussis Agreement and to complement the operations of ECOWAS and French forces for an initial period of six months. In the following months, the efforts of ECOWAS and France to promote a peaceful settlement of the conflict proved insufficient to stabilise the country (UNSC, 2004a). The ineffectuality of MINUCI was the reason France lobbied for the establishment UNOCI under Resolution 1528 dated 24 February 2004 (UNSC, 2004b). As the President of the UN General Assembly (UNGA) underlined in his letter of 8 January 2004, the UNSC determined that 'the situation in Côte d'Ivoire continues to pose a threat to international peace and security in the region' (UNSC, 2004c).

UNOCI was established in accordance with Chapter VII of the Charter with a military strength of maximum of 6,240 UN personnel for an initial period of 12 months. By this resolution, the mandate was transferred from MINUCI and ECOWAS forces to UNOCI, wherein the latter was to carry out its tasks in coordination with the French forces. A detailed and robust mandate with 17 subheadings was established for monitoring the ceasefire and armed groups movements, as well as protecting 'civilians under imminent threat of physical violence, within its capabilities and its areas of deployment' (UNSC, 2004b). As in most operations, the peacekeepers were allowed to use 'all necessary means' to protect civilians. Yet, once they were deployed it was seen that they lacked the necessary resources to fulfil their mandate. Even though UNOCI was collaborating with the French troops already present and operational in Côte d'Ivoire, the mission stayed as a traditional peace operation playing the role of an interposition between the protagonists and failed to provide protection to civilians. France was the leading state behind UNOCI. Since the day the UNSC decided to establish this operation, France was present at all the stages, especially when adopting resolutions and deploying troops. UNOCI's formation is one of the examples where an operation was backed up by a permanent member, and also where there was unity in the Council (Novosseloff, 2018).

At the end of 2004, President Gbagbo who once insisted for French intervention in Côte d'Ivoire turned against French presence in his country. FANCI did not respect the ceasefire and continued to attack *Forces Nouvelles*, and UNOCI was unable to stabilise the country. When nine French peacekeepers were killed by Gbagbo's forces on 6 November, French forces retaliated, and this became the reason of the conflict between the Ivorian President and France (Livre Blanc, Les Débats, 2008b). On the one hand, the Government of National Reconciliation was unable to carry out the disarmament, demobilisation and reintegration (DDR) process (Olonisakin, 2004). On the other hand, the question about the definition of *Ivoirité* and all the disagreements mentioned in the annex of the Linas-Marcoussis Agreement were left without a concrete resolution plan. Consequently, the elections were delayed several times. From November 2004 to January 2007, the UNSC adopted 17 resolutions concerning the situation in Côte d'Ivoire but without concrete progress in the resolution of the crisis.

It is within this context that the Ougadougou Agreement was signed on 4 March 2007. As mentioned in the Secretary-General's report, the agreement sought to resolve the crisis in Côte d'Ivoire by implementing two follow-up mechanisms (UNSC, 2007). First, President Gbagbo, Prime Minister Soro, former President Bedié, former Prime Minister Ouattara and the facilitator, President of Burkina Faso Blaise Compaoré would be part of a consultative mechanism. Second, an evaluation and monitoring committee consisting of three members would be created with representatives from each party with the mandate of implementation of the agreement. The key actor in this agreement was Guillaume Soro who would remain as prime minister until the presidential election. He was given specific powers to implement the Ouagadougou Agreement and organise national elections. A new transitional Government was formed and the withdrawal process of UNOCI and French forces was scheduled for after the presidential election that took place on 31

October 2010. As noted in the Secretary-General's report, 'the overall security situation in Côte d'Ivoire remained stable but still fragile, given the ongoing sensitive electoral process and the unresolved aspects of the peace process, including the uncompleted disarmament and reintegration of former combatants and the reunification of the country' (UNSC, 2010). Moreover, under the Ouagadougou Agreement, millions of Ivorian people received their national identity and voter cards, and hence, an important task was accomplished.

From Linas-Marcoussis Agreement to the elections of 2010, we observe R2P in practice in. The Government of National Reconciliation's every initiative to secure the country such as the DDR process or the establishment of an evaluation and monitoring committee can be considered as measures pertaining to Pillar One, and thus as an attempt to realise the protection responsibilities of the State. Meanwhile, the assistance provided by France, ECOWAS, UNOCI or other local and/or international actors falls under Pillar Two, wherein the international community is tasked with assistance and capacity-building. A working Pillar Two is considered to be a strong instrument in preventing crimes and especially regarding to the protection of the disadvantaged groups (UNGA, 2009). Nevertheless, neither the measures adopted by the Government of National Reconciliation nor the international community's efforts in line with Pillar Two proved sufficient to prevent the post-electoral crisis in 2010.

The Post-Electoral Crisis: From Pillar Three to Sustainable Protection

The first round of the presidential elections was conducted peacefully, and thus considered mostly successful. With a turnout rate of 83.73%, the election raised hopes for an end to the crisis. While Gbagbo and Ouattara were to run for a second round on 28 November 2010, the situation got complicated because the population was polarised over the *Ivoirité* question. UNOCI military and police personnel were present to monitor the security situation (Darracq, 2011). As in the first round, more than 300 international observers were deployed to observe the whole process. The day before the election, on 27 November, Gbagbo decided to impose a curfew 'as a preventive security measure aimed at deterring violence during the elections' (UNSC, 2011a)'. Perceiving the curfew as an obstruction, Ouattara's supporters seized the streets of Abidjan. After the polls were closed, Gbagbo's representatives alleged that the elections were not conducted transparently in the northern and western parts of the country because of the violence committed by *Forces Nouvelles*.

Four days after the election, on 2 December the Chair of the Independent Electoral Commission announced the results of the second round. With an 81% overall participation, Ouattara got 54.10% of the votes while Gbagbo got 45.90% (UNSC 211). However, on 3 December, the President of the Constitutional Council 'proclaimed the final results of the presidential elections, with Laurent Gbagbo having received 51.45% of the vote and Alassane Ouattara 48.55%, and with a voter turnout of 71.28%' (UNSC 211). The change was mostly due to the cancellation of 660,000 votes coming from seven departments in the north of the country where Ouattara was largely ahead (Darracq, 2011).

The same day, the Special Representative of the Secretary-General, Choi Young-jin held a press conference. He stated that the results announced by the Independent Electoral Commission were the certified one and rejected the result announced by the President of the Constitutional Council. The Special Representative's conclusions were based on a 'detailed analysis of more than 20,000 tally sheets that UNOCI had received from the Ivorian polling authorities' (UNSC 211). The alleged massive irregularities claimed by the representatives of Gbagbo and the President of the Constitutional Council were not considered sufficient to change the election results the Independent Electoral Commission announced.

After the press conference things changed drastically for Côte d'Ivoire. First, the Special Representative of the Secretary-General expressed his certainty about the election results and dismissed the allegations. Then, the Secretary-General expressed his full support for Special Representative Choi, and called Ouattara to congratulate him on his victory on 3 December without waiting for the official results from Ivorian authorities. Choi's determination and the Secretary-General's clear stance regarding the results had very much influenced the international response to the post-electoral crisis, and the international community soon declared Ouattara as the President-elect of Côte d'Ivoire. However, on 4 December, Gbagbo took the oath of office as did Ouattara while he was under a blockade in the Golf Hotel. Consequently, two distinct governments were formed in the next few days, and that is how Côte d'Ivoire had two presidents each claiming to be the legitimate one: 'Gbagbo had power without legitimacy, while Ouattara had legitimacy without power' (Novosellof, 2018).

On 7 December, ECOWAS recognised Ouattara as the president-elect. On 8 December, the UNSC, pleased by the decision of ECOWAS as the regional organisation that monitored the election process, endorsed the outcome of the election in favour of Ouattara. On 9 December, the African Peace and Security Council positioned itself with ECOWAS. It recognised Ouattara as the president-elect and urged Gbagbo to respect the results of the election. The support of two regional organisations was an important step in the concretisation of the international community's reaction. Few days later, the United States (US) and the European Union decided to impose visa bans and financial sanctions on Gbagbo and his close entourage. Over the following months diplomatic efforts of various actors to persuade Gbagbo to peacefully step down and respect the free will of the Ivorian people proved unsuccessful. Rejecting all proposals, Gbagbo continued to claim that he was the legitimate president of his country until he was apprehended on 11 April 2011.

On 20 December 2010 the UNSC unanimously adopted Resolution 1962 and recognised Ouattara as Côte d'Ivoire's president-elect. Acting under Chapter VII of the Charter, the Council renewed the mandate of UNOCI and decided that 500 additional personnel were to join UNOCI to strengthen its dissuasive presence on the ground with 8,650 personnel in total. With this resolution, the UNSC compromised its impartiality and decided that Gbagbo had to step down to ensure that UNOCI achieves its mandate (Novosseloff, 2018). In other words, the UNSC skipped a vital step and did not seek the host State's consent (Bellamy & Williams, 2011). Ultimately, Resolution 1962 put an end to Gbagbo's hope to impose a *fait accompli* by playing for time until the international community forgot about the crisis.

Confronted with the deteriorating situation and escalating violence on the ground, the UN's first reference to R2P was made in a press release. On 29 December 2010, the Secretary-General's Special Advisers on the Prevention of Genocide and the Responsibility to Protect reminded all the parties of their responsibility to protect all persons in Côte d'Ivoire and that they are accountable for their actions under international law (UNSC, 2011a). Three weeks later, on 19 January 2011, driven by a grave concern about the possibility of mass atrocity crimes in Côte d'Ivoire, Special Advisers released their second statement wherein they called on the international community to take action in line with R2P.

By that time, 23,500 Ivorians have fled to neighbouring countries while another 16,000 were internally displaced (UNSC, 2011a). The threat of ethnic clashes spreading across the country and transforming into mass atrocities was imminent.

While the army pledged its support to Gbagbo, on 17 March when an attack on Abidjan killed more than 100 people, President Ouattara established the Republican Forces of Côte d'Ivoire (RFCI) including *Forces Nouvelles* in this new structure and ordered the military offensive to Abidjan (UNSC, 2011b). As for UNOCI, Gbagbo perceived it as a collaborator of Ouattara's forces, and hence, on 8 December he asked it to leave the country. From this moment on, UNOCI stayed operational without the consent of the host State in a situation where Gbagbo was not internationally recognised as the president and was considered to be holding a form of de facto power. Under the deteriorating conditions in Côte d'Ivoire, the UN force's impartiality was compromised when it protected Ouattara by securing the perimeter of the Golf Hotel (Darracq, 2011).

The debate on the consent of the parties and impartiality for a UN mission dates back to the 1960 UN Operation in Congo (UNOC). At the time, the then Secretary-General Dag Hammarskjöld asserted that consent and impartiality are bedrock principles for peacekeeping, and the use of force could only be in self-defence (UNSC, 2000). In 2000, the Brahimi Report stated that 'impartiality is not the same as neutrality or equal treatment of all parties in all cases for all time', and that 'the consent in the context of intra-State/transnational conflicts, may be manipulated in many ways' (UNSC, 2000). In early January 2011, the Secretary-General pointed in his letter to the UNSC that 'UNOCI is operating in an openly hostile security environment with direct threats from regular and irregular forces loyal to former President Gbagbo' (UNSC, 2011c). He also called on Member States to urgently strengthen the capacity of UNOCI so that it could carry out its mandate. After several attacks against civilians that killed more than 400 people, UNOCI warned the UN about possible crimes against humanity.

It can be argued that throughout the electoral process state authorities have failed to uphold their Pillar One responsibility and dragged the country into a crisis. Meanwhile, from the lens of Pillar Two, we may argue that the international community aided Côte d'Ivoire to help the State to protect its population. The fact that the polls were observed by local and international observers and that UNOCI was present to secure the situation were positive contributions on the part of the international community. Nevertheless, these measures fell short in terms of securing the country as well as protecting the population, and thus, failed to stop the mass atrocity crimes.

Resolution 1975 and Pillar Three

Given the imminent threat posed by the situation, one might argue that when the UNSC adopted Resolution 1962 and recognised Ouattara as president-elect of Côte d'Ivoire, it also decided to implement the principle of subsidiarity under Pillar Three because the Ivorian national authorities were 'manifestly failing' to protect their population. However, the wide range of non-coercive measures adopted under Chapters VI and VIII of the Charter were not efficient for stopping the mass atrocity crimes in the country. That is why the UNSC decided to adopt coercive action. It was on 30 March that the UNSC unanimously adopted Resolution 1975 submitted by the delegations of France and Nigeria. The Resolution's decisions were consistent with the fact that 'the precarious security situation could quickly degenerate into widespread conflict' (UNSC, 2011c). The UNSC provided a possibility for UNOCI to actualise its strong protection of civilian mandate by authorising it to 'use all necessary means to carry out its mandate to protect civilians under imminent threat of physical violence' (Evans, 2016). In compliance with Resolution 1962, Ouattara was recognised as the legitimate president. The UNSC condemned Gbagbo for not accepting a peaceful solution and urged him to immediately step aside. Acting under Chapter VII, it also authorised UNOCI 'to prevent the use of heavy weapons against the civilian population' which was in line with complex and risky mandates that have been the rule rather than the exception since the end of the Cold War (UNSC, 2000). The control of heavy weapons may also be the outcome of the 'new politics of protection' as described by Bellamy and Williams (2011) because Resolution 1975 was adopted only 13 days after Resolution 1973 on Libya, which was the first authorisation of use of force in the case of an R2P crisis. Nonetheless, neither Resolution 1973 nor 1975 referred to Paragraph 139 of the 2005 World Summit Outcome Document. Throughout Resolution 1975, the UNSC recalls three times the government's responsibility to protect but does not make an explicit or implicit reference to the international community's responsibility. The

R2P literature nonetheless draws a link between the decisions of the Resolution and Pillar Three as the measures decided overlap with R2P's toolkit and the mandate of the Resolution raised the prospect of the protection of the population.

It is also noteworthy that there were concerns raised by the Member States, although the Resolution was adopted unanimously. As the representative of India noted in the UNSC meeting, for some Member States there was a 'growing concern at the tendency to hurry the process of adopting resolutions' and that 'there should be enough time for deliberations and consultations with all countries concerned' (UNSC, 2011d). Besides, in their statements following the voting some Member States highlighted the importance of UNOCI implementing its mandate impartially, which was a condition that was abandoned long before (UNSC, 2011d).

While Resolution 1975 strengthened the mandate of UNOCI in terms of the protection of civilians, there have been criticisms that UNOCI interpreted this 'as authorization to send attack helicopters in support of a French operation to capture Gbagbo. While Russia, which had close ties with Gbagbo, condemned this manoeuvre' and accused the French Forces and UNOCI for having used excessive force, 'the Secretary-General and other UN officials flagged it as a great success for peacekeeping' (Gowan, 2018). With the assistance of UNOCI and French forces, especially by the air strikes against the heavy weapons of the forces loyal to Gbagbo, RFCI took control of Abidjan and Gbagbo was apprehended on 14 April 2011. Then, he was transferred to the Hague to wait for his trial in January 2016 during which he pleaded not guilty to charges of crimes against humanity and war crimes. To end a ten-year painful crisis in the history of Côte d'Ivoire 'it took five months of convincing Gbagbo to hold elections, four months of diplomatic negotiations, and one week of war' (Novosseloff, 2018). As Hunt (2016) observes, 'it was a combination of diplomatic measures, economic sanctions, arms embargo, and force that unseated Gbagbo and ended the crisis'.

The use of force by the UN peacekeepers and French troops ignited debates on different questions. One was that whether the Secretary-General has exceeded his responsibility by claiming the victory of Ouattara right after the second round by disregarding the position of the Constitutional Council (UNSC, 2011e)? The general debate on the role of the Secretary-General has been continuing since the 1960 intervention in

Congo. During this operation, much was decided with the then Secretary-General Dag Hammarskjöld's personal initiatives, and he was criticised for surpassing the mandate of the operation. Since then, a rather firm control over the role and competence of the Secretary-General has been enforced by Member States especially by those called the 'sovereigntists' such as China and Russia vis-à-vis the 'legalists' such as France, United Kingdom and the US (Novosseloff, 2018). Countering the claims, in May 2011, the Secretary-General stated: 'at no time has the UN exceeded its UNSC mandates. In Côte d'Ivoire, UN forces undertook a limited military operation whose sole purpose was to protect innocent people. The only targets of armed action were the heavy weapons used by the former regime to attack civilians and our own headquarters and peacekeepers' (Ban, 2011).

The other question sparking a debate concerned UNOCI's impartiality, which emerged as another disagreement between the Member States. In the post-Cold War period, robust peace enforcement operations replaced traditional peacekeeping providing a definition of aggressor and victim. As the Brahimi Report made it clear, 'no failure did more to damage the standing and credibility of United Nations peacekeeping in the 1990s than its reluctance to distinguish victim from aggressor' (UNSC, 2000). From the moment that UNOCI and French troops joined forces to protect Ouattara and his government at Golf Hotel, it was impossible to treat the parties to the conflict equally. Nonetheless, 'the operation in Côte d'Ivoire managed to prevent a severe post-electoral crisis, despite experiencing severe harassment' (Gowan, 2018). In Côte d'Ivoire, a decision was made to endorse RFCI, and the close monitoring of the Secretary-General and his Special Representative 'helped to stabilize the situation and minimize casualties, but things could have turned out very differently' (Bellamy & Williams, 2011). The case of Côte d'Ivoire has seriously challenged the UN's credibility because when it was impossible to reach a peaceful solution, opting for the use of force through Resolution 1975 was not an easy task given the earlier reluctance of Russia and South Africa for a more decisive action (Gowan, 2011).

Ultimately, it can be argued that the international response was timely and decisive as R2P would require. As Hunt (2016) claims, alongside the complexity of the Ivorian crisis, R2P played an important role 'in informing and justifying the action through statements on the crisis, language in mandates, and authorizing certain actions'. The Secretary-General claimed success arguing that 'the international community stood firm on a fundamental principle, and it did not back down. What is happening in Libya, Côte d'Ivoire and elsewhere is an historic precedent, a watershed in the emerging doctrine of the responsibility to protect' (Ban, 2011).

Drawdown and Transition of UNOCI

After President Ouattara assumed his rightful duties, the main goal was first to stabilise the security situation in the country. Although things remained fragile, Ouattara had the opportunity to improve the country's economy with international assistance (UNSC, 2012). In his March 2013 Report, the Secretary-General noted that 'despite persistent fragility, Côte d'Ivoire was entering a phase of consolidation since the end of the 2011 post-elections crisis' (UNSC, 2013). In his evaluation of the overall situation, Ban observed that 'President Ouattara's leadership has been critical to addressing immediate security challenges, accelerating economic recovery and initiating sensitive processes such as disarmament, demobilization and reintegration (DDR) and security sector reform' (UNSC, 2013). With the growing effectivity of the local administration and the National Assembly, it became possible to organise legislative elections on 20 February 2013 (UNSC, 2013). In early 2013, the country was ready to initiate a normalisation of relations and dialogue between various actors to prepare for the 2015 presidential elections (Piccolino, 2017). Despite this Western perception of positive progress and development, so little was accomplished on the ground as demonstrated by the Dialogue, Truth and Reconciliation Commission, which was founded in July 2011 with high expectations but has been absent on local ground (Charbonneau, 2013). Notwithstanding the inconsistencies between the reality on the ground and the better picture the government was drawing, the relative stability of political and economic conditions made it possible to allow UNOCI to begin its withdrawal with the aim of preparing the country for the transition to a post-peacekeeping presence.

The drawdown was seen as a benefit for both the UN and Côte d'Ivoire. From an R2P point of view, after the Libyan intervention, it was crucial for the UN to perform a successful peace operation and set a good example. Especially, the military intervention led by France in Libya, the day after the adoption of Resolution 1973 generated criticisms about France's real intentions and led to accusations of being an opportunist as well as of conducting a military operation for its own interests. Therefore, France was planning to reduce the number of its military forces in Côte d'Ivoire. There was also a plan to cut the budget of peacekeeping operations because of the implementation of two new operations in Mali and the Central African Republic. As for Côte d'Ivoire, the new government 'wanted to show the rest of the world that with 9 percent annual growth, their country did not need that kind of help anymore, particularly as it was getting ready to join the Security Council itself' (Novosseloff, 2018).

On 25 October 2015, Ouattara obtained 83.6% of the votes and won the presidential election for a second and final term. The election was held peacefully and transparently but there was tension because of the antagonistic political divisions. UNOCI supported the Ivorian authorities throughout the election process by providing logistical help and implementing a 'comprehensive election security plan' (UNSC, 2015a). On 28 April 2016, with Resolution 2284 the UNSC extended the mandate of UNOCI for a final period until 30 June 2017. The referendum in October 2016 for adopting a new Constitution and the legislative election in December 2016 were seen as the evidence of trust for Ivorian authorities to govern democratically despite persisting political and ethnic tension in the country.

In 2015, the Secretary-General noted that a true reconciliation of the population would require the implementation of the fundamental principle of equality before the law and to 'bring to justice some of the alleged perpetrators of crimes committed against the State during the post-elections crisis' (UNSC, 2015b). Nevertheless, those efforts were never made while the supporters of former President Gbagbo were persecuted for committing crimes against the State. After his second win, President Ouattara aimed to endorse national reconciliation and social cohesion, and encountered various political, religious and local actors (Piccolino, 2017). As a result, on 31 December 2016, he announced a 'presidential pardon for 3,100 prisoners, as well as the release of individuals detained in connection with the post-elections crisis' (UNSC, 2016). However, stability in Côte d'Ivoire has always been fragile because President Ouattara could not manage to address the root causes of the Ivorian conflict in order to consolidate peace which requires 'the full commitment of all citizens to a comprehensive and meaningful process of national reconciliation' (UNSC, 2016). As for the new Constitution, which aimed to promote ethnic, cultural and religious diversity of the country, it could not provide social cohesion and stability. Despite the efforts for reconciliation at a national level, the country remained divided.

Moreover, local people displayed a preference for amnesty and mechanisms of conflict resolution over the alternative of seeking prosecution through the International Criminal Court (Malu, 2019).

In March 2020, after ten years in office Ouattara declared that he would not seek for a third term and that he would hand the power over to the new generation (Bado, 2021). To run for the forthcoming October elections, Prime Minister Amadou Gon Coulibaly was chosen as the candidate of the ruling Rally of Houphouëtists for Democracy and Peace Party (RHDR)—which is a political alliance of five political parties established in 2018—but he suddenly died in July. Since the whole strategy was forged around a single person, accepting to be the candidate of RHDR in August, Ouattara had to seek re-election in October 2020, which he considered a 'real sacrifice' given his previous promise (Coulibaly, 2020). This marked the beginning of a tumultuous era as well as a constitutional debate until the presidential elections on 31 October 2020. Practically, the new Constitution that was accepted in 2016 forbid a third term in presidency. Hence, his opponents argued that the two-term limit should be applied for banning Ouattara from running for elections again, whereas Ouattara asserted that his first two mandates did not count under the new Constitution. Owing to their brave effort for democratisation, the opponents of Ouattara became the ones who had to bear with several sanctions, and that is why the presidential election of 2020 was seen by the opposition as 'the revenge' (Bado, 2021). However, when they could not ban Ouattara from running for the presidency, they called on their supporters to boycott the election. As declared by the Electoral Commission, the voter turnout remained at 53.90% wherein Ouattara received 94.27% of the votes and won the election. Since the latest presidential election, the country remains highly unstable with a high risk of turmoil between different ethnic and political groups. According to official records, at least 85 people have been killed and 8,000 had to flee the country since August 2020 due to election-related violence (GCR2P, 2020).

Conclusion

From 2011 to the present day, Libya and Côte d'Ivoire remain as the two exceptional cases wherein the use of military force was consecutively employed as a UNSC sanctioned measure under Pillar Three of R2P, yet the two cases are very different from each other. The 2011 post-election crisis in Côte d'Ivoire that resulted in the death of 3,000 people and the displacement of 600,000 is quite a unique R2P crisis in many respects. As noted in several Secretary-General reports, there were too many challenges obstructing stability in the country. Though the presence of regional and/or international forces on the ground prevented a complete collapse of state institutions, neither the Government of National Reconciliation created by the Linas-Marcoussis Agreement, nor the international community could prevent the post-electoral crisis. What happened in Côte d'Ivoire was a failure in terms of the responsibility to prevent under Pillars One and Two. One might argue that this failure happened because none of the international actors sought to understand or question Gbagbo's real intentions: Was he ever ready to hand over power peacefully? Since the day he became president, he insisted on keeping the *Ivoirité* doctrine and tried to consolidate it through the Constitution. When we look at the big picture and the way events unfolded, his refusal of stepping down peacefully was not a surprise at all.

Given the continuous engagement in Côte d'Ivoire, carrying out the responsibility to react was arguably an ongoing requirement. In the years following the UN Secretary-General's introduction of the three-pillar implementation strategy, we can talk about academic and to some extent political will to give life to R2P. There was a growing sensibility in the international community regarding prevention of mass atrocity crimes as we saw it in Resolution 1973 on Libya. Concerning the case of Côte d'Ivoire, the role played by France—one of the staunch supporters of R2P—was crucial, because it managed to mobilise the UNSC members despite its colonial past with the host State. It is noteworthy that the decision to react in a timely and decisive manner was not without controversies. When the UNSC reaffirmed its full support to UNOCI backed by French forces and authorised the use of all necessary means for civilian protection, it emphasised impartial operation. However, impartiality was compromised when the UNSC recognised Ouattara as the President of the Republic of Côte d'Ivoire despite the officially contested election results. Moreover, the Council condemned Gbagbo's denial to step down and passed a judgement on a Member State's internal issue. Furthermore, while adopting Resolution 1975 and deciding action under Chapter VII, it did not seek the consent of the Ivorian State.

Although criticised by some Member States because of the excessive use of force and lack of impartiality, the operation authorised by Resolution 1975 under Pillar Three was generally conceived as a success because it was a timely, decisive and unanimous response delivered in the face of mass atrocities. The case of UNOCI also showed that a peace operation backed by a robust mandate could use its presence on the ground effectively to prevent the killings unlike the bitter example of UNAMIR in Rwanda. After Gbagbo's apprehension in April 2011, President Ouattara managed to stabilise the country and despite persistent fragility Côte d'Ivoire entered a phase of consolidation. Given the environment of relative political stability in the country, the UNSC ended the mandate of UNOCI in June 2017.

To date, the case of Côte d'Ivoire is arguably the only successful example of the responsibility to react under Pillar Three wherein military force was employed. Though we may consider Côte d'Ivoire a successful example of Pillar Three implementation, this case provides us with an additional important lesson on sustainable protection, which seems to be a vital point yet to be taken seriously by the international community. Since August 2020 internal violence has escalated in Côte d'Ivoire, and the presidential elections held in late 2020 were not enough to soothe the underlying ethnic and political tensions. The gravity of the situation in 2020 necessitates a deeper analysis of the national reconciliation process and highlights the problems of transparency and accountability. While ending UNOCI's mandate was approved both by the UN Member States and the Ivorian government, the atrocities of the last year make us question that perhaps the departure of UNOCI happened too soon, too quickly, resulting in a failure what the responsibility to rebuild would achieve.

Given the history of civil war and the cycle of election-related violence, as well as the lack of an effort to rebuild the country post-military intervention, it can be claimed that sustainable protection has not been achieved in the case of Côte d'Ivoire. The country's population is still at risk because of political instability and the lingering threat of mass atrocities. Moreover, after spending almost eight years in prison and two years on parole in Brussels, on 31 March 2021, Laurent Gbagbo was acquitted from all the accusations of committing war crimes and crimes against humanity and has returned to Côte d'Ivoire on 17 June 2021 (Lankoandé, 2021). While his return can be a new opportunity for a real national reconciliation, it also presents a potential challenge for the Ivorian political system. Hence, Côte d'Ivoire remains a case that requires constant attention of the international community if mass atrocity prevention is the desired objective.

References

Babo, A. (2012). L'étranger à travers le prisme de l'*ivoirité* en Côte d'Ivoire: Retour sur des regards nouveaux. *Migrations Société, 6*(6), 99–120.

Bado, A. B. (2021). La Côte d'Ivoire au lendemain de l'élection présidentielle. *Études, 2*(2), 19–30.

Bah, A. B. (2010). Democracy and civil war: Citizenship and peacemaking in Côte d'Ivoire. *African Affairs, 109*(432), 597–615.

Bellamy, A. J., & Williams, P. D. (2011). The new politics of protection? Côte d'Ivoire, Libya and the responsibility to protect. *International Affairs, 87*(4), 825–850.

Ban, K. M. (2011, May 6). *Address to the Sofia platform*. https://www.un.org/sg/en/content/sg/speeches/2011-05-06/address-sofia-platform. Accessed 15 March 2021.

Banga, A. (2020). Chefs politiques et chefs militaires en Côte d'Ivoire depuis 1960. *Histoire, Économie & Société, 4*(4), 110–126.

Charbonneau, B. (2013). Côte d'Ivoire: Possibilités et limites d'une réconciliation. *Afrique Contemporaine, 1*(1), 111–129.

Coulibaly, L. (2020, August 6). Ivory coast President Ouattara says he will run for third term. *Reuters*.https://www.reuters.com/article/us-ivorycoast-politics/ivory-coast-president-ouattara-says-he-will-run-for-third-term-idUSKCN252354. Accessed 20 May 2021.

Crook, R. C. (1997). Winning coalitions and Ethno-regional politics: The failure of the opposition in the 1990 and 1995 elections in Côte d'Ivoire. *African Affairs, 96*(383), 215–242.

Darracq, V. (2011). Côte d'Ivoire: Le monde et la crise ivoirienne. In T. De Montbrial (Ed.), *Les États submergés: Ramses 2012* (pp. 206–209). Institut Français des Relations Internationales.

Blanc, L. (2008a). *Défense et sécurité nationale: Le livre blanc*. Odile Jacob/La Documentation Française.

Blanc, L. (2008b). *Défense et sécurité nationale: Le livre blanc, les débats*. Odile Jacob/La Documentation Française.

Evans, G. (2016). R2P: The next ten years. In A. J. Bellamy & T. Dunne (Eds.), *The Oxford handbook of the responsibility to protect* (pp. 913–932). Oxford University Press.

Gautier, L. (2011). Les guerres de François Mitterrand. *Matériaux Pour L'histoire De Notre Temps, 1*(1–2), 64–70.

Global Center for the Responsibility to Protect (GCR2P). (2020, November 15). *Côte d'Ivoire. Populations at risk*. https://www.globalr2p.org/countries/cote-divoire/. Accessed 10 May 2021.

Gowan, R. (2011). *The security council's credibility problem*. Friedrich-Ebert-Stiftung. https://cic.nyu.edu/sites/default/files/gowan_security_council_credibility.pdf. Accessed 12 March 2021.

Gowan, R. (2018). Peacekeeping operations. In T. G. Weiss T. G., & S. Daws, *The Oxford handbook on the United Nations* (2 ed.) (pp. 420–446). Oxford: Oxford University Press.

Human Rights Watch. (2010). Afraid and forgotten lawlessness, rape, and impunity in Western Côte d'Ivoire. https://www.hrw.org/sites/default/files/reports/cotedivoire1010webwcover_0.pdf. Accessed 15 January 2021.

Hunt, C. (2016). Côte d'Ivoire. In A. J. Bellamy & T. Dunne (Eds.), *The Oxford handbook of the responsibility to protect* (pp. 693–717). Oxford University Press.

Langer, A. (2005). Horizontal inequalities and violentg group mobilization in Côte d'Ivoire. *Oxford Development Studies, 33*(1), 25–45.

Lankoandé, W. H. (2021, June 17). Why is Laurent Gbagbo returning to Côte d'Ivoire? *International Crisis Group.* https://www.crisisgroup.org/africa/west-africa/côte-divoire/retour-de-laurent-gbagbo-en-cote-divoire-une-nouvelle-occasion-de-reconciliation. Accessed 20 June 2021.

Marshall, R. (2005). La France en Côte d'Ivoire: l'interventionnisme à l'épreuve des faits. *Politique Africaine, 2*(2), 21–41.

Mitchell, M. I. (2018). Land conflict and electoral violence in Côte d'Ivoire: A micro-level analysis. In M. Söderberg Kovacs, & J. Bjarnesen (Eds.), *Violence in African elections: Between democracy and big man politics* (pp. 67–87). Zed Books.

Malu, L. N. (2019). *The international criminal court and peace processes.* Côte d'Ivoire, Kenya and Uganda. Palgrave Macmillan.

Mitterand, F. (1994, November 8). *Speech of François Mitterand at the XVIe sommet franco-africain de La Baule.* https://www.elysee.fr/front/pdf/elysee-module-8181-fr.pdf. Accessed 10 March 2021.

Novosseloff, A. (2018). *The many lives of a peacekeeping mission: The UN operation in Côte d'Ivoire.* International Peace Institute.

Olonisakin, F. (2004). Windows of opportunity for conflict prevention: Responding to regional conflict in West Africa 1. *Conflict, Security & Development, 4*(2), 181–198.

Piccolino, G. (2017). Rhétorique de la cohésion sociale et paradoxes de la «paix par le bas» en Côte d'Ivoire. *Politique Africaine, 4*(4), 49–68.

Toungara, J. (2001). Ethnicity and political crisis in Cote d'Ivoire. *Journal of Democracy, 12*(3), 63–72.

United Nations General Assembly (UNGA). (2005, October 24). Resolution Adopted by the General Assembly on 16 September 2005, '60/1. 2005 World Summit Outcome', A/Res/60/1.

United Nations General Assembly (UNGA). (12 January 2009). *Implementing the responsibility to protect.* Report of the Secretary-General, A/63/677.

United Nations General Assembly–Security Council (UNGA–UNSC). (2000, August 21). Report of the Panel on United Nations Peace Operations, A/55/305–S/2000/809.
United Nations Security Council (UNSC). (2003a). Report of the Secretary General on Côte d'Ivoire, S/2003/374.
United Nations Security Council (UNSC). (2003b). Annex I to the letter dated 27 January 2003 from the Permanent Representative of France to the United Nations addressed to the President of the Security Council, S/2003/99.
United Nations Security Council (UNSC). (2003c). Resolution adopted by the Security Council at its 4700th meeting, S/2003/1464.
United Nations Security Council (UNSC). (2004a). Report of the Secretary-General on the United Nations Mission in Côte d'Ivoire submitted pursuant to Security Council resolution 1514 (2003) of 13 November 2003, S/2004/3.
United Nations Security Council (UNSC). (2004b). Resolution Adopted by the Security Council at its 4918th meeting, S/2004/1528.
United Nations Security Council (UNSC). (2004c). *Letter dated 8 January 2004 from the President of the General Assembly to the President of the Security Council, S/2004/100.*
United Nations Security Council (UNSC). (2007, 14 May). Thirteenth progress report of the Secretary-General on the United Nations Operation in Côte d'Ivoire, S/2007/275.
United Nations Security Council (UNSC). (2010, November 23). Twenty-sixth progress report of the Secretary-General on the United Nations Operation in Côte d'Ivoire, S/2010/600.
United Nations Security Council (UNSC). (2011a). Twenty-seventh progress report of the Secretary-General on the United Nations Operation in Côte d'Ivoire, S/2011/211.
United Nations Security Council (UNSC). (2011b). Twenty-eighth report of the Secretary-General on the United Nations Operation in Côte d'Ivoire, S/2011/387.
United Nations Security Council (UNSC). (2011c). Letter dated 7 January 2011 from the Secretary-General to the President of the Security Council, S/2011/5.
United Nations Security Council (UNSC). (2011d). The situation in Côte d'Ivoire, S/PV.6508.
United Nations Security Council (UNSC). (2011e). Protection of civilians in armed conflict, S/PV.6531.
United Nations Security Council (UNSC). (2012, December 31). Thirty-first progress report of the Secretary-General on the United Nations Operation in Côte d'Ivoire, S/2012/964.

United Nations Security Council (UNSC). (2013, March 28). Special report of the Secretary-General on the United Nations Operation in Côte d'Ivoire, S/2013/197.

United Nations Security Council (UNSC). (2015a). Thirty-seventh progress report of the Secretary-General on the United Nations Operation in Côte d'Ivoire, S/2015/940.

United Nations Security Council (UNSC). (2015b). Thirty-sixth progress report of the Secretary-General on the United Nations Operation in Côte d'Ivoire, S/2015/320.

United Nations Security Council (UNSC). (2016, March 31). Special report of the Secretary-General on the United Nations Operation in Côte d'Ivoire, S/2016/297.

CHAPTER 7

Libya and Syria: The Protection of Refugees and R2P

Selin Kul

The Arab uprisings that started in Tunisia in 2010 and spread to various countries in the Middle East deeply impacted Libya and Syria as well. The rapidly escalating situations and threat of mass atrocity crimes made the two cases an immediate concern from a Responsibility to Protect (R2P) point of view. The somewhat convergent evolution of the two humanitarian crises resulted in disparate international response with the decision to militarily intervene in Libya at an early stage. After ten years of internal unrest and international involvement of different sorts, Libya and Syria remain as prominent R2P concerns. Despite visible accumulation of scholarly works on Libya and Syria in relation to the implementation of R2P, and more specifically Pillar Three, there remain neglected but significant aspects of the two cases. Diverging from previous accounts, this chapter focuses on the humanitarian crises in Libya and Syria based

S. Kul (✉)
Department of International Relations, Hacettepe University, Ankara, Turkey

P. Gözen Ercan (ed.), *The Responsibility to Protect Twenty Years On*,
https://doi.org/10.1007/978-3-030-90731-0_7

on the inherent interrelation between R2P and the protection of refugees, which has been underexplored in the literature.[1]

As Bellamy (2016) argues, R2P and the protection of refugees has always been linked. When atrocity crimes are being committed in a region against a certain population, people usually flee to ensure their security. In such cases those who are forcibly displaced but remain within the boundaries of the State are labelled as internally displaced persons (IDPs), while those who cross an international border are considered as refugees. Though the latter seek refuge in the borders of another country, this does not mean that they are secure. Many civilian casualties occur during their attempts to flee due to the unsafe escape routes they have to take. Moreover, they usually have to seek refuge first in the neighbouring countries, and they remain vulnerable because they are most often unable to meet their basic needs such as shelter, food and health services due to the mass influx and/or internal conditions of these States. The circumstances may get even more troubling in terms of the protection of refugees due to the unequal distribution of burden sharing between States. In particular, developing countries host a large portion of refugees not only because of their geographical proximity to the country of origin but also because of developed countries' policies aiming to prevent refugees from arriving at their territories (Coen, 2015, p. 1054). Because of the ever-tightening refugee and immigration policies that developed countries adopt, 86% of the world's refugee population is living in low- and middle-income countries that are close to the regions of conflict (UNHCR, 2020). This inequality has become even more visible with the Libyan and Syrian refugee protection crises post-Arab uprisings. In this regard, bringing an additional aspect of discussion into the picture, this chapter studies the cases of Libya and Syria from the lens of the protection of refugees. Accordingly, it scrutinises the depth of R2P's implementation and persisting issues as to the realisation of the responsibility to protect at the national and international levels.

The chapter starts off with a general overview of how the situations have unfolded in Libya and Syria and the initial international response. Afterwards, conducting a pillar-by-pillar analysis, the chapter dwells into the question of to what extent and how R2P has been implemented in

[1] For exceptions see, Barbour and Gorlick (2008), Francis (2012), Achiume (2015), Coen (2015), Maley (2015), Bellamy (2016), Souter (2016), Ralph and Souter (2017), and Gözen Ercan and Kul (2021).

these two cases with respect to the protection of refugees. To this end, it first focuses on the actions of the States receiving the refugees, i.e. the host States[2] under Pillar One, and then reflects on the measures the international community has adopted under Pillars Two and Three. Finally, comparing practice with what could have been done in theory, the chapter concludes by arguing that the protection of refugees is an inherent part of R2P, which if realised would contribute to sustainable protection in the mid- to long-term for not only the population residing in the conflict zones but also those who had to leave their countries.

Unfolding Crises and International Response

In Libya, the protests that began in February 2011 turned into demands for President Muammar Gaddafi's resignation. As the demonstrations grew, the government's response turned violent. According to the estimates expressed by the United Nations (UN) Secretary-General, more than a thousand people lost their lives right before the international military intervention (UNGA–SC, 2011a). As the conflict in Libya reached an alarming level, many international and regional organisations as well as UN Member States immediately expressed their concern about the escalating situation. The then Secretary-General Ban Ki-moon drew attention to the rising number of Libyan refugees and displaced persons based on the data provided by the UN High Commissioner for Refugees (UNHCR) (*UN News*, 2011a). On 26 February, the UN Security Council (UNSC) unanimously adopted Resolution 1970 and urged the Libyan authorities to immediately end the conflict. It also decided to refer the issue to the International Criminal Court (ICC) as well as to implement an arms embargo against Libya and assets freeze on certain Libyan officials (UNSC, 2011a, p. 3). However, as the desired result was not achieved and the death toll continued to increase, on 17 March 2011, the UNSC adopted Resolution 1973, which authorised 'all necessary measures' to end the violence against civilians and for their protection. After the UN Member States unanimously adopted R2P in 2005, for the first time in an R2P situation, on the basis of Chapter VII of the UN Charter and for the purpose of protection of civilians, the UNSC decided

[2] Hereinafter, as the refugees' country of origin, Libya and Syria will be labelled as home States. It should be reminded that due to being a transit country for those aiming to reach Europe, Libya will also be considered as a host state.

to adopt military measures against a state that had effective control over its territory (UNSC, 2011b). Following this, on 19 March, the coalition of States that was formed by the United States (US), the United Kingdom (UK), Canada and France began their operations.[3] Later, on 31 March, the North Atlantic Treaty Organization (NATO) took full command and began Operation Unified Protector (NATO, 2011). Despite the ongoing clashes in the country the operation was ceased right after Muammar Gaddafi was captured and lynched by the rebels. Such timing fed the criticisms that the military intervention in Libya was a regime change operation (UNSC, 2011c). While some did not consider the deployment of special forces to help rebels in Libya a violation of international law, they still regarded it as a betrayal to the 'spirit of Resolution 1973' (Schmitt & Myers, 2011). As Evans et al. (2013) observe, far from targeting threats to the civilian population, the coalition operations rather aimed to provide military aid to the rebels, which resulted in further civilian casualties.

Unlike in the case of Syria, since the Libyan government was not supported by international allies or a Permanent Member, the UNSC was able to adopt decisions swiftly. Backed by the US, the UK and France (P3) arguing for the immediacy of the situation, with the measures adopted under Resolution 1973, Pillar Two was bypassed in favour of a more coercive response that fell under the scope of Pillar Three. R2P advocates celebrated the 'timely and decisive' response in the early days of the situation (Evans, 2011) and labelled it as 'the first instance of the implementation of the sharp edge of the new norm of the responsibility to protect' (Thakur, 2011, p. 13). Nevertheless, as Adams (2012, p. 8) observes, many of those who have been critical of the intervention argue that Libya's geopolitical position and natural resources had an important role in the decision to intervene. Hence, the controversial aspects of the military operations sparked major criticisms (Pattison, 2011), which eventually led to the perception of the Libyan case as an 'R2P failure' (see, for instance, Hehir, 2013; Nahlawi, 2018; Zifcak, 2012).

The Libyan experience had its toll also on the Syrian case. In the UNSC deliberations of the rapidly escalating situation, Russia, and from time-to-time China cited Libya as a negative precedent to block any R2P

[3] The operations were as follows: Operation Odyssey Dawn (led by the US), Operation Harmattan (led by France); Operation Ellamy (led by the UK), Operation Mobile (led by Canada).

response in Syria. The anti-government demonstrations in Syria started one month into the events in Libya (Black & Bowcott, 2011). Unlike previous cases of the Arab uprisings, the movement against the Bashar Al-Assad government rapidly evolved into a large-scale civil war (Coutts, 2011), which has caused the loss of hundreds of thousands of lives and a very large number of displaced people. The government systematically used military force against the people and according to the data of the UN Office of the High Commissioner for Human Rights (OHCHR), in the period between March and November, at least 3,500 civilians lost their lives while thousands were unlawfully arrested and tortured (*UN News*, 2011b). Institutional dysfunction accompanied the ongoing unrest while the power vacuum created an advantage for different groups to surface. Radical Islamic militants from different regions of the world, especially from North Africa and the Middle East, flocked into the country.

Beginning with regional and international terrorist attacks—such as that of the Islamic State of Iraq and Levant (ISIL)—conflicts between different armed groups in the region became a matter of international concern. After the onset of the incidents, most UNSC Member States expressed their concern and called for an immediate stop to the violence (Zifcak, 2012, p. 16). Three months after the conflict in Syria began, on 21 June 2011, the UN Secretary-General's Special Advisors on the Prevention of Genocide and the Responsibility to Protect issued a declaration cautioning that given their size and gravity the violations can be regarded as crimes against humanity, and they invoked the Syrian government's responsibility to protect its population from atrocity crimes (UN Press Release, 2011). Iran and Saudi Arabia's regional confrontation over Syria and Russia's support to Iran and the Baath regime, along with the efforts of the US to assert its influence over the region by supporting certain groups (AbuKhalil, 2014) were arguably the main determinants that made it difficult for the UNSC to take decisive action in the Syrian case. Since 2013, China and Russia have rejected ten draft resolutions together, and Russia alone has vetoed six resolutions (GCR2P, 2021). They grounded their vetoes on the non-intervention principle and the need to respect the national sovereignty and territorial integrity of Syria (See, UNSC, 2014; UNSC, 2017a; UNSC, 2017b). Thus, unlike in the case of Libya, the UNSC has not adopted any resolutions authorising the use of force or any other decisive measure. The absence of a timely and decisive action has brought about a civil war that has been going on ceaselessly since 2011. Consequently, as Thakur (2013, p. 61) observes, 'Syrians have paid the price of NATO excesses in Libya'.

Overall, the intervention in Libya which failed to bring sustainable protection for the Libyan population also served as an excuse for inaction in Syria. Consequently, the growing situations in both countries resulted in an unprecedented number of displaced persons. Against this backdrop, the following sections question the implementation of R2P vis-à-vis its three-pillar implementation strategy from the aspect of the protection of refugees.

Protection of Responsibilities of Host States

As Gallagher (2014, p. 9) posits, the mass movement of refugees is an important sign that a State is not (capable of) fulfilling its responsibility to ensure the safety and welfare of its population. Such failure to uphold Pillar One responsibilities have been clearly visible in the cases of both the Libyan and Syrian authorities. After the civil war began, portions of the Libyan population started to take refuge in the neighbouring countries such as Tunisia, Egypt and Chad, as well as Europe by crossing the Mediterranean. As early as February 2011, the International Organization for Migration (IOM) reported the number of Libyan refugees who fled the region as 790,000 (Aghazarm et al., 2012, p. 5). Though the 2011 military intervention may have limited the number of refugees initially, the uncontrolled Mediterranean crossings have continued as the political crisis in Libya persisted in the absence of an effective post-intervention rebuilding (Coen, 2015, p. 1053). Although many people returned to their country of origin when the first civil war ended, as the turmoil of the post-Gaddafi period dragged the country into a second civil war in 2014 (Stephen, 2016), the number of refugees leaving Libya continued to increase. According to Amnesty International (2020), with unceasing conflict between opposing factions, the region has turned into an environment where refugees and asylum seekers cannot be protected properly.[4] Having stuck in a cycle of internal conflict for the last decade, Libya

[4] In terms of protection, there are various aspects that need to be considered. For instance, 71% of the refugees and asylum seekers in the region are deprived of health services, and the situation has turned into a major health crisis after the COVID-19 pandemic (Migration Policy Institute, 2020).

now has more than 927,000 people of concern according to UNHCR's (2021a) data.

In the current state of affairs, and as evinced by mass refugee movements, Libya is capable of providing the necessary protection neither to the people habiting in its borders nor to those who are trying to reach Europe. Hence, Libya has not been a preferable target/end State for asylum seekers and refugees, but it continues to be a transit country and a gateway to Europe.[5] Prior to February 2011, Libya hosted approximately 1.5 million refugees (Amnesty International, 2011), and this number is now down to 43,870 (UNHCR, 2021a). Nevertheless, combined with factors such as the power vacuum resulting from the existence of two governments since 2014, and the absence of a fully functioning institutional structure, the Libyan route has become even more convenient for trans-Mediterranean irregular migration flows and smuggling activities. Furthermore, the mass influx of Syrian refugees to Libya especially after 2013 has exacerbated the issue of human smuggling (Toaldo, 2015, p. 1) and fuelled Europe's refugee protection crisis.

In the case of Syria, the civil war has caused more than 6 million Syrians to leave their homes (UNHCR, 2021b). As the UN Secretary-General António Guterres remarked, the Syrian refugee protection crisis has been 'the most dramatic humanitarian crisis the world has faced' (UNHCR, 2014). Since the early days of the conflict, large numbers of people have been moving to the neighbouring countries to escape from the conflict zones and meet their basic needs in another country. To this end, some Syrians have tried to reach Greece or Italy through dangerous sea routes forcing the capacity of boats and such attempts have usually resulted in tragedies. While many accidents made the world face with the severity of the crisis, the image of the lifeless body of Alan Kurdi, a Syrian toddler trying to make it to Greece with his family and died in the crash of September 2015 and found at the shores of Bodrum, Turkey became the symbol of the tragedy (Smith, 2015). Although this triggered an international outcry, it was not enough to change the policies of States, and especially of the European Union (EU) Member States that wish to keep refugees outside their borders. Hence, it has mostly been the

[5] Many refugees who reached Lampedusa expressed how dangerous it was for them to stay in Libya (Kingsley, 2015). According to the IOM, at least 1,200 people died trying to cross the Mediterranean to reach Europe in 2020 with plastic boats that are not suitable for open sea conditions (DW, 2021).

neighbouring States that have assumed the responsibility to protect the incoming refugees in a manner consistent with Pillar One of R2P.

Over the last decade, Turkey, Lebanon, Jordan, Iraq and Egypt have been hosting the vast majority of refugees, and it is important to look at their practices to understand what sort of a protection they can provide. As of July 2021, with 3,688,093 people of concern, Turkey is the country hosting the largest number of registered asylum seekers (UNHCR, 2021c). Concerning Syrian refugees, Turkey has adopted an 'Open Door Policy' from the beginning of the Syrian civil war (TUR–MFA, 2016). Yet, because Turkey imposes the geographic limitation as a right arising from the 1951 Convention, only those who take refuge in the country due to 'events occurring in Europe' are legally categorised as refugees and able to assume the rights granted under the refugee status (UN Treaty Collections, 2021). Thus, the Syrians who took refuge in Turkey are not legally considered as refugees but are placed under temporary protection based on the regulation adopted by the Council of Ministers of the Republic of Turkey on 22 October 2014 pursuant to Article 91 of the Foreigners and International Protection Act of 4 April 2013 (NLB/NA, 2021). This status enables people with registered access to fundamental services such as health and education but are much more limited compared to the rights granted under the refugee status.[6] Moreover, as they cannot apply for asylum, this situation is highly likely to result in secondary movements from the region, and hence, may cause instability in the mid- to long-term.

As for the other neighbouring countries—namely Lebanon, Jordan and Iraq—which are hosting the highest number of Syrian refugees following Turkey, we see that they are not parties to the 1951 Convention (Janmyr, 2016, p. 10; ILO, 2015, p. 19; Sadek, 2013, p. 5). Therefore, they do not grant refugee status to the people fleeing Syria. The lack of an official status and insufficient internal conditions cause these people to experience serious difficulties in accessing services, particularly healthcare, as well as obtaining residence permits, while they face the risk of being returned to their countries involuntarily at any time (NRC, 2014, pp. 5–6). More

[6] For instance, persons under temporary protection need to obtain specific permissions to go to another city or another country, and they face various restrictions to obtain work permits.

importantly, millions of refugees in refugee camps or host communities with limited infrastructure find it difficult to meet their basic needs (UNHCR, 2013).

While the neighbouring States have welcomed the refugees to their borders in a spirit that conforms with the objectives of R2P and sovereignty as responsibility, it is questionable if they have enough capacity to provide sustainable protection for these people. Most of these host States have fundamental problems of their own that have become aggravated with the refugee influx. A prominent example is the water scarcity in Jordan (Mercy Corps, 2014). In the case of Lebanon which hosts the greatest number of refugees from Syria in proportion to its own population (McPhilips, 2016) a large portion of Syrian refugees in this country are unable to meet their basic needs and most of them are exposed to safety risks. Finally, when we consider Libya as a host State for refugees, besides the fact that it is neither a party to the 1951 Convention nor the 1967 Protocol and that it has not been allowing UNHCR's activities in the region (Bialasiewicz, 2012, p. 843; Tucci, 2012, p. 49), it is clear that the Libyan authorities are failing to provide the necessary protection to refugees because of the ongoing political turmoil.

As Former Special Adviser to the UN Secretary-General on the Responsibility to Protect, Jennifer Welsh (2014, p. 3) argues, those States that have accepted Syrian refugees are fulfilling their responsibility to protect. Following from this, from the perspective of Pillar One, we may argue that the neighbours of Libya and Syria that have accepted the refugees into their territories are practically providing protection to these people in compliance with their sovereign responsibilities. Notwithstanding their positive contribution to resolution of the refugee protection crisis, we also need to consider the aforementioned economic, social, physical and political inadequacies of these States, as well as their non-recognition of the refugee status, which consequently deprives these people from legal protection under an international regime. This leads to the conclusion that these States have limited capacity to provide protection to the people fleeing conflict zones, and that other States with better conditions need to step up. At the international level, there is great imbalance in burden sharing between the global north—which have undertaken only a small part of the burden—and the global south—which are already overburdened. This brings to the fore the question of the responsibility of the international community in assisting host States as well as responding to the humanitarian crises in the home States.

Protection of Responsibilities of the International Community

Pillar Two of R2P covers not only the responsibility of the international community to support and assist the country of origin in order to increase its capacity to protect its population, but also the international community's responsibility towards host States to ensure that they can provide the necessary protection for the refugees they have opened their borders to. In this regard, we can talk about a variety of forms of assistance. For example, if a country is lacking the capacity to host refugees, most basically, the international community through financial assistance can help these States and share the burden within the scope of Pillar Two. As the States affected by the mass refugee movement the most, on various occasions Syria's neighbours have expressed their concerns about countering the negative consequences of the protection crisis and their need for international support (Achiume, 2015, p. 725).

Considering the dire conditions of the neighbouring countries, which host 5.6 of over 6.6 million Syrian refugees in total, such request is more than valid and one that needs to be addressed under Pillar Two of R2P. Some of these neighbouring countries have become unable to properly meet the humanitarian needs of the refugees despite support from UN agencies, non-governmental organisations and individual states. The COVID-19 pandemic has further aggravated the existing problems (UNHCR, 2021d). For instance, Lebanon as a State hosting the largest number of Syrian refugees in proportion to its population has been facing serious economic difficulties since 2020, and refugees have been vastly affected by this economic crisis (Vohra, 2021). On the one hand, international actors such as the EU and the World Bank have tried to tackle the refugee crisis by concluding a series of agreements and organising donation programmes with the neighbouring countries such as Turkey (European Council, 2016), Lebanon (European Commission, 2021a) and Jordan (European Commission, 2021b). On the other hand, financial support alone has so far proven adequate neither to improve the living conditions of the refugees, nor the internal conditions of the host States. As for the EU's bilateral agreements with the States that have assumed the larger portion of the burden, these agreements are considered morally and legally unacceptable as they are perceived to be conscious policies to simply keep refugees outside the Union's borders[7] (Human Rights Watch, 2016). Likewise, Gilgan (2017, p. 367) observes that 'States like the UK are avoiding asylum by making regional agreements aimed at containing refugees within the region in order to prevent them from making it to their territories where they have a right to claim asylum'.

In the light of this, in the specific cases of Libya and Syria, it can be argued that the method of capacity-building and financial aid to host countries have not always been applied in a manner consistent with the R2P mindset/objectives and have proven to be an inadequate form of support in terms of fulfilling the international responsibility. Hence, the internal conditions of host countries have to be taken into consideration and a tailored approach needs to be devised not for the purpose of containing refugees but for bringing them to safety. Accordingly, the international community has to seek ways to provide a safer environment for asylum seekers and the necessary conditions to allow them to make their asylum applications (Gözen & Kul, 2021). When we look at it as a host State, the Libyan experience constitutes a controversial example in this regard. As a consequence of the EU's desire to use Libya as a gatekeeper, the Libyan Coast Guard has been pursuing smugglers' boats at the sea. As it is smuggling in question, such efforts would be deemed legal and appropriate, yet there are widespread allegations that many refugees escaping from Libya were ill-treated by the Coast Guard, arrested, and put in detention centres where they were subjected to torture and other forms of abuse (Bellis, 2017).[8]

In cases where Pillar Two measures of assistance and capacity-building fall short, and where a host State is struggling internally, the international community needs to remain seized of the early warning signs,

[7] Furthermore, for purposes of border management, EUNAVFOR MED (2016) has been carrying out rescue operations (first Operation Sophia, and then Operation Irini) in the Central Mediterranean route since 2015. While these operations have led to the capture of many smugglers and the rescue of many people's lives, they have also been perceived as a way to relieve the EU from mass movements of refugees (Bialasiewicz, 2012, p. 845). As a consequence of these operations those who escaped from Libya, in violation of the principle of non-refoulement, were sent back to the land they escaped without any consideration of their lives and freedoms being in danger (Butler & Ratcovich, 2016, p. 235).

[8] Some of the refugees confirmed these claims remarking that they would prefer to die in the sea rather than to return to Libya (Ghoneim, 2016). Moreover, asylum seekers from Libya expressed that their main objective is to be protected and they cannot find this protection in Libya, so they preferred the European route (Malakooti, 2013, p. 110).

and if necessary, should be ready for a timely peaceful response under Pillar Three in order not to further aggravate the situation either for the refugees or the permanent population. For example, the already existing sectarian divisions in Lebanon are becoming even more critical with the Syrian refugees' arrival at the region, and there is the risk of atrocity crimes against these populations as the long-term divisions have become even more acute (Achiume, 2015, p. 725).

Given that the international community has been failing to devise a sustainable solution to the ongoing humanitarian crises in Libya and Syria through Pillar Three, hence not been able to create a safe environment for the return of the refugees, we need to seek for alternative ways for the international community and individual States to uphold their responsibility towards the refugees. Gilgan suggests the solution of linking resettlement with Pillar Three of R2P. She notes that.

> [r]esettlement is a concrete expression of international solidarity and a responsibility sharing mechanism that encourages states that host the majority of the world's refugees to keep their borders open to those fleeing mass atrocities, which saves lives and demonstrates sovereign equality by sharing responsibility in the response to a humanitarian crisis more evenly (Gilgan, 2017, pp. 377–378).

She further argues that 'offering resettlement encourages those states surrounding the crisis to keep their borders open and prevents refoulement by ameliorating the enormous burden felt by states proximate to those conflicts producing mass refugee flows' (Gilgan, 2017, p. 393). That said, the Libyan and Syrian experiences have proven the international community generally unwilling to take a part in such a solution. Overall, it can be observed that in both cases the international community has failed within the scope of Pillars Two and Three of R2P.

Conclusion

In the early days of the conflicts in Libya and Syria, the gravity of the situations made both cases an immediate R2P concern. Yet, Libya and Syria, which have completed their tenth year of bloody civil wars, are still grappling with internal conflicts today. While the arguably failed military intervention in Libya served as an excuse for inaction in Syria, many States have been militarily present on the territory of the latter without a concern of delivering responsible protection for the population. Hence, unsurprisingly, R2P cynics have been referring to the cases of Libya and Syria as the 'death of R2P'. Nevertheless, despite being major failures on the part of the international community in terms of upholding the responsibility to protect, both cases offer important lessons as to the depth of R2P. Hence, moving beyond the discussions solely focusing on the use of force under Pillar Three, this chapter has evaluated the two cases from the viewpoint of the protection of refugees.

By scrutinising the place of refugee protection within the three-pillar implementation strategy of R2P, this chapter not only offers a more straightforward way to protect refugees as potential victims of atrocity crimes and to prevent their further victimisation but also reminds of various peaceful methods available in the R2P toolkit. As Valentino (as cited in Coen, 2016) claims, a vast majority of the twentieth-century genocides can be overcome by giving a more significant international response to refugees. Accordingly, this chapter argues that assuming the responsibility to protect refugees fleeing from mass atrocity crimes is a natural/inherent part of the global responsibility to protect, and thus, it does not require a reformulation of the norm.

When people who are subjected to or under threat of atrocity crimes take shelter in the territory of another country, the responsibility to protect is borne with the State hosting these people as part of its sovereign responsibility. Consequently, refugees are placed under the protection of the host State within the scope of Pillar One. Even if these people take refuge in the territory of a State that is not a party to the 1951 Convention or its 1967 Protocol, and/or have a temporary status in that country, they will be able to benefit from the protection framework offered by R2P. As former UN Secretary-General Kofi Annan reminds, R2P includes 'potential or actual victims of massive atrocities' (UNGA–SC, 2005, Para. 132). Thus, R2P by providing protection to refugees enables a preventive response against potential genocide, ethnic cleansing, war crimes and crimes against humanity.

This is not to suggest that R2P is a substitute for the existing refugee protection regime. It is a complementary mechanism to invoke international responsibility as well as the individual responsibility of the host States. Most often R2P is viewed within the limits of the protection of the people in the conflict zones. Nevertheless, those who flee from mass atrocities are also in desperate need of such protection. An additional concern about the safety of the refugees in the host countries and invocation of the international responsibility especially under Pillar Two for assistance and capacity-building is therefore of utmost importance.

All in all, it can be argued that considering the protection of refugees as an inherent part of the R2P framework would not only help to make States receiving refugees and/or asylum seekers act more responsibly, but also make the international community realise that this is a responsibility for all and help those States that are trying to fulfil their Pillar One responsibilities. Therefore, including refugees within the framework of R2P will not only be a step towards increasing consciousness about the obligations of States arising from the refugee law, and reconsider their asylum and/or resettlement policies, but also will invoke an understanding that would avoid further refugee movements when the international community is taking action in conflict zones. The internalisation of such an inclusive understanding and responsible protection mindset can contribute to sustainable protection of populations, and eventually make an actual change in the behaviour of States and the international community. In this vein, moving the focus away from the counterproductive intervention debates, as future work it is important to conduct case-based studies focusing on the interrelation between R2P and refugee protection to understand different ways to provide better protection.

References

AbuKhalil, A. (2014). The 8 proxy wars going on in Syria right now. *HuffPost*. https://www.huffpost.com/entry/syria-proxy-wars_b_5874488. Accessed 7 August 2021.

Achiume, T. (2015). Syria, cost-sharing and the responsibility to protect refugees. *University of Minnesota Law Review, 100*(2), 687–761.

Adams, S. (2012). Libya and the responsibility to protect. *Global Centre for Responsibility to Protect, Occasional Paper Series, 3*, 1–23.

Aghazarm, C., Quesada, P., & Tishler, S. (2012). The IOM experience in Libya. *IOM*, 1–36.

Amnesty International. (2011). *North Africa's refugees suffer pattern of displacement*. https://www.amnesty.org/en/latest/news/2011/09/north-africaes-refugees-suffer-pattern-displacement/. Accessed 15 May 2021.

Amnesty International. (2020). *Annual report: Libya*. https://www.amnesty.org/en/countries/middle-east-and-north-africa/libya/report-libya/. Accessed 14 February 2021.

Barbour, B., & Gorlick, B. (2008). Embracing the 'responsibility to protect': A repertoire of measures including asylum for potential victims. *International Journal of Refugee Law, 20*(4), 533–566.

Bellamy, A. J. (2016). *Safe passage and asylum key to fulfilling responsibility to protect*. https://theglobalobservatory.org/2015/09/syria-refugees-unhcr-aylan-kurdi/. Accessed 20 March 2021.

Bellis, M. (2017). *The human cost of European hypocrisy on Libya*. https://www.amnesty.org/en/latest/news/2017/03/the-human-cost-of-european-hypocrisy-on-libya/. Accessed 20 February 2021.

Bialasiewicz, L. (2012). Off-shoring and out-sourcing the borders of Europe: Libya and EU border work in the Mediterranean. *Geopolitics, 17*(4), 843–866.

Black, I., & Bowcott, O. (2011). Libya protests: Massacres reported as Gaddafi imposes news blackout. *The Guardian*. https://www.theguardian.com/world/2011/feb/18/libya-protests-massacres-reported. Accessed 22 April 2017.

Butler, G., & Ratcovich, M. (2016). Operation Sophia in uncharted waters: European and International Law Challenges for the EU Naval Mission in the Mediterranean Sea. *Nordic Journal of International Law, 85*(3), 235–259.

Coen, A. (2015). R2P, Global governance, and the Syrian refugee crisis. *International Journal of Human Rights, 19*(8), 1044–1058.

Coen, A. (2016). *The responsibility to protect and the refugee crisis*. https://sustainablesecurity.org/2016/03/09/the-responsibility-to-protect-and-the-refugee-crisis/. Accessed 10 December 2020.

Coutts, A. (2011). Syria's uprising could have been avoided through reform. *The Guardian*. https://www.theguardian.com/commentisfree/2011/may/18/syria-uprising-reform-bashar-al-assad. Accessed 1 March 2021.

DW. (2021). *Uluslarası Göç Örgütü'nden Libya'ya uyarı*. https://www.dw.com/tr/uluslarası-göç-örgütünden-libyaya-uyarı/a-57044909. Accessed 2 April 2021.

Evans, G. (2011, April 15). *Interview with Nayan Chanda, Yale Global Online*.

Evans, G., Thakur, R., & Pape, R. A. (2013). Correspondence: Humanitarian intervention and the responsibility to protect. *International Security, 37*(4), 199–214.

EUNAVFOR MED. (2016). *EUNAVFOR MED: Operation Sophia flagship ITS GARIBALDI rescued over one thousand igmrants*. Press release 001/2016.

European Commission. (2021a). *Lebanon*. https://ec.europa.eu/neighbourhoodenlargement/neighbourhood/countries/lebanon_en. Accessed 3 March 2021.

European Commission. (2021b). *Jordan*. https://ec.europa.eu/echo/where/middle-east/jordan_en. Accessed 17 April 2021.

European Council. (2016). *EU-Turkey statement*. http://www.consilium.europa.eu/en/press/press-releases/2016/03/18-eu-turkeystatement/. Accessed 13 March 2021.

Francis, A. (2012). The responsibility to protect and the international refugee regime. In A. Francis, V. Popovski & C. Sampford (Eds.), *Norms of protection: Responsibility to protect, protection of civilians and their interaction*. United Nations University Press.

Gallagher, A. (2014). Syria and indicators of 'Manifest Failing.' *The International Journal of Human Rights, 18*(1), 1–19.

Ghoneim, N. (2016). Refugees: Better to 'Die at Sea' than return to Libya. *Al Jazeera*. http://www.aljazeera.com/blogs/europe/2016/07/refugees-die-sea-return-libya-160718165132671.html. Accessed 3 March 2021.

Gilgan, C. M. (2017). Exploring the link between R2P and refugee protection: Arriving at resettlement. *Global Responsibility to Protect, 9*, 366–394.

Global Centre for the Responsibility to Protect (GCR2P). (2021). *Syria*. https://www.globalr2p.org/countries/syria/. Accessed 3 May 2021.

Gözen Ercan, P. & Kul, S. (2021). Ülkeleri İçinde Yerinden Edilmiş Kişilerin ve Mültecilerin Koruma Sorumluluğu Çerçevesinde Korunması. *Uluslararası İlişkiler* (pp. 1–19). Online First.

Hehir, A. (2013). The permanence of inconsistency: Libya, the security council, and the responsibility to protect. *International Security, 38*(1), 137–159.

Human Rights Watch. (2016). *EU: Don't send Syrians back to Turkey*. https://www.hrw.org/news/2016/06/20/eu-dont-send-syrians-back-turkey. Accessed 29 March 2021.

International Labour Organization (ILO). (2015). *Access to work for Syrian refugees in Jordan: A discussion paper on labour and refugee laws and policies*.

Janmyr, M. (2016). The legal status of Syrian refugees in Lebanon. *Issam fares institute for public policy and international affairs* (Working Paper 33).

Kingsley, P. (2015). Risking Death in the Mediterranean: The least bad option for so many migrants. *The Guardian*. https://www.theguardian.com/world/2015/apr/17/death-mediterranean-africans-migrant-sea-libya. Accessed 2 February 2021.

Malakooti, A. (2013). Mixed migration: Libya at the crossroads. *Altai consulting report*. http://www.refworld.org/docid/52b43f594.html. Accessed 2 February 2021.

Maley, W. (2015). Humanitarian law, refugee protection and the responsibility to protect. In R. Thakur & W. Maley (Eds.), *Theorising the responsibility to protect* (pp. 249–265). Cambridge University Press.

McPhilips, D. (2016). The tragic numbers behind Syria's refugees. *US News*. www.usnews.com/news/best-countries/articles/2016-12-19/countries-hosting-the-highest-proportion-of-syrian-refugees. Accessed 20 March 2021.

Mercy Corps. (2014). *Water scarcity and the Syrian refugee crisis*. https://www.mercycorps.org/articles/jordan/water-scarcity-and-syrian-refugee-crisis. Accessed 7 March 2021.

Migration Policy Institute. (2020). *Once a destination for migrants, post-Gaddafi Libya has gone from transit route to containment*. https://www.migrationpolicy.org/article/once-destination-migrants-post-gaddafi-libya-has-gone-transit-route-containment. Accessed 24 February 2021.

Nahlawi, Y. (2018). The legality of NATO's pursuit of regime change in Libya. *Journal on the Use of Force and International Law, 5*(2), 295–323.

National Legislative Bodies/National Authorities (NLB/NA). (2021). *Temporary protection regulation*. https://www.goc.gov.tr/turkiye-de-gecici-koruma. Accessed 12 March 2021.

North Atlantic Treaty Organization (NATO). (2011). *NATO takes command in Libya air*. Operations. https://www.nato.int/cps/en/natolive/news_71867.htm. Accessed 25 February 2021.

Norwegian Refugee Council (NRC). (2014). *Lebanon field assessment–The consequences of limited legal status for Syrian refugees in Lebanon*.

Pattison, J. (2011). The ethics of humanitarian intervention in Libya. *Ethics & International Affairs, 25*(3), 271–277.

Ralph, J., & Souter, J. (2017). Introduction: The responsibility to protect and the refugee protection regime. *Ethics & International Affairs, 31*(1), 47–50.

Republic of Turkey–Ministry of Foreign Affairs (TUR-MFA). (2016). Press Release. http://www.mfa.gov.tr/no_-83_-3-april-2016_-press-release-regarding-the-allegations-that-turkey-has-sent-some-syrians-back-to-their-countries-by-force.en.mfa. Accessed 12 March 2021.

Schmitt, E & Myers, S. L. Surveillance and coordination with NATO aided Rebels. *New York Times*. http://www.nytimes.com/2011/08/22/world/africa/22nato.html. Accessed 5 February 2021.

Sadek, G. (2013). *Legal status of refugees: Egypt, Jordan, Lebanon, and Iraq*. The Law Library of Congress Report, Global Legal Research Center.

Smith, H. (2015). *Shocking images of drowned Syrian boy show tragic plight of refugees*. https://www.theguardian.com/world/2015/sep/02/shocking-image-of-drowned-syrian-boy-shows-tragic-plight-of-refugees. Accessed 12 March 2021.

Souter, J. (2016). Good international citizenship and special responsibilities to protect refugees. *British Journal of Politics and International Relations, 18*(4), 795–811.

Stephen, C. (2016). Five years after Gaddafi, Libya Torn by civil war and battles with Isis. *The Guardian*, https://www.theguardian.com/world/2016/feb/16/libya-gaddafi-arab-spring-civil-war-islamic-state. Accessed 20 January 2021.

Thakur, R. (2011). Libya and the responsibility to protect: Between opportunistic humanitarianism and value-free pragmatism. *Security Challenges, 7*(4), 13–25.

Thakur, R. (2013). R2P after Libya and Syria: Engaging emerging powers. *The Washington Quarterly, 36*(2), 61–76.

Toaldo, M. (2015). Migrations through and from Libya. *Istituto Affari Internazionali Working Papers, 15*, 1–20.

Tucci, S. (2012). Libya and international refugee and asylum law: Addressing the protection of refugees and migrants displaced by the 2011 conflict. *Oxford Monitor of Forced Migration, 2*(2), 48–54.

UN General Assembly–Security Council (UNGA–SC). (2005). *In larger freedom: Towards development, security and human rights for all*. A/59/2005.

UN General Assembly–Security Council. (UNGA–SC). (2011a). *Remarks to security council meeting on peace and security in Africa*. https://www.un.org/sg/en/content/sg/speeches/2011-02-25/remarks-security-council-meeting-peace-and-security-africa. Accessed 18 April 2021.

UN High Commissioner for Refugees. (UNHCR). (2013). *UNHCR report shows health services for Syrian refugees increasingly overstretched*. http://www.unhcr.org/news/briefing/2013/4/517a58af9/unhcr-report-shows-health-services-syrian-refugees-increasingly-overstretched.html. Accessed 7 March 2021.

UN High Commissioner for Refugees (UNHCR). (2014). *Remarks by António Guterres, United Nations High Commissioner for refugees*. Conference on The Syrian Refugee Situation—Supporting Stability in The Region, Berlin. http://www.unhcr.org/admin/hcspeeches/544fb4189/remarks-antonio-guterres-united-nations-high-commissioner-refugees-conference.html. Accessed 12 March 2021.

UN High Commissioner for Refugees (UNHCR). (2020). *Refugee data finder*. https://www.unhcr.org/refugee-statistics/. Accessed 22 February 2021.

UN High Commissioner for Refugees (UNHCR). (2021a). *Fact sheet–Libya*. https://reporting.unhcr.org/sites/default/files/UNHCR%20Libya%20Factsheet%20-%20February%202021.pdf. Accessed 4 April 2021.

UN High Commissioner for Refugees (UNHCR). (2021b). *Syria emergency*. https://www.unhcr.org/syria-emergency.html. Accessed 20 March 2021.

UN High Commissioner for Refugees (UNHCR). (2021c). *Syria regional refugee response–Turkey*. https://data2.unhcr.org/en/situations/syria. Accessed 4 December 2020.

UN High Commissioner for Refugees (UNHCR). (2021d, February 5). *Syria refugee crisis explained*. https://www.unrefugees.org/news/syria-refugee-crisis-explained/. Accessed 22 February 2021.

UN News. (2011a). *Ban calls on security council to consider immediate steps to stop killings in Libya*. https://news.un.org/en/story/2011/02/367

622-ban-calls-security-council-consider-immediate-steps-stop-killings-libya. Accessed 09 July 2021.

UN News. (2011b). *Death toll passes 3,500 as Syrian crackdown continues*. http://www.un.org/apps/news/story.asp?NewsID=40326#.WNDHBzuLTIU. Accessed 20 February 2020.

UN Press Release. (2011). *Security council fails to adopt draft resolution to end attacks on Aleppo as two permanent members Cast Veto*. SC/12609. https://www.un.org/press/en/2016/sc12609.doc.htm. Accessed 6 March 2021.

UN Security Council. (UNSC). (2011a). *Resolution 1970, adopted by the security council at its 6491st meeting*. S/RES/1970.

United Nations Security Council. (UNSC). (2011b). *Resolution 1973, adopted by the security council at its 6498th meeting*. S/RES/1973.

UN Security Council. (UNSC). (2011c). *6620th meeting*. S/PV.6620.

UN Security Council. (UNSC). (2014). Draft resolution. *On Syria*. S/PV.7180.

UN Security Council. (UNSC). (2017a). Draft resolution. *On a sanctions regime for the use and production of chemical weapons in Syria*. S/PV.7893.

UN Security Council. (UNSC). (2017b). Draft Resolution. *On condemning the Khan Shaykhun chemical weapons attack*. S/PV.7922.

UN Treaty Collections. (2021). *Refugees and stateless persons*. https://treaties.un.org/Pages/ViewDetailsII.aspx?src=TREATY&mtdsg_no=V-2&chapter=5&Temp=mtdsg2&clang=_en#EndDec. Accessed 20 February 2021.

Vohra, A. (2021). Syrian refugees' plight in Lebanon 10 years after the uprising. *Al Jazeera*. https://www.aljazeera.com/news/2021/3/19/syrian-refugees-in-lebanon-ten-years-after-the-uprising. Accessed 10 April 2021.

Welsh, J. (2014). Fortress Europe and the responsibility to protect: Framing the issue. *EUI forum on migration, citizenship and demography*. https://www.eui.eu/Documents/RSCAS/PapersLampedusa/FORUM-Welshfinal.pdf. Accessed 20 March 2021.

Zifcak, S. (2012). The responsibility to protect after Libya and Syria. *Melbourne Journal of International Law, 13*(1).

CHAPTER 8

Gaza: R2P and Selective Implementation

Özgecan Eskiduman

In December 2008 and July 2014, Israel carried out two of its deadliest operations on the Gaza Strip, wherein a significant number of civilian causalities were incurred. Considered as an interstate conflict (Hehir, 2014), the situation in Gaza and the Israeli offensives have mainly been studied under the title of the Arab-Israeli conflict. Since Israel is a party to the Fourth Geneva Convention, the crisis has been considered as a matter of international law as well (Rudolph, 2014). However, the human rights violations amounting to mass atrocity crimes evinces the manifest failure of the sovereign parties involved in the situation and makes the situation extend beyond the confines of an interstate problem, which requires the invocation of the Responsibility to Protect (R2P) (Adams, 2014; Bayeh, 2014; Gözen Ercan, 2015; Hehir, 2015; Kearney, 2014; Rieff, 2014).

In this regard, different from other chapters of this edited volume that provide a broader view into intrastate conflicts, this chapter develops a more specific focus to highlight a core problem in R2P practice, that is the issue of selectivity. Accordingly, it places under focus two major Israeli

Ö. Eskiduman (✉)
Department of International Relations, Hacettepe University, Ankara, Turkey

P. Gözen Ercan (ed.), *The Responsibility to Protect Twenty Years On*,
https://doi.org/10.1007/978-3-030-90731-0_8

operations, namely Operation Cast Lead in December 2008 and the Operation Protective Edge in July 2014, wherein war crimes and crimes against humanity were reported by independent United Nations (UN) fact-finding missions (UNGA, 2009c, 2015a). To this end, this chapter conducts a pillar-by-pillar analysis, and studies what has happened in Gaza during both operations and the international response that followed to reveal how and why R2P's implementation has failed in this specific case. Regarding Pillar One of R2P, the chapter first addresses the question of who is the sovereign in Gaza that is responsible for the protection of the Gazan population? The case of Gaza presents us with a unique example in R2P's history, due to the existence of multiple sovereigns having a responsibility over a specific population on the very same territory. After establishing that there are three different sovereigns that have failed to protect the population, the chapter then briefly focuses on the Pillars Two and Three responsibilities of the international community, and determines the reasons as to why the international community could not fulfil its responsibility. The case of Gaza also allows us to test the efficacy of the UN Security Council (UNSC) in carrying out R2P practices in cases where immediate interests of the Permanent Members of the UNSC (P5) are involved. Hence, as for analysing the responses of the international community under Pillars Two and Three, the chapter builds its analysis mainly on the UNSC processes and draft resolutions and draws attention to elements of great power politics.

Accordingly, the chapter argues that the non-implementation of R2P in the case of Gaza evinces the issue of selective implementation of international norms, and in the specific case of R2P, it hints at the fragility of the international responsibility which is dependent on the will and authority of the UNSC. This selective implementation poses a major question as to what will happen when a state supported by one or more of the five Permanent Members of the UNSC (P5), or one of the P5 itself commits mass atrocity crimes. Finally, the chapter concludes that R2P's selective implementation stemming from the structural limitations of the UNSC and the policies its Permanent Members pursue constrains the attempts of various agents of the international community in fulfilling their responsibility.

Background to the Gazan Crisis

The conflict in Gaza reflects the complexities of the Israeli-Palestinian dispute. Although the problem is rooted in the establishment of the Jewish state on the Palestinian Arab land, the dynamics of the issue have become far more complex with the involvement of third parties over the years. One of the initial issues that the UN General Assembly (UNGA) dealt with in the early years of the UN's establishment was partitioning the Palestinian lands between Arabs and Jews. In November 1947, the UNGA adopted Resolution 181 to settle the long-lasting dispute. However, the Resolution produced a disproportionate partition as 55% of the Palestinian lands was given to the Jewish population, which owned only 7% prior to the UN decision (Khalidi, 1997).

While the UN failed to provide a sustainable solution, four major Arab–Israeli wars determined the future of the dispute. The first war broke out right after the partition plan when Israel declared its independence. At the end of the war, Israel had annexed more than its actual share in the UN partition, and a majority of Palestinian Arabs became immigrants. Israel also declared Jerusalem as its capital, which was placed formerly under an international regime by the UN (Khalidi, 1997). To date, issues that stem from this first war, such as Palestinian refugees' right to return to their lands and Jerusalem's status persist as major obstacles to a possible peace settlement between the parties. In 1956, the second war—namely the Suez War—broke out between Egypt-led unified Arab forces and Israel. Winning a political victory, Egypt nationalised the Suez Canal, while Israel established the Dimona Nuclear Facility owing to its alliance with France, which gave them an advantage in the Israeli-Palestinian conflict (Cleveland & Bunton, 2016). Nevertheless, it was the third major war that was a game-changer in the Israeli-Arab conflict. In the 1967 War, Israel defeated the united Arab army only in six days and annexed the Golan Heights from Syria, Gaza and the Sinai Peninsula from Egypt, as well as the West Bank from Jordan (Cleveland & Bunton, 2016). Among the Arab States, only Egypt regained the Sinai Peninsula with the 1979 Egyptian Israeli Peace Agreement that was concluded after the 1973 War, which was the fourth major Arab-Israeli war. The status of the rest of the territories gained by Israel in the 1967 War continues to serve as the main causes of the Arab-Israeli conflicts.

Following the wars that changed the balance, in November 1988, Palestinian Liberation Organisation's (PLO) chairman Yasser Arafat established the State of Palestine *ex parte*. However, Israel did not recognise this claim until the 1993 Oslo Accords (Cleveland & Bunton, 2016). A year after the Accords, the Palestinian Authority (PA) was established to rule over the West Bank and Gaza. However, Gaza and major parts of the West Bank were still under Israeli occupation. Moreover, central aspects of the Israeli-Palestinian conflict—namely, the right of return, the status of Jerusalem and the Israeli settlement projects in occupied territories—were not included among the negotiation items in the Oslo Accords (Cleveland & Bunton, 2016). Hence, the peace achieved was not long-lasting, and the Al-Aqsa Intifada—the second Palestinian uprising—started in the occupied Palestinian territories.

Hamas's terrorist attacks and the disproportionate Israeli reprisal raids resulted in serious humanitarian costs. Israel's presence in Gaza was considered by many, including the UN Secretary-General Ban Ki-moon, as an occupation (Levs, 2009). The exacerbated humanitarian losses led to international pressure and resulted in the Israeli withdrawal from Gaza in 2005 (Brugnola, 2015). One year later, Hamas won the parliamentary elections in Gaza. Such victory of its biggest nemesis was alarming for Israel. Hence, it started to impose a blockade on the Gaza Strip as of June 2007 (Brugnola, 2015). Israel restricted the freedom of movement and the flow of goods since the first days of the blockade, which was considered a de facto occupation.

The cycle of violence was fuelled by the ongoing Israeli military operations and numerous Hamas attacks targeting Israeli civilians, which led to more Israeli reprisal raids in return. These raids have arguably been the main causes of the humanitarian crisis in Gaza, which fits perfectly into the R2P context as it concerns the protection of the Gazan population regardless of Hamas's actions. Of these raids, this chapter focuses on the two of the deadliest operations, namely Operation Cast Lead of December 2008 and Operation Protective Edge of July 2014 as its main concerns.

Operation Cast Lead began in December 2008 with the claim of self-defence to prevent further rocket attacks from the Gaza Strip. However, the scope of the operation went far beyond the declared intention and turned to be a systemic violation of the rights of the population in Gaza (Kattan, 2009). Even if the military operation could be justified as self-defence under Article 51 of the UN Charter, the fundamental requirement of distinguishing between civilian and military targets was not accomplished. According to the report of Amnesty International (July 2009), civilians were directly and indiscriminately targeted by the Israeli air attacks in which high-tech weaponry were used and resulted in increased civilian casualties.

Operation Protection Edge was launched in July 2014. This was the deadliest military campaign against Gaza since the 1967 War (Brugnola, 2015). Although the officially claimed objective was to save the kidnapped Israeli soldiers, the operation turned into a war between Hamas and the Israeli Defence Forces (IDF). Once again, human rights were violated, and the operation resulted in a devastating humanitarian crisis. Overall, the gravity of the human rights violations amounting to alleged war crimes in both Israeli operations makes Gaza an R2P concern. In this regard, the subsequent section addresses the Pillar One responsibility under R2P.

Whose Responsibility?

As the UN Secretary-General notes, all three pillars of R2P are interrelated, and there is no formal sequence among them in terms of implementation (UNGA, 2009a). In the case of Gaza, the interrelation between the three pillars of R2P can be clearly seen due to the way the crisis has unfolded. However, it is important to analyse Pillar One separately, since Gaza is an exceptional case due to the possibility to claim responsibility on the part of three different sovereign authorities.

Pillar One is based on the notion of sovereignty as responsibility, which establishes that the primary responsibility to protect populations rests with the States. In this regard, within the specific context of Gaza, we first need to answer the question whose sovereign responsibility is it to protect the Gazan population? Given their different levels of control over the territory, Hamas, PA and Israel can be argued to have a responsibility over the Gazan population. Hence, we can talk about a shared, tripartite responsibility in Gaza. Both this multiplicity and the human rights violations committed by all three authorities present us with a complex problem. After Operation Cast Lead in 2009, the UN established a fact-finding mission to investigate the alleged violations committed by all three parties. The Mission prepared the Goldstone Report to share the results of their final investigations. In the aftermath of Operation Protective Edge, again an independent commission was established pursuant to UN Human

Rights Council Resolution S-21/1 to investigate all human rights violations in the Occupied Palestinian Territory and to prepare a report based on their findings (UNGA, 2015b). Moreover, Human Rights Watch prepared a report in 2015, considering the humanitarian costs of Operation Protective Edge and the ongoing blockade. The common conclusion in all the three reports was that all parties to the conflict—namely Israel, Hamas and the PA—committed serious human rights violations. As they all played a part in the failure to protect the Gazan population, it is important to consider their actions one-by-one under Pillar One of R2P.

As for Hamas, since it is the ruling party, it can be considered as the first sovereign authority in Gaza. Nevertheless, there is also the fact that the Hamas's sovereignty is undermined by the international community due to its consideration as a terrorist organisation. While it is outside the scope of this chapter to evaluate the actions and status of Hamas as terrorist organisation, there is the fact that it is the government-elect in Gaza. As Pourmokhtari (2013) contends, Hamas's non-recognition as a sovereign authority reflects the Western-centric construction of reality. Such outside determination of who the sovereign is undermines the free will of Gazans, together with their representation at the international level. On the other hand, it is important to establish Hamas's responsibility as the sovereign authority of the territory, since it is one of the primary perpetrators in Gaza. This owes to the fact that its attacks against Israel constitute the reason for the massive Israeli raids in the very first place, and that its unlawful practices towards the population to investigate pro-Israelis and/or members of Fatah—that is the ruling party of the Palestinian State—result in further humanitarian crises.

The Goldstone Report notes the violations, war crimes and crimes against humanity committed by the PA and Hamas, and indicates that internal violence between the two parties increases the humanitarian costs of the conflict. The Report finds that after its electoral victory, Hamas systematically detained the Fatah members in Gaza, and that members of domestic and international human rights organisations were also targeted (UNGA, 2009c). Moreover, the Report establishes as a war crime the use of human beings as shields as part of Hamas's combat strategy during both Israeli operations (UNGA, 2009c, p. 23). All the mortars and rocket attacks and indiscriminate killings are considered to amount to war crimes, and 'may amount to crimes against humanity' (UNGA, 2009c, p. 366).

The 2015 Report issued after the second operation also finds that Palestinian armed groups directly targeted Israeli civilians, which resulted in additional Israeli attacks on Gaza (UNGA, 2015b). Also, the ongoing political division between Hamas and Fatah has had devastating effects on the Palestinians, who have already suffered from the Israeli operation (UNGA, 2015b). In its report, Human Rights Watch (2015) identifies Hamas as one of the perpetrators in Gaza during the 2015 Israeli Operation. Besides the mortal attacks that directly caused civilian casualties, Hamas also arbitrarily arrested protestors and its opponents accusing them of collaborating with Israel. Moreover, freedom of speech and display of any kind of political dissent were prohibited.

The second sovereign, which has also failed to protect the population in Gaza, is the PA since it is the central authority of the Palestinian State. The 2015 Fact Finding Mission reports that Palestinian groups are 'inherently indiscriminate' towards Israeli targets, which amount to war crimes (UNGA, 2015b, p. 20). While these attacks provoked further Israeli attacks, the PA has failed to bring the perpetrators to justice. Moreover, the Goldstone Report identifies that Hamas members were targeted in the West Bank after the electoral victory of Hamas. Unlawful arrests and ill-treatment of suspected Hamas members were reported as well as the suspension of the freedom of the press and systematic repression of the political opposition (UNGA, 2009c). Such treatment of their members provoked Hamas to respond in the same manner against the Fatah members in Gaza, and consequently the PA's actions contributed to the human rights violations in Gaza. Nevertheless, it is noteworthy that aiming to bring the perpetrators to justice, the PA brought the allegations before the ICC for investigation. While on the part of the PA this was a major positive step in the name of upholding its responsibility towards the population, this attempt was undermined by the US as will be discussed further in the subsequent section.

As it is the occupying power, we can determine Israel as the third sovereign authority in Gaza that is capable of exerting its power. Since it is the Israeli military operations that was the main cause of the humanitarian crisis in the very first place, it can be argued that Israel has manifestly failed to protect the Gazan population. The Goldstone Report underlines that the IDF has failed to take the necessary measures to protect the civilian population in Gaza during its operation (UNGA, 2009c). Moreover, the IDF indiscriminately targeted civilian infrastructures as well as UN facilities, food production facilities, water installations, treatment plants and civilian housings without any military justification. The Report considers all these actions as war crimes (UNGA, 2009c, pp. 21, 23, 32), and crimes against humanity (UNGA, 2009c, pp. 32, 284). Moreover, the IDF's containment policies justified under counterterrorism measures are among the causes of the human suffering. This situation can be considered as collective punishment, and as the Secretary-General underlines, this is strictly prohibited under Article 32 of the Fourth Geneva Convention, to which Israel is a State party (UNGA, 2015a).

Furthermore, the 2015 UNGA report underlines that the IDF attacked civilian infrastructures by using explosive weapons especially in populated areas (UNGA, 2015b), which suggests that the aim of the Operation Protective Edge deviated from the officially claimed objective of destructing military infrastructures of Hamas to prevent further rocket attacks on the Israeli territory. The IDF's direct targeting of civilian infrastructures has also increased the number of internally displaced persons during the 2014 operation (Brugnola, 2015). Moreover, the UN Report identifies that Israeli military officials' actions could be considered as war crimes (UNGA, 2015b). Confirming the numbers of the UN, Human Rights Watch (2015) reports 2,100 Palestinians killed, of whom more than 1,500 were civilians. More than 108,000 people were displaced, and a large portion of the population remaining in Gaza did not have access to water and electricity since the Israeli attacks targeted Gaza's water resources and power plants.

As a result, in both operations, Israel has manifestly failed to protect the population in Gaza. First of all, while indiscriminate attacks resulting in civilian casualties raised concerns about possible war crimes and crimes against humanity, in both operations civilian infrastructures and facilities that have been used to meet the basic needs were targeted. This raised the question of collective punishment. Second, the continuing blockade over Gaza has dramatically increased the humanitarian cost. Although Israel had officially withdrew its military presence in Gaza in 2005, due to the blockade it continues to apply, it is still considered to be a de facto occupying power. Over the years, this effective blockade and de facto occupation have systematically weakened Gaza's administrative structure and made it impossible to govern properly, turning it to the largest open-air prison (Gözen Ercan, 2015, p. 1104).

Given that all three sovereign authorities in Gaza have failed to protect the population, we should look into the efforts of the international community under Pillars Two and Three. Accordingly, the subsequent section examines what sorts of measures have been undertaken, and evaluates to what extent they achieved their purpose.

The International Community's Involvement in Gaza

Pillar Two of R2P concerns the responsibility of the international community to assist the State in fulfilling its responsibility while Pillar Three underlines the international community's responsibility to react in a timely and decisive manner in cases of the State's manifest failure. As mentioned previously, the three pillars of R2P do not have to follow a sequenced order (UNGA, 2009a), and the three pillars may have to be applied together. Such a need has manifested itself in the case of Gaza due to the fact that the alleged mass atrocities have taken place during military operations, which is yet to be realised.

Regarding the situation in Gaza as to the fulfilment of Pillar Two responsibilities, we observe that the UN has been involved in the process through establishing fact-finding missions and attempting to determine the characteristics of assistance that could be provided. For instance, making a direct reference to the 2005 World Summit Outcome Document and the 2009 Report of Secretary-General, the Goldstone Report reminded the necessity to uphold the responsibility to protect and invoked the international community's responsibility in the case of the State's failure (UNGA, 2009c), but this did not yield immediate action. Given that fact-finding missions' reports do not have any binding power over the Member States, the impact of the reports on Gaza remained limited to defining the problem, establishing the existence of mass atrocity crimes as well as providing suggestions on the characteristics of the assistance that could be provided. While on the basis of the Goldstone Report in 2009 that established the immediacy of the situation we could have expected further efforts to prevent future crimes, any attempt at such did not find an answer in the UNSC, as evinced by the repetition of the alleged mass atrocity crimes in 2014.

On grounds of Paragraph 139 of the World Summit Outcome Document, the gravity of the situation and the manifest failure of the authorities directs our attention to the response of the UNSC. Since 2009, three draft resolutions on Palestine were brought before the Council. The 2011 draft resolution that 'call[ed] upon both parties to act on the basis of international law and their previous agreements and obligations…' (UNSC, 2011a), and the draft resolution on the Status of Jerusalem in 2017 demanding all parties to comply with the UNSC resolutions (UNSC, 2017a) were vetoed by the US delegation. As it wanted to avoid any compelling action against Israel, in justifying its veto, the US put forth Israel's inherent right to self-defence (UNSC, 2011b, 2017b). Similarly, the 2018 draft resolution 'urg[ing] the provision of immediate and unimpeded humanitarian assistance to the Palestinian civilian population in Gaza Strip…' (UNSC, 2018a) was vetoed by the US delegation. Pinpointing Hamas as the one responsible for the situation, the US once again asserted that Israel was acting in self-defence (UNSC, 2018b).

Considering that these draft resolutions addressed all the parties involved and constituted attempts to place the situation under control, we may argue that it was not a total indifference about the situation but rather a deadlock by veto that prevented UNSC-sanctioned responses. In this regard, while the establishment of the fact-finding missions and their reports can be evaluated as efforts under Pillar Two that could have triggered action under the authority of the UNSC pertaining to Pillar Three, we observe that they did not yield concrete steps for either prevention or reaction as they lacked the binding power to enforce action in the absence of the political will of the UNSC.

It is noteworthy that also the Palestinian State's full membership[1] to the UN was blocked by the US. Under Pillar Two, it is imperative that the international community assists the State in meeting its responsibility to protect. However, in the case of Gaza, all positive attempts to strengthen the Palestinian statehood have been prevented by the US. Consequently, the international community through the UNSC has failed to adopt assertive preventive and reactive measures and to end the Israeli blockade, which has worsened the humanitarian crisis in Gaza.

Likewise, threatening the Court and its members, the US attempted to prevent the ICC's further investigation into possible war crimes in Palestine (Human Rights Watch, 2020). We may consider the PA's referral of its case to the ICC as part of the peaceful measures of Pillar Three, which can also be considered as an act in fulfilment of the Palestinian State's

[1] Despite the non-recognition of the Palestinian State by Israel and the US, 'the UN has upgraded Palestine's status from an "observer entity" to a "nonmember observer state" in November 2012, and currently there are 134 member states of the UN and international organizations such as the ICC that recognize Palestine as a state and the PA as its national representative' (Gözen Ercan, 2015, p. 1103).

responsibility.[2] Being a State party to the Rome Statute,[3] the PA took the next step by bringing the issue to the ICC as one of the primary sovereign authorities in Gaza in search of accountability and ending impunity. The ICC's Chief Prosecutor Fatou Bensouda concluded the preliminary examination in January 2019, wherein it was found that there was considerable evidence to open a formal investigation for possible war crimes committed in Gaza by both Palestinian armed groups and Israel (BBC, 2019). Following this, as it did with the UNSC draft resolutions, the US attempted at blocking the investigations.

Both to counter the allegations against itself in the case of Afghanistan as well as the allegations against its ally, Israel in the specific case of Gaza, to prevent potential judicial processes, President Donald J. Trump authorised an executive order on 11 June 2020 to impose sanctions against the ICC, including travel bans on its officials and those who support the ICC investigations on Afghanistan and Palestine (Human Rights Watch, 2020). Nonetheless,

> [o]n 3 March 2021, the Prosecutor announced the opening of the investigation into the Situation in the State of Palestine. This followed Pre-Trial Chamber I's decision on 5 February 2021 that the Court could exercise its criminal jurisdiction in the Situation and, by majority, that the territorial scope of this jurisdiction extends to Gaza and the West Bank, including East Jerusalem. (ICC, n.d.)

Hence, unlike the developments in the UNSC, without comprising its impartiality, the ICC continues to consider the case. As for the implementation of R2P, this plays a complementary role by holding the perpetrators accountable for their actions and deterring future crimes by helping to end impunity. Nevertheless, as the proceedings take a long time to be

[2] 'In his 2009 report, Ban reminds that the crimes committed which lead to states' manifest failure can be referred to the ICC, since of the four grave crimes that determine the scope of R2P, genocide, war crimes and crimes against humanity fall under the jurisdiction of the ICC. As suggested by his call for states to join "the relevant international instruments on human rights, international humanitarian law and refugee law, as well as to the Rome Statute of the International Criminal Court", Ban sees such involvement as an initial step in the full implementation of R2P' (Gözen Ercan, 2015, p. 1105).

[3] There are three ways to bring a case before the ICC. According to Article 13 of the Rome Statute, there can be either referral by a State party, an initiation of investigation by the Prosecutor, or a referral by the UNSC under Chapter VII of the UN Charter (Mills, 2013).

completed, we cannot consider the ICC processes as an immediate source of solution to the ongoing humanitarian crisis. Regardless of what the final judgement of the Court will be, there is still need for other Pillar Three measures to stop the ongoing mass atrocity crimes committed by all sides of the conflict over Gaza, yet we are facing a UNSC deadlock because of the stronghold of the US wielding the veto as a Permanent Member.

What happened—or did not happen—in Gaza tells us about the neo-colonial tendencies in the way of R2P's implementation as a universal norm. The gravity of the situation has already been established by the fact-finding missions that were authorised by the UN organs, and there was considerable voice within the UN implying that international attention was there. For instance,

> [f]ollowing the collapse of the ceasefire, on 3 August 2014 Ban condemned the IDF's attack near a UN school in Rafah as a 'moral outrage and criminal act'. He further noted: 'United Nations shelters must be safe zones not combat zones [...] the Israel Defense Forces (IDF) have been repeatedly informed of the location of these sites. This attack, along with other breaches of international law, must be swiftly investigated and those responsible held accountable.' (Gözen Ercan, 2015, p. 1104)

As Gözen Ercan (2015, p. 1105) notes, unlike in the former instances in which UN-protected shelters were targeted, the UN Secretary-General dropped the diplomatic language and expressly pointed at Israel for the alleged violations of international law. Hence, it may be argued that as the severity and the impact of the situation grew, so did the attitude of the agents of the international community, which was also evinced with the two consecutive draft resolutions in 2017 and 2018. Nevertheless, this was not enough to change the attitude of the US, which rendered the UNSC at a deadlock. Therefore, it can be argued that the absence of action/reaction pertained mainly to the UNSC, which had lost its impartiality despite the fact that the consideration of the situation in the Council meetings did not target only Israel but instead addressed all responsible actors.

Conclusion

In the twenty-year old history of R2P, Gaza remains an exceptionally important example due to various reasons. The first is that there is a tripartite responsibility, which makes three different authorities, namely Hamas, the PA and Israel responsible for the protection of the Gazan population. Second, Gaza presents us with a perfect display of power politics in play and exemplifies how the case-by-case approach can be interpreted as selectivity in implementation. Looking at the precedent of Libya wherein the US and its allies hastily pushed for military intervention despite the early stage of an unfolding crisis and without exhausting possible measures short of use of force (Kelleci & Bodur Ün, 2017), the case of Gaza can be interpreted as a controversy. This is not to suggest that a military intervention should have been authorised by the UNSC under Chapter VII of the UN Charter as it was the case in Libya. On the contrary, such a response under Pillar Three would only exacerbate the already dismal conditions for the Gazan population. Rather, it is to suggest that universal norms can be implemented arbitrarily in convenience of the great powers. As Bilgin (2018, p. 53) underlines, '[a]rbitrary application of universals has long constituted a challenge for the notion of universals'. In this regard, the mindset behind the hasty action in Libya and inaction in Gaza are quite similar, as at the end of the day in both cases 'geopolitics prevails over norms' (Mahdavi, 2015, p. 12).

Overall, analysing the case of Gaza from an R2P lens is important since it evinces the selective implementation of international norms driven by the self-interested motivations of the implementors. In the case of Gaza, the responses to both Israeli operations reveal a total failure of all sides to protect the Gazan population. It tells us that interventions do not only take a military form anymore. That is to say, selective implementation of international norms serves as another form of systemic intervention.

Consequently, the interruption of prevention attempts under Pillar Two and the non-implementation of Pillar Three in Gaza are rooted in the dependency of R2P on the UNSC as the 'right authority'. Similar to the case of the Uyghurs in Xinjiang wherein the national interests of China are at stake (see Chapter 12), the direct involvement of the US in the case of Gaza reveals how the great power interests may drive decision-making processes in the UNSC and rendering attempts at protection of populations useless. Such direct dependency on the will of the P5, and selectivity in protection of populations can be considered as indirect forms of manipulation and control to achieve the agenda of the great powers. Accordingly, the UNSC is placed in a position where it can decide who is worth to be saved or not under the current operational framework of R2P. The dependency of R2P's implementation on the mercy of the P5's veto power also leads to the assumption that the P5 would not lose their impartiality, and they themselves would not be the perpetrators of mass atrocity crimes. Nevertheless, twenty years of R2P experience tells otherwise. As the representative of Darfur remarked in the first formal debate on R2P in 2009, '[t]o give the Security Council the privilege of being executor of the concept of the responsibility to protect would be tantamount to giving a wolf the responsibility to adopt a lamb' (UNGA, 2009b, p. 11).

All in all, the failure in Gaza demonstrates the systemic problems pertaining to R2P's practice. As for Pillar One, deciding who the sovereign of Gaza is has posed a major challenge in implementation. Multiple sovereignty problem not only makes it difficult to determine who is responsible for the protection of Gazan population, but also to determine the characteristics of the assistance. When it is an authority that is not considered to be legitimate one by the international community, as in the case of Hamas, this also undermines the international representation of the concerned population. As for Pillars Two and Three, although the UN made several attempts to identify the characteristics of the assistance, further action was prevented repetitively due to the deadlock in the UNSC. Accordingly, the case of Gaza teaches us that the structural dependency of the R2P on the UNSC needs to change. Within this existing framework, R2P cannot be implemented consistently and without prejudice.

This brings us to standards to ensure that arbitrary implementation of universal norms is prevented. Although R2P is not an inherently postcolonial norm, leaving its implementation to the mercy of P5 makes it a neo-colonial practice as mentioned. The universal norms have been used and abused for the interests of hegemonic powers. Within this existing structure, the Global North is able to produce norms and values and use them as a tool to reconstruct their interests. The case of Gaza reveals that R2P's implementation needs to be free from the neo-colonial structural limitations of the UNSC. Although numerous fact-finding missions investigated and established Israeli violations amounting to war crimes and crimes against humanity, the US never considered Israel as the wrongdoer but instead put the blame on the 'other'. This suggests that the P5's perception of the world and their evaluation of ongoing mass atrocities do matter within this existing structure. Therefore, a deep structural reform in the UN is necessary.

Secondly, there has to be an independent checks-and-balances body to investigate both the violations of four main atrocity crimes and the possible abuses in the implementation of R2P. While the ICC can be a strong candidate for this balance, its long proceedings would not yield an R2P response in the desired short-term. Hence, it is important to explore other possibilities such the UNHRC.

Finally, we need to acknowledge that interventionism does not only take a military form. The selective implementation of norms can also be considered as a kind of intervention. Silence is as equally dangerous as the human rights violations themselves. Overall, it can be concluded that in the case of Palestine, the human rights violations in Gaza are not the causes but the symptoms of the conflict. Avoiding to address the core issues of the conflict such as the right of return, settlement projects and the status of Jerusalem, the international community's silence only worsens the situation in Gaza.

References

Adams, S. (2014, July 25). *Both Israel and Hamas have a responsibility to protect civilians*. https://justiceinconflict.org/2014/07/25/both-israel-and-hamas-have-a-responsibility-to-protect-civilians/. Accessed 25 May 2020.

Amnesty International. (2009, July). *Operation 'cast lead': 22 days of death and destruction*. https://www.amnesty.org/download/Documents/48000/mde150152009en.pdf. Accessed 25 May 2020.

Bayeh, E. (2014). The current war on Gaza: A challenge to R2P. *International Journal of Political Science and Development, 2*(9), 205–210.

BBC. (2019). *ICC wants to open 'war crimes' investigation in West Bank and Gaza*. https://www.bbc.com/news/world-middle-east-50871337. Accessed 30 May 2020.

Bilgin, P. (2018). Securing the Postcolonial. In O. U. Rutazibwa & R. Shilliam (Eds.), *Routledge handbook of postcolonial politics* (pp. 48–57). Routledge.

Brugnola, S. (2015). *Who protects the Palestinians in Gaza: Analysis of the legal basis for responsibility of the international community and obstacles for implementation* (M.A. Thesis), National University of Ireland. https://repository.gchumanrights.org/handle/20.500.11825/269. Accessed 18 June 2020.

Cleveland, W., & Bunton, M. (2016). *A history of the modern Middle East* (6th ed.). Routledge.

Gözen Ercan, P. (2015). Responsibility to protect and inter-state crises: Why and how R2P applies to the case of Gaza. *The International Journal of Human Rights, 19*(8), 1098–1111.

Hehir, A. (2014, July 23). *Is Gaza in Israel? R2P and inter-state crisis*. https://justiceinconflict.org/2014/07/23/is-gaza-in-israel-r2p-and-inter-state-crises/. Accessed 15 May 2020.

Hehir, A. (2015, July 15). *A propensity to ignore? R2P advocacy and the crisis in Gaza*. https://www.e-ir.info/2014/07/15/a-propensity-to-ignore-r2p-advocacy-and-the-crisis-in-gaza/. Accessed 15 May 2020.

Human Rights Watch. (2015). *World report 2015: Israel/Palestine*. https://www.hrw.org/world-report/2015/country-chapters/israel/palestine. Accessed 3 May 2020.

Human Rights Watch. (2020). *US sets sanctions against International Criminal Court*. Retrieved May 26, 2020, from https://www.hrw.org/news/2020/06/11/us-sets-sanctions-against-international-criminal-court. Accessed 3 May 2020.

International Criminal Court (ICC). (n.d.). *State of Palestine*. https://www.icc-cpi.int/palestine. Accessed 11 August 2021.

Kattan, V. (2009). Operation cast lead: Use of force discourse and jus ad bellum controversies. *The Palestine Yearbook of International Law Online, 15*(1), 95–118.

Kearney, M. (2014, July 24). *In Palestine R2P isn't dead, it could never have existed*. https://justiceinconflict.org/2014/07/24/in-palestine-r2p-isnt-dead-it-could-never-have-existed/. Accessed 10 May 2020.

Kelleci, T., & Bodur Ün, M. (2017). TWAIL ve yeni bir hakimiyet aracı olarak koruma sorumluluğu (R2P): Libya örneği. *Uluslararası İlişkiler, 14*(56), 89–104.

Khalidi, W. (1997). Revisiting the UNGA partition resolution. *Journal of Palestine Studies, 17*(1), 5–21.

Levs, D. (2009, January 6). Is Gaza 'occupied territory?. *CNN*. https://edition.cnn.com/2009/WORLD/meast/01/06/israel.gaza.occupation.question/. Accessed 12 May 2020.

Mahdavi, M. (2015). Post-colonial critique to responsibility to protect in the Middle East. *Perceptions, 10*(1), 7–36.

Mills, K. (2013). R2P3: Protecting, prosecuting, or palliating in mass atrocity situations? *Journal of Human Rights, 12*(3), 333–356.

Pourmokhtari, N. (2013). A postcolonial critique of state sovereignty in IR: The contradictory legacy of a 'West-centric' discipline. *Third World Quarterly, 34*(10), 1767–1793.

Rieff, D. (2014. July 25). *R2P isn't a useful framework for Gaza–or anything*. https://justiceinconflict.org/2014/07/25/r2p-isnt-a-useful-framework-for-gaza-or-anything/#more-5512. Accessed 12 May 2020.

Rudolph, J. (2014, July 24) *Gaza and Israel: A case for international law*. https://justiceinconflict.org/2014/07/24/gaza-and-israel-a-case-for-international-humanitarian-law-not-r2p/. Accessed 9 May 2020.

United Nations General Assembly (UNGA). (2005, October 24). *Resolution Adopted by the General Assembly on 16 September 2005, 60/1. 2005 World Summit Outcome*. A/Res/60/1.

United Nations General Assembly (UNGA). (2009a, January 12). *Implementing the responsibility to protect*. Report of the Secretary-General, A/63/677).

United Nations General Assembly (UNGA). (2009b, July 28). *Sixty-third session, 101st plenary meeting*, A/63/PV.101.

United Nations General Assembly (UNGA). (2009c, September 25). *Human Rights and other occupied Arab territories*. Report of the United Nations Fact Finding Mission on the Gaza Conflict, A/HRC/12/48.

United Nations General Assembly (UNGA). (2015a, March 5). *Human rights situation in the occupied Palestinian territory, including East Jerusalem*. Report of the Secretary-General, A/HRC/28/45.

United Nations General Assembly (UNGA). (2015b, June 24). *Human rights situation in Palestine and other occupied Arab territories*. Report of the Independent commission of inquiry established pursuant to Human Rights Council resolution S-21/1, A/HRC/29/52.

United Nations Security Council (UNSC). (2011a, February 18). *Draft resolution 24*, S/2011/24.

United Nations Security Council (UNSC). (2011b, February 18). *6484th meeting*, S/PV.6484.

United Nations Security Council (UNSC). (2011c, March 17). Resolution 1973, Adopted by the Security Council at its 6498th meeting, S/RES/1973.

United Nations Security Council (UNSC). (2017a, December 18). Draft Resolution 1060, S/2017/1016.

United Nations Security Council (UNSC). (2017b, December 18). 8139th Meeting, S/PV.8139.

United Nations Security Council (UNSC). (2018a, June 1). Draft Resolution 516, S/2018/516.

United Nations Security Council (UNSC). (2018b, June 1). 8274th Meeting, S/PV.8274.

CHAPTER 9

The Forsaken War in Yemen: R2P as Mere Rhetoric?

Haseenah Huurieyah Wan Rosli

The tumultuous armed conflict in Yemen has culminated in the 'gravest humanitarian crisis' in the world, with the unrelenting indiscriminate armed attacks and violence against civilians (Kahwati, 2019). As of 21 March 2020, a study conducted by the Armed Conflict Location and Event Data Project (ACLED) approximated the death toll in Yemen to have exceeded 112,000 since 2015 (ACLED, 2020)[1] in addition to the unprecedented figure of 16.6 million Yemenis confronted with acute food insecurity (WFP & FAO, 2021).

The skyrocketing number of casualties begs us to inquire whether the present crisis in Yemen evinces the 'manifest failure' of the government as well as the international community to protect the Yemeni population from mass atrocity crimes. While the Responsibility to Protect (R2P) language has been present in the justifications of the intervention with

[1]Specifically, over 12,690 civilians were killed as a result of targeted attacks (ACLED, 2020).

H. H. Wan Rosli (✉)
Hacettepe University, Ankara, Turkey

P. Gözen Ercan (ed.), *The Responsibility to Protect Twenty Years On*,
https://doi.org/10.1007/978-3-030-90731-0_9

references to the protection of 'Yemen and its people from the ongoing Houthi aggression' (UNSC, 2015b, p. 3), it is questionable whether the R2P mindset has truly been present during operationalisation.

The case of Yemen has rather been disregarded in the R2P literature, yet it is noteworthy of analysis for several reasons. Unlike in Libya and Syria, the primary actor of the humanitarian crisis in Yemen was not the incumbent government itself but non-state actors—namely Houthi armed rebels who committed acts amounting to 'threat of atrocity crimes'. Moreover, this case is also exceptional in terms of the operationalisation of the response through intervention by invitation (IvI). The subsequent analysis looks into the situation through the three pillars of R2P and also reflects on the parameters on the use of force—i.e. five basic criteria for legitimacy—that was proposed in the 2004 Report of the High-level Panel on Threats, Challenges and Change.

Tracing back to the key events prior to the military operations, this Chapter aims to gradually dissect the three-pillar implementation of R2P in Yemen specifically focusing on the initial phase of the Saudi-led intervention in 2015. The first part of this Chapter critically analyses the manifold attempts of the incumbent government and the international community as being instrumental in preventing the outbreak of atrocity crimes. The subsequent part addresses the crux issue on the use of force vis-à-vis Pillar Three. The contentions put forth are the following: When incumbent governments are unable to protect their populations from atrocity crimes, even in the absence of a United Nations (UN) Security Council (UNSC) authorisation, States are empowered to issue invitations to the international community to protect their population from atrocity crimes. Yet, this does not mean that the UNSC is released from its international responsibility including monitoring operationalisation to ensure responsible protection.

In the case of Yemen, a valid invitation for military intervention couched in the language of R2P was issued by President Hadi to the regional bodies. In response, a military intervention was carried out by the Saudi-led coalition with the claim of protecting the Yemeni population from mass atrocity crimes. However, in the aftermath of the intervention, it was evinced that the underlying motivation for the intervention was to restore and maintain President Hadi's sovereign powers which ultimately fortifies Saudi Arabia's hegemony over Yemen. Set against this background, this Chapter provides a critical assessment on the adverse implementation of R2P by Saudi-led interveners based on the pretext of protecting the Yemeni population. Last but not least, this Chapter evaluates the (mis)use of force under Pillar Three vis-à-vis the criteria laid down in the 2004 Report and argues for the adoption of these criteria to ensure an effective and responsible implementation of R2P in the near future.

Background to the Crisis in Yemen

The Republic of Yemen was established in 1990 and prior to its formation, the State was comprised of different areas governed by multiple regimes (Dingli, 2013). The northern part of Yemen was ruled by a Shi'ite group, namely the Qasimi Imams, since the sixteenth century but its control over the territory eventually waned with the arrival of the Ottoman and British Empires (Clausen, 2018).

After the collapse of both empires, a civil war broke out leading to the formation of Yemen Arab Republic (YAR) in the north and People's Democratic Republic of Yemen (PDRY) in the south (Brehony, 2011). In the wake of the Soviet Union's disintegration, PDRY began to lose influence, which resulted in YAR members having greater political control prior to unification, with the agreement appointing Ali Abdallah Salleh as the president of Yemen in 1990 (Dingli, 2013). Salleh's continued allegiance towards YAR was reflected in his policies of infrastructure development and his lack of determination to integrate PDRY and YAR military forces. The political and economic exclusion of PDRY in the Yemeni governance further exacerbated the strained relationship between Salleh and PDRY, eventually culminating into a civil war in 1994 (Hathaway et al., 2018). Although Salleh's government managed to defeat PDRY's forces, Salleh did not honour his undertaking for unification but instead augmented the suppression of the southern population (Dingli, 2013).

These policies prompted the southern opposition to intensify its protests in 2003 and sparked a smouldering unrest between these two forces. To quell this, Salleh's government initiated a crackdown on Houthi[2] forces. This resulted in the death of the Houthi leader Husayn al Houthi (Nußberger, 2017), which impelled other southerners to partake in an armed rebellion against Salleh's government with persistent attacks

[2] The Houthis are predominantly Zaiddiyah (a Shi'ite Muslim sect) and are allegedly backed up by Iran, which is a long-time adversary of Saudi Arabia (Popp, 2015).

in the Sa'ada region (Hathaway et al., 2018). Consequently, the Houthis and President Salleh's government have been engaged in armed hostilities in a span of six years from 2004 to 2010.

Notwithstanding Salleh's effort to improve relations with the rebel forces, the widespread protests that were taking place during the Arab uprisings in 2011 sparked a 'Yemeni Revolution'. This became an unprecedented wave of protests in Yemen partaken not only by the Houthis but extending to the Yemeni population as a whole (Popp, 2015). In the wake of this uprising, the Yemeni population took to the streets demanding an immediate dismissal of President Ali Salleh and an end to his authoritarian rule over Yemen (ICG, 2012). However, on 18 March 2011, the minor and purportedly peaceful protests turned violent when pro-Salleh military forces killed more than 50 demonstrators under the pretext of suppressing public discontentment (Clausen, 2018).

Due to escalation, the Gulf Cooperation Council (GCC) proposed an initiative entailing a 'two-phase transitional process'. In the first phase, Salleh was requested to resign in exchange for immunity from prosecution while Vice President Mansur Hadi was temporarily appointed as the head of state (Buys & Garwood-Gowers, 2019, p. 4). The UNSC adopted a resolution condemning the human rights violations perpetrated by Salleh's government and expressing support for the GCC initiative (UNSC, 2011). Owing to international pressure, Salleh officially handed over his resignation on 23 November 2011 whereupon elections took place on 21 February 2012 as agreed in the initiative.

Upon Hadi's appointment, the second phase was initiated with the convening of a 'National Dialogue Conference', which was subsequently enforced with the backing of the UN (Ruys & Ferro, 2016). As agreed in the GCC Initiative, the Conference was intended to bring about a negotiation on a feasible plan for a 'peaceful political transition' amongst key political actors of Yemen, and particularly the Houthis (Buys & Garwood-Gowers, 2019, p. 4). At the end of the Conference, participants agreed upon recommendations on pressing issues such as the 'Houthi issue', the political system of Yemen and governance in the southern part of Yemen (Popp, 2015).

However, the Houthis rejected the 'six-region structure' proposal and resorted to brutal territorial expansion, taking advantage of the 'power vacuum' and the growing 'security void' due to the political instability in Yemen (ICG, 2012). Concurrently, the offshoots of Salleh's government aligned with the Houthis to overthrow Hadi's government to further expand their influence in Yemen. The Houthi-Salleh alliance joined forces to take over the northern region and became the de facto government in the capital, Sana'a (Popp, 2015). Due to the aggravating security and political instability in Yemen, the UNSC (2014) adopted Resolution 2140 and imposed stern measures such as assets freeze and travel bans on the Houthis. Despite international condemnation, the Houthi forces persisted with their efforts in overthrowing Hadi's government by taking control of Sana'a in addition to seizing all the key functions of the government (UNSC, 2015c).

To quell the insurrection, Hadi's government entered into a Peace and National Partnership Agreement (PNPA) with the Houthis on 21 September 2014 wherein their demands were set out and agreed to be satisfied accordingly (Ruys & Ferro, 2016). On 7 January 2015, a draft constitution was proposed to President Hadi but was categorically rejected on the grounds that it contravened the terms of the PNPA (Nußberger, 2017). The lingering mistrust led the Houthis to resume their efforts by placing Hadi and his top officials under house arrest in addition to dissolving the parliament and setting up a new 'Presidential Council' upon Hadi's removal as head of state (Buys & Garwood-Gowers, 2019). In response, the UNSC adopted Resolution 2201, strongly deploring the unilateral actions of the Houthis and demanding them to inter alia, participate in the UN-brokered negotiations, remove forces from governmental institutions and safely release those who were arbitrarily detained (UNSC, 2015e, Para. 7).

Upon his release, Hadi successfully fled to Aden and subsequently proclaimed it as the temporary capital of Yemen. Meanwhile, on 21 February 2014, he publicly revoked his resignation which in turn prompted Houthi forces to advance towards Aden culminating in a successful seizure of the new Yemeni capital. With no other option left, Hadi eventually escaped to Riyadh and officially invited GCC members[3] for a military intervention in Yemen (UNSC, 2015c). In response to Hadi's invitation, a Saudi-led military coalition provided military assistance to Hadi's forces in Yemen comprising of 'military units, tribal militias, and Islamic militants' (UNSC, 2014). The coalition launched Operation Decisive Storm on 26 March 2015 followed by Operation 'Renewal of Hope' on 22 April 2015 (Buys & Garwood-Gowers, 2019).

[3] The GCC members consist of Saudi Arabia, United Arab Emirates, Bahrain, Omar, Kuwait and Qatar.

Owing to these operations, the coalition managed to successfully recapture the city of Aden and the Sunni populated regions in southern Yemen. Meanwhile, western Yemen remained under the authority of the Houthi-Salleh alliance (Ruys & Ferro, 2016).

In view of the ongoing human rights violations committed against the Yemeni population, in April 2015, former UN Secretary-General Ban Ki-moon appointed UN Special Envoy Ismail Ahmed to assist both parties in reaching a temporary settlement (UN News, 2015). However, his endeavour was proven futile as the parties failed to even agree on 'a basic framework for peace' (Hathaway et al., 2018, p. 6). In December 2017, Salleh announced his support for the Saudi-led coalition, the Houthi-Salleh alliance was disbanded, and this resulted in Salleh's assassination (Wintour, 2017). In response, the Saudi coalition launched a drone strike killing the President of Houthi's Supreme Political Council on 23 April 2018 (UNSC, 2018). The Yemeni crisis that is currently labelled as the 'worst humanitarian crisis in the world' (UN News, 2019) remains unabated until this day. Despite several attempts by the international community to reach a temporary ceasefire, both warring parties are still locked in a violent cycle of military strikes undeterred by the surge in civilian deaths (ACLED, 2020).

Pillar One: Successive Preventive Measures by the Yemeni Government

Even though the Saudi-led intervention couched in the language of R2P took place under Hadi's administration, the key events precipitating the intervention need to be traced back to the acts and omissions of the previous government under President Salleh. Therefore, it helps to briefly evaluate Salleh's administration in fulfilling Pillar One responsibilities.

In the light of the pivotal episodes, I argue that there was an attempt by President Salleh as the then incumbent government to prevent the outbreak of mass atrocity crimes during the 2011 uprising. Paragraph 138 of World Summit Outcome Document (WSOD) states that 'Each individual state has the responsibility to protect its populations from genocide, war crimes, ethnic cleansing and crimes against humanity. This responsibility entails the prevention of such crimes, including their incitement, through appropriate and necessary means' (UNGA, 2005). Considering that civilian casualties occurred as a result of Salleh's crackdown on peaceful protestors, also owing to insurmountable international pressure, the State is argued to have later upheld Pillar One responsibility by acquiescing to the Yemeni population's demand for Salleh's resignation. This is evinced in the agreement to implement the two-phased transition period under the GCC initiative for a power transfer to the then Vice President Hadi who received popular support at the material time (Ruys & Ferro, 2016).

Nevertheless, Hadi's appointment as the head of state did not ease the situation. Unable to fulfil its Pillar One responsibilities, the incumbent Hadi government requested for military assistance to protect the Yemeni population. It is well established that within the R2P framework, absolute sovereignty orthodoxy is transformed into 'sovereignty as responsibility'. Hence, the ensuing question is how did Hadi's government uphold its Pillar One responsibility? Hathaway et al. (2013, p. 540) argue that in the event where there is a breakdown of state institutions—for instance the police force, military and judiciary—states 'may consent to intervention by others when they cannot meet their responsibilities alone'. Accordingly, the discharge of Pillar One responsibility by the State may also be evinced by its request for external assistance to protect its population from atrocity crimes. Hadi made his request with an official letter addressed to the GCC members[4] dated 24 March 2015 (UNSC, 2015b). The letter started off with the allegation that the current instability in Yemen is caused by the Houthis in the form of 'ongoing acts of aggression and incessant attacks against the country's sovereignty' (UNSC, 2015b, p. 3). At the same time, Hadi claimed that his government pursued every action to protect its population from 'heinous, criminal attacks being committed by Houthis' (UNSC, 2015b), but these were rendered futile owing to the categorical rejection by the Houthis. Hadi also insinuated the involvement of 'external forces' supporting the Houthis to further expand their influence in Yemen. Establishing the 'inability' of his government to effectively protect the Yemeni population from 'threats of mass atrocity crimes', he recalled his state's responsibility to protect and requested military assistance from allied states to 'protect Yemen and its people from the ongoing Houthi aggression' (UNSC, 2015b, p. 5).

The UNSC has also affirmed 'acts of violence' perpetrated against the Yemeni people by the Houthis in their attempt to overthrow Hadi's government and overtake governmental institutions (UNSC, 2015d). If

[4] Specific reference to the head of states of Saudi Arabia, United Arab Emirates (UAE), Bahrain, Oman, Kuwait and Qatar (see UNSC, 2015b).

we take Hadi's letter at face value, his government's 'inability' to prevent the commission of mass atrocity crimes would entitle him to request for military assistance from the GCC members for the main purpose of fulfilling the State's Pillar One responsibility.

In a similar vein, based on Paragraph 138, I argue that President Hadi's issuance of the invitation for military intervention can be deemed as 'appropriate and necessary means' to prevent mass atrocity crimes from taking place. Meanwhile, pursuant to the 'dual responsibility' as established in the Report of the International Commission on Intervention and State Sovereignty (ICISS), this Chapter contends that such an act is an internal manifestation of President Hadi's responsibility towards the population and an external manifestation towards the international community. In the latter, Hadi's government ensures that by issuing consent, prompt military assistance is provided to prevent any spill over of mass atrocity crimes that could also negatively affect neighbouring sovereign states. However, the right to issue external intervention is circumscribed by the question of the government's legitimacy and ultimately boils down to the question of whose right is it to request for external intervention. As Buys and Garwood-Gowers (2019) contend, since the invitation was issued when Yemen was in a state of civil war and thus bound by the negative equality doctrine,[5] neither Hadi nor the Houthis had the right to request for external intervention. However, it could be argued that if the primary purpose is to protect the population from mass atrocity crimes, Hadi could still be deemed to retain the right to issue the intervention.

Pillar Two: Manifold Attempts by the International Community

As the UN Secretary-General notes, '[i]nternational actors can provide advice and expertise to support local mediation and dispute resolution efforts' (UNGA–SC, 2014, Para. 62). In the light of the escalating and unabating conflict between the incumbent government of Yemen and the Houthi rebels, the first attempt of the international community in

[5] This doctrine is known as 'negative equality' whereby each side is 'equally unable to invite outside assistance' in situations of civil war (Fox, 2015, p. 827).

preventing the outbreak of atrocity crimes is reflected in the Qatari mediation efforts. In May 2007, Qatari delegates were appointed to personally meet with representatives from both warring factions, followed by a Qatari peace plan—also known as the Doha Agreement—and a ceasefire in mid-June 2007 (Winter, 2011). The salient peace plan laid down key principles encompassing not only Houthi's pledge to surrender the use of heavy armoury but also a consensual endeavour towards a legitimate peace settlement. Albeit the collapse of the agreement due to lack of implementation and influence of external forces, it is argued that the Qatari government, as representative of the international community[6] carried out Pillar Two responsibilities by assuming the role of mediator and spearheading dispute resolution efforts, which in effect prevented the outbreak of atrocity crimes at the material time (Boucek, 2010).

Subsequently, the international community attempted to uphold its Pillar Two responsibility during the 2011 Arab uprisings which had thrusted Yemen into a civil war. During this period, increasing civilian deaths and casualties due to use of excessive force against peaceful protestors were reported during Salleh's armed confrontations with the Houthi rebels (Arimatsu & Choudhury, 2014). It was on 18 March 2011 that Salleh's government forces opened fire on the demonstrators in Sana'a, resulting in more than 45 people killed (Arraf, 2017). The exacerbation of the humanitarian crisis prompted the GCC to assist the Yemeni government in restoring stability and preventing further outbreak of atrocity crimes.

On 21 February 2012, phase two was implemented and presidential elections were carried out—wherein Hadi, by receiving considerable mandate from the Yemeni population, was proffered as the 'sole consensus candidate'. Such an endeavour of the international community can be deemed as another initiative falling under Pillar Two. As the Secretary-General notes in his 2013 Report, 'encourag[ing] intercommunal political cooperation can help to prevent tensions that may spiral into atrocity crimes' (UNGA-SC, 2013, Para. 37).

It was on 21 October 2011 that the UNSC (2011) adopted Resolution 2014 wherein it fortified and accorded legitimacy to the GCC initiative as an appropriate measure to resolve the political crisis in Yemen. Moreover,

[6] I argue that the 'international community' referred to is not solely confined to the organs of the UN per se but also encompasses key actors, such as individual Member States, and in this case Qatar and/or regional bodies.

the Resolution also underscored the aspirations of the Yemeni people by 'stressing that the best solution to the current crisis in Yemen is through an inclusive and Yemeni-led political process of transition that meets the legitimate demands and aspirations of the Yemeni people for change' and urged 'all parties in Yemen to commit themselves to implementation of a political settlement based upon this initiative' (UNSC, 2011). Pursuant to this, the UN and the GCC proposed and mediated the consensus amongst political parties in Yemen on the 'Agreement on the implementation mechanism for the transition process in Yemen in accordance with the initiative of the Gulf Cooperation Council' in December 2011.

At this juncture, the cardinal role of the UN in preventing the outbreak of atrocity crimes went further than mere extension of support to the GCC initiative. In view of the issues arising from the failed implementation of the two-phased transition process, the UNSC adopted Resolution 2051 on 12 June 2012. Regarding the first stage of the transition, it expressed 'concern at the recent deterioration of cooperation among some political actors and actions that could adversely affect or delay the political transition process' and 'demand[ed] the cessation of all actions aimed at undermining the Government of National Unity and the political transition' (UNSC, 2012).

Notwithstanding Yemen's current state, the deals and proactive negotiations by the UN and GCC prior to the outbreak of atrocity crimes were laudable attempts by the international community to assist the State in protecting the Yemeni population from atrocity crimes (Kahwati, 2019). I argue that the successive actions of regional bodies and the UN, and timely implementation of the proposed measures under Pillar Two has subverted the smouldering unrest of 2011 from abruptly spiralling into mass atrocity crimes at the time.

Pillar Three: Circumventing the Quandary on the Use of Force

In the light of the appalling situation as asserted in President Hadi's letter, the representatives from Bahrain, Kuwait, Qatar, Saudi Arabia and UAE issued a joint statement to the UN. While explaining their stance, they referred to their responsibility to protect the Yemeni population in the following words:

> We are mindful of our responsibility towards the Yemeni people. We note the contents of President Hadi's letter, which asks for immediate support in every form and for the necessary action to be taken in order to protect Yemen and its people from the aggression of the Houthi militias. [... We] therefore have decided to respond to President Hadi's appeal to protect Yemen and its great people from the aggression of the Houthi militias. (UNSC, 2015b, p. 5)

The joint statement also claimed that the Houthis were supported by 'regional forces, which are seeking to extend their hegemony over Yemen and use the country as a base from which to influence the region' therefore the threat could destabilise not only Yemen, but also adversely affect regional and global stability (UNSC, 2015b, p. 5). Apart from the military support provided by the GCC members, the 'logistical and intelligence support' rendered by the United States (US) was purported to 'defend Saudi Arabia's border and to protect Yemen's legitimate government' (UNSC, 2015b), without any mention of the Yemeni population's protection.

According to the GCC's joint statement, the intervening states invoked the doctrine of 'Intervention by Invitation' (IvI), as evinced by their explicit reference in their response to Hadi's invitation. Moreover, the official statements by Saudi representatives affirm IvI as a ground for intervention as they claim that 'Saudi Arabia has launched military operations in Yemen ... in response to a direct request from the legitimate government of Yemen' (Saudi Embassy, 2015). Furthermore, the express reference to the Yemeni population's protection in the GCC's statement establishes that R2P was invoked alongside IvI, implying that the intervention was aimed to protect the Yemeni population.

In line with Paragraph 139 of the WSOD, I argue that the invited interveners (i.e. the Saudi-led coalition) were prepared to use force in a timely and decisive manner at a time when the UNSC was silent and merely acknowledged the then-ongoing Operation Decisive Storm led by Saudi Arabia (UNSC, 2015f). Although the deafening silence and lack of criticism did not result in an explicit authorisation for the use of force, it implies that the UNSC has acquiesced to the operation, which then fortifies the role assumed by the Saudi-led interveners as legitimate parties of the international community to uphold Pillar Three responsibility, with the purported objective of protecting the Yemeni population from atrocity crimes. In view of the above argument, I propose that the five basic criteria for legitimacy laid out in the 2004 Report of Kofi Annan should be adopted to question the effective role of the international responsibility.

Parameters on the Use of Force

The parameters on the use of force, which are based on the 2001 Report of the ICISS and found voice in the 2004 Report of the High-level Panel on Threats, Challenges and Change, are essential to scrutinise the Saudi-led coalition's intervention vis-à-vis the R2P framework as to determine whether or not it abided by the *jus ad bellum* conditions. Hence, we should first look at the criterion of 'seriousness of threat'.

The pertinent question to address is if the state is 'manifestly failing' to protect its population from mass atrocity crimes either due to inability or unwillingness? According to the letters issued, it appears that the alleged crimes—i.e. crimes of aggression and criminal attacks—committed by the Houthis have not reached the threshold of mass atrocity crimes. Accordingly, the analysis is not predicated upon the 'actual commission of mass atrocity crimes' but on the 'threats or risks' that may precipitate the commission of these crimes. To ascertain whether the acts in question constituted 'threats of mass atrocity crimes', the 'Framework of Analysis for Atrocity Crimes' (FAAC) that was advanced by former Secretary-General Ban Ki-moon in 2014 serves as a guideline. On the basis of the information provided in UNSC Resolution 2201 and the 2018 UN Human Rights Council (UNHRC) Report, only indicators of Risk Factor 1 seem pertinent to the Yemeni crisis.

Risk Factor 1 concerns situations of instability that could trigger the commission of mass atrocity crimes. In view of the factual background, the ongoing-armed conflict between Hadi's government and Houthi militias since 2004, which eventually resulted in a takeover by the Houthis, is classified as Non-International Armed Conflict (NIAC). Pursuant to the assessment made by the International Court of Justice (ICJ), the Yemeni crisis fits the criteria of NIAC on the following grounds: (a) the opposition group that is in conflict with Hadi's government is an 'organised armed group' as manifested in their de facto control of Yemen and its capital city Sa'ada in addition to its authority over Yemeni military (Clausen, 2018), and (b) there is high intensity of hostilities in view of the deployment of armed forces at government institutions and arbitrary detention of President Hadi and his key ministers (ICJ, 2018). Considering Indicator 1.2, the Houthi's defection from the PNPA, which aimed at undermining the political transition process (UNHRC, 2018), has led to a security crisis, and caused political instability in Yemen. Furthermore, Indicator 1.4 is also relevant as the abrupt 'transfer of power' through a coup d'état also gave rise to political instability (UN, 2014).

Based on this assessment alone, the severe political instability in Yemen caused by the Houthi takeover may lead to a conclusion that there is the likelihood of escalation into actual mass atrocity crimes. However, given that the threshold is a 'manifest failure', there is no clear evidence of alleged 'criminal attacks' or 'acts of violence' against the Yemeni people. If we look into the acts committed by the Houthis including, inter alia, 'arbitrary detention of Hadi's supporters and usage of media to incite violence' (UNSC, 2015c) and 'intimidation, arbitrary detention, ill-treatment and torture of vocal critics, in addition to raids on media outlets in Sana'a' (UNHRC, 2018, pp. 11–12), I argue that these acts cannot be considered as imminent threats of mass atrocity crimes that would cause the State's manifest failure.

The allegations of 'acts of violence', 'criminal attacks' and 'acts of aggression' that might precipitate preventive deployment under Pillar Two are not corroborated by credible reports. Thus, it can be deduced that the acts perpetrated by the Houthis were not 'sufficiently clear and serious, to justify prima facie use of force' and that they do not involve mass atrocity crimes that are 'imminently apprehended' (UNGA, 2004). Accordingly, although Hadi's government was deemed to have the legitimacy, I argue that since the threat was not serious enough to qualify as a manifest failure, Hadi was thus not entitled to request for external intervention.

Next, we should consider the criterion of proper purpose. Supposing that Hadi's letter would be taken as a *prima facie* evidence, it would be presumed that he has acted in accordance with the State's Pillar One responsibility to the best of his ability, wherein his government has been unable to protect the Yemeni population from mass atrocity crimes. The allegation that the Houthis have persisted with acts of aggression may be deemed as threats of mass atrocity crimes thereby triggering the responsibility of the international community either under Pillar Two or Three. Yet, further analysis allows us to observe that the acts were perpetrated against Yemeni sovereignty not the population. Consequently, it is rather Hadi's sovereign authority that was at stake. If the primary purpose for military assistance is to reinstate Hadi's sovereignty, this does not justify the hasty exercise of the use of force by the Saudi-led coalition either in the form of preventive deployment or military intervention.

However, if there is cogent evidence proving that the 'acts of aggression' were specifically perpetrated against the Yemeni population that may lead to the actual commission of mass atrocity crimes, in such situation, Hadi has the right to request for external intervention. Since the joint statement refers to the protection of the Yemeni people, we may conclude that the intervention was carried out to protect the Yemeni population from mass atrocity crimes. However, in view of the data gathered on civilian casualties, it appears that the primary purpose was to reinstate Hadi's sovereignty by defeating Houthi militias even at the expense of committing mass atrocity crimes against the Yemeni population. According to a report published by Human Rights Watch (HRW), the Saudi-led intervention resulted in a sharp increase on the death toll up to 4,000 civilians and 7,000 wounded. Meanwhile, the coalition airstrikes have deliberately targeted public facilities involving 800 civilian casualties (HRW, 2017). The UNHRC (2018) report also affirms that the Saudi-led coalition's intervention has resulted in the highest number of civilian casualties thus strengthening the argument that the purpose of the intervention was to regain sovereign control as opposed to protecting the Yemeni population from mass atrocity crimes.

The claim that the intervention was carried out to achieve ulterior political, economic and religious motives seem to be tenable vis-à-vis credible reports. The political purpose stems from Iran's rising dominance over Yemen in view of the allegation that Iran extends support to the de facto authority of Houthi militias. This political rivalry has impelled Saudi Arabia to exert its hegemony over Yemen by intervening on behalf of President Hadi (Matthiesen, 2013). Matthiesen (2013) also asserts that the political rivalry is also tied with the sectarian affiliation between Saudi Arabia of Sunni influence and Iran of Shia dominance. Thus, Yemen's instability would adversely affect Saudi Arabia's oil exportation that passes through Yemen's ports. However, there is no cogent evidence that proves military assistance provided to the opposition group or the militarily involvement of the regional power in carrying out acts of aggression on behalf of the Houthis. Thus, this claim is tenuous and should merely remain a 'speculation' (US–DoS 12 February, 2015).

As such, the assessment of proper purpose entails us to look beyond the official assertions made by the interveners. The Saudi-led intervention couched in the language of R2P bears similarities with the military intervention in Libya, which effectuated a regime change instead of protecting the Libyan population from mass atrocity crimes (Kuperman, 2013). As Buys and Garwood-Gowers (2019, p. 27) argue, 'the perceived appropriateness (and thus, legitimacy) of the military action was bolstered by Saudi Arabia's humanitarian and R2P rhetoric, prompting perceptions that the Operation [Decisive Storm] aimed to avert the greater crime of human suffering'. Given Saudi Arabia's substandard human rights record and the casualties caused by the military operations, it is not really conceivable for the international community to believe that the intervention carried out upon Hadi's request was for the primary purpose of protecting the Yemeni population. Bearing in mind the large number of civilian casualties and the claim that the intervention was requested to prevent Iran's hegemonic influence—which was supporting the Houthi rebels in Yemen (Kutsch, 2015)—we may assert that the primary purpose was to reinstate Hadi's sovereignty.

In view of the 'last resort' criterion, if the alleged acts committed by Houthi aggression amounted to 'threats of mass atrocity crimes', preventive deployment under Pillar Two or measures short of use of force under Pillar Three would have been prioritised over military intervention. Tzimas (2018) asserts that in the light of the peaceful political transition comprising of all key internal actors prior to the issuance of invitation, President Hadi should have requested for a UNSC mandate to 'establish peacekeeping and peace-building mission' (p. 181). Hence, Hadi's invitation should have entailed establishing preventive deployment to ensure that the peace plans are abided by the Houthis and at the same time to steer clear of military escalation that could lead to mass atrocity crimes. However, since Hadi and the Saudi-led coalition have resorted to military intervention even though the situation did not require such a coercive 'timely and decisive response', we may argue that the use of force was not employed as a 'last resort'.

In terms of proportionality, again there are important concerns. The Saudi-led coalition became embroiled in the Yemeni crisis on 26 March 2015. The initial response was the launching of Operation Decisive Storm wherein Saudi Arabia took the lead whilst receiving assistance from other Arab countries.[7] It is alleged that the coalition included 'indiscriminate use of airstrikes and attacks using surface-to-surface missile' (Strategic Comments). According to the UNHRC report, this operation went on for less than a month with the objective of undermining the Houthi's stronghold by targeting their 'ballistic missile capabilities, troop concentrations, leadership locations, military camps and arms depots' (UNHRC, 2018) but the reality on the ground was proven otherwise as the air attacks seemed to have also targeted non-combatants (Strategic Comments, 2017). The first mission began with naval operations with the objective of completely obstructing military vessels from entering territorial waters of Yemen (Fink, 2017). To achieve this, an intensive air campaign was carried out with unceasing shelling of the Houthi targets to effectively weaken their authority (Orkaby, 2015). On 22 April 2015, this operation formally came to a close upon attaining its military objectives (Ruys & Ferro, 2016).

In terms of its legitimacy, the launching of this operation received general approval and acquiescence from the international community except for Iran and Russia. In July 2015, the UK expressed its approval in the following words: The 'Operation has a clear and lawful basis in response to President Hadi's request' (UK–GFCO, 2015). Germany, Japan and Turkey followed suit (Buys & Garwood-Gowers, 2019), while several UN Member States, such as China,[8] acquiesced to it. However, given that Resolution 2216 does not mention anything about the operation, the UNSC's silence can thus be interpreted as acquiescing to the operation (UNSC, 2015f). On the other hand, Iran and Russia strongly condemned the Operation, with Iran describing it as 'flagrant defiance of the most basic principles of international law, flouting the purposes and principles of the Charter of the United Nations, in particular the obligation to refrain from the threat or use of force in international relations' (UNSC, 2015a).

[7] Sudan, Egypt and Senegal undertook deployment of ground troops whereas the other GCC member states pledged up to 30 fighter jets. Furthermore, Egypt provided naval support, while the US and the United Kingdom (UK) provided 'intelligence and logistical support'. At the same time, Somalia allowed the use of its territory to assist the operation (Ruys & Ferro, 2016).

[8] For instance, China stated that it was concerned with the humanitarian crisis in Yemen and urged all actors to act accordingly (CMFA, 2015).

At the end of the Operation Decisive Storm, the coalition initiated Operation Renewal of Hope 'at the request of the legitimate government of Yemen' with the main objective of facilitating political and humanitarian process in addition to protecting 'the Yemeni population from Houthi aggression' (UNSC, 2018, p. 18). Despite the claim that the military bombardment ended, there were reports alleging that the coalition resumed its military onslaught to use force 'as necessary' against the Houthis under the disguise of 'Renewal of Hope' (Nußberger, 2017). In July 2015, with the launching of Operation Golden Arrow, the balances in the Yemeni conflict changed in favour of Hadi's government as the weapons used, such as heavy artillery and military tanks, were influential enough to allow the coalition to regain control of the Houthi strongholds (Ruys & Ferro, 2016).

The data gathered by the Yemen Data Project indicate that the Saudi-led air campaign was 'severe' as there were roughly 18,000 raids carried out from 1 March 2015 to 30 June 2018 (UNHRC, 2018). On 12 May 2015, the deteriorating humanitarian crisis and pressure from the international community compelled the coalition to agree to a five-day humanitarian ceasefire contingent upon the Houthis honouring the agreement (Black, 2015). The UNHRC (2018) Report further asserts that the coalition's air campaigns 'have been and continue to be the leading direct cause of civilian deaths' (p. 38). Additionally, the targets of coalition airstrikes are also questionable given that they hit 'residential areas, markets, funerals, weddings, detention facilities, civilian boats and even medical facilities' (UNHRC, 2018, p. 6).[9]

Since there is no established evidence proving mass atrocity crimes committed against the Yemeni population at the time when the invitation was issued, the operations launched by the Saudi-led coalition thus can be considered as disproportionate vis-à-vis the existing situation. Additionally, given the high number of civilian casualties resulting from these operations, the force used also contravenes the proportionality criterion. If the invited interveners have assumed the UN's responsibility as representatives of the international community, they are also responsible to

[9] In another report published by HRW, it is categorically affirmed that the 'coalition has conducted scores of indiscriminate and disproportionate airstrikes killing thousands of civilians and hitting civilian objects in violation of the laws of war, using munitions sold by the United States, the United Kingdom, and others, including widely banned cluster ammunition' (HRW, 2018, p. 1).

assess whether the situation on the ground necessitates a military intervention to either prevent or react to real or potential mass atrocity crimes. Since they have failed to adopt proportionate measures in meeting the alleged threat in question, the Saudi-led interveners have evidently failed to satisfy this criterion.

This leads us to the question of reasonable chance of success—i.e. the balance of consequences—in carrying out the intervention. The Saudi-led coalition as invited interveners should have known that if they were to pursue 'Operation Decisive Storm' entailing indiscriminate airstrikes in Yemen in addition to the disproportionate deployment of armed forces, the consequence would undoubtedly be worse than inaction. This argument is also tenable in view of the available evidence as established above wherein the collateral damage inflicted as a direct result of the intervention did not only exacerbate the conflict but also led to the actual commission of mass atrocity crimes against the Yemeni population. This has been affirmed by UN Human Rights Experts who reported that the Saudi-led coalition has committed acts amounting to war crimes in view of the sharp rise on civilian death toll (UNHRC, 2018). Furthermore, since the alleged acts of violence perpetrated by the Houthis did not involve any civilian casualties prior to intervention, a reasonable assessment would have undoubtedly pointed to unsuccessful military action in meeting the slight threat in question.[10] To answer the UN Secretary-General's question, the consequences of the Saudi-led operations are arguably much worse than the consequences of inaction. In this regard, the Saudi-led interveners have also failed to satisfy the necessities of the balance of consequences criteria.

In this vein, the available information on the Saudi-led intervention points towards a contravention of all *jus ad bellum* guidelines proposed in the 2004 Report. As a corollary, the Saudi-led coalition has failed to uphold its responsibility to protect on behalf of the international community. It is noteworthy that the adverse ramifications of the Saudi-led intervention did not only contravene proposed guidelines but also International Humanitarian Law. UN Human Rights Council reported that the Saudi-led coalition has intentionally targeted the destruction of 'medical facilities and educational, cultural and religious sites', with at least

[10] The situation bears a similarity with Libya. As Kuperman (2013, p. 207) claims, the military intervention has further prolonged the conflict by 30 weeks in Libya while it has 'multiplied the deaths in Tripoli and Misurata about tenfold'.

32 reported incidents since the launching of the 'Operation Decisive Storm' (UNHRC, 2018, p. 6). To make matters worse, the coalition has also conscripted child soldiers specifically from Darfur into the armed forces (Kirkpatrick, 2018). The Panel of Experts on Yemen affirmed that these acts have violated not only International Humanitarian Law but also International Human Rights Law and amounted to war crimes (UNHRC, 2018, p. 13). In a deliberate attempt to use 'starvation as a method of warfare', the coalition's obstruction of humanitarian assistance into Yemen has further exacerbated the situation rendering it as the 'worst humanitarian crisis in the world' (ICJ, 2018; UNHRC, 2019). While the question of the consequences of intervention is beyond the scope of this Chapter, it is important to note that this is another aspect that requires special focus in relation to the reasonable prospects criterion.

Conclusion

Building on the three-pillar implementation strategy of R2P, this Chapter revealed that there were several attempts by various stakeholders in upholding the responsibility to protect the Yemeni population. Despite the ultimate collapse of peacebuilding initiatives and mediation efforts, Pillar One and Two responsibilities were carried out by the incumbent governments with assistance rendered by the international community to the best of their ability. However, this Chapter also reveals that there were serious problems with regard to implementation under Pillar Three. It can be observed that the aggravated humanitarian crisis in Yemen stems from the failure of the Saudi-led interveners to embed the R2P mindset into their actions. This includes the lack of adherence to the prerequisites on the use of force vis-à-vis Pillar Three. The precipitating events leading to the commission of atrocity crimes in Yemen took place when the Saudi-led interveners misused the R2P doctrine to restore Hadi's sovereignty. Under normal circumstances, although a 'swift' Saudi-led intervention grounded on the IvI doctrine may have circumvented the dilemma of the 'political deadlock of the UNSC', the lack of accountability mechanisms on invited interveners appears to be the underlying issue that was similarly faced by the UNSC in the Libyan crisis.

Accordingly, I argue that the lack of a true implementation of R2P, and the interveners' failure to adhere to the proposed guidelines on the use of force have further exacerbated the Yemeni crisis as proven by the high number of civilian casualties as it did in the case of Libya. Hence, the consequences of action have been worse than inaction. The Yemeni case demonstrates that although the R2P norm is essentially focused on protecting the population from atrocity crimes, the failure of the UNSC to oversee the operations carried out by the Saudi-led interveners have contributed to the excessive use of force, eventually resulting in a humanitarian catastrophe. It is noteworthy that the UNSC addressed the military intervention approximately three weeks after the first operation was launched. In Resolution 2216, whilst noting the request from Yemen for military support and the response letter by the regional forces, the UNSC did not raise any issues regarding the unauthorised use of force by the interveners (UNSC, 2015f). In this regard, my contention is that the UNSC has failed to uphold its Pillar Three responsibility as the WSOD explicitly states that the UN is 'prepared to take collective action, in a timely and decisive manner, through the Security Council, in accordance with the Charter, including Chapter VII…' (UNGA, 2005).

Furthermore, the lack of accountability mechanisms has also gravely contributed to the worsening of the Yemeni crisis. While the ICISS Report underscored the issue of the lack of accountability with reference to the case of Somalia, this was subsequently dropped in the WSOD and later UN reports on R2P. With reference to the ICISS Report, the discussion on sovereignty of states is tied to the accountability aspect internally and internationally (ICISS, 2001, p. 11). However, there seems to be a chasm between the State's and the international community's responsibilities regarding their accountability for their actions. As in the case of Libya, this pivotal issue remains the crux of the unrestrained use of force.[11]

The case of Yemen clearly demonstrates that this issue will persist and eventually continue to discredit R2P if the international community is not subjected to the same level of accountability as individual States. As a concluding remark, I would like to reiterate Sussman and Nicolaidis's (2016, p. 17) proposal:

> Imagine if every R2P intervention required a follow-up evaluation one year after atrocities began, in which a public hearing held at the United Nations would scrutinise the ways the international community had chosen to act,

[11] It should be reminded that the foregoing analysis is limited to the initial phase of the Saudi-led intervention in 2015, in line with the scope of the three-pillar implementation of R2P.

or not act as the case may be. It would hear testimonies from citizens on the ground, legal experts, journalists who covered the intervention, as well of course as those who led it. Supporters and critics of the intervention would be able to make their case–or their mea culpa.

All in all, the case of Yemen leaves us with questions of accountability not only for the States but also for the international community, as well as reconsideration of the 'five basic criteria of legitimacy' for responsible use of force under R2P.

References

Arimatsu, L., & Choudbury, M. (2014). *The legal classification of the armed conflicts in Syria, Yemen and Libya*. The Chatham House.

Arraf, S. (2017). *The armed conflict in Yemen: A complicated Mosaic* (The War Report 2017). Geneva Academy.

Black, I. (2015). Yemen conflict continues despite Saudi Arabia claiming to have ended campaign. *The Guardian*. https://www.theguardian.com/world/2015/apr/22/yemen-crisis-air-strike-hits-adenafter-saudiarabia-ends-bombing-campaign. Accessed 8 November 2020.

Boucek, C. (2010). Yemen: Avoiding a downward spiral. In C. Boucek & M. Ottaway (Eds.), *Yemen on the brink* (pp. 1–30). The Carnegie Endowment.

Brehony, N. (2011). *Yemen divided: The story of a failed state in South Arabia*. I.B. Tauris.

Buys, E., & Garwood-Gowers, A. (2019). The (Ir)relevance of human suffering: Humanitarian intervention and Saudi Arabia's operation decisive storm in Yemen. *Journal of Conflict & Security Law, 24*(1), 1–33.

China Ministry of Foreign Affairs (CMFA). (2015). *Foreign ministry spokesperson Hua Chunying's regular press conference*. Foreign Ministry People's Republic of China. www.fmprc.gov.cn/mfa_eng/xwfw665399/s2510_665401/t1248965.shtml. Accessed 15 March 2021.

Clausen, M.-L. (2018). Competing for control over the state: The case of Yemen. *Small Wars & Insurgencies, 29*(3), 560–578.

Dingli, S. (2013). Is the failed state thesis analytically useful? The case of Yemen. *Politics, 33*(2), 91–100.

Fink, M. D. (2017). Naval blockade and the humanitarian crisis in Yemen. *Netherlands International Law Review, 64*(2), 291–307.

Fox, G. H. (2015). Intervention by Invitation. In M. Weller (Ed.), *The oxford handbook of the use of force in international law*. Oxford: Oxford University Press.

Hathaway, O. A., Brower, J., Liss, R., Thomas, T., & Victor, J. (2013). Consent-based humanitarian intervention: Giving sovereign responsibility back to the sovereign. *Cornell International Law Journal, 46*(3), 499–568.

Hathaway, O. A., Haviland, A., Kethireddy, S. R., & Yamamoto, A. T. (2018). Yemen: Is the U.S. breaking the law? *Harvard National Security Journal, 10*, 1–74.

Human Rights Watch (HRW). (2017). *Yemen: Events of 2016* (World report 2017). https://www.hrw.org/world-report/2017/country-chapters/yemen. Accessed 21 September 2020.

Human Rights Watch (HRW). (2018). *Yemen: Events of 2017* (World report 2018). https://www.hrw.org/world-report/2018/country-chapters/yemen. Accessed 21 September 2020.

International Commission on Intervention and State Sovereignty (ICISS). (2001). *The responsibility to protect*. http://responsibilitytoprotect.org/ICISS%20Report.pdf. Accessed 15 May 2020.

International Commission of Jurists (ICJ). (2018). *Bearing the brunt of war in Yemen: International Law violations and their impact on the civilian population*. A Briefing Paper. http://www.icj.org/wp-content/uploads/2018/09/Yemen-War-impact-on-populations-Advocacy-Analysis-Brief-2018-ENG.pdf. Accessed 11 February 2021.

International Crisis Group (ICG). (2012). *Yemen: Enduring conflicts, threatened transition*. Crisis Group. https://www.crisisgroup.org/middle-east-north-africa/gulf-and-arabian-peninsula/yemen/yemen-enduring-conflicts-threatened-transition. Accessed 14 January 2021.

Kahwati, A. A. (2019). *Peace in Yemen*. The Swedish Institute of International Affairs. https://www.ui.se/globalassets/ui.se-eng/publications/ui-publications/2019/ui-paper-no.-5-2019.pdf. Accessed 22 February 2021.

Kirkpatrick, D. (2018). On the front line of the Saudi war in Yemen: Child Soldiers from Darfur. *The New York Times*. https://www.nytimes.com/2018/12/28/world/africa/saudi-sudan-yemen-child-fighters.html. Accessed 23 March 2021.

Kuperman, A. J. (2013). NATO's intervention in Libya: A humanitarian success. In A. Hehir & R. W. Murray (Eds.), *Libya, the responsibility to protect and the future of humanitarian intervention* (pp. 191–221). Palgrave Macmillan.

Kutsch, T. (2015). US says Houthis "obviously" receive Iran support, but experts not so sure. *Al Jazeera America*. http://america.aljazeera.com/articles/2015/4/10/kerry-accuses-iran-of-yemen-meddling-but-level-of-its-support-un-clear.html. Accessed 14 February 2021.

Matthiesen, T. (2013). *Sectarian Gulf: Bahrain, Saudi Arabia, and the Arab Spring That Wasn't*. Stanford University Press.

Nußberger, B. (2017). Military strikes in Yemen in 2015: Intervention by invitation and self-defence in the course of Yemen's 'model transitional process.' *Journal on the Use of Force and International Law, 4*(1), 110–160.

Orkaby, A. (2015). Yemen's humanitarian nightmare. *Foreign Affairs*. https://www.foreignaffairs.com/articles/yemen/2017-10-16/yemens-humanitarian-nightmare. Accessed 18 January 2021.

Popp, R. (2015). War in Yemen: Revolution and Saudi intervention. *CSS Analyses in Security Policy, 175*, 1–5.

Ruys, T., & Ferro, L. (2016). Weathering the storm: Legality and legal implications of the Saudi-led military intervention in Yemen. *International and Comparative Law Quarterly, 65*(1), 61–98.

Saudi Embassy. (2015). *Statement by Saudi ambassador Al-Jubeir on military operations in Yemen*. The Embassy of the Kingdom of Saudi Arabia: Press Releases. https://www.saudiembassy.net/press-release/statement-saudi-ambassador-al-jubeir-military-operations-yemen. Accessed 29 June 2021.

Strategic Comments. (2017). The percolating proxy war in Yemen. *Strategic Comments, 23*(1), iv–vi.

Sussman, S., & Nicolaidis, K. (2016). R2P: "State of play." *The International Spectator, 51*(2), 9–18.

The Armed Conflict Location & Event Data Project (ACLED). (2020). *Research hub: War in Yemen*. Yemen data project. https://acleddata.com/research-hub-war-in-yemen/. Accessed 29 March 2021.

Tzimas, T. (2018). Legal evaluation of the Saudi-Led intervention in Yemen. *Zaörv, 78*, 147–187.

UK Government Foreign and Commonwealth Office (UK–GFCO). (2015). *Yemen–in-year update July 2015. Corporate report*. www.gov.uk/government/publications/yemen-in-year-update-july-2015/yemen-in-year-update july-2015. Accessed 9 January 2021.

United Nations (UN). (2014). *Framework of analysis for atrocity crimes: A tool for prevention*. http://www.un.org/en/genocideprevention/documents/about-usDoc3.FrameworkofAnalysisforAtrocityCrimes_EN.pdf. Accessed 7 January 2021.

United Nations General Assembly (UNGA). (2004). *A more secure world: Our shared responsibility: Report of the high-level panel on threats, challenges and change*. Report of the Secretary-General, A/59/565.

United Nations General Assembly (UNGA). (2005). *Resolution adopted by the general assembly on 16 September 2005: '60/1. 2005 World Summit Outcome'*, A/Res/60/1.

United Nations General Assembly–Security Council (UNGA–SC). (2011). *Responsibility while protecting: Elements for the development and promotion of a concept*. A/66/551–S/2011/701.

United Nations General Assembly–Security Council (UNGA–SC). (2013). *Responsibility to protect: State responsibility and prevention*. Report of the Secretary-General, A/67/929–S/2013/399.

United Nations General Assembly–Security Council (UNGA–SC). (2014). *Fulfilling our collective responsibility: International assistance and the responsibility to protect*. Report of the Secretary-General, A/68/947–S/2014/449.

United Nations Human Rights Council (UNHRC). (2018). *Situation of human rights in Yemen, including violations and abuses since September 2014*. Report of the United Nations High Commissioner for Human Rights. A/HRC/39/43.

United Nations Human Rights Council (UNHRC). (2019). *Yemen: Collective failure, collective responsibility–UN expert report*. Feature stories. https://www.ohchr.org/EN/HRBodies/HRC/Pages/NewsDetail.aspx?NewsID=24937&LangID=E. Accessed 11 June 2021.

United Nations News (UN News). (2015). Secretary-General appoints Ismail Ould Cheikh Ahmed as new special envoy for yemen. https://news.un.org/en/story/2015/04/497042-secretary-general-appoints-ismail-ould-cheikh-ahmed-newsspecial-envoy-yemen. Accessed 21 December 2020.

United Nations News (UN News). (2019). *Humanitarian crisis in Yemen remains the worst in the world, warns UN*. Humanitarian Aid. https://news.un.org/en/story/2019/02/1032811. Accessed 29 February 2021.

United Nations Security Council (UNSC). (2011). *Resolution 2014* (2011). S/RES/2014.

United Nations Security Council (UNSC). (2012). *Resolution 2051 (2012)*. S/RES/2051.

United Nations Security Council (UNSC). (2014). Resolution 2140 (2014). S/RES/2140.

United Nations Security Council (UNSC). (2015a). *Annex to the Letter dated 17 April 2015 from the Permanent Representative of the Islamic Republic of Iran to the United Nations Addressed to the Security Counci*l Doc S/2015/263.

United Nations Security Council (UNSC). (2015b). *Identical letters dated 26 March 2015 from the Permanent Representative of Qatar to the United Nations addressed to the Secretary-General and the President of the Security Council.* S/2015/217.

United Nations Security Council (UNSC). (2015c). *Letter dated 20 February 2015 from the Panel of Experts on Yemen established pursuant to Security Council resolution 2140 (2014) addressed to the President of the Security Council*. S/2015/125.

United Nations Security Council (UNSC). (2015d). *Record of UN Security Council Meeting 7411*. UN Doc S/PV.7411.

United Nations Security Council (UNSC). (2015e). *Resolution 2201 (2015)*. S/RES/2201.

United Nations Security Council (UNSC). (2015f). *Resolution 2216 (2015)*. S/RES/2216.

United Nations Security Council (UNSC). (2018). *Final report of the Panel of Experts on Yemen*. S/2018/594.

United States Department of State (US–DoS). (2015). *Daily press briefing*. https://2009-2017.state.gov/r/pa/prs/dpb/2015/02/237453.html. Accessed 13 July 2021.

Winter, L. (2011). Conflict in Yemen: Simple people, complicated circumstances. *Middle East Policy, 18*(1), 102–120.

Wintour, P. (2017). Yemen Houthi rebels kill former president Ali Abdullah Saleh. *The Guardian*. https://www.theguardian.com/world/2017/dec/04/former-yemen-president-saleh-killed-in-fresh-fighting. Accessed 1 August 2020

WFP and FAO. (2021). *Hunger Hotspots. FAO-WFP early warnings on acute food insecurity: August to November 2021 outlook*. http://www.fao.org/3/cb6054en/cb6054en.pdf. Accessed 5 September 2021.

CHAPTER 10

Afghanistan: An R2P Concern

Sevgi Balkan-Şahin

The engagement of a large coalition of international forces, most notably the United Nations (UN), North Atlantic Treaty Organization (NATO), the United States (US) and the European Union (EU) in Afghanistan following the 9/11 terrorist attacks coincided with the emergence of the Responsibility to Protect (R2P) norm in 2001. Although R2P has not been invoked in the Afghan case, the large-scale political, financial and military support provided by the international community, as well as the comprehensive capacity-building measures taken by the Afghan governments since 2001 to transform the country into a self-sustained democratic state that is capable of protecting its population mirrors many aspects of R2P, which are reflected in the 2009 Report of the UN Secretary-General on implementing the responsibility to protect. In this vein, from an R2P lens, this chapter examines the case of Afghanistan wherein the population has been suffering from mass atrocities due to the breakdown of the central authority, the devastation of the national economy, and external interference by regional and global actors after decades-long armed conflict (Rubin, 2020).

S. Balkan-Şahin (✉)
Department of International Relations, Çağ University, Tarsus, Turkey

P. Gözen Ercan (ed.), *The Responsibility to Protect Twenty Years On*,
https://doi.org/10.1007/978-3-030-90731-0_10

The legacy of the nineteenth century British-Russian competition over the control of Central Asia, the 1979 Soviet occupation, the ethnic/regional civil war and the 2001 military intervention led by the US to topple the Taliban regime had laid the seeds of the ongoing violence in Afghanistan. Particularly with the rise of the Taliban insurgency, both security and human rights conditions have deteriorated in Afghanistan, claiming the lives of more than 150,000 Afghans by 2019 (Watson Institute, 2019). Due to the deterioration of health services, infrastructure and security under the extensive use of air strikes and night raids on residential areas in pursuit of suspected insurgents, 43,000 civilians were killed (Watson Institute, 2019). Being exposed to the detrimental impact of the armed conflict, children and women amounted to an important bulk of these civilian casualties (UNAMA, 2020a, p. 6; UNGA–UNSC, 2020a). The endurance of the conflict has also led to the emergence of 2.6 million registered refugees from Afghanistan (Amnesty International, 2019). The February 2019 US-Taliban peace deal wherein the US committed to withdraw its forces over a 14-month period and the Taliban's engagement in intra-Afghan peace talks in September 2020 seem to have opened a more peaceful future for the country. Nevertheless, from an R2P perspective, under the complex and unstable political, economic and security environment in Afghanistan, a large number of civilians remain under the threat of mass atrocity crimes. With the Taliban's use of residential areas for military purposes, its intentional targeting of civilians in health centres, markets or schools, as well as its use of sexual abuse as a tool of war and prevention of humanitarian agencies' access to areas under its control have considerably weakened the Afghan government's ability to ensure individuals' security (UNAMA, 2020b). The ongoing chaotic situation in Afghanistan makes this chapter a timely contribution for examining the implementation of the R2P norm pillar-by-pillar in a complex conflict situation such as the Afghan case.

To this end, after providing a brief background on the protracted armed conflict in which mass atrocities that have been committed by various state and non-state actors in Afghanistan, focusing on Pillar One, this chapter studies the measures the Afghan governments have taken to improve their capacity to protect the Afghan population and the level of its failure to uphold R2P since 2001. Then, focusing on Pillar Two, it examines the international community's preventive response(s) to a war-torn country suffering from severe human rights abuses. Finally, this chapter concludes that to improve the country's capacity to achieve stable and self-sustaining political, economic and security structures that can survive the withdrawal of external support, Afghanistan should develop a national ownership of R2P while the international community, in a complementary manner, should privilege the implementation of Pillar Two besides embarking on competing objectives such as counterterrorism.

Background

Considering Afghanistan as a buffer zone for the protection of their respective imperial interests, the Great Britain and Russia engaged in a geopolitical struggle, better known as 'The Great Game' in Afghan territories in the nineteenth century (Barfield, 2010). Britain intended to control Afghanistan to prevent any potential Russian occupation of India and nearby territories crucial for British naval and trade interests. Motivated by a similar desire to prevent any potential invasion of its territories by Britain through India, and to expand its trade interests into Eastern Asia, Russia confronted Britain over Afghanistan (Berkowitz, 2007; Rashid, 2000). As of the second half of the twentieth century, the British–Russian Great Game was replaced by the American and Soviet confrontation over Afghanistan under the Cold War conditions. Particularly, after the December 1979 Soviet invasion of Afghanistan to ensure the consolidation of the Afghan communist regime—i.e. the Democratic Republic of Afghanistan—the magnitude of the new Great Game between the two superpowers intensified. Threatened by a potential Soviet incursion into the Middle East that would endanger US oil interests in the region, the US extended support to Afghan resistance groups, namely the so-called Mujahedeen to expel the Soviet Union from Afghanistan (Rashid, 2000).

The US and its collaborators, including Saudi Arabia and Pakistan, engaged in strengthening the jihadi groups that emerged as a reaction to foreign occupation by a non-Muslim country (Rashid, 2000). The collaboration between the American and Pakistani intelligence agencies provided the jihadi groups with military equipment, logistical supplies and financial means. Moreover, the Central Intelligence Agency (CIA)'s training of new fighters recruited from the large Afghan population in Pakistani refugee camps provided Mujahedeen with a constant flow of manpower to fight against the Soviet army. With the financial and military assistance of the Western powers and their allies, the Afghan jihadi fighters succeeded in their insurgency against the Soviet forces that suffered heavy casualties. Given its economic and military decline by the end of the 1980s, unable to continue fighting the Soviet Union, the US withdrew from Afghanistan in accordance with the Geneva Accords concluded in 1988 (Barfield, 2010).

The Soviet occupation of Afghanistan created heavy political, economic and social upheavals that still have a paralysing impact on Afghanistan today (Rubin, 2020). While the destruction of critical infrastructures and agricultural lands of the country devastated the Afghan economy, the Soviet occupation also led to the flow of millions of Afghan refugees to Pakistan and Iran (Rubin, 2020). Moreover, the death of tribal and traditional religious leaders coupled with the escape of urban and educated peoples of the Afghan society throughout the Afghan-Soviet war created a political vacuum at the national and regional levels. The urban elites' loss of power on regional areas paved the way for the emergence of an illicit narcotics economy as well as an ethnic and tribal turmoil in the following years.

Given the ethnically divided composure of the society, ethnic conflict has been an inescapable part of Afghan political history. Out of the 14 major ethnic groups recognised by the Afghan Constitution, it has been the Pashtuns—the largest ethnic group in the country—that predominantly controlled national power since the establishment of the Afghan state in the mid-eighteenth century (Barfield, 2011; Riphenburg, 2005). Overall, along with the Pashtuns (38%), the Tajiks (25%), Hazaras (19%) and Uzbeks (6%) constitute almost 90% of the population (Riphenburg, 2005). Being exposed to intra-group divisions within itself, the Pashtuns historically tried to dominate non-Pashtun ethnic groups in Afghanistan. The confrontation between Pashtun and non-Pashtun ethnic groups created centuries old instability in the country (Barfield, 2011). Although various rival ethnic and tribal groups had united throughout the Afghan-Soviet war, the national unity quickly faded soon after the invader withdrew from Afghanistan, opening space for a full scale inter-ethnic struggle for power (Barfield, 2011).

The ethnic and tribal divisions made it impossible for the interim government established under the 1992 Peshawar Accord to function properly. Aspiring a Pashtun-dominated Afghanistan, the Pashtuns refused to sign the Accord that reflected a power-sharing agreement with the Tajik and Uzbek groups. The ensuing inter-ethnic violence after the fracturing of the interim government led to the death of thousands of

Afghan people, widespread human rights violations, and consequently, the emergence of millions of internally displaced people (IDPs) as well as refugee flows to Pakistan and Iran (Rashid, 2000). The lack of a central government capable of enforcing its authority nationwide coupled with the drug-based economy supported by warring factions led to the emergence of the Taliban that enforced its authority throughout Afghanistan (Rashid, 2000).

Through the indoctrination of many Pashtun refugees against Western norms in its madrassas and refugee camps, Pakistan played a crucial role in the emergence of the Taliban in 1994 (Barfield, 2010). The Taliban grew stronger quickly and outpaced various warlords in the struggle for power thanks to the modern military equipment, intelligence, as well as logistical and financial support provided by Pakistan (Rashid, 2000). After capturing Kabul in 1996, the Taliban established the Islamic Emirate of Afghanistan as a centralised and authoritarian regime based on a strict interpretation of Sharia Law embedded in Wahhabi principles. In 1998, the Taliban became powerful enough to control 90% of the Afghan territory (Goodson, 2001). The rising power of the Taliban triggered further ethnic and tribal cleavages in Afghanistan.

Under the Taliban's rule, the economic situation deteriorated considerably. As the Taliban replaced qualified administrators and employees of previous governments with unqualified but loyal staff, the devastated Afghan economy under decades of war took a further blow. In order to strengthen its power militarily and financially, the Taliban supported drug trade, and this led to the collapse of formal economy. Moreover, imposing radical social rules, the Taliban urged women to cover all parts of their body, banned women's participation in public life on their own without male family members accompanying them and banned their access to education. Men were required to grow a beard, while recreational activities, including listening to music, watching TV or sports were prohibited (Goodson, 2001). The Taliban's repressive regime had to come to an end when in 2001 the US and its allies invaded Afghanistan under the war on terror they initiated in response to the 9/11 attacks by Al-Qaida.

The Protection Responsibilities of the Afghan State

An analysis of the situation in Afghanistan from an R2P lens requires a twofold approach. In this regard, before focusing on the efforts of the international community and various external actors, first there is need to address the primary responsibility of the State to prevent its population from genocide, war crimes, crimes against humanity and ethnic cleansing. Hence, this section examines to what extent Afghanistan has developed a capacity to fulfil its Pillar One responsibilities. After the US-led military intervention which ousted the Taliban regime, with the 2001 Bonn Agreement that established a roadmap, arguably the capacity of the Afghan government to enforce its authority and fulfil its responsibilities towards the population has increased. With this agreement, Afghanistan assumed the responsibility to establish an interim government and adopt a consensus-based constitution that would lay the foundation of a legitimate democratic state (Murray, 2011). After intense debates over the role of religion, protection of fundamental rights, as well as power-sharing at the national and local levels, Afghanistan adopted its constitution in 2004. By organising presidential and parliamentary elections, reforming its judicial system and establishing crucial institutions, such as the independent human rights commission, the government showed its determination to increase its capacity to govern responsibly.

The adoption of the 2005 Afghanistan Compact that ensured the support of the international community to help Afghanistan achieve a comprehensive progress in security, governance, development and the transformation of the drug-based economy served as an important stimulus for rebuilding the country (ANDS, 2008). To achieve the targets outlined in the Compact, in 2008 Afghanistan National Development Strategy (ANDS) was put in action. Founded on the three pillars of security, governance, and economic and social development, the ANDS aimed at consolidating law enforcement and democratic institutions nationwide, tackling widespread poverty, endorsing sustainable development and ensuring the security of all citizens (ANDS, 2008).

An important step undertaken to strengthen the capacity of the country to fulfil the state's Pillar One responsibility has been the empowerment of the Afghan security forces since 2001. With the support of the international community, both the Afghan National Army and Afghan National Police were offered extensive training and most of the former fighters were either demobilised and disarmed or embedded into the Ministry of Defence (ANDS, 2008). In addition to military and police reforms, substantial measures were taken to modernise the judicial system and strengthen the efforts to fight against the narcotics industry. Moreover, investments made for improving the infrastructural conditions in rural and urban areas enabled easier access to education and health services, employment opportunities as well as social services. Such measures increased the prospects for political and economic stability, which in turn led to the return of many Afghan refugees to their country (ANDS, 2008). As noted in the Afghanistan National Peace and Development Framework 2017–2021 (ANPDF, 2016), Afghanistan also achieved significant progress in increasing school enrolment rates, life expectancy and access to clean water.

Such achievements are quite impressive compared to the desperate security, economic and political conditions of the country prior to the 2001 intervention. Various UN Secretary-General reports on R2P highlight the responsibility of the State to prioritise atrocity prevention, and thus, strengthen its resilience to pre-emptively address root causes of tension before they escalate (UNGA–UNSC, 2013, 2015, 2019). The Secretary-General, for instance, puts forward structural and operational measures needed for building national resilience, such as preventing political and gender discrimination, strengthening women, creating a dynamic civil society, fostering an independent press, ending sexual violence and holding perpetrators responsible, and reforming the justice and the security sector in a way to ensure that law enforcers respect human rights (UNGA–UNSC, 2013, pp. 6–14; 2019, pp. 5–7; 2020b, pp. 2–3). In this regard, continued progress would help the State authorities to uphold their responsibility towards the Afghan population. Nevertheless, after almost two decades of international engagement to support the Afghan government militarily and financially, the mounting violence committed by anti-government forces, notably the Taliban, the perseverance of the drug-based economy that finances extremist fractions of society, the prevalence of corruption, poor investment prospects for the private sector, increasing unemployment and migration flows, as well as dependency on foreign aid (Berdal, 2019) pose a great threat to the ability of the Afghan government to fulfil its Pillar One responsibilities in a sustainable manner.

Despite being overthrown with the 2001 military intervention, by mobilising Pashtun nationalism, the Taliban re-emerged as an anti-government force composed of various local tribal networks—including the Quetta Shura (remnants of the Taliban led by Mullah Omar), a fraction led by a former jihadi prime minister, Gulbuddin Hekmatyar, and the Pakistan-based Haqqani network (Murray, 2011, p. 44). Particularly, after the end of the NATO-led International Security Assistance Force (ISAF) mission that led to a substantial reduction of foreign troops in 2014, the Taliban began to exert its influence in almost half of the country. With the resumption of the Taliban insurgency as well as the rising attacks of the Afghan branch of the Islamic State, the Afghan security forces have been able to exert their authority only in less than 60% of the Afghan territory (Rahman, 2019, p. 88). Almost two and a half million Afghans live in areas under the control of the Taliban while nine million live in contested areas leading to the suffering of civilians, financial devastation and continuance of human rights abuses, specifically violations against women's rights (Rahman, 2019, p. 88; UNAMA, 2020b, p. 21).

As Taliban engaged in targeted attacks on civilians, civilian casualties surged in Afghanistan. Almost 6000 civilians were either killed or injured between January and October 2020 (UNAMA, 2020a, p. 1). The Taliban continued its military campaign against civilians even after it engaged in peace talks with the US in December 2018. For instance, its use of suicide attacks and improvised explosive devices during political rallies before the 28 September 2019 Presidential elections led to hundreds of civilian casualties (Human Rights Watch, 2020). Just a week after concluding a peace agreement with the US on 29 February 2020, the Taliban carried out 76 attacks across 24 provinces targeting civilian-populated areas, including healthcare facilities and places of worship. Condemning such incidents as unjustifiable, the UN Special Representative for Afghanistan Tadamichi Yamamoto called for the protection of civilians from being subjected to indiscriminate attacks in the following words: 'Those who are responsible for enabling this attack must be brought to justice and held to account. These brutal and senseless attacks against people at prayer are atrocities. Such attacks at congregations and places of worship may amount to war crimes' (GCR2P, 2019).

In its special report on attacks against healthcare facilities during the COVID-19 pandemic, the UN Assistance Mission in Afghanistan (UNAMA) (2020c, p. 8) reminded the conflicting parties of their responsibility to take the necessary measures to ensure that health facilities and staff are protected from attack. Uttering the R2P language, UNAMA (2020b, p. 19) condemned targeted attacks on healthcare facilities for endangering the lives of Afghan civilians who were deprived of their right to attain physical and mental health and urged for the prioritisation of the health and well-being of Afghan citizens. UNAMA (2020c, p. 8) highlighted that attacks on healthcare facilities and staff constitute war crimes.

Accounting for seven per cent of the total civilian casualties in 2020, Islamic State-Khurasan Province (ISKP) has emerged as another anti-government force posing a great threat to the Afghan population (UNAMA, 2020a, p. 8). In 2020, hundreds of people either lost their lives or were injured in several suicide attacks committed by the ISKP at various venues such as the Dharamshala Sikh Temple in Kabul, health facilities, funerals and wedding halls (Human Rights Watch, 2020). For these civilian targeting attacks, the Taliban and the ISKP were held responsible for almost 60% of the casualties in 2020 (UNAMA, 2020a, p. 8).

From an R2P perspective, the Afghan population has also been subjected to atrocities committed by the Afghan security forces as well as international military forces during their counter attacks against the Taliban and the ISKP (UNAMA, 2020a, 2020b). The use of air strikes and night raids by NATO and Afghan security forces led to more than 1000 civilian casualties, including 100 children between January and September 2019, which led to a 45% increase compared to the previous year (GCR2P, 2019; Human Rights Watch, 2020). In 2020, in several attacks of the Afghan National Army in response to Taliban attacks in a residential area and also a busy market-place, many civilians (mostly children and women) were killed or injured. Pro-government forces were held responsible for 1640 civilian casualties—that is 28% of total number of casualties—between January and October 2020 (UNAMA, 2020a, p. 11). Both pro-government forces and Taliban were responsible for the death of more than 700 children in the same period (UNAMA, 2020a, p. 6). Another heinous crime committed both by the Taliban and Afghan national security forces has been the recruitment of child soldiers who are trained and armed for combat missions and sexual exploitation (UNAMA, 2020a, p. 7; 2020b, p. 19).

Considering Pillar One, it is the responsibility of a sovereign state to cooperate with the International Criminal Court (ICC) and other international tribunals in the apprehension of those who are accused of alleged mass atrocity crimes (UNGA, 2009). Being a party to the Rome Statute since 2003, Afghanistan has a responsibility to fulfil its duty stemming from the Rome Statute to prosecute crimes against humanity, war crimes and genocide, and to cooperate with the ICC. UNAMA () has documented torture and other forms of inhuman or degrading treatment of detainees under custody by Afghan authorities, including the National Police and the National Army, as well as the local police. Similarly, investigating the use of systemic torture against detainees in Afghanistan since 2007, the Office of the Prosecutor (OTP) of the ICC reported that both anti-government (Taliban and the Haqqani Network) and pro-government forces (Afghan security forces and international military forces) committed crimes against humanity and war crimes in Afghanistan by torturing detainees and carrying out summary executions (Hazim, 2019).

Moreover, as documented by the UN and human rights organisations, the non-accountable use of Afghan militias to defeat the Taliban and strengthen the US war on terror in Afghanistan by the CIA since 2001 has further exacerbated human rights abuses and the sufferings of the Afghan population amounting to possible war crimes (De Lauri & Suhrke, 2020). UNAMA (2019) reports the crimes committed by Afghan militias, including illegal detainment of individuals, intentional killing of civilians and damaging their property. Most of these acts failed to be investigated and prosecuted by the Afghan authorities (De Lauri & Suhrke, 2020). Although for decades anti- and pro-government forces have committed atrocities against the Afghan people, neither side has been held accountable for their crimes (Hazim, 2019).

Criticising the failure of the government of Afghanistan to bring such crimes before the ICC for holding the perpetrators accountable, international human rights groups such as the Human Rights Watch and Amnesty International demanded the trial of Taliban leaders by the ICC for alleged war crimes—including intentional targeting of health facilities and religious sites (such as mosques) as well as humanitarian aid organisations. The trial for investigating the alleged crimes committed in Afghanistan seems to have proceeded as the Appeals Chamber of the ICC approved in 2020 the request of authorisation that Chief Prosecutor Fatou Bensouda made in 2007 for investigating war crimes committed in Afghanistan since 2003.

Although the 2009 UN Secretary-General Report identifies the three pillars of R2P as having equal weight, Welsh (2016) points out the recent emphasis on the importance of State responsibility (i.e. Pillar One) when implementing R2P. The Afghan population's exposure to widespread atrocities committed by the Taliban, the Islamic State, the Afghan security forces and international military forces, as well as the failure of Afghan governments to hold the perpetrators responsible through either domestic courts or the ICC demonstrate that the State authorities' ability to fulfil their Pillar One responsibilities in a sustainable manner has not fully developed. In this regard, such insufficiency of national capacity in a complex conflict situation makes the role of the international community in helping Afghanistan live up to its responsibility to protect much more crucial under Pillar Two of R2P.

International Response, Assistance and Capacity-Building Efforts

As the UN Secretary-General establishes as to Pillar Two, the international community needs to undertake preventive measures and positive incentives to help States to protect their populations from mass atrocity crimes (UNGA, 2009). In the specific case of Afghanistan, from an R2P point of view, the necessary measures and incentives have been taken by a combination of actors, including the UN, NATO, the EU, the US-led coalition and various civil society organisations. Hence, numerous influential actors have collectively contributed to the capacity-building processes of the consecutive Afghan governments by providing military assistance, political support and development aid since the fall of the Taliban regime in 2001. In order to consolidate central governments established in the post-Taliban period, the international community has prioritised the implementation of capacity-building measures for Afghanistan where national authority has been weak and divided for decades.

The UN has played a crucial role in coordinating the international community to end the decades-long conflict in Afghanistan, toppling the Taliban regime that provided safe haven to Al-Qaeda, as well as creating a stable government strong enough to impose its authority nationwide. The UN Security Council (UNSC) (2001a; 2001b) encouraged the efforts to establish a transitional government that would support the war on terror and embark on humanitarian missions, including the organisation of the return of the refugees and IDPs. It then made a plea to the international community to participate in the efforts for the reconstruction of the post-Taliban Afghanistan and encouraged the conclusion of the Bonn Agreement (UNSC, 2001c).

The Bonn Agreement laid out the guidelines to be followed by both the Afghan government and the international community to transform Afghanistan into a stable democratic state. To help Afghanistan achieve this objective, the US, Germany, the United Kingdom, Japan and Italy assumed pioneering roles in strengthening the Afghan military forces; training the Afghan police; fighting against the narcotics industry; coordinating disarmament, demobilisation and reintegration efforts; as well as modernising the Afghan justice system, respectively (Murray, 2011, p. 47). In order to assist the Afghan interim government to maintain security in Kabul, the UNSC (2001d) authorised the establishment of ISAF. It also encouraged the initiation of a broadly participated political process for drafting a new constitution endorsed by all ethnic groups in Afghanistan (Nuruzzaman, 2009, p. 284).

In terms of the implementation of Pillar Two responsibilities, another major step taken by the UNSC (2002) was arguably the establishment of UNAMA in March 2002 to help Afghanistan increase its capacity for achieving sustainable political and economic stability. The mandate of UNAMA has so far been annually renewed in order to coordinate international civilian efforts in collaboration with the Afghan government. Most recently, UNSC Resolution 2543 (2020) assigned UNAMA with the responsibility to continue to help the Afghan government gain its financial independence and achieve full ownership over areas of security, governance and development as envisioned for the period between 2015–2024, which is referred to as the 'Transformation Decade'.

One of the crucial roles UNAMA has played in Afghanistan in terms of Pillar Two has been constantly reminding the conflicting parties of their primary responsibility under international humanitarian law to respect and protect the rights of the Afghan population and prevent incidental loss of civilian lives (UNAMA 2020b, p. 15). Endorsing the position of the UN Secretary-General emphasising the no tolerance stance for the 'dehumanizing, cruel, inhuman and degrading practice of public executions', UNAMA (2020b, p. 13) urged the Taliban 'to immediately cease imposing cruel, inhuman, or degrading punishment on individuals'. Criticising the Afghan National Army's use of weapons that have wide area effects resulting in high civilian casualties in its attack against the anti-government forces, UNAMA (2020b, p. 18) highlighted the need to restrict the use of indirect fire in civilian-populated areas in cases where anti-government forces attack from residential areas. UNAMA (2020b, p. 15) also reminded the Afghan government to act in accordance with the accountability principle by investigating the attacks that harmed civilians, to hold those who are responsible accountable and to inform the public about the whole process.

From an R2P point of view, a government should ensure the economic and social rights of the underprivileged segments of the society and minority groups (UNGA, 2009, p. 19). Accordingly, parallel to the understanding laid out in Pillar Two, UNAMA (2020b, p. 13) highlighted the need for the Afghan government to increase its capacity to provide all its citizens the right to education, the right to food, clothing and housing, the right to have access to health care services, the right to work, and the right to participate in social and cultural life. Hence, a combination of multiple donors, including the US, the EU, the World Bank and the Organization for Economic Cooperation and Development (OECD) have all engaged in providing development assistance to Afghanistan since 2001. In a study conducted through collaboration between the World Bank, the UN Development Program (UNDP) and the Asian Development Bank (ADB) in 2002, it was suggested that $9–12 billion should be provided to Afghanistan to finance the reconstruction process for five years.

Since 2002, the International Development Association (IDA) of the World Bank has provided almost $5 billion for development projects that would enable Afghanistan to achieve inclusive growth and reduce vulnerability among the underprivileged sections of the society, and thus, fulfil its primary responsibility to deliver basic services to all its population (World Bank, 2020, p. 5). The Afghanistan Reconstruction Trust Fund (ARTF) that was established in 2002 to coordinate the reconstruction efforts of the international community, and the Afghan Government have received more than $12 billion from 34 donors by February 2020. The OECD countries have also been important donors as they have provided $58 billion assistance between 2002 and 2017 for Afghanistan's reconstruction. Of this, 47% came from the US while 24% came from the EU and its Member States (Hassan, 2020, p. 87).

Foreign aid by multiple donors has led to substantial improvement in areas such as health, education, life expectancy, maternal and child mortality, as well as access to food (Rubin, 2020, p. 182). Moreover, between 1990 and 2018 the Human Development Index (HDI) value of Afghanistan increased by 66.4%, that is from 0.298 to 0.496 (UNDP, 2019, pp. 2–3). However, Afghanistan is still classified as having low human development with a rank of 170 out of 189 countries (UNDP, 2019, pp. 2–3). Despite the generous amount of development aid Afghanistan has received for almost two decades, most Afghans still have no secure access to food, water or electricity as significant parts of foreign aid have been stolen by the Taliban, warlords or government officials due to widespread corruption in the country. Afghanistan Millennium Development Goals Report indicates that only three per cent of Afghans have access to safe drinking water, 12% to adequate sanitation and six per cent to electricity. The same report notes that 40% of the Afghan population remains unemployed and another 37% suffers from hunger (UNESCO, 2010, p. 8).

As the Afghan government was still in need of international support to provide the basic needs of its population, the World Bank (2019) made a call to international donors to help Afghanistan overcome its fiscal challenges by providing a sum of $6 billion to $8 billion annually, which is crucial to finance peace in Afghanistan after the inter-Afghan peace deal with the Taliban. Such amount would contribute to the maintenance and preservation of peace by encouraging more investments for faster economic growth, increasing employment levels and decreasing violence in the country (World Bank, 2019). In its recent report, the World Bank (2020, p. 4) noted that Afghanistan needed an annual amount of $11 billion to finance its public expenditure for basic services.

The EU stands out as another crucial member of the international community that has been taking part in the stabilisation and reconstruction processes of Afghanistan in the post-Taliban era. The EU adopted European Rapid Reaction Mechanism (RRM) in Afghanistan to support the objectives envisaged in the Bonn Agreement, including the promotion of human rights, enhancing the position of Afghan women in society, supporting the delivery of humanitarian assistance to those in need and triggering rural development (Hassan, 2020). Assuming a leading role in financing development projects in Afghanistan, the EU has provided €5.1 billion for the reconstruction of the country between 2002 and 2020 (European Commission, 2020). In the EU-Afghanistan Joint Declaration adopted in 2005, the European Council (2005) declared its commitment to help Afghanistan create an economically and politically stable democratic country free from terrorist threats, radicalism and organised crime. In the Country Strategy Paper on Afghanistan (2007–2013), the European Commission (2007) declared the EU's commitment to support measures for reforming the legal system and the security sector, achieving rural development, social justice and women empowerment.

By providing soldiers to the ISAF mission and assuming responsibility in NATO's Provincial Reconstruction Teams, the EU Member States also contributed to the efforts for creating security in Afghanistan. Moreover, with the initiation of the EU Police Mission to Afghanistan (EUPOL) in 2007, the EU undertook to train Afghan police forces and judicial authorities and support Afghanistan's law enforcement efforts. In addition to its mission of ensuring Afghan police's respect to fundamental rights and the rule of law while conducting operations, the EUPOL has also been involved in designing a comprehensive anti-corruption strategy.

After the end of the NATO-led ISAF mission in 2014, the international community focused on the achievement of a permanent inter-Afghan peace, democratisation and the establishment of a prosperous society in the so-called transformation decade (2015–2024). The EU continued its commitments in Afghanistan within this framework. At the October 2016 Brussels Conference on Afghanistan, the EU and its member states pledged €5 billion out of a total of €13.6 billion in support for Afghanistan in the period between 2016 and 2020 (European Commission, 2016). With the Cooperation Agreement on Partnership and Development (CAPD) concluded with Afghanistan in 2017, the EU declared its determination to support initiatives for enhancing the rights of women and children, improving access to education, science and technology, tackling corruption, terrorism and organised crime, as well as addressing global issues including climate change (European Parliament, 2019).

Highlighting that the realisation of these objectives fully depended on the achievement of peace and security in Afghanistan, the European Council (2018) called for a sustainable resolution of the armed conflict through an inclusive Afghan-led and Afghan-owned peace process, in which the Afghan Government and the Taliban would play a crucial role. At the Geneva Ministerial Conference on Afghanistan in 2018, the EU declared its commitment to provide €474 million to help finance public sector reforms in the fields of education, health, justice and elections (European Commission, 2018).

On the other hand, invoking the collective defence obligation of the organisation—i.e. Article 5 of the Atlantic Charter—on 12 September 2001, NATO emerged as a crucial actor that helped Afghanistan increase its capacity to fulfil its responsibility to protect its population. Undertaking the command of ISAF in 2003 and assuming the mandate of ensuring security and extending the central government's authority to the whole of Afghanistan, NATO established multinational Provincial Reconstruction Teams (PRTs) that combined civilian and military objectives for achieving political and economic stability (Berdal, 2019; Maley, 2020). The PRTs that were run from local bases by individual countries were vital for facilitating the operations of NGOs and international organisations for implementing the development projects. These projects were designed in a way to contribute to the attainment of objectives outlined in the Afghanistan Compact and the Afghanistan National Development Strategy (Giegerich & Hlatky, 2020).

At its Bucharest Summit, NATO (April 2008) declared a strategic military-political plan to create an 'enduring stable, secure, prosperous and democratic state, respectful of human rights and free from the threat of terrorism' in Afghanistan. In 2009, the NATO Training Mission-Afghanistan was designed to train the military, police and gendarmerie for anti-terrorism and counter-narcotics operations as well as border control (Murray, 2011, p. 54). However, the rising insurgency since 2006 challenged the successful implementation of NATO's strategic plan in Afghanistan despite a substantial increase in the number of its troops in the country (Berdal, 2019). By announcing that the Afghan forces would assume full responsibility for the country's own security, NATO declared the gradual withdrawal of its forces from Afghanistan by the end of 2014 at its Lisbon Summit in 2010. Ending its combat mission in Afghanistan in 2014, NATO continued to train Afghan national forces to fight against insurgency through the non-combat mission, Resolute Support (Schmitt, 2017).

After a comprehensive engagement in Afghanistan for almost two decades, NATO's objective of fully stabilising Afghanistan, which was of great significance for the Afghan state in upholding its responsibility to protect its population seems to have failed. Unequal burden-sharing within the alliance; disagreements over whether to prioritise the war on terror or to focus on the humanitarian aspects and rebuilding Afghanistan; intra-alliance reluctance to engage further in Afghanistan in the long-term; and the resurgence of Taliban can be cited as notable reasons for such a failure. From an R2P lens, NATO's cooperation with corrupt regional warlords who had privileged access to development assistance compared to other segments of the society has arguably weakened NATO's efforts to bring stability to Afghanistan.

As noted in various UN Secretary-General reports, providing international assistance under Pillar Two requires the prevention of inequalities in access to development funding, which would weaken social harmony and trigger further conflicts (UNGA, 2009, pp. 19–20; UNGA–UNSC, 2014, p. 5). Analysing the Afghan case, Karell and Schutte (2018) show how unequal access to the distribution of resources led to the subsequent intensification of insurgency in Afghanistan. Furthermore, Berdal (2019) demonstrates how NATO's efforts to ensure security and provide development assistance for reconstruction were compromised with the resentment of the Afghan population due to NATO's cooperation with corrupt regional warlords to defeat the Taliban and Al-Qaeda. Following the toppling of the Taliban in 2001, former warlords managed to have access to the development aid at the local level by using tribal networks and consolidating their link with the central government. The exclusion of other local groups not affiliated with corrupted networks of aid distribution undermined their trust to Afghan institutions (Berdal, 2019). Briefly, the increasing power of local power networks based on tribal and patronage networks played an important role in undermining NATO's efforts to stabilise Afghanistan. Moreover, the increasing number of civilian casualties from NATO operations on the one hand, and the Afghan people's accusing of NATO forces for not respecting their culture and way of life on the other added on to the reasons for the failure of NATO in putting an end to the increasing insurgency of the Taliban (Berdal, 2019).

Overall, from a Pillar Two perspective, the improvement of human development indicators and security situation in the country and international engagement has been crucial to contribute to the protection of the Afghan population affected by a complex conflict situation. Nevertheless, the international community's privileging of counterterrorism has led to inequalities in access to development funding while the strengthening of corrupt warlords has increased tensions among various sections of the Afghan society. This has created a clash between the international community's responsibility to protect the Afghan population on the one hand and its pursuit of counterterrorism measures on the other (Welsh, 2016). Hence, there is a vital need for the international community to focus on the establishment of an inclusive and sustainable political, economic and security structure that would help to fulfil the responsibility to protect rather than prioritising competing objectives such as counterterrorism.

Conclusion

This chapter has examined the case of Afghanistan in the post-intervention period from an R2P perspective vis-à-vis the three-pillar implementation strategy with a primary focus on Pillars One and Two. It has highlighted the ongoing gross violations of human rights of the Afghan population committed both by anti- and pro-government forces despite intensive international engagement, and why it is important to approach this case from an R2P point of view. The comprehensive analysis of the reports released by the Afghan government and the international community with respect to the first two pillars of R2P has revealed that Afghanistan has undertaken comprehensive measures for strengthening its resilience capacity to prevent atrocities against the Afghan population. This chapter has also emphasised how the political, military and financial contribution of the international community has helped Afghanistan increase its resilience to protect its population vulnerable to mass atrocities. Nevertheless, illustrating the unstable political, economic and security situation in Afghanistan since 2001, it argues that the implementation of comprehensive preventive measures, which have also been consistent with the various aspects and measures of R2P, has failed to end the sufferings of the Afghan population resulting from the ongoing violence. This argument speaks to the debate on the challenges of implementing R2P successfully in practice despite the capacity-building efforts of the national governments and international community in line with Pillars One and Two.

The emphasis on national resilience and national ownership has been promoted by the UN Secretary-General as effective ways for the successful operationalisation of Pillar One in national contexts. While the former requires measures such as rebuilding the security forces, modernising the judicial system, consolidating law enforcement nationwide, tackling widespread poverty and providing public services for its citizens, the latter requires the declaration of atrocity prevention and response a national priority as well as setting up early warning systems to deal with threats of mass atrocity crimes (UNGA–UNSC, 2016, p. 20; 2019, p. 3). National ownership further requires the active involvement of civil society actors, including NGOs, religious leaders and private sector in the implementation of R2P's preventive measures. The UN Secretary-General considers these non-state actors crucial for encouraging states to act in an accountable way, counselling victims of atrocity crimes, mediating local disputes, calming tensions, promoting tolerance, providing life-saving humanitarian aid, and mobilising human and financial resources (UNGA–UNSC, 2016, p. 14). Moreover, national ownership requires the investigation and prosecution of those responsible for atrocity crimes to encourage the reconciliation of conflicting parties of society, and thus, preventing future violations (UNGA–UNSC, 2017, p. 8). Accordingly, this chapter has demonstrated that despite its substantial progress in increasing national resilience capacity and ownership of R2P, Afghanistan is still far from protecting its population from atrocity crimes. Therefore, it is of paramount importance to complement Pillar One with a comprehensive international engagement to help Afghanistan undertake its responsibility to protect.

An important finding of this chapter in terms of the implementation of Pillar Two is that using military force even by one of the most powerful members of the international community, or providing billions of development assistance for reconstruction efforts in a conflict-ridden country like Afghanistan does not ensure sustainable peace and stability. In one of his reports, former UN Secretary-General Ban Ki-moon highlights the importance of aligning foreign assistance with national strategies that reflect the priorities of the whole society (UNGA–UNSC, 2015, p. 5). Accordingly, this chapter has revealed how the use of thousands of NATO and ISAF forces predominantly with the objective of eliminating global terror has undermined the efforts that prioritised the objective of rebuilding Afghanistan to become atrocity-free in a sustainable way (Maley, 2020, p. 247). It has also highlighted how the increasing number of civilian casualties from the operations of international forces and the perceived lack of respect of foreign soldiers to Afghan culture and way of life has struck a further blow to the effective implementation of atrocity prevention measures in Afghanistan. Ban makes it clear that the international community can fulfil its responsibility to help prevent atrocities successfully only by inclusively engaging with national and local authorities, human rights organisations, traditional leaders and women's groups (UNGA–UNSC, 2015, p. 5). The situation in Afghanistan confirms such observation with the specific example of NATO's engagement with corrupt warlords, which has triggered inter-regional and inter-ethnic competition for access to resources among Afghan population.

Furthermore, this chapter demonstrated that the joint action of national, regional and global actors for maximising capacity to prevent atrocities does not assure sustainable success. The UN Secretary-General encourages the effective coordination of national, regional and subregional arrangements to achieve best results in atrocity prevention (UNGA–UNSC, 2017, p. 9; 2016, p. 14). Although the distinctive engagements of the UN, NATO, the EU and the World Bank in Afghanistan have complemented each other's capacity-building contributions, their combined efforts have failed to prevent the continuation of the conflict. Afghanistan's limited national resilience capacity to protect its population from human rights violations without the help of the international community shows the limits of international engagement.

All in all, these findings demonstrate that the primary challenge to building a coherent prevention capability from an R2P perspective has not been a shortage of financial or military means but rather the absence of a commitment to prioritise national and local priorities, and engagement with all segments of society equally. The international community should take this point into consideration while developing relevant strategies for the prevention of atrocities, and the protection of populations should be there as the main drive and/or mentality.

In the light of the lessons that can be drawn from case of Afghanistan, given the importance of national ownership of the responsibility to protect in atrocity prevention at the earliest stage possible, future research may examine the roles non-state actors, particularly the private sector, can play in atrocity prevention efforts at the national level. The issue of engaging non-state actors for increasing national resilience capacity becomes more critical as the international community is committed to withdraw its forces from Afghanistan in the summer of 2021.

References

Amnesty International. (2019). *Afghanistan's refugees: Forty years of dispossession*. https://www.amnesty.org/en/latest/news/2019/06/afghanistan-refugees-forty-years/. Accessed 21 September 2020.

Afghanistan National Development Strategy (ANDS). (2008). *Afghanistan National Development Strategy (2008–2013)*. The Islamic Republic of Afghanistan. https://www.refworld.org/docid/5b28e5864.html. Accessed 18 September 2020.

Afghanistan National Peace and Development Framework (ANPDF). (2016). *Afghanistan National Peace and Development Framework (2017–2021)*. The Islamic Republic of Afghanistan. http://policymof.gov.af/home/afghanistan-national-peace-and-development-framework-anpdf/. Accessed 15 September 2020.

Barfield, T. (2010). *Afghanistan: A cultural and political history*. Princeton University Press.

Barfield, T. (2011). Afghanistan's ethnic puzzle: Decentralizing power before the U.S. Withdrawal. *Foreign Affairs, 90*(5), 54–65.

Berdal, M. (2019). NATO's landscape of the mind: Stabilisation and state-building in Afghanistan. *Ethnopolitics, 18*(5), 526–543.

Berkowitz, B. (2007). The Great Game and the endgame in Afghanistan. *Orbis, 51*(1), 165–174.

De Lauri, A., & Suhrke, A. (2020). Armed governance: the case of the CIA-supported Afghan militias. *Small Wars & Insurgencies*. https://www.cmi.no/publications/file/7258-armed-governance-the-case-of-the-cia-supported-afghan-militias.pdf. Accessed 8 October 2020.

European Commission. (2007). *Country Strategy Paper (CSP) Afghanistan 2007–2013*. https://eeas.europa.eu/sites/eeas/files/csp_afg_07-13_en.pdf. Accessed 12 November 2020.

European Commission. (2016). *Brussels conference on Afghanistan: Continued international support for Afghanistan's political and economic stability and development*. https://ec.europa.eu/commission/presscorner/detail/en/IP_16_3329. Accessed 15 November 2020.

European Commission. (2018). *New €474 million co-operation package for Afghanistan*. https://ec.europa.eu/commission/presscorner/detail/en/IP_18_6565. Accessed 11 November 2020.

European Commission. (2020). *Afghanistan*. https://ec.europa.eu/international-partnerships/where-we-work/afghanistan_en. Accessed 10 November 2020.

European Council. (2005). EU-Afghanistan joint declaration: Committing to a new EU-Afghan partnership.

European Council. (2018). *Council conclusions on Afghanistan*. https://reliefweb.int/sites/reliefweb.int/files/resources/st13823-en18.pdf. Accessed 14 November 2020.

European Parliament. (2019). *EU-Afghanistan cooperation agreement*. https://www.europarl.europa.eu/RegData/etudes/ATAG/2019/635555/EPRS_ATA(2019)635555_EN.pdf. Accessed 14 November 2020.

Giegerich, B., & von Hlatky, S. (2020). Experiences may vary: NATO and cultural interoperability in Afghanistan. *Armed Forces & Society, 46*(3), 495–516.

Global Centre for the Responsibility to Protect (GCR2P). (2019, October 23). *Atrocity Alert No. 177: South Sudan, Afghanistan and Syria*. https://www.globalr2p.org/. Accessed 25 September 2020.

Goodson, L. (2001). *Afghanistan's endless war: State failure, regional politics, and the rise of the Taliban*. University of Washington Press.

Hassan, O. (2020). The evolution of the European Union's failed approach to Afghanistan. *European Security, 29*(1), 74–95.

Hazim, A. M. (2019). A critical analysis of the Rome statue implementation in Afghanistan. *Florida Journal of International Law, 31*, 1–31.

Human Rights Watch. (2020). *Afghanistan. Events of 2019*. https://www.hrw.org/world-report/2020/country-chapters/afghanistan. Accessed 3 October 2020.

Karell, D., & Schutte, S. (2018). Aid, exclusion, and the local dynamics of insurgency in Afghanistan. *Journal of Peace Research, 55*(6), 711–725.
Maley, W. (2020). Civil-military relations and R2P: The Afghan experience. In C. Jacob & M. Mennecke (Eds.), *Implementing the responsibility to protect: A future agenda* (pp. 236–250). Routledge.
Murray, T. (2011). Security sector reform in Afghanistan, 2002–2011: An overview of a flawed process. *International Studies, 48*(1), 43–63.
NATO. (2008). *ISAF's strategic vision.* https://www.nato.int/cps/en/natolive/official_texts_8444.htm. Accessed 30 September 2020.
Nuruzzaman, M. (2009). Revisiting the category of fragile and failed states in international relations. *International Studies, 46*(3), 271–294.
Rahman, M. (2019). The US state-building in Afghanistan: An offshore balance? *Jadavpur Journal of International Relations, 23*(1), 81–104.
Rashid, A. (2000). *Taliban: The power of militant Islam in Afghanistan and beyond.* Yale University Press.
Riphenburg, C. J. (2005). Ethnicity and civil society in contemporary Afghanistan. *The Middle East Journal, 59*(1), 31–51.
Rubin, B. R. (2020). *Afghanistan: What everyone needs to know.* Oxford University Press.
Schmitt, O. (2017). International organization at war: NATO practices in the Afghan campaign. *Cooperation and Conflict, 52*(4), 502–518.
United Nations Assistance Mission in Afghanistan (UNAMA). (2015). *Update on the treatment of conflict related detainees in Afghan custody: Accountability and implementation of presidential decree 129.* https://www.ohchr.org/Documents/Countries/AF/UNAMA_OHCHR_Detention_Report_Feb2015.pdf. Accessed 5 October 2020.
United Nations Assistance Mission in Afghanistan (UNAMA). (2017). *Treatment of conflict-related detainees: Implementation of Afghanistan's National Plan on the elimination of torture.* https://www.ohchr.org/Documents/Countries/AF/AfghanReportApril2017.pdf. Accessed 5 October 2020.
United Nations Assistance Mission in Afghanistan (UNAMA). (2019). *Afghanistan: protection of civilians in armed conflict: Annual report 2018.* https://unama.unmissions.org/protection-of-civilians-reports. Accessed 12 September 2020.
United Nations Assistance Mission in Afghanistan (UNAMA). (2020a). *Afghanistan protection of civilians in armed conflict. Third Quarter Report: 1 January to 30 September 2020.* https://reliefweb.int/sites/reliefweb.int/files/resources/unama_protection_of_civilians_in_armed_conflict_-_3rd_quarter_report_2020.pdf. Accessed 15 November 2020.
United Nations Assistance Mission in Afghanistan (UNAMA). (2020b). *Afghanistan protection of civilians in armed conflict Midyear Report: 1 January-30 June 2020.* https://reliefweb.int/sites/reliefweb.int/files/resour

ces/unama_poc_midyear_report_2020_-_27_july.pdf. Accessed 12 September 2020.
United Nations Assistance Mission in Afghanistan (UNAMA). (2020c). *Protection of civilians in armed conflict special report: Attacks in healthcare during the Covid-19 pandemic*. https://unama.unmissions.org/sites/default/files/unama_special_report_attacks_on_healthcare_during_the_covid-19_pandemic_20_june_2020.pdf. Accessed 12 September 2020.
United Nations Development Program (UNDP). (2019). *Inequalities in human development in the 21st century*. Afghanistan. http://hdr.undp.org/sites/all/themes/hdr_theme/country-notes/AFG.pdf. Accessed 10 October 2020.
United Nations Educational, Scientific and Cultural Organization (UNESCO). (2010). *Afghanistan millennium development goals report 2010*. http://planipolis.iiep.unesco.org/sites/planipolis/files/ressources/afghanistan_mdg_2010.pdf. Accessed 5 October 2020.
United Nations General Assembly (UNGA). (2009, January 12). *Implementing the responsibility to protect* (Report of the Secretary-General, A/63/677).
United Nations General Assembly–Security Council (UNGA–UNSC). (2013, July 9). Responsibility to Protect: State responsibility and prevention. Report of the Secretary-General, A/67/929-S/2013/399.
United Nations General Assembly–Security Council (UNGA–UNSC). (2014, July 11). Fulfilling our collective responsibility: International assistance and the responsibility to protect. Report of the Secretary-General, A/68/947-S/2014/449.
United Nations General Assembly–Security Council (UNGA–UNSC). (2015, July 13). *A vital and enduring commitment: Implementing the responsibility to protect* (Report of the Secretary-General, A/69/981-S/2015/500).
United Nations General Assembly–Security Council (UNGA–UNSC). (2016, July 22). *Mobilizing collective action: The next decade of the responsibility to protect* (Report of the Secretary-General, A/70/999-S/2016/620).
United Nations General Assembly–Security Council (UNGA–UNSC). (2017, August 10). *Implementing the responsibility to protect: Accountability for prevention* (Report of the Secretary-General, A/71/1016 S/2017/556).
United Nations General Assembly–Security Council (UNGA–UNSC). (2019, June 10). *Responsibility to protect: Lessons learned for prevention* (Report of the Secretary-General, A/73/898-S/2019/463).
United Nations General Assembly–Security Council (UNGA–UNSC). (2020a, August 18). *The situation in Afghanistan and its implications for international peace and security* (Report of the Secretary-General, A/74/993-S/2020/809).
United Nations General Assembly–Security Council (UNGA–UNSC). (2020b, July 23). *Prioritizing prevention and strengthening response: Women and*

the responsibility to protect (Report of the Secretary-General, A/74/964-S/2020/501).
United Nations Security Council (UNSC). (2001a, September 12). Resolution 1368 adopted by the Security Council at its 4370th meeting, S/RES/1368.
United Nations Security Council (UNSC). (2001b, November 14). Resolution 1378 adopted by the Security Council at its 4415th meeting, S/RES/1378.
United Nations Security Council (UNSC). (2001c, December 6). Resolution 1383 Adopted by the Security Council at its 4434th meeting, S/RES/1383.
United Nations Security Council (UNSC). (2001d, December 20). Resolution 1386 adopted by the Security Council at its 4443rd meeting, S/RES/1386.
United Nations Security Council (UNSC). (2002, March 28). Resolution 1401 adopted by the Security Council at its 4501st meeting, S/RES/1401.
United Nations Security Council (UNSC). (2020, September 15). Resolution 2543 Adopted by the Security Council at its 8759th meeting, S/RES/2543.
Watson Institute. (2019). *Human cost of post-9/11 Wars*. https://watson.brown.edu/costsofwar/files/cow/imce/papers/2019/Direct%20War%20Deaths%20COW%20Estimate%20November%2013%202019%20FINAL.pdf. Accessed 5 October 2020.
Welsh, J. (2016). R2P's next ten years, deepening and extending the consensus. In A. J. Bellamy & T. Dunne (Eds.), *The Oxford handbook on the responsibility to protect* (pp. 984–999). Oxford University Press.
World Bank (2020). *World Bank Group in Afghanistan*. Country Update. Issue:056. http://documents1.worldbank.org/curated/en/968941585747221862/pdf/The-World-Bank-Group-in-Afghanistan-Country-Update.pdf. Accessed 18 October 2020.
World Bank (2019). *Financing peace. Fiscal challenges and implications for a post-settlement Afghanistan*. https://openknowledge.worldbank.org/handle/10986/32815. Accessed 18 October 2020.

CHAPTER 11

The Rohingya of Myanmar: R2P, International Justice and Accountability

Vildan Taştemel Kapucu

On 1 February 2021, Myanmar hits the headlines once again as the army staged a coup, ending the relatively short-lived democratic experience of the country. This is arguably a consequence of the highly delicate social and political landscape of Myanmar as a multi-ethnic and multi-religious country. Although present-day Myanmar became independent in 1948 under the name of the Union of Burma, the process of nation-building has been severely hindered by ethnic and religious divisions and tensions that have given rise to many conflicts throughout the country. One of them is the Rohingya crisis, and it has recently drawn a great deal of international attention when violence and displacement in the Rakhine State of Myanmar reached an alarming level. This chapter examines the Rohingya crisis of Myanmar from a Responsibility to Protect (R2P) lens and reflects on the role of the international justice system as a non-coercive measure under R2P.

V. T. Kapucu (✉)
Department of International Relations, Hacettepe University, Ankara, Turkey

P. Gözen Ercan (ed.), *The Responsibility to Protect Twenty Years On*,
https://doi.org/10.1007/978-3-030-90731-0_11

The Rohingya crisis is a multi-dimensional and complicated one, and so far, a substantial literature has developed on various aspects of the issue. These studies mainly highlight grave human rights violations arising from forced displacement, forced labour, rape, as well as destruction of property and even refer to ethnic cleansing and an intention of genocide (Barany, 2019; Beyrer & Kamarulzaman, 2017; Dussich, 2018). Also, as the human rights violations in the country and mass refugee movements in the region have turned into a humanitarian catastrophe, the plight of the Rohingya has come to be addressed under the broader concept of protection. With grave concerns of possible ethnic cleansing and genocide, the question of responsibility has been widely discussed in relation to the Rohingya.

As part of the above-mentioned discussions, studies have examined the plight of the Rohingya from an R2P perspective mainly with a focus on the relevance and applicability of R2P to this specific case (see Beyrer & Kamarulzaman, 2017; İbrahim & Nordin, 2015; Kingston, 2015; Khan & Ahmad, 2020; Nishikawa, 2018). Yet, the discussion on the Rohingya and R2P has been rather limited in scope and depth since the non-coercive measures of R2P in general, and the role of the international justice system in particular, are missing in the literature with the exception of the brief reference by Kingston (2015) who argues that R2P is more than the use of force and provides a wide array of tools. In this vein, this chapter aims to fill a gap in the literature by focusing on the actions that have been taken within the international justice system as part of the peaceful measures envisaged within the framework of R2P.

To this end, the chapter first provides a historical overview of the case to shed light on the root causes of the conflict. Then, conducting a pillar-by-pillar analysis, it questions how and to what extent R2P has been implemented in the case of the Rohingya. While doing so, it places a special emphasis on judicial settlement as a peaceful measure under R2P and examines the actions taken within the international justice system as per this case. Such an analysis aims to determine the implications of the involvement of international tribunals in the Rohingya crisis with a specific focus on the concepts of justice and accountability under R2P. Following from this, the chapter purports that the actions taken under the international justice system have raised awareness about the case and increased the prospects for the group having access to protection, justice and accountability. Arguably, the ongoing judicial processes are expected to prevent further escalation of the crisis and sufferings on the part of the Rohingya by becoming a deterrent factor for the perpetrators, mainly the Tatmadaw (official armed forces of Myanmar). Finally, the chapter concludes that the international justice system has now become instrumental in helping the protection of populations from mass atrocity crimes and it complements the R2P norm in terms of achieving sustainable protection.

Myanmar and the Protracted Rohingya Crisis

The Rohingya, a Muslim minority and one of the hundreds of ethnic groups in Myanmar, are commonly cited among the most persecuted or discriminated minorities of the world (BBC, 2020a; OHCHR 2017; UNHCR n.d.). Although figures are not precise, it is estimated that there are currently about four million Rohingya around the world, and the number of the Rohingya living in Myanmar has reduced from around 3.6 million in the 1970s to about one billion today (Alam, 2019). Predominantly followers of Sunni Islam, they mainly live in the Rakhine State along with the ethnic Rakhine. Regarding the history of the group in Myanmar, there are certain conflicting views. Under the British colonial rule, many Muslims from Bengal were brought to Burma as labour force for rice production, and the Muslim population is said to have tripled during this period (Abdelkader, 2017; Blakemore, 2019). Thus, both the Myanmar authorities and ethnic and religious majority groups associate the presence of the Rohingya with this era and deny their inherent rights in the country. This deep and large-scale denial is also reflected in the use of the name Rohingya for the group. According to Albert and Maizland (2020), the name Rohingya has a meaning similar to 'those coming from Arakan' in the Rohingya dialect and shows the connection of the group to the State which was previously known as Arakan. Chan (2005), on the other hand, argues that this name was adopted by some Bengali Muslim intellectuals only in the 1950s. Although the group calls itself as the Rohingya and claims historical connections with the country, the Myanmar government, the ethnic Rakhine in the Rakhine State and the Buddhist majority of the country perceive the use of the name Rohingya as a threat, making its use a taboo. The government officially refers to the group as Bengalis or illegal migrants and deliberately avoids using the name Rohingya (Blakemore, 2019). Burke (2016, p. 265) explains this refusal on the part of the government and Buddhist majority with 'the logic of ethnic territorial politics' dominant in Myanmar where recognising the ethnic label or identity of a certain group brings a territorial claim.

Present-day Myanmar was founded after World War II (WWII) with the organisation of the Panglong Conference by Aung San, who is accepted as the father of the nation. The independence agreement signed by the national leader—who was a member of the ethnic Bamar group—with the representatives of major ethnic groups—namely, Shans, Kachins and Chins—resulted in the formation of the Union of Burma but left many ethnic problems unresolved and planted the seeds of conflict (Walton, 2008). Although the Rohingya were both discontent and resentful at the end of the independence process, they had no problem of recognition and were among the groups recognised by the State. It was the rise of the military junta to power in 1962 that deteriorated the already tense relations between the ethnic groups of the country and triggered systematic discrimination and oppression on the part of the Rohingya. As Smith (2002, p. 8) notes, federalism attempts of ethnic minority groups were accelerating at that time, and this paved the way for the military to oust the democratic government on the grounds that federalism was separatism and would destroy the nation. Thus, the military junta adopted an alleged agenda of 'Burmanisation', further fuelling tension across the country. Yegar (2018, p. 200) reports that the displacement and expulsion of the Rohingya towards Bangladesh started as early as the 1970s, and at least two waves of mass movements took place, first due to persecution of the Buddhist ethnic groups and then, the infamous Dragon King Operation of the army. By the end of the 1970s, hundreds of thousands of the Rohingya had taken shelter in nearby Bangladesh. As part of its attempts to suppress all minority movements throughout the country, the military regime of General Ne Win adopted the 1982 Citizenship Law and introduced new requirements for entitlement to citizenship. This law drastically changed the situation of the Rohingya in Myanmar and effectively rendered them stateless, which started a decades-long process through which the Rohingya lost their civil and political rights (Beyrer & Kamarulzaman, 2017, p. 1571).

The deeply rooted tensions between the residents of the Rakhine State, namely Buddhist Rakhine and Muslim Rohingya, are decades-old and have turned into direct conflict from time to time. However, the conflict has drawn international attention only after the last wave of violence against the Rohingya started in 2017 when a militant Rohingya organisation known as the Arakan Rohingya Salvation Army (ARSA) staged attacks on the army and police posts and caused casualties. In response to the attacks of ARSA, which is referred to as a terrorist organisation by the Myanmar government, Tatmadaw launched so-called clearance operations (Barany, 2019; Dussich, 2018, p. 8). However, it has been reported that civilians were also targeted, and the operations of the military quickly turned into communal violence against the Rohingya with the help of the ethnic Rakhine. The deteriorating conditions in the country inevitably triggered an exodus of the Rohingya from the Rakhine State. In this tragic phase of the humanitarian crisis, the death toll reportedly reached at least 6,700 in the first months, which included hundreds of children and women. Also, it was confirmed with satellite images that the Rohingya villages were burnt down to prevent the return of the Rohingya to their homeland (BBC News, 2020a; CoFR, 2020). Thus, the Rohingya have suffered from not only systematic discrimination, social exclusion, suppression and communal violence but also persecution, mass killings, rape and abuses, deportation and forced displacement. Although the Myanmar government asserted that there were no human rights violations, the excessive use of force and grave human rights violations have been reported by numerous parties on grounds of witness accounts and other evidence (AI, 2017; Barany, 2019; Dussich, 2018, p. 3).

Adding to the decades-old sufferings of the Rohingya, the escalation of violence during the 2010s and, especially the events unfolding in the Rakhine State from 2017 onward led to discussions on how to frame the plight of this group with definitions ranging from 'mere' human rights violations to ethnic cleansing and from crimes against humanity to genocide. Kingston (2015), Beyrer and Kamarulzaman (2017), Rahman et al. (2018) and Barany (2019) describe the plight of the Rohingya as ethnic cleansing committed by the Myanmar government and the military. Ibrahim and Nordin (2015) argue that the sufferings of the Rohingya amount to ethnic cleansing and crimes against humanity and also refer to a serious threat of genocide. Lee (2021) states that the Rohingya of Myanmar suffered from acts amounting to genocide first gradually and then suddenly. Likewise, Dussich (2018, p. 3) uses the term genocide for the plight of the Rohingya and states that

> ... forced labour, removal of citizenship, depopulation of their communities, severe abuse of children, elders and women (including use of rape as a

> weapon), prohibition of freedom of movement, confiscation and destruction of property (including schools, homes and religious centres), denial of education, religious and ethnic discrimination, restrictions on marriage, systemic persecution and racism, mass rapes, massacres, ethnic cleansings and forced expulsions. It is these grievous human rights violations which clearly justify the use of the term genocide.

In the light of this, this chapter acknowledges that the grave human rights violations that the Rohingya have suffered from for decades with obvious escalation in the last decade, may amount to ethnic cleansing and crimes against humanity, and there is a non-negligible risk of genocide for the Rohingya population of Myanmar. Under these circumstances, the Rohingya crisis clearly qualifies as an R2P case and requires R2P action. Thus, in what follows, through a pillar-by-pillar analysis, this chapter examines how and to what extent R2P has been implemented in the Rohingya case before elaborating on the role of international justice system within R2P as a non-coercive measure.

Pillar One: Statelessness and Responsibility of Myanmar

Paragraph 138 of the World Summit Outcome Document (WSOD) starts by stressing the individual responsibility of each State. The 2009 Report of the United Nations (UN) Secretary-General reiterates the approach adopted in the Outcome Document by specifying that, 'the state, however, remains the bedrock of the responsibility to protect' (UNGA, 2009, p. 10) and emphasises that the purpose here is to promote sovereignty as responsibility, not to weaken sovereignty itself in general. The Report also makes it clear that this obligation and responsibility of individual States are closely associated with fundamental human rights, which are already codified in numerous treaties, conventions as well as customary international law. Hence, the obligations of States to protect their populations are based on firm legal grounds, but practices may always go in the opposite direction and a State may be unable or unwilling to protect its population. Yet, it is noteworthy that the Rohingya case is different from many R2P crises due to the stateless status of the group. Thus, before elaborating on the responsibility of the State of Myanmar to protect the Rohingya, the question of statelessness needs to be addressed.

A person 'who is not considered as a national by any state under the operation of its law' is stateless by the definition accepted by the 1954 Convention Relating to the Status of Stateless Persons. While this definition refers to *de jure* statelessness, there is also another category as de facto statelessness. In the latter case, although a person theoretically has a nationality, she/he cannot enjoy protection or related rights in that specific country (Massey, 2010). In this sense, the Rohingya constitute a *de jure* stateless group. As explained before, statelessness and systematic discrimination of the group by successive governments are a significant part of the decades-old crisis, and this process is usually traced back to the 1982 Citizenship Law, which officially rendered most of the Rohingya stateless by bringing new requirements for citizenship. Although it is beyond doubt that this date became a turning point in the case of the Rohingya, Kyaw (2017) argues that the problem is not the Citizenship Law itself but the governments which intentionally refrained from recognising the Rohingya as citizens, and hence, lack of political will. Likewise, Ullah (2016, p. 289) posits that 'Rohingyas are deliberately excluded from being citizens of Myanmar to build a mono-religious nation, and as a result of depriving of citizenship, they are subjected to state-sponsored violence'. Regarding this issue, Kipgen (2019) states that contestation of identity might pave the way for conflicts among different ethnic groups as well as repression by the state, which totally holds true for the case of the Rohingya.

Besides its impact on the plight of the Rohingya, statelessness has also been a point of discussion in relation to R2P. Nishikawa (2018, p. 10) associates the concept of R2P with citizenship and membership in the political community of a State and asserts that R2P does not offer a feasible framework for the protection of the Rohingya. She further implies that the government of Myanmar is not responsible for protecting the Rohingya since they are stateless and outside the recognised political community, and Myanmar can be held responsible for protecting these people just like any other country on the basis of their basic human rights. However, this is an exceptional interpretation of R2P's scope, and such an argument cannot be grounded on the main documents regarding the norm. The WSOD on which the current practice is based refers to populations, not citizens (UNGA, 2005). Moreover, the 2009 Report of the Secretary-General clearly states that the responsibility to protect is extended to populations, whether or not nationals (UNGA, 2009).

Likewise, vast majority of the literature on the Rohingya directly acknowledge the responsibility of the State of Myanmar for the protection of the Rohingya regardless of the statelessness of the group (İbrahim & Nordin, 2015; Islam, 2019; Khan & Ahmed, 2020). We also observe that the international community has repeatedly accepted the responsibility of the State of Myanmar by calling it to take action for protecting the people living on the territories under its control (see, for instance, UNGA, 2017; UNSC, 2017). Consequently, while this Chapter acknowledges that statelessness is obviously a factor that has deteriorated the plight of the Rohingya by depriving them of even the most fundamental human rights and the protection of the State of Myanmar, it argues that this circumstance cannot be formulated as an obstacle or limitation to the applicability of R2P in the case of the Rohingya. On the contrary, within the scope of R2P, Myanmar has the primary responsibility to protect the Rohingya as part of the population living on the territories over which it holds effective control.

In humanitarian crises like the one addressed in this chapter, there are victims on the one side and the perpetrators on the other. In this case, the victims are obvious, the Rohingya. Yet, when it comes to the perpetrators, they range from other ethnic groups or Buddhist militias to the Myanmar armed forces and respective governments (Seth, 2018). Thus, direct or indirect involvement of State authorities in the grave offences described above further complicates the issue. While systemic exclusion and discrimination of the Rohingya by the State for decades have had severe consequences on them, statelessness and lack of protection being the primary ones, the operations led by the military targeting an already unprotected group have clearly demonstrated that the State of Myanmar is not willing to protect the Rohingya. In this respect, detailed findings of the Independent International Fact-Finding Mission on Myanmar are of great importance. The Mission reports that the 'Rohingya remain the target of a Government attack aimed at erasing the identity and removing them from Myanmar' and holds mainly the Tatmadaw but also other government authorities responsible for the crimes committed (HRC, 2019, p. 5). Thus, this Chapter acknowledges that the State of Myanmar—with its military and civilian authorities—has manifestly failed to protect the Rohingya. Given the failure at the level of Pillar One, we need to address the international community's responsibility under Pillar Two and Three.

Pillar Two: Failure of the International Community to Prevent

Introducing the three-pillar structure envisaged by the Secretary-General for R2P's implementation, the 2009 Report makes it clear that this structure does not imply any sequence or degree of significance. While Pillar One focuses on State responsibility for the prevention of mass atrocities, Pillars Two and Three elaborate on the role of the international community in preventing and responding to humanitarian crises requiring R2P action (UNGA, 2009).

The Report defines the main task of the international community under Pillar Two as providing assistance and helping the capacity-building efforts of States. This task can be fulfilled in four main ways, which include reminding and persuading States to fulfil their responsibilities arising from international law; helping States in their efforts for this purpose; helping States to build capacity in this respect; and assisting States under stress before the breakout of any conflict or crisis. While the measures envisaged under Pillar Two might include public diplomacy of the UN, its agencies and officials and regional and sub-regional organisations; training programmes, education and other forms of assistance directed to capacity building; and even military assistance in some cases, they are firmly based on the existence of cooperation and partnership between the parties. Thus, the Report of the Secretary-General acknowledges that the impact of these measures might be weak in cases where the government is unwilling to protect the populations and even is involved in the crimes committed (UNGA, 2009). In the case of the Rohingya, this calls into question the involvement of the UN as the world organisation and the Association of Southeast Asian Nations (ASEAN) as the main regional organisation.

The UN presence in Myanmar can be traced back to the 1950s and has continued even during the most difficult times of military regime with varying levels of engagement. As Myanmar has opened up to the external world following its democratisation efforts, the involvement of the UN in the country has naturally increased. However, the UN has mainly focused on developmental aspects in its relations with Myanmar by refraining from being directly involved in sensitive issues like ethnic conflicts and problems of the country. Rosenthal (2019, p. 15) explains this approach by stating that the UN preferred to pursue 'quiet diplomacy' instead of 'public advocacy' in Myanmar, especially in the first years of increased engagement with the Myanmar government. However, this approach of the UN has been criticised with arguments that the UN team ignored the signs of escalating violence and failed to prevent the latest surge of violence in the Rakhine State in 2016 and 2017 (Fisher, 2017). Overall, it can be argued that because of the increase in the extent of violence and sufferings of the Rohingya, the UN had to change its discourse in and approach to the Rohingya crisis and eventually brought human rights and protection issues to the fore only in the last decade.

On the other hand, ASEAN as the leading organisation of the region remained indifferent to the plight of the Rohingya due to the dominant understanding of non-intervention in domestic affairs of Member States, which is referred to as the 'ASEAN-way' (Jati, 2017; Limsiritong, 2017). China and India, major powers in the region, followed suit by regarding the Rohingya issue as a domestic problem of Myanmar and refrained from criticising or condemning Myanmar for its actions (Joy, 2018; Taufiq, 2019). To sum up, as the violence and human rights violations that the Rohingya have suffered have intensified in Myanmar, there have been no meaningful efforts towards prevention at the regional and international levels. Given the failure to prevent the Rohingya's protection crisis at the national and international levels, the question then becomes what can be done under Pillar Three.

Pillar Three: Response of the International Community

It is unfortunate but true that the Rohingya could attract the attention of the international community only in the last decade, that is, following the deterioration of the situation with alleged crimes amounting to ethnic cleansing and genocide. In the international arena, the UN General Assembly (UNGA) addressed the human rights situation in Myanmar in general and urged the government to accelerate its efforts towards a solution in 2012 (UNGA, 2013). In 2015, the UNGA again expressed serious concern over the human rights situation in Myanmar but put higher stress on the violence and abuses that the Rohingya suffered. Following the so-called clearance operations that resulted in the surge of violence and persecution for the Rohingya in 2016 and 2017, the UN adopted a firmer position in defining the situation in Myanmar. Zeid Ra'ad al-Hussein, the then UN High Commissioner for Human Rights stated in reference to the Rohingya crisis that 'the situation seems a textbook example of ethnic cleansing' (UN News, 2017) while Secretary-General Antonio Guterres was more precise in describing the plight of the Rohingya as ethnic cleansing (Besheer, 2017). As a highly significant step, the UN Human Rights Council established the Independent International Fact-Finding Mission on Myanmar in 2017. In 2018, after a thorough investigation into the case, the Mission reported serious violations of international humanitarian law and stated that the acts of the security forces and the army in particular constitute mass atrocity crimes, and that leaders and senior members of the army should be investigated and prosecuted on these grounds (UNGA, 2018). This view was reiterated one year later in another report of the Mission. Highlighting the lack of cooperation by and support from the Myanmar government, the report stated that the mission had 'reasonable grounds to conclude that there is a strong inference of genocidal intent on the part of the State, that there is a serious risk that genocidal actions may recur' in Myanmar (UNGA, 2019a, pp. 14–15).

Regarding R2P's implementation, the UN Secretary-General states in the 2009 Report that the scope should be narrow, but the response should be deep through the use of a 'wide array of prevention and protection instruments available to Member States, the UN system, regional and sub-regional organisations and their civil society partners' (UNGA, 2009, p. 8). Hence, as Bellamy (2015) argues, Pillar Three should not be solely associated with resort to military action, and non-coercive measures should come first as the default response of the international community under this pillar. Likewise, this chapter assumes that the undermining of Pillar Three to the military use of force should be overcome, and other available measures, especially the peaceful ones should be brought to the fore to strengthen R2P and help discover its true potential. In this regard, the Rohingya case allows us to focus on the peaceful measures of R2P. Accordingly, within the broader framework of such measures, the subsequent section discusses the international justice system and actions undertaken to achieve accountability and justice for the Rohingya.

The Role of International Justice in the Rohingya Case

The 2009 Report states that the UN prefers 'dialogue and peaceful persuasion', and thus, Pillar Three encompasses not only coercive measures but also peaceful ones. However, it falls short of providing further details on the peaceful measures of this pillar. Drawing attention to the importance of peaceful measures that he refers to as 'Pillar 3a', Bellamy (2015) argues that they are not adequately understood and are commonly ignored. To demonstrate their potential, he provides a 12-item list of peaceful measures or strategies which include but are not limited to information gathering and reporting, diplomacy, judicial settlement, human rights mechanisms and unarmed civilian protection.

As mentioned previously, in the case of the Rohingya, international awareness and involvement increased, and the UN changed its course of action to some extent only after the last wave of violence and conflict started in 2017. Since then, under the auspices of the UN, efforts for information gathering and reporting have intensified, and the human rights violations as well as the plight of the Rohingya have been frequently underlined. Although UN organs like the Security Council (UNSC) and the UNGA have pointed out grave human rights violations, condemned escalating violence and called on the authorities of Myanmar to take the necessary actions on various occasions (UNSC, 2017; UNGA, 2017, 2018, 2019a), no resolution with binding force has yet been adopted by the UNSC. It was in 2018 that Secretary-General Guterres paid a visit to Bangladesh and visited the refugee camps in the Cox Bazaar region. Upon his return, he addressed the UNSC for more concerted action in the Rohingya crisis (UNSG, 2018). Meanwhile, the detailed reports of the independent fact-finding mission on the situation in Myanmar, including the plight of the Rohingya, documented the gravity of the crisis. The conclusions of the Mission are particularly important since it highlighted on several occasions that the human rights abuses in the country, and the Rakhine State in particular, met the criteria for mass atrocity crimes of genocide, crimes against humanity and war crimes. According to the report, although the main perpetrator of crimes has been the Tatmadaw, the civilian authorities of the country and mainly Aung San Suu Kyi are blamed for not doing their best to prevent the events. The Mission urged the international community to act for bringing justice to the victims on the basis of the apparent unwillingness of the Myanmar authorities to do so (UNGA, 2018, , 2019a). Arguing that the government of Myanmar is far from prosecuting and punishing the perpetrators, the members of the Mission suggested the way forward to hold those responsible accountable for the alleged mass atrocity crimes through the International Criminal Court (ICC), International Court of Justice (ICJ), an ad hoc tribunal or a hybrid model with national and international participation (UNGA, 2019a).

When it comes to accountability and justice, two pathways are available in the international justice system, namely, the responsibility of the State based on international humanitarian law and human rights law, and criminal responsibility of individuals based on international criminal law (GCR2P, 2019). In this regard, the Rohingya became the subject of a case first before the ICC, which deals with individual criminal responsibility, and then the ICJ regarding the responsibility of the State of Myanmar within the framework of the Genocide Convention. In the meantime, another lawsuit was filed before a national court in Argentina by civil society organisations in line with the principle of universal jurisdiction to try the individuals involved in the crimes committed against the Rohingya in Myanmar (Guardian, 2019).

Individual criminal responsibility is in close relation with the concept of impunity, and for centuries, the issue of impunity has been overshadowed by the principle of sovereignty. As the World witnessed mass atrocity crimes during and after World War II, this balance has changed, and the ad hoc tribunals established have tried the individuals for the crimes they committed under the shield of state sovereignty. As Robertson (2005, p. 655) posits, 'it was the judgment at Nuremberg which heralded the removal of the shield of state sovereignty for crimes against humanity'. However, it was not until the end of the Cold War that the attempts to end sovereignty-related impunity and to incorporate criminal responsibility of wrongdoers in international law on a permanent basis bore fruits with the approval of the Rome Statute establishing the ICC in 1998 (Kibler, 2019).

Since the authorities of Myanmar are accused of mass atrocity crimes, which are the crimes that the ICC has jurisdiction over, the expectation was that the ICC could investigate the case of the Rohingya. However, the ICC has limited jurisdiction, for which being a State party to the Rome Statute is a prerequisite. Since Myanmar is not a State party, the only way for the ICC to open an investigation is a UNSC referral. As stated by Lee (2019), due to the strong support extended to Myanmar by China and Russia, the UNSC has failed to refer the Rohingya case to the ICC. Nevertheless, in 2018, the ICC Prosecutor opened a preliminary examination to investigate the crimes of forced displacement and deportation, which involved Bangladesh as a State party. On grounds of the preliminary examination, the Prosecutor then requested authorisation for a full investigation on the alleged crimes, mainly crimes against humanity (Lee, 2019, pp. 243–244). In November 2019, the ICC judges granted authorisation for investigations into alleged crimes taking place in Bangladesh as well as any other crimes with sufficient links to the former (ICC, 2019). In response to these developments, the Myanmar government declared that the ICC has no jurisdiction over Myanmar, and that they are not liable to comply with any ICC decision (Aydın, 2019). Despite all the drawbacks, the ICC Prosecutor finally opened an investigation into the crimes committed against the Rohingya. As reported by Amnesty International (2019), this is a highly important development for bringing justice to the Rohingya and holding the perpetrators of mass atrocity crimes accountable in the long-term.

Regarding the responsibility of the State of Myanmar, the ICJ as the world court offers the main legal path. In the case of the Rohingya, Gambia—a small Muslim country in Africa—filed a lawsuit against Myanmar before the ICJ in late 2019. Abubacarr Tambadou, the Gambian Justice Minister and a former judge in the UN Tribunal for Rwanda, decided to file a case against Myanmar as he likened what happened in Myanmar to the tragic events in Rwanda. In this case, Gambia had the support of the Organisation of Islamic Cooperation (BBC, 2020b). As both Gambia and Myanmar are parties to the Genocide Convention, Gambia took Myanmar before the ICJ for not fulfilling its obligations arising from the Convention by committing genocidal acts against the Rohingya. In its application, Gambia requested an order for provisional measures for the protection of the Rohingya minority pending a final verdict (HRW, 2019). In a surprising manner, Aung San Suu Kyi represented her country in the trials held in The Hague, described the events unfolding in her country as an internal conflict and depicted the operations of the military as a response to the attacks by ARSA. Although Aung San accepted the use of disproportionate force by the army and the sufferings of the Rohingya, she strongly argued against the genocide allegations (Aljazeera, 2019). However, the ICJ deciding in favour of Gambia adopted its first order on provisional measures in January 2020. It is noteworthy that 17 Judges of the ICJ unanimously voted for these measures. Accordingly, the Court ruled that,

> Myanmar must, in accordance with its obligations under the Convention, in relation to the members of the Rohingya group in its territory, take all measures within its power to prevent the commission of all acts within the scope of Article II of the Convention, in particular: (a) killing members of the group; (b) causing serious bodily or mental harm to the members

> of the group; (c) deliberately inflicting on the group conditions of life calculated to bring about its physical destruction in whole or in part; and (d) imposing measures intended to prevent births within the group (ICJ, 2020).

Moreover, Myanmar was held liable to report to the Court on its implementation of the preventive measures first within four months and then every six months.

Although the action to be taken by the Myanmar authorities, who must have been disappointed by the first decision of the Court on the case, was an issue of concern, the government of Myanmar submitted its first report to the ICJ in May and the second report in November 2020 (Khaliq, 2020). However, the two reports submitted to the ICJ court were not made public. This has been subject of severe criticisms as non-disclosure of the reports prevents the ICJ's provisional measures from fulfilling their intended purpose. Also, there have been suspicions about the accuracy of the reports and whether they reflected the real intentions of the Myanmar government or were the products of mere rhetoric (Ibrahim, 2020). On the political side, the situation has become even more complex with the military coup staged in February 2021, which led to human rights abuses and violations across the country. In legal terms, it is almost beyond doubt that this is only the beginning of a contentious case which will take years until a final decision or a charge of genocide on the part of Myanmar will be reached. Barelli (2019) implies that it will be challenging for the ICJ to charge Myanmar with the crime of genocide based on the previous cases heard by the Court. To date, no country was held responsible for the crime of genocide by the ICJ since the threshold of evidence is extremely high for this crime. Furthermore, the enforcement of the provisional measures and even the judgement of the Court (when it is adopted) will be restrained by the level of cooperation that Myanmar is ready to make. In the event of an unwilling Myanmar, the political will of major powers will be required to put pressure on Myanmar. Although the UNSC and the UNGA might take action to urge Myanmar to comply with the order of the ICJ, considering the strong support of China and Russia that Myanmar has enjoyed so far, an action by the UNSC is unlikely and the UNGA remains the only platform for possible action to pressure Myanmar under the roof of the UN (HRW, 2019). Despite such shortcomings and the deteriorating situation in Myanmar, the case brought before the ICJ and the unanimous adoption of the first order by the judges constitute a hopeful milestone in terms of accountability and justice in the case of the Rohingya.

Last but not least, the Rohingya became the subject of a case filed in a national court in Argentina under the principle of universal jurisdiction. Defined as 'the ability of the court of any state to try persons for crimes committed outside its territory which are not linked to the state by the nationality of the suspect or the victims or by harm to the state's own national interests' (AI, 2009: 13), universal jurisdiction provides another venue for ending impunity for the perpetrators. In this way, national courts also play key roles as alternatives to international courts that can be incapacitated on certain occasions due to procedural or political reasons. Besides its symbolic importance, the lawsuit filed in Argentina is important because it can investigate a wider scope of crimes not having cross-border links to Bangladesh, as is the case with the investigation launched by the ICC (Khin, 2020).

Acknowledging that the actions taken within the scope of the international justice system are relatively new and any concrete decision by international courts will take time and any meaningful result will require international political support, this chapter argues that even the involvement of international tribunals in the case of the Rohingya is highly important. Lee (personal communication, June 2021) states that the cases brought before the ICC and the ICJ represent an innovative use of R2P to help the Rohingya and argues that despite the symbolic importance that the ICJ has in this respect, it is the ICC that may have a real impact on the plight of the Rohingya in the long-term.

Criminal law, domestic and international alike, arguably rests on two philosophical camps regarding the rationale behind it. These are retribution and deterrence, the latter being more prominent (Rosenberg, 2015). Thus, the potential impact of the cases brought before the ICC and the Argentinian court regarding the plight of the Rohingya can be analysed from two aspects. In Myanmar, the Tatmadaw—which is accepted as the main perpetrator of the crimes committed along with other Security Forces and some civilian groups—seized power once again following the military coup of February 2021 and thus is likely to engage in similar acts. As the country has been drawn into ambiguity with the recent developments, the cases brought before international tribunals have gained even more importance. The ICC prosecution, in particular, aims to end the impunity of military and civilian leaders and key authorities who are allegedly involved in the crimes investigated to hold them accountable for their roles in the plight of the Rohingya. In this respect, this chapter purports that the fear of punishment can serve as a deterrent to the persons and groups involved—mainly the Tatmadaw—in future, and further sufferings can be prevented on the part of the Rohingya.

Secondly, as the cases were brought before the ICC, the ICJ and a national court in Argentina, the Rohingya crisis hit the headlines and received widespread media coverage. These have led to an increased awareness about the plight of the Rohingya and made the voice of the victims heard. Considering that national courts and legal venues in Myanmar are closed to the victims seeking justice,[1] the international justice system remains the only option left for the Rohingya. Thus, these pending cases have the potential to help the Rohingya have the protection that they desperately need and ensure that accountability and justice are served. Furthermore, from a very optimistic point of view, these cases might even pave the way for domestic changes that are essential for a durable solution to the Rohingya's protection crisis driven by ethno-religious, socio-economic and political causes.

Conclusion

The situation concerning the Rohingya is a multi-dimensional and complicated one, and ethnic and religious divisions of the country as well as social, economic and political factors are all of paramount importance. In this respect, the recent developments in the country will certainly have an impact on the case of the Rohingya, most likely in a negative manner. The military coup that took place following the latest general elections brought new uncertainties regarding the future of Myanmar as well as the Rohingya. However, the protection needs of the Rohingya are still there, and the response and action by the international community are more meaningful and essential than ever. Thus, the international community should uphold its responsibility to protect by giving weight to peaceful measures so as not to exacerbate the suffering of the Rohingya, as well as its 'responsibility to prosecute' through the international justice system.

[1] The ICC Prosecutor, in her request for authorisation, clearly states that the case is admissible on the basis of the principle of complementarity since national efforts and actions addressing the 2017 incidents, in particular, lack genuinity and aim at shielding the military and civilian leaders from any criminal responsibility.

As argued by Mills (2015), although the latter comes after the commitment of violations and abuses and might be considered as a late response, it is beyond doubt that it is 'better late than never'.

Based on the case of the Rohingya, this chapter argues that peaceful measures in general, and international justice system in particular, have greater potential than envisaged within the scope of the R2P norm. In a case where national courts have been rendered ineffective and domestic legal venues have been closed, the international justice system has provided a feasible alternative, and the cases brought before the ICC, the ICJ and an Argentinian court with the aim of ending impunity of the wrongdoers and helping victims have access to accountability and justice, have made limited but important contributions. Along with the symbolic importance that all these cases have, they are expected to have a deterring impact for the future actions of the military and other groups involved in mass atrocity crimes by holding the perpetrators accountable. Moreover, when justice is served, this would also help to prevent the surge of the sense of revenge for the victims. At the current state of affairs, the Rohingya case shows us how the international justice system can be engaged in the protection of populations. Provided that the actions taken result in meaningful action in the long-term with respect to accountability and justice, the Rohingya case may also become exemplary of components of success wherein we may highlight the impact of peaceful measures and particularly the international justice system within the broader R2P framework, and Pillar Three.

All in all, accountability and justice are two vital but overlooked components of R2P, but as emphasised by the Secretary-General, they are 'essential for resolving past conflicts and grievances while also contributing to the prevention of future violations and abuses' (UNGA, 2019b). Therefore, a greater focus on accountability and justice mechanisms with their mid- to long- term implications can help strengthen the R2P norm and contribute to sustainable protection for populations.

References

Abdelkader, E. (2017). *The history of the persecution of Myanmar's Rohingya*. The Conversation. https://theconversation.com/the-history-of-the-persecution-of-myanmars-rohingya-84040. Accessed on 18 June 2021.

Alam, S. (2019). *Infographic—Top Rohingya-hosting countries*. Anadolu Agency. https://www.aa.com.tr/en/asia-pacific/infographic-top-rohingya-hosting-countries/1563674. Accessed 19 June 2020.

Albert, E., & Maizland, L. (2020). *The Rohingya crisis*. https://www.cfr.org/backgrounder/rohingya-crisis. Accessed 9 June 2020.

Aljazeera. (2019). *Aung San Suu Kyi defends Myanmar against genocide allegations*. https://www.aljazeera.com/news/2019/12/myanmar-suu-kyi-stand-genocide-case-hague-191211054254397.html. Accessed 24 June 2020.

Amnesty International (AI). (2009). *Ending impunity: Developing and implementing a global action plan using universal jurisdiction*. https://www.amnesty.org/download/Documents/48000/ior530052009en.pdf. Accessed 10 June 2021.

Amnesty International (AI). (2017). *Myanmar: Crimes against humanity terrorize and drive Rohingya out*. https://www.amnesty.org/en/latest/news/2017/10/myanmar-new-evidence-of-systematic-campaign-to-terrorize-and-drive-rohingya-out/. Accessed 20 June 2020.

Amnesty International (AI). (2019). *Myanmar: ICC decision to investigate Rohingya atrocities an important step towards justice*. https://www.amnesty.org/en/latest/news/2019/11/myanmar-icc-referral/. Accessed 24 June 2020.

Aydın, N. (2019). *Myanmar rejects jurisdiction of ICC for Rohingya Muslim*. Anadolu Agency. https://www.aa.com.tr/en/asia-pacific/myanmar-rejects-jurisdiction-of-icc-for-rohingya-muslim/1648020. Accessed 24 June 2020.

Barany, Z. (2019). The Rohingya predicament: Why Myanmar's army gets away with ethnic cleansing. *IAI Papers, 19*, 1–27. https://www.iai.it/en/pubblicazioni/rohingya-predicament. Accessed 20 June 2020.

Barelli, M. (2019). *Why Aung San Suu Kyi is in The Hague defending Myanmar against allegations of genocide*. The Conversation. https://theconversation.com/why-aung-san-suu-kyi-is-in-the-hague-defending-myanmar-against-allegations-of-genocide-125102. Accessed 25 June 2020.

BBC News. (2020a). *Myanmar Rohingya: What you need to know about the crisis*. https://www.bbc.com/news/world-asia-41566561. Accessed 18 April 2020.

BBC News. (2020b). *Rohingya crisis: The Gambian who took Aung San Suu Kyi to the world court*. https://www.bbc.com/news/world-africa-51183521. Accessed 24 June 2020.

Bellamy, A. J. (2015). *The first response: Peaceful means in the third pillar of the responsibility to protect*. The Stanley Foundation. http://www.stanleyfoundation.org/publications/pab/Bellamy3rdPillarPAB116.pdf. Accessed 18 April 2020.

Besheer, M. (2017). *UN chief assails 'ethnic cleansing' of Myanmar's Rohingyas*. Voice of America. https://www.voanews.com/east-asia-pacific/un-chief-assails-ethnic-cleansing-myanmars-rohingyas. Accessed on 22 June 2020.

Beyrer, C., & Kamarulzaman, A. (2017). Ethnic cleansing in Myanmar: The Rohingya crisis and human rights. *The Lancet, 390*(10102), 1570–1573.

Blakemore, E. (2019). *Who are the Rohingya people?* https://www.nationalgeographic.com/culture/people/reference/rohingya-people/. Accessed 9 June 2020.

Burke, A. (2016). New political space, old tensions: History, identity and violence in Rakhine State, Myanmar. *Contemporary Southeast Asia, 38*(2), 258–283.

Chan, A. (2005). The development of a Muslim enclave in Arakan (Rakhine) State of Burma (Myanmar). *SOAS Bulletin of Burma Research, 3*(2), 396–420. https://www.soas.ac.uk/sbbr/editions/file64388.pdf. Accessed 8 June 2021.

Council on Foreign Relations (CoFR). (2020). *Global conflict tracker*. https://www.cfr.org/global-conflict-tracker/conflict/rohingya-crisis-myanmar. Accessed 20 June 2020.

Dussich, J. P. J. (2018). The ongoing genocidal crisis of the Rohingya minority in Myanmar. *Journal of Victimology and Victim Justice, 1*(1), 4–24.

Fisher, J. (2017). UN failures on Rohingya revealed. *BBC News*. https://www.bbc.com/news/world-asia-41420973. Accessed 23 June 2020.

Global Centre for the Responsibility to Protect (GCR2P). (2019). *Q&A: The Gambia v. Myanmar Rohingya Genocide at the International Court of Justice*. https://www.globalr2p.org/publications/myanmarqav2/. Accessed 7 July 2021.

Human Rights Council (HRC). (2019). *Detailed findings of the independent international fact-finding mission on Myanmar*. A/HRC/42/CRP.5.

Human Rights Watch (HRW). (2019). *Questions and answers on Gambia's genocide case against Myanmar before the International Court of Justice*. https://www.hrw.org/news/2019/12/05/questions-and-answers-gambias-genocide-case-against-myanmar-international-court. Accessed 24 June 2020.

Ibrahim, A. (2020, May 21). *No place for optimism: Anticipating Myanmar's first report to the International Court of Justice*. https://newlinesinstitute.org/rohingya/no-place-for-optimism-anticipating-myanmars-first-report-to-the-international-court-of-justice/. Accessed 19 May 2021.

Ibrahim, H., & Nordin, R. (2015). The principle of responsibility to protect: The Case of Rohingya in Myanmar. *Pertanika Journal of Social Sciences & Humanities, 23*(S), 1–18.

International Court of Justice (ICJ). (2020, January 23). *Application of the convention on the prevention and punishment of the crime of genocide* (The Gambia v. Myanmar). https://www.icj-cij.org/files/case-related/178/178-20200123-ORD-01-00-EN.pdf. Accessed 24 June 2020.

International Criminal Court (ICC). (2019, November 22). *Statement of the prosecutor of the International Criminal Court, Fatou Bensouda, following judicial authorisation to commence an investigation into the situation in Bangladesh/Myanmar*. https://www.icc-cpi.int/Pages/item.aspx?name=20191122-otp-statement-bangladesh-myanmar. Accessed 24 June 2020.

Islam, M. S. (2019). Understanding the Rohingya crisis and the failure of human rights norm in Myanmar: Possible policy responses. *Jadavpur Journal of International Relations, 23*(2), 158–178.

Jati, I. (2017). Comparative study of the roles of ASEAN and the organization of Islamic cooperation in responding to the Rohingya crisis. *Indonesian Journal of Southeast Asian Studies, 1*(1), 17–32.

Joy, A. (2018). *Understanding China's response to the Rakhine crisis*. United States Institute of Peace Special Report, 419. https://www.usip.org/sites/default/files/2018-02/sr419-understanding-chinas-response-to-the-rakhine-crisis.pdf. Accessed 28 February 2021.

Khaliq, R. (2020, November 24). *Myanmar submits 2nd Rohingya report to top UN court*. Anadolu Agency. https://www.aa.com.tr/en/asia-pacific/myanmar-submits-2nd-rohingya-report-to-top-un-court/2054175#:~:text=Myanmar%20has%20submitted%20a%20second,order%20to%20protect%20Rohingya%20community.&text=The%20second%20report%20was%20filed,elections%20held%20early%20this%20month. Accessed 19 May 2021.

Khan, M. T., & Ahmed, S. (2020). Dealing with the Rohingya crisis: The relevance of the general assembly and R2P. *Asian Journal of Comparative Politics, 5*(2), 121–143.

Khin, T. (2020). *Universal jurisdiction, the International Criminal Court, and the Rohingya genocide*. http://opiniojuris.org/2020/10/23/universal-jurisdiction-the-international-criminal-court-and-the-rohingya-genocide/. Accessed 20 July 2021.

Kibler, T. (2019). *The Nuremberg trials and their profound impact on International Law*. https://home.heinonline.org/blog/2019/10/the-nuremberg-trials-and-their-profound-impact-on-international-law/. Accessed 9 June 2021.

Kingston, L. N. (2015). Protecting the world's most persecuted: The responsibility to protect and Burma's Rohingya minority. *The International Journal of Human Rights, 19*(8), 1163–1175.

Kipgen, N. (2019). The Rohingya crisis: The centrality of identity and citizenship. *Journal of Muslim Minority Affairs, 39*(1), 61–74.

Kyaw, N. N. (2017). Unpacking the presumed statelessness of Rohingyas *Journal of Immigrant & Refugee Studies, 15*(3), 269–286.

Lee, R. (2019). Myanmar's citizenship law as state crime. A case for the International Criminal Court. *State Crime Journal, 8*(2), 241–279.

Lee, R. (2021). *Myanmar's Rohingya genocide: Identity, history and hate speech*. I.B. Tauris.

Limsiritong, N. (2017). Why ASEAN fails to play role in the Rohingya situation from the perspective of ASEAN Charter. *Asian Political Science Review, 1*(2), 73–79.

Massey, H. (2010). *UNHCR and de facto statelessness*. https://www.unhcr.org/4bc2ddeb9.pdf. Accessed 28 February 2021.

Mills, K. (2015). *International responses to mass atrocities in Africa: Responsibility to protect, prosecute, and palliate*. University of Pennsylvania Press.

Nishikawa, Y. (2018). The reality of protecting the Rohingya: An inherent limitation of the responsibility to protect. *Asian Security, 16*(1), 90–106.

Office of the High Commissioner for Human Rights (OHCHR). (2017, December 5). *Human Rights Council opens special session on the situation of human rights of the Rohingya and other minorities in Rakhine State in Myanmar*. https://www.ohchr.org/EN/NewsEvents/Pages/DisplayNews.aspx?NewsID=22491&LangID=E. Accessed 19 May 2021.

Rahman, Z., Anusara, J., Chanthamith, B., Hossain, S., & Amin, A. (2018). Rohingya crisis: Identity of Rohingya Muslim in Myanmar. *International Research Journal of Social Sciences, 7*(12), 12–16.

Robertson, G. (2005). Ending impunity: How international criminal law can put tyrants on trial. *Cornell International Law Journal, 38*(3), 649–671.

Rosenberg, S. P. (2015). Audacity of hope: International criminal law, mass atrocity crimes, and prevention. In S. Rosenberg, T. Galis, & A. Zucker (Eds.), *Reconstructing atrocity prevention* (pp. 151–174). Cambridge University Press.

Rosenthal, G. (2019). *A brief and independent inquiry into the involvement of the United Nations in Myanmar from 2010 to 2018*. https://www.un.org/sg/sites/www.un.org.sg/files/atoms/files/Myanmar%20Report%20-%20May%202019.pdf. Accessed 23 June 2020.

Seth, A. (2018). *Myanmar's armed forces and the Rohingya crisis* (Peaceworks No. 140). https://www.usip.org/publications/2018/08/myanmars-armed-forces-and-rohingya-crisis. Accessed 28 February 2021.

Smith, M. (2002). *Burma (Myanmar): The time for change*. Minority Rights Group International. https://www.refworld.org/pdfid/469cbf8cd.pdf. Accessed 10 June 2020.

Taufiq, H. A. (2019). China, India, and Myanmar: Playing Rohingya roulette? In I. Hussain (Ed.), *South Asia in global power rivalry inside-out appraisals from Bangladesh* (pp. 81–99). Palgrave Macmillan.

The Guardian. (2019). *Myanmar's Aung San Suu Kyi faces first legal action over Rohingya crisis*. https://www.theguardian.com/world/2019/nov/14/myanmars-aung-san-suu-kyi-faces-first-legal-action-over-rohingya-crisis. Accessed 26 July 2021.

Ullah, A. K. M. A. (2016). Rohingya crisis in Myanmar: Seeking justice for the "stateless." *Journal of Contemporary Criminal Justice, 32*(3), 285–301.

UN News. (2017). *UN human rights chief points to 'textbook example of ethnic cleansing' in Myanmar*. https://news.un.org/en/story/2017/09/564622-un-human-rights-chief-points-textbook-example-ethnic-cleansing-myanmar. Accessed on 18 April 2020.

United Nations General Assembly (UNGA). (2005, October 24). *Resolution adopted by the general assembly on 16 September 2005, 60/1.* 2005 World Summit Outcome, A/Res/60/1.

United Nations General Assembly (UNGA). (2009, January 12). *Implementing the responsibility to protect* (Report of the Secretary-General, A/63/677).

United Nations General Assembly (UNGA). (2013, April 8). *Resolution adopted by the General Assembly on 24 December 2012.* A/RES/67/233.

United Nations General Assembly (UNGA). (2017, October 31). *Draft resolution on the situation of human rights in Myanmar.* A/C.3/72/L.48.

United Nations General Assembly (UNGA). (2018, September 12). *Report of the independent international fact-finding mission on Myanmar*. A/HRC/39/64.

United Nations General Assembly (UNGA). (2019a, August 8). *Report of the independent international fact-finding mission on Myanmar*. A/HRC/42/50.

United Nations General Assembly (UNGA). (2019b, July 19). *Report of the Secretary-General on the work of the Organization*. A/74/1.

United Nations High Commissioner for Refugees (UNHCR). (n.d.). *Rohingya refugee crisis*. https://www.unrefugees.org/emergencies/rohingya/. Accessed 18 April 2020.

United Nations Secretary-General (UNSG). (2018, August 28). *Secretary-General's remarks to the Security Council on Myanmar* [as delivered]. https://www.un.org/sg/en/content/sg/statement/2018-08-28/secretary-generals-remarks-security-council-myanmar-delivered. Accessed 25 June 2020.

United Nations Security Council (UNSC). (2017, November 6). *Statement by the President of the Security Council*, S/PRST/2017/22.

Yegar, M. (2018). The plight of the Rohingya in Myanmar. *Israel Journal of Foreign Affairs, 12*(2), 197–207.

Walton, M. J. (2008). Ethnicity, conflict and history in Burma: The myths of Panglong. *Asian Survey, 48*(6), 889–910.

CHAPTER 12

'Three Evils' of Xinjiang: Suppression, Violent Separatism and R2P

İrem Karamık

Xinjiang Uyghur Autonomous Region has been home to a myriad of Uyghurs, who are a Turkic-originated Muslim community that identify themselves as distinct from the Han Chinese culturally, religiously and linguistically. Since the beginning, the Uyghur story was interwoven with a self-claim attempt. Uyghurs used radio broadcasts to announce their self-determination requests and claim their homeland as East Turkestan (Bovingdon, 2004, p. 11). A Chinese official's speech in 1957 clearly illustrated that the central government was indeed aware of the Uyghur pledges of self-governance. Nonetheless, China did not just stay myopic to the Uyghur demands but also suppressed the cultural, religious and ethnic differences through its homogenisation practices.

As van Wie Devis (2008, p. 16) recalls, while China was first announced to be a multinational and multicultural State, starting from 1957 and inflamed by the Cultural Revolution, the Communist Party

İ. Karamık (✉)
Department of International Relations, Hacettepe University, Ankara, Turkey

P. Gözen Ercan (ed.), *The Responsibility to Protect Twenty Years On*,
https://doi.org/10.1007/978-3-030-90731-0_12

refrained from local nationalism. Ethnic minorities and other religions conveyed social unrest. In recent years, both the names Xinjiang and Turkic-originated Uyghurs started to echo in a plethora of politics, human rights and media platforms. The salience of the region and the community is wedded to the intensified Chinese restrictions on religious and cultural life in Xinjiang and in return, growing separatist movements on the Uyghur crowds which are often violent due to the fear of cultural degradation, persistent identity denial and religious inhibition. Amplified with the *ad placitum* 'War on Terror' agenda that ravaged throughout the world, China's counterterrorism and deradicalisation agenda went too far that it turned into the detention of Uyghurs and raised questions on human rights abuses and violations. Reportedly, since 2017, at least one million Uyghurs are taken to the so-called *Re-education Camps* and have been ill-treated, malnourished and indoctrinated (Feng, 2018; Phillips, 2018). Hence, the ongoing situation in Xinjiang is of significance for the implication of human rights and the maintenance of international peace and security.

With the concern arising from these, it is this chapter's aim to discuss the uneasiness in the region and approach it from the perspective of the Responsibility to Protect (R2P). While the literature on the historical construction of the Uyghur identity and the current human rights conditions are rich and abundant (see, for instance, Bovingdon, 2004; Foot, 2020; Fung, 2021; Millward, 2004; Rogers & Sidhu, 2016), the evaluation of Xinjiang as an R2P case is disregarded by the literature, although the R2P framework serves as an antidote for State-caused mass atrocity crimes and human rights violations. In this regard, this chapter conducts its analysis based on the three-pillar implementation strategy of R2P to reflect on the stage the crisis has developed into and how close China—the primary holder of the responsibility—and the international community are to fulfil this responsibility.

Historical Roots of the Uyghur Case

The word *Xinjiang* (新疆) connotes to *New Frontier* or *New Dominion* in Chinese. This meaning is deeply tied to the history of the region. It was not until the 1750s that Xinjiang came under the rule of the Chinese and integrated into the Chinese borders as a province in 1884, forming the Western border shared with Russia (van Wie Davis, 2008, p. 16). According to Millward (2004, p. 3), after the capture of Xinjiang, the Qing dynasty initiated certain provincialisation and redistribution programmes that aimed to even and fill the region. As a result, many Taranchis (known as Uyghurs today) immigrated through the province and became the initial settlers. Whereas there were ongoing in-province settlement movements, the community was divided and as Brophy (2005, p. 166) and Millward (2004, p. 3) reveal, political upheavals in the region forced many East Turkestanis to take refuge in Russia.

When the Qing dynasty was overthrown and replaced by the Republic of China (1912–1949), the Xinjiang region or Xinjiang's Sunni Muslims were not particularly on the agenda of the Republic. This was of importance only when a rebellious period instigated by the Uyghur enlightenment disrupted the peace in Xinjiang. The ethnic make-up of the people living in the region has been intricate with the sole immutable information being that these were Turkic originated people. It was an intellectual Abdullah Rozibaqiev who, for the first time, referred to this community as *Uyghur.*

In the 1920s, the elite Turkics who have travelled to Europe pioneered the process to modernise Uyghur education and instil Uyghur nationalist ideas (Millward, 2004, p. 4). In the meantime, the Uyghur declaration of cultural existence was under close surveillance of Chinese warlords. However, they could not foresee the rest of the iceberg: the initial small-scale jacquerie paved the way for the rise of a fully fledged rebellion. In pursuit of establishing an independent government for the Turkic peoples—Uyghurs, Qazaqs, Hui (Chinese Muslim) and others—Ili National Army (INA) was formed and brought together under different regiments and subdivisions. In 1933, Turkic originated peoples declared the first East Turkistan Republic (ETR)—or with its official name Turkish Islamic Republic of Eastern Turkistan (TIRET)—a regime to this date effectuates the Uyghur independence claims. This cooperative attempt by the peoples was followed by the Second Eastern Turkistan Republic of 1944–1949. This time, it was a Soviet-backed, socialist, secular but still ethnically Turkic regime. However, after the Sino-Soviet Treaty of Friendship and Alliance (1945), ETR was coerced to agree on a ceasefire with the Guomindang (Nationalist Party of China) forces (Millward, 2004, p. 6). Furthermore, in the period between 1946 and 1949, ETR and Nationalist Party co-governed the Xinjiang region. Although the Soviet Union's support defined the birth of the regime, eventually, Turkic originated people could not evade being tied to the consequences of band-wagoning.

Prior to the advancement of the Chinese Communist Party, expectance of full political independence was flamed within Uyghurs (Bovingdon, 2004, p. 4). In the end, despite all the independence efforts, the region was handed over to the People's Liberation Army and became a territory of the People's Republic of China (PRC). Mumford (2018, p. 19) suggests that the region, in addition to the ethnically and religiously different Turkic Muslims, were fully incorporated into the political lineup after 1949: the founding of the People's Republic of China. Hence, the Xinjiang Uyghur Autonomous Region (XUAR) was established in October 1955, in a context of great political ambiguity for Xinjiang and its residents.

For the construction of a 'New China', there was a need for restructuring policies effective throughout the country. Even before the region was labelled as XUAR, in the 1950s, the government propelled a Han immigration from other parts of China to the XUAR (Dillon, 1994, p. 82). The increase in the Han Chinese population in the area proved to have certain consequences. First and foremost, it manifested the ruling party's intention to uniform and homogenise the overall texture of the country's population. The flow of Han Chinese to the region helped evening out the ethnic distribution of people with the rest of the country. As van Wie Davis (2008, p. 20) comments, the Han settlement further reinforced the minority status of Uyghurs and puts them in a less-advantageous and/or lower-ranked position within the society since jobs with higher income rates and prestige were given to the Han Chinese. Moreover, by encouraging the ethnic placement of Hans, the government has also placed demography in the realm of security. This demographic securitisation goes hand-in-hand with the perception of cultural, ethnic and religious differences as a security threat.

This belief has also laid out the basis for certain other policies that will further damage the cultural climate of the country. One of these policies, the Great Leap Forward, was launched in 1958 and aimed to drive radical collectivisation and industrialisation, perceived ethnicity, cultural or religious difference as obstacles to progress (Bovingdon, 2004, p. 18). It can be asserted that this period planted the seeds for a more assimilationist and homogenising thrust. The disruption of everyday life, constant propaganda and annihilation of the cultural-self drove residents to flee from the country. Data reveals that more than 60.000 Turkic people crossed the Soviet border only in 1962 (Bovingdon, 2004, p. 18). This was exacerbated by the Cultural Revolution of 1965–1976, formally known as the

'Great Proletariat Cultural Revolution'. This movement itself caused a death toll of hundreds of thousands Pye, 1986). Millward (2004, p. 7) reminds that one of the most violent acts in the PRC history had little to do with minority peoples but rather was caused by Han Chinese fractions, yet the minorities bore the brunt.

The bloody Cultural Revolution originally aimed to uniform and foist *Zhōngguó rén* (mainstream Chinese) culture that is considered to be superior compared to the existing endonyms (Dillon, 1994, p. 71). Moreover, party leader Mao Zedong announced other cultures and religious practices as 'backward customs' (McMillen, 1979). Therefore, the 'inferior' Uyghur Muslim culture was faced with a breakdown of the traditional culture and religious independence. Their mosques were destroyed, copies of the Quran were demolished, all religious and cultural activities were banned and religious leaders were persecuted (Bovingdon, 2004; Dillon, 1999; van Wie Davis, 2008). These assimilationist practices went extreme. As Bovingdon (2004, p. 18) and Denyer (2014) claim, certain religious leaders were forced to raise pigs and use alcohol, which are considered as sinful acts in Islam. Additionally, in 1966, certain Uyghurs who were in significant positions in the society, such as the Governor of Xinjiang, the Vice-Chairman, along with the former members of ETR, were accused of treason (Rogers & Sidhu, 2016, p. 114). This wave of robbery of fundamental freedoms, coupled with the demographic alteration in Xinjiang, helped PRC bring 'Others' under control and employ biopolitics (Foucault, 1997).

On the contrary, starting from the 1970s, the PRC adopted opening policies in which restrictions on minorities, religious and cultural events were softened (van Wie Davis, 2008, p. 17). The underlying incentives in doing so can be traced back to the political and economic goals of the PRC. As Dillon (1994, p. 71) reveals, China aimed at convincing the Muslim world along with others in the religious freedom in China so that it can further establish trade relations and political exchange. To this end, in this period mosques were rebuilt, newspapers, Qurans and journals were re-published. However, meanwhile, the spark of freedom had already been triggered within the Uyghur community. Uyghurs started to form organised movements with certain political aims such as full autonomy, secession and/or cultural, social and political freedom. Thereby, the unrest in the region evolved into a mutually constructed and collectively harming series of acts from both sides.

Starting from the late 1980s, some parts of the PRC and Xinjiang specifically experienced terrorist attacks in an increasing frequency. Chinese sources reported the activities of an 'East Turkistan Independence Organization', led by a seventeen-year-old along with another group called the 'Spark Alliance' brought together by separatist students (Millward, 2004, p. 8). In 1985, the Xinjiang University students protested the Han immigration and family planning policies of the government along with nuclear testing which are believed to be damaging the health of Uyghurs (Millward, 2004, p. 8). In parallel to the events articulated since the Cultural Revolution, the general demand for respect for Uyghur lives, their religion and cultural identity was sensible. China's propaganda of spreading disparaging publications on Uyghurs was also on the agenda of student demonstrations that took place in 1988 as well as 1989.

The year 1989 is, especially notable for Uyghur households in two ways. One of the widely known Uyghur armed groups, the East Turkestan Islamic Movement (ETIM) was established with the claim of fighting against Chinese oppression and building a separate Uyghur State (van Wie Davis, 2008). ETIM is recognised internationally as a terrorist organisation that has close ties with Al-Qaida. Due to intensifying suppression, ETIM had transformed and re-branded itself as Turkestan Islamic Party (TIP) in 2006.

Another breaking point the year 1989 brought was the Tiananmen Square Protests, i.e. 4 June Incidents that took place in Beijing. These six-week-long student protests were a part of the new democratisation and political openness movement initiated by the Chinese public, they assembled in the historically significant Tiananmen Square. Initially, the government took no action. However, on 4 June, the People Liberation Army troops began to flow into the square and opened fire on the protesters to regain control (BBC, 2019). While China reported 200 civilians dead, the then British ambassador to China, Sir Alan Donald disclosed the causalities to be more than 10,000 in a secret cable (South China Morning Post, 2018). According to Rogers and Sidhu (2016, p. 119), it was not until this event that the human rights violations in Xinjiang were internationalised. Mass killings of civilians resonated in the eyes and ears of the international community. The internationalisation of this incident had the potential to reveal the internal conflicts within China which sparked hope in the Uyghur community that their voice could be heard. Nevertheless, Mumford (2018, p. 70) observes that in the aftermath of these events, the divisions within the society and the State amplified, and the separatist demand was entrenched.

The seeds of the violent acts of Uyghurs gave its fruits in the 1990s and onwards. Intensified with the Baren violent protests in April 1990, Uyghur Muslims opted for spreading the idea of resistance. The concomitant of this resistance was the 'Strike Hard (*Yanda*) Campaign' launched by the Chinese government in 1990 to fight increasing crime (Trevaskes, 2010). Beijing announced that more than 160 people were killed and 440 injured due to Uyghur violence between 1990 and 2001 (Mumford, 2018). These attacks did not solely target Chinese authorities but also civilians. The bus bombings in Urumqi that occurred in 1992 and 1997 clearly revealed that separatist Uyghurs were indeed venturing to lose their legitimacy in order to strike back and leave scars on the Chinese government. Moreover, in the 1990s, building bombings, poisonings, gunfire and stabbings took place (Millward, 2004).

It is possible to purport that in these attacks, there was also an underlying attempt of gathering international attention. Violent Uyghur resistance was not confined to Xinjiang or the PRC borders, many violent incidents took place in the name of Uyghur independence in the territories of neighbouring countries such as Kazakhstan and Kyrgyzstan (Millward, 2004, p. 4). Xinjiang region, in fact, constitutes a border to many Turkic-originated countries. Being surrounded by Turkic communities who established their own country inspired the Uyghur community. Violent parties of the Uyghur resistance opted for establishing militant training camps in these countries (van Wie Davis, 2008). Like Uyghurs carrying their objectives into the territories of others, after the establishment of the Shanghai Five in 1996, China pressured its co-member States to eradicate the Uyghur presence in their territories (Bovingdon, 2004, p. 22).

Starting from the 1990s, the United States (US) piqued interest in the human rights violations in Xinjiang, however, faced with adamant Chinese denial (Rogers & Sidhu, 2016, p. 128). One the one hand, the US was condemning human rights conditions, on the other, its 2001 Global War on Terror agenda exacerbated Chinese suppression. According to Mumford (2018, p. 19), associating Islamic extremism with the Uyghur separatist movement served as a Trojan Horse. First, by siding with the US in its fight, China gained legitimacy and international approval in its actions towards Uyghurs. Through the discourse of the War on Terror, China could easily label a group of separatists as Islamic extremists.

Second, by being allies, Chinese authorities meliorated Sino-American relations that were somewhat shaky.

Chinese Communist Party adjusted its Strike Hard Campaign parallel to the War on Terror narrative. In January 2002, China officially announced a list of nine main East Turkestan terrorist groups (van Wie Davis, 2008). Subsequently, the US Embassy in Beijing declared ETIM as a terrorist organisation that is linked to Al-Qaida in addition to holding it responsible for all violent incidents in Xinjiang (Millward, 2004, p. 13). Attributing the Uyghur movement, an Islamic objective also attracted the extremists. For instance, in 2009, a high-ranking Al-Qaida commander invoked a holy war against China, expressed his support to Uyghur Muslims and announced that Islamic fighters are ready to help (Potter, 2013, p. 74).

Deriving from the Strike Hard policies as well as the increasing unrest in the region, Xinjiang's public security budget rocketed to ¥2.89 billion in 2010 (Potter, 2013, p. 73). In May 2014, the Chinese government reiterated the 'Strike Hard Campaign against Violent Terrorism' (Finley, 2019; Mumford, 2018). Through this campaign, the Chinese government further incorporated its policies into the War on Terror narrative and declared 'People's War on Terror'. Moreover, the 'Three Evils' against the Chinese State was identified as 'separatism, extremism, and terrorism'. This renewed set of policies was laden with provisions on increasing military presence, adamant prohibitions on free mobility and eradicating cultural and religious differences. According to the Wall Street Journal, in 2014—the year Strike Hard Campaign was initiated—the arrests tallied in Xinjiang were almost double compared to the previous year (Arreddy, 2015).

The Strike Hard approach also projected the establishment of the so-called Vocational Education and Training Centres or Re-education Centres. These camps are designated to be a part of counterterrorism measures and aimed at indoctrinating Uyghurs who are claimed to be radical Muslims. Chinese language and history, Han cultural values and Han practices are taught in a continuous cycle in these propaganda facilities (Feng, 2018), while it is ensured that the detainees will renounce their religion and mother-tongue and announce their loyalty to Han identity. According to Finley (2019), starting from 2014, XUAR residents were asked to obtain new identity cards, and hence, have been stripped from their identities while the Uyghur identity was being re-engineered.

In addition, the 'guests' of these re-education camps are not volunteers or free individuals who receive this education and continue their daily lives but are taken there forcefully and detained from their free lives (Phillips, 2018). With an intensifying commonality, hundreds of thousands Turkic-originated people (predominantly Uyghurs and Kazakhs) have gone and are still going missing since 2017 (Phillips, 2018). As Byler observes, since then the phrases 'everyone is gone' or 'disappeared' (that is '*Adem yok*' in Uyghur) have become common among Uyghurs and are occasionally used in everyday conversations. Furthermore, contrary to what the Strike Hard Campaign purports, the detainees are far from being limited to people who are involved in terrorist activities or people who are religious extremists but instead are a mix of scholars, students, artists, journalists and ordinary citizens (Duara, 2019).

China Director of Human Rights Watch Sophie Richardson (2019) discloses that the detained people were not evidently charged with any crimes, but the mere reason was that the Chinese government declared these people to be 'politically unreliable'. The entrenched terrorism measures and the long-fabricated homogenisation attempts were pregnant to these dystopian internment or detention camps. Although the 1989 Tiananmen Square events drew the attention of the international community greatly for the first time, the stories resonated from the detention camps served as a tipping point, now many eyes and ears are on the human rights conditions in Xinjiang. However, since China claims to have its historical reservations on international interference and frames this issue solely as an internal affair, all the information the international community and the human rights bodies can gather is confined to inside agents and satellite images. Gunawan (2019) claims that in the span of two years (2017–2019), the number of people who have been detained and/or disappeared amounted approximately to 10% of the Xinjiang population. According to the data of Chinese Human Rights Defenders (2019), at least one million Uyghurs are held in these camps. Several reports indicate that detainees suffer from malnourishment, food poisoning and starvation along with mental distress and suicidal or self-harming behaviour (Denyer, 2014; Shih, 2018). Deprivation of sleep, beating, being shackled and hung upside down by their feet are among additional sorts of maltreatment mentioned by former detainees (Human Rights Watch, 2018a). Furthermore, there is a salient paranoia among the non-detained Uyghur community due to constant Orwellian surveillance, as well as fear of being abducted.

A Scotoma in R2P Implementation: The Uyghur Case

In the light of the overview of how the Uyghur case historically accumulated, this chapter suggests that the Xinjiang case is, indeed, an R2P crisis and there is a need for an R2P response to prevent further suffering of the Uyghur population in Xinjiang. The Global Centre for the Responsibility to Protect lists Uyghurs in China as one of the 'populations at risk' and labels the case as a 'current crisis' (GCR2P, 2020). Although the 1989 events hinted at how China tends to handle public opposition to its policies, mass detention and abduction of minorities, the securitisation of terrorism coupled with the uncooperative and conservative/protectionist temper of China evidently indicated the erosion in its 'sovereignty as responsibility'. Deriving from the aforementioned reports on Uyghurs in Xinjiang, this chapter bases China's failure to protect its population on four of the elements of crimes against humanity[1] as established under Article 7(1) of the Rome Statute of the International Criminal Court. These are:

d. Deportation or forcible transfer of population;
e. Imprisonment or other severe deprivation of physical liberty in violation of fundamental rules of international law;
h. Persecution against any identifiable group or collectivity on political, racial, national, ethnic, cultural, religious, gender [...];
i. Enforced disappearance of persons. (ICC, 1998)

Moreover, in February 2021, Canada's 43rd Parliament voted unanimously (266–0) and hence formally recognised Uyghur suffering as a genocide. In the following days, the Dutch Parliament reiterated this recognition. In June 2021, the German Parliament acknowledged the crimes against humanity committed towards Uyghurs (World Uyghur Congress, 2021). As crimes against humanity and alleged genocide are

[1] The GCR2P (2020) and the January report of the Congressional-Executive Commission on China (2020) also claim that the Chinese actions may amount to crimes against humanity. Furthermore, China is also violating its commitment to the International Convention on the Elimination of All Forms of Racial Discrimination, which it ratified in 1981.

two of the four crimes[2] that defines the scope of R2P, the subsequent sections of the chapter examine whether or not the three-pillar implementation strategy of R2P is being applied to the Xinjiang case.

The Unbearable Lightness of Protecting: China and Pillar One

The 2009 Report of the UN Secretary-General titled 'Implementing the responsibility to protect' (A/63/677) stipulates an implementation strategy consisting of three main pillars. Based on Paragraph 138 of the World Summit Outcome Document (WSOD), under Pillar One States bear the primary responsibility to shield their populations from mass atrocity crimes. With regard to the Xinjiang case, the preceding evidence demonstrates that above and beyond falling short of meeting this capability or simply disregarding it, China has displayed victimising policies. Furthermore, it persistently denied notifying the international community of its policies and prohibited any international assessments in this regard. Coupled with the rigid concealing scheme, China failed miserably at implementing Pillar One, which is of importance for successful prevention of mass atrocity crimes.

Recalling the roundtable discussions on the draft of the Responsibility to Protect Report of the International Commission on Intervention and State Sovereignty (ICISS), Thakur (2006) notes that China had its reservations on R2P since it perceived it as 'humanitarian intervention in disguise' and claimed that humanitarian intervention was 'tantamount to marrying evil to good'. When the focus is brought to the XUAR, initially, China denied the rumours and even the existence of these internment camps (Watson & Westcott, 2020). Since the Uyghur case is interwoven with violent actions that are disrupting security not only in the Xinjiang region but throughout China and in certain other neighbouring countries, China acquired the upper hand and covered up human rights abuses as counterterrorism measures. It was not until November 2019 when the 'China Cables'[3] leaked that the Chinese narrative of Xinjiang cascaded (Watson & Westcott, 2020). When the systematic prosecution

[2] These are genocide, war crimes, crimes against humanity and ethnic cleansing, and hereinafter will be referred to as atrocity crimes.

[3] A group of exiled Uyghurs leaked strong evidence on the situation in Xinjiang through the International Consortium of Investigative Journalists on 24 November 2019 (Watson & Westcott, 2020).

and detention was brought to light, international allegations and pleas for human rights assessments were amplified. The Chinese response to these allegations was simply playing the 'sovereignty and non-interference to domestic affairs card' (Hirono et al., 2019; Human Rights Watch, 2018a; Weinian, 2019). It accused the international community of applying double standards and ignoring the countries with worse human rights conditions. Moreover, China framed the allegations as a part of the interplay between communism and capitalism by purporting that Western States are purely imposing their political systems and preventing China's freedom of choice. The Chinese scheme of international manipulation and the historically mounted abuses applied to Uyghurs, thereby, is the confirmation that there is little to none that Pillar One can promise in the case of Xinjiang.

International Repercussions and Pillar Two: On a Slow Boat to China

Pillar Two, 'international assistance and capacity-building', distributes the responsibility for the protection of populations between the State and the international community. Despite the responsibility to prevent chiefly being attributed to the State itself, the international community is required to encourage, assist and supervise States in their mission of protection. Paragraph 139 of the WSOD emphasises further involvement of the international community by offloading some of the responsibility. It prescribes the international community with the responsibility to assist States in establishing and maintaining their capacity to protect as well as to prevent conflicts or crises by helping States under stress. These efforts, however, can only be effective if the State is 'incapable' of meeting its responsibility. In the case of the ruling power's 'unwillingness', this assistance can do little. For those situations, the 2009 Report of the Secretary-General suggests the international community to gather the 'capacity and will for timely and decisive action'. Paragraph 30 of the Report also highlights the significance of creating a dialogue through good offices and diplomatic efforts[4] in order to negotiate with the unwilling State (UNGA, 2009).

For the Xinjiang case, international repercussions were rich and loud, however, were voiced at the eleventh hour and practically little. It was only in the 2000s that the human rights conditions in Xinjiang were verbalised and put on the table in the United Nations (UN). In 2009, the then UN High Commissioner for Human Rights Navi Pillay brought to attention the growing number of deaths and called on both the concerned parties of the Uyghur resistance and the Chinese government to retreat and stop the violence (UN News, 2009). The same year, during its non-permanent membership to the UN Security Council (UNSC), Turkey tried to bring the Xinjiang case before the Council. Considering that the accused State is a Permanent Member State of the UNSC (P5), it was a bold but necessary move. In 2010, during the 15th Session of the UN Human Rights Council (UNHRC), the poor conditions were raised by two human rights organisations—namely, the Society for Threatened Peoples and the International Society for Human Rights and International Education Development, Inc. (Rogers & Sidhu, 2016). However, they were immediately castigated by the Chinese delegation. The same year, the UN Universal Periodic Review (UPR) initiated the assessment of ethnic minorities within Xinjiang camps. Yet, it could not be instigated since China prohibited the UPR evaluation of any kind (Human Rights Watch, 2018b). Not until 2018, the UN Committee on the Elimination of Racial Discrimination (CERD) confirmed the detention of up to a million people in these camps. The intellectual community could not stay oblivious to these violations. On 26 December 2018, 646 scholars from 40 countries released the 'Statement by Concerned Scholars on China's Mass Detention of Turkic Minorities' (Al Jazeera, 2018).

Arguably, due to the emerging power politics between the US and China and America's 'democratic hero' identity, the US paid close attention to the victimising Chinese policies. In the 2018 UPR at the UN,

[4] Namely, the 'regional and sub-regional mechanisms, the United Nations High Commissioner for Human Rights, the United Nations High Commissioner for Refugees, the Emergency Relief Coordinator, the Special Adviser on the Prevention of Genocide, other special advisers, special representatives and envoys of the Secretary-General, and ranking officials of the United Nations, its development agencies and the Bretton Woods institutions' (UNGA, 2009).

the US primarily pledged China to 'abolish all forms of arbitrary detention, including internment camps in Xinjiang, and immediately release the hundreds of thousands, possibly millions, of individuals detained in these camps'. Furthermore, the human rights violations in XUAR were brought up in several public speeches by Republican politicians such as Mike Pence and Mike Pompeo (Szadziewski, 2020).

In March 2016, twelve countries—namely, Australia, Denmark, Finland, Germany, Iceland, Ireland, Japan, the Netherlands, Norway, Sweden, the UK and the US—signed a joint letter to the UNHRC to express their concerns about the deteriorating human rights record of China, unexplainable disappearances and the lack of judicial process in some cases (US-MIOG, 2016). Following the CERD affirmation on detainees, on 8 July 2019, eighteen European countries[5] joined by Canada, Japan and New Zealand delivered another letter to the UNHRC (A/HRC/41/G/11). This letter reiterated the concerns indicated in the 2016 letter and emphasised the freedom of belief and the application of human rights. It is noteworthy that this time despite acknowledging and speaking out about this issue many times on various platforms, the US was not a signatory to the 2019 letter.

Only four days later, 50 countries[6] united to indicate their opposition to 'politicizing human rights issues, by naming and shaming, and publicly exerting pressures on other countries' (A/HRC/41/G/17). Moreover, they underlined the supposed human rights achievements of China and claimed that its actions were justifiable due to these being counterterrorism and deradicalisation measures (Global Times, 2019).

[5] Namely, Australia, Austria, Belgium, Denmark, Estonia, Finland, France, Germany, Iceland, Ireland, Latvia, Lithuania, Luxembourg, the Netherlands, Norway, Spain, Sweden, Switzerland and the UK.

[6] Namely, Algeria, Angola, Bahrain, Bangladesh, Belarus, the Plurinational State of Bolivia, Burkina Faso, Burundi, Cambodia, Cameroon, Comoros, the Congo, Cuba, the Democratic People's Republic of Korea, the Democratic Republic of the Congo, Djibouti, Egypt, Equatorial Guinea, Eritrea, Gabon, the Islamic Republic of Iran, Iraq, Kuwait, the Lao People's Democratic Republic, Mozambique, Myanmar, Nepal, Nigeria, Oman, Pakistan, the Philippines, the Russian Federation, Saudi Arabia, Serbia, Somalia, South Sudan, Sri Lanka, Sudan, the Syrian Arab Republic, Tajikistan, Togo, Turkmenistan, Uganda, the United Arab Emirates, Uzbekistan, the Bolivarian Republic of Venezuela, Yemen, Zambia, Zimbabwe and the State of Palestine.

In October 2019, 23 countries[7] renewed their suggestions and stressed their stance on the misconduct and securitisation of terrorism course of action (Human Rights Watch, 2019). This statement was delivered by the UK Permanent Representative to the UN, Karen Pierce during the Third Committee session on the Committee for the Elimination of Racial Discrimination. In the following month, Belarus voiced the approval of Chinese policies on behalf of 54 countries.[8] The content of the statement was similar to the one in July 2019, congratulating terrorism-free China.

It is noteworthy to analyse Ambassador Pierce's concluding remark (UKGFCO, 2019): 'What measures should the Chinese government undertake to address the concerns raised in CERD's Concluding Observations regarding restrictions on the right to freedom of religion or belief and the right to freely participate in cultural life'? While delivering the uneasiness of fellow countries, she also clearly manifested that these countries still seek a solution and protection within the Chinese administration. The discourse of Pierce's statement reveals that as of October 2019, the international community has eluded from sharing the responsibility and insisted on attributing it to China, which has obviously been failing. Hence, considering certain countries' international prevention efforts along with the opposition of some others and the Chinese consistency in persisting its harmful policies, it can be concluded that the strategies within Pillar Two provided no ease to Xinjiang.

[7] Albania, Australia, Austria, Belgium, Canada, Denmark, Estonia, Finland, France, Germany, Iceland, Ireland, Japan, Latvia, Liechtenstein, Lithuania, Luxembourg, the Netherlands, New Zealand, Norway, Sweden, the UK and the US.

[8] Angola, Antigua and Barbuda, Bangladesh, the Plurinational State of Bolivia, Burkina Faso, Burundi, Cambodia, Cameroon, the Central African Republic, Chad, China, Comoros, the Congo, Cuba, the Democratic People's Republic of Korea, the Democratic Republic of the Congo, Djibouti, Egypt, Equatorial Guinea, Eritrea, Gabon, Guinea, Guinea Bissau, Iraq, the Islamic Republic of Iran, the Lao People's Democratic Republic, Mauritania, Mozambique, Myanmar, Nepal, Nicaragua, the Niger, Nigeria, Oman, Pakistan, the State of Palestine, the Philippines, the Russian Federation, Serbia, Sierra Leone, the Solomon Islands, South Sudan, Sri Lanka, Sudan, Suriname, the Syrian Arab Republic, Togo, Uganda, the United Arab Emirates, the United Republic of Tanzania, the Bolivarian Republic of Venezuela, Zambia, Zimbabwe and Belarus.

Pillar Three, the UNSC, UNGA and China

As stated in Paragraph 139 of the WSOD, 'the international community, through the UN, also has the responsibility to use appropriate diplomatic, humanitarian and other peaceful means, in accordance with Chapters VI and VIII of the Charter, to help protect populations from genocide, war crimes, ethnic cleansing and crimes against humanity'. Therefore, timely and decisive action entails both coercive and non-coercive measures in pursuit of protecting populations under stress. However, Paragraph 139 also stipulates two preliminary criteria to invoke these measures, which are 'should peaceful means be inadequate' and 'national authorities are manifestly failing to protect their populations'. Accordingly, the UNSC is determined as the sole authority to decide which measures should be adopted in cases of the manifest failure of States (UNGA, 2005). Although Pillar Three repetitively highlights its preference for peaceful, non-coercive and non-violent measures (see, Para. 51, UNGA, 2009), it also focuses on the deterring actions that the international community could adopt to save lives and restore order. Concisely, these can be compiled as investigation (Para. 53), referral to the ICC (Para. 54), sanctions (Para. 57), restrictions of weapons (Para. 58) and application of more robust measures through either the UNSC, the UN General Assembly (UNGA) or regional arrangements (Para. 56)[9] (UNGA, 2009).

Investigation is emphasised as an extension of preventive pillars and a measure that would be adopted before resorting to coercive measures. As mentioned previously, in the Xinjiang case, China turned down any assessment, refused to share information voluntarily and no official investigation was instigated by any UN body. Saving the lives of Uyghurs, freeing them from detention, restoring order and reminding China of its responsibility through Paragraph 56 (UNGA, 2009) are merely lost causes. This is simply because the *carte blanche* of R2P is in the hands of the UNSC, and specifically the P5 that wields the veto power, and therefore, serves as a shield for them. The PRC as one of the P5 can veto any decision against itself. Hence, in the case of Uyghurs, any resolution or even the discussion of the case in the UNSC seems unlikely.

[9] In Paragraph 56, the actions of the regional organisations are preconditioned with a UNSC authorisation, while the General Assembly may operate on the basis of the Uniting for Peace Resolution in the case of a deadlock without any prior authorisation provided from UNSC.

It is noteworthy that with its representative structure and recommendatory powers, the UNGA oftentimes serves as a moral authority that sets decisive routes on the course of an R2P crisis. Accordingly, it has the capability to encourage the Member States to take the necessary steps in an R2P crisis through its resolutions. However, in the case of Uyghurs, the UNGA has not yet adopted any decisions. Similarly, the Uyghur case is not situated anywhere in the UNHRC decisions and resolutions either.

While there is legally no obstacle for the Xinjiang case to be discussed in the UNGA, with a high probability there will be political and economic incentives of other countries on the way. China is a country that is high up in the political food chain and there are only a few privileged States that could undertake an efficacious opposition against China. Moreover, these sessions require a 2/3 majority of those present. Considering the letters written in support of China (the most recent one signed by 54 countries in total), it is dubious if the 2/3 majority can be achieved. Moreover, contributing to China's narrative of deradicalisation benefits and consolidates economic and political relations with China in the eyes of certain countries. Hence, once again, underlying incentives and interests prevail over human suffering and substantiate how politically shaky the bedrock that the UN system was built on.

Another option under Paragraph 56 is the application of R2P through regional or sub-regional arrangements. Although for some cases (see Chapters 3–6) this may be an alternative that could ease the argument that the UNSC reproducing colonial hegemony, for the Xinjiang case, it is proved to be futile. First and foremost, as regulated under Article 53 of the UN Charter, regional arrangements are only entitled to exercise coercive measures if the UNSC refers them the case. As mentioned earlier, referral aside, this chapter foresees little to no possibility for the UNSC to trigger R2P for the Uyghur suffering.

Regional or sub-regional organisations may decide on imposing sanctions on China without a need for UNSC authorisation. Since there are no binding requirements for regional powers, sanctions would simply be voluntary actions to deter China. In this case, the relations within the region should be heeded. The chief regional organisations, namely, the Association of Southeast Asian Nations (ASEAN) or the Shanghai Cooperation Organisation (a.k.a. the Shanghai Five), have been eerily silent on the human rights abuses and violations. As for the former, as we have also seen in Chapter 10, it rather strictly adheres to the principle of non-interference in internal affairs. In the case of the latter, although it has three members that are Turkic-originated countries,[10] it is unlikely for the Organisation to condemn and/or react to these events, because Russia as another key actor in the region and a partner in the Shanghai Five, allies itself with China on critical matters. The underlying reasons for this 'Double Trouble' alliance may be found in their shared power struggle with the US, strong-State emphasis on both States, regional proximity and interdependence. At the end of the day, this silent stance stems from China being in a key position in the region and within the Shanghai Five, holding the ropes and being of significance for the well-being of these Member States. Moreover, these organisations share a tradition of strong and persistent non-interference in each other's domestic affairs.

Alternatively, the possibility to end Uyghur suffering lies with the ICC. As Mills (2014) explains, as a last resort court in the cases of political unwillingness or incapability of State parties, the ICC can exercise jurisdiction after the fact in three ways: if a State Party refers a case, if the Prosecutor initiates an investigation, or if the UNSC refers a situation to the Court. The UNSC and the ICC are mutually reinforcing and complementary in the prosecution of R2P crimes. The PRC, due to its reservations on definitions (Wuthnow, 2012), is neither a signatory to the Rome Statute nor it has accepted the Court's jurisdiction. Therefore, the mere possibility for the ICC prosecution is the UNSC referral. However, given the political dynamics of the UNSC and China's permanent membership, there is no such prospect. Even though the ICC takes over the case, the jurisdiction process goes a long way and hence, is unhelpful for a population under an urgent risk. Therefore, the international community should prioritise preventing further escalation of the crisis through the immediately accessible political tools of the R2P framework.

As might be predicted, there are no debates within the UNSC on a collective sanction or restriction plan to be imposed on China. Nevertheless, as a fellow P5, the US drafted the 'Uighur Intervention and Global Humanitarian Unified Response Act of 2019' or the 'UIGHUR Act of 2019' on 3 December. This bill passed by a unanimous vote of the US Senate and entered into force on 17 June 2020 following President Donald Trump's approval. This act adopted sanctions on 'senior officials

[10] Kazakhstan, Kyrgyzstan and Uzbekistan.

of the Government of the People's Republic of China whom the President determines are responsible for or who have knowingly engaged in serious human rights abuses', namely, Communist Party Secretary Chen Quanguo, along with sanctions on the importation of goods that would be determined by the President. While it is hoped that this bill will mitigate human rights abuses in China even slightly, this legislation should not be read separately from the dynamics of the US–China relations. Over the course of the ongoing Trade Wars and powerplay among these countries, the Uyghur Bill may engender an upper hand for one and a point of vulnerability for the other. It is also noteworthy how America's stance has shifted over the years. While in the 2000s, it supported the War on Terror agenda of China, the extreme and systematic exercise of counterterrorism measures, also possibly coupled with the gradually strengthening position of China in the world, made America retreat its support.

In the light of this, the chapter argues the measures taken under Paragraphs 57 and 58 to be the most realistic resolution for the Uyghur suffering. For unilateral sanctions, prior UNSC or UNGA authorisation is not required. However, as Bapat and Morgan (2009) remind, sanctions are more effective when they are applied collectively. The international community is expected to act on human rights abuses in the form of sanctions or restrictions on weapons. As previously mentioned, the US initiated a set of sanctions, export controls and limitations for the goods imported to China through a bill. Like the US, the UK, Canada and the European Union (EU) have laws enabling sanctions against human rights abuses. In December 2020, the European Parliament passed a resolution (2020/2913(RSP)) banning the freedom of travel of certain Chinese officials, freezing assets and limiting the EU funds. Canada, recognised the Uyghur genocide in the Parliament, coordinated with the rest in 'a united transatlantic response' (USDS, 2021) and authorised sanctions against Chinese officials.

In October 2020, Member of Parliament Shabana Mahmood called for British lawmakers to impose sanctions on China and uttered 'No amount of trade can wipe out the actions of a regime that is committed, in the case of the Uighur population, to genocide' (Alecci, 2020). It is worthy of consideration that the UK is already applying an arms embargo on China-related to the 1989 Tiananmen Square Events and extended its embargo to Hong Kong due to the intensifying anti-democratic exercises of the Chinese government. Until 22 April 2021, the UK did not extend its Magnitsky sanctions to the Uyghur issue. As of late April, the UK adopted sanctions complementary to the EU and US ones and targeted Chinese officials.

The Netherlands officially recognised the Uyghur genocide but did not impose any political and/or economic sanctions on China. The Dutch sanction agenda is deeply tied to the EU's and/or UN's sanction decisions (Dutch government, 2021). Although the EU has enabled a set of sanctions, the UN has been silent. This is merely because the decision-maker position on the sanctions is attributed to the UNSC under Chapter VII of the UN Charter, specifically Article 41. Therefore, the possibility of collective sanctions under the UN umbrella is affixed to political confrontations once more. On the bright side, however, countries still can individually cry foul in the form of sanctions and/or restrictions. The effectiveness of these probable sanctions is still dubious since China does not rely on foreign allies fully in its financial affairs, but it indeed is a coercive response.

This section has tried to revisit the international community's probable route on the way of stopping the human rights violations in the XUAR and how far it is from meeting its responsibility. Hitherto, the response of the international community has not been anything else than a failure, wherein the perpetrator country holds such a position in the international arena that blurs the gain–loss axis.

Conclusion

The systematic discrimination, suppression, deprivation from daily life and violence through victim-blaming in XUAR left no room for suspense on China's failure in meeting its responsibility to protect. There is a salient need for the international community to ensure the safety and freedom of Uyghurs. However, China is positioned in a high castle, the international community is reluctant to exchange its stake with its duties. China, as a vigorous wing of the international arena, especially in economic terms, is capable of offering the international community a myriad in return for their silence. Therefore, Uyghurs are not victimised only by China but also imprisoned in the individual political and economic ideals of the silent international community members. It is required for the international community to break down the post-Cold War bamboo curtain, this time made out of Uyghur suffering.

The Xinjiang case as a protection crisis attests to certain gaps in R2P's implementation strategy. In the scholarship, there is a vast contention that R2P has an ineffective, inapplicable and a politically driven nature due to political unwillingness, deadlocks, overuse of veto powers and late responses. However, the possibility of the P5's failure in their responsibility and committing these crimes is often neglected. The current system of the norm works on the basis of 'be your own judge' for the P5 countries and cannot exceed Pillar One, which solely underlines sovereignty as responsibility. There is no specific prudence on the P5 either in the R2P framework or implementation. The self-serving position of the P5 within the R2P norm raises the question 'who do you call when the police murders?' at the international level. Consequently, the Uyghur case also constitutes a point of reference to the imagined UN reform agenda by unfolding the lacunae within the existing system that cripples two of the three pillars that the UN was built on: human rights, peace and security and development.

Furthermore, the Uyghur history is blended with the self-determination claims that target a separate Uyghur State in the Xinjiang region. The R2P framework also neglects how self-determination claims may alter into a violent clash between the two parties and further engender mass atrocity crimes. Therefore, any self-determination attempt should be closely watched by the international community and for the prevention efforts that are necessary in order for it to not evolve into human rights violations, the necessary framework should be provided by the R2P norm.

References

Al Jazeera. (2018, November 27). *Academics condemn China over Xinjiang camps, urge sanctions*. https://www.aljazeera.com/news/2018/11/27/academics-condemn-china-over-xinjiang-camps-urge-sanctions/. Accessed 21 May 2021.

Alecci, S. (2020, October 14). *British lawmakers call for sanctions over Uighur human rights*. International Consortium of Investigative Journalists. https://www.icij.org/investigations/china-cables/british-lawmakers-call-for-sanctions-over-uighur-human-rights-abuses/. Accessed 12 February 2021.

Areddy, S. (2015). Xinjiang Arrests Nearly Doubled in '14, Year of 'Strike-Hard' Campaign. *The Wall Street Journal*. https://www.wsj.com/articles/BL-CJB-25742. Accessed 21 June 2021.

Bapat, N., & Morgan, T. (2009). Multilateral versus unilateral sanctions reconsidered: A test using new data. *International Studies Quarterly, 53*(4), 1075–1094.

BBC. (2019, June 4). *Tiananmen Square: What happened in the protests of 1989?* https://www.bbc.com/news/world-asia-48445934. Accessed 14 March 2021.

Bovingdon, G. (2004). Autonomy in Xinjiang: Han nationalist imperatives and Uyghur discontent. *East-West Center Policy Studies, 11*, 1–74.

Brophy, D. (2005). Taranchis, Kashgaris, and the 'Uyghur question' in Soviet Central Asia. *Inner Asia, 7*(2), 163–184.

Chinese Human Rights Defenders. (2019). *Defending human rights in the era of dystopia: The situation of defenders in China.* https://www.nchrd.org/2020/02/defending-human-rights-in-the-era-of-dystopia-the-situation-of-defenders-in-china-2019/. Accessed 25 June 2020.

Denyer, S. (2014). China's war on terror becomes all-out attack on Islam in Xinjiang. *The Washington Post*. https://www.washingtonpost.com/world/chinas-war-on-terror-becomes-all-out-attack-on-islam-in-xinjiang/2014/09/19/5c5840a4-1aa7-4bb6-bc63-69f6bfba07e9_story.html. Accessed 21 June 2021.

Dillon, M. (1994). Muslim communities in contemporary China: The resurgence of Islam after the cultural revolution. *Journal of Islamic Studies, 5*(1), 70–101.

Dillon, M. (1999). *China's Muslim Hui community: Migration, settlement and sects*. Routledge.

Duara, P. (2019). *AAS statement on extra-judicial detention of Turkic Muslims in Xinjiang, PRC*. Association for Asian Studies. https://www.asianstudies.org/aas-statement-on-extra-judicial-detention-of-turkic-muslims-in-xinjiang-prc/. Accessed 25 June 2020.

Dutch Government. (2021). *Policy Dutch government on international sanctions.* https://www.government.nl/topics/international-sanctions/policy-international-sanctions. Accessed 16 April 2020.

European Parliament. (2020, December 16). *Resolution on forced labour and the situation of the Uyghurs in the Xinjiang Uyghur autonomous region*, 2020/2913(RSP).

Feng, E. (2018). Crackdown in Xinjiang: Where have all the people gone? *Financial Times*. https://www.ft.com/content/ac0ffb2e-8b36-11e8-b18d-0181731a0340. Accessed 25 June 2020.

Finley, J. S. (2019). Securitization, insecurity and conflict in contemporary Xinjiang: Has PRC counterterrorism evolved into state terror? *Central Asian Survey, 38*(1), 1–26.

Foot, R. (2020). *China, the UN, and human protection: Beliefs, power, image*. Oxford University Press.

Foucault, M. (1997). *Society must be defended: Lectures at the Collège de France, 1975–1976*. Martin's Press.

Fung, C. (2021). Just not in the neighbourhood: China's views on the application of the responsibility to protect in the DPRK. *The China Quarterly, 246*, 565–585.

Global Centre for the Responsibility to Protect (GCR2P). (2020). *China*. https://www.globalr2p.org/countries/china/. Accessed 25 June 2020.

Global Times. (2019). *Support of 50 countries on governance in Xinjiang redefines human rights*. https://www.globaltimes.cn/content/1159375.shtml. Accessed 25 June 2020.

Gunawan, Y. (2019). Responsibility of People's Republic of China for minority based on ICERD: Uyghur Case. *Varia Justicia, 15*(2), 65–73.

Hirono, M., Jiang, Y., & Lanteigne, M. (2019). China's new roles and behaviour in conflict-affected regions: Reconsidering non-interference and non-intervention. *The China Quarterly, 239*, 573–593.

Human Rights Watch. (2018a). *Eradicating ideological viruses*. https://www.hrw.org/report/2018/09/09/eradicating-ideological-viruses/chinas-campaign-repression-against-xinjiangs. Accessed 25 June 2020.

Human Rights Watch. (2018b). *Submission to the universal periodic review of China*. https://www.hrw.org/news/2018/03/29/submission-universal-periodic-review-china. Accessed 25 June 2020.

Human Rights Watch. (2019). *Countries blast China at UN over Xinjiang abuses*. https://www.hrw.org/news/2019/10/30/countries-blast-china-un-over-xinjiang-abuses. Accessed 25 June 2020.

International Criminal Court (ICC). (1998). *Rome statute of the international criminal Court*.

McMillen, D. H. (1979). *Chinese Communist power and policy in Xinjiang, 1949–1977*. Boulder, Colo: Westview Press.

Mills, K. (2014). The responsibility to protect and the International Criminal Court: Complementary or conflicting? *Asia Pacific Centre for the Responsibility to Protect (AP R2P) Brief, 4*(2), 1–17.

Millward, J. (2004). Violent separatism in Xinjiang: A critical assessment. *East West Center Policy Studies, 6*, 1–73.

Mumford, A. (2018). Theory testing Uyghur terrorism in China. *Perspectives on Terrorism, 12*, 18–26.

Phillips, T. (2018, January 25). China 'holding at least 120,000 Uighurs in re-education camps'. *The Guardian*. https://www.theguardian.com/world/2018/jan/25/at-least-120000-muslim-uighurs-held-in-chinese-re-education-camps-report. Accessed 12 May 2021.

Potter, P. (2013). Terrorism in China: Growing threats with global implications. *Strategic Studies Quarterly, 7*(4), 70–92.

Pye, L. (1986). Reassessing the cultural revolution. *The China Quarterly, 108*, 597–612.

Richardson, S. (2019). *Unprecedented UN critique of China's Xinjiang policies*. Human Rights Watch. https://www.hrw.org/news/2019/11/14/unprecedented-un-critique-chinas-xinjiang-policies. Accessed 25 June 2020.

Rogers, R. A., & Sidhu, J. S. (2016). International Norms And Human Rights Conditions In The Xinjiang Uyghur Autonomous Region (Xuar). *Malaysian Journal of International Relations, 4*(1), 109–137. https://doi.org/10.22452/mjir.vol4no1.6.

Shih, G. (2018, May 18). *China's mass indoctrination camps evoke cultural revolution*. Associated Press. https://apnews.com/6e151296fb194f85ba69a8babd972e4b. Accessed 25 June 2020.

South China Morning Post. (2018). *Sir Alan Donald, British ambassador at time of Tiananmen killings, dies*. https://www.scmp.com/news/china/diplomacy-defence/article/2156285/sir-alan-donald-british-ambassador-beijing-during. Accessed 25 June 2020.

Szadziewski, H. (2020). The push for a Uyghur human rights policy act in the United States: Recent developments in Uyghur activism. *Asian Ethnicity, 21*(2), 211–222.

Thakur, R. (2006). *The United Nations, peace and security: From collective security to the responsibility to protect*. Cambridge University Press.

The United Kingdom Government Foreign & Commonwealth Office (UKGFCO). (2019). *Joint statement on human rights violations and abuses in Xinjiang*. https://www.gov.uk/government/speeches/joint-statement-on-xinjiang. Accessed 25 June 2020.

Trevaskes, S. (2010). *Policing serious crime in China*. Routledge.

UN News. (2009, July 7). *UN human rights chief alarmed by 'major tragedy' in western China*. https://news.un.org/en/story/2009/07/305782-un-human-rights-chief-alarmed-major-tragedy-western-china. Accessed 25 June 2020.

United Nations General Assembly (UNGA). (2005, October 24). *Resolution adopted by the general assembly on 16 September 2005*, '60/1. 2005 World Summit Outcome', A/Res/60/1.

United Nations General Assembly (UNGA). (2009, January 12). *Implementing the responsibility to protect*. Report of the Secretary-General, A/63/677.

United States Department of State (USDS). (2021, April 20). *2020 Country reports on human rights practices*. https://www.state.gov/reports/2020-country-reports-on-human-rights-practices/. Accessed 9 August 2021.

US Mission to International Organizations in Geneva (US-MIOG). (2016). *Joint statement—Human rights situation in China*. https://geneva.usmission.gov/2016/03/10/item-2-joint-statement-human-rights-situation-in-china/. Accessed 25 June 2020.

Uyghur Human Rights Policy Act of 2019, S.178, 116th Congress. (2019). https://www.congress.gov/bill/116th-congress/senate-bill/178/text?format=txt. Accessed 11 June 2021.

van Wie Davis, E. (2008). Uyghur Muslim ethnic separatism in Xinjiang, China. *Asian Affairs, 35*(1), 15–29.

Watson, I., & Westcott, B. (2020). China's Xinjiang records revealed: Uyghurs thrown into detention for growing beards or bearing too many children, leaked Chinese document shows. *CNN.* https://edition.cnn.com/interactive/2020/02/asia/xinjiang-china-karakax-document-intl-hnk/. Accessed 11 June 2021.

Weinan, Z. (2019). US Uyghur bill grossly violates international law. *Global Times.* https://www.globaltimes.cn/content/1172565.shtml. Accessed 11 June 2021.

World Uyghur Congress. (2021, June 24). *Press release: The Wuc welcomes the declaration in German parliament recognizing crimes against humanity.* https://www.uyghurcongress.org/en/the-world-uyghur-congress-welcomes-the-declaration-in-german-parliament-recognizing-crimes-against-humanity/. Accessed 11 June 2021.

Wuthnow, T. (2012). *China and the ICC.* The Diplomat. https://thediplomat.com/2012/12/china-and-the-icc/. Accessed 11 June 2021.

CHAPTER 13

Venezuela: An R2P Impasse?

Hazal Arslan

Venezuelan people have been living in a politically and economically deteriorating country and struggling with mass violations of human rights for some time now. While the economic crisis became apparent after the death of Venezuela's charismatic leader Chavez in 2013, it was during Maduro's administration, which assumed power with a barely won election (J. S. Gonzalez, 2019a) that the humanitarian crisis became more visible. The first instance that was followed by further authoritarianism was when the security forces used excessive force in anti-government demonstrations following the April 2013 elections.

In the International Relations literature, the case of Venezuela has mostly been studied with respect to the political and economic aspects of the ongoing crisis (see, for instance, Duddy, 2015; Kahn, 2017; Briceño-Ruiz, 2019, 2020; J. S Gonzalez, 2019a; M. Gonzalez, 2019b; Weisbrot & Sachs, 2019). Nevertheless, as it can be observed in the United Nations (UN) reports, such as that of the 2020 report of the Human Rights Council (UNHRC), due to the alleged mass atrocity crimes, the case of Venezuela also qualifies as an R2P concern, wherein the

H. Arslan (✉)
Department of International Relations, Hacettepe University, Ankara, Turkey

P. Gözen Ercan (ed.), *The Responsibility to Protect Twenty Years On*, https://doi.org/10.1007/978-3-030-90731-0_13

Venezuelan population is regarded as a population under risk (GCR2P, 2021). In this regard, while studying this overlooked R2P situation, this chapter asks the question of how and to what extent R2P has been implemented in the humanitarian crisis in Venezuela. With the aim of understanding the reasons for the failure to protect the Venezuelan population which has already been vulnerable due to the economic crisis, the chapter approaches the case through the lens of the three-pillar implementation strategy of R2P. Accordingly, it first provides a historical background of the conflict and traces how the situation has escalated. Then, from the perspective of Pillar One, it studies the root causes of the crisis and the failure of the Venezuelan government to fulfil its responsibility to protect its population. After establishing the State's manifest failure, the chapter goes on to analyse the international community's response to the crisis. Given the simultaneous implementation of measures pertaining to Pillars Two and Three, this chapter questions the effectiveness of preventive measures as well as the larger consequences of the coercive ones. Finally, questioning the harmony among the members of the international community and the genuine intentions of the actors that took part in the process, it argues that in the absence of an R2P mindset in the policies pursued towards Venezuela and the persisting crisis, the self-interested motives of the involved internal and external actors have resulted in the failure to protect the Venezuelan population. Hence, it is not the idea behind the R2P norm that failed in Venezuela but the priorities and policy choices of those who were to implement it.

Historical Background of the Venezuelan Crisis

In Venezuela, Hugo Chavez came to power in 1999 and consecutively won the elections, which allowed him to hold the power until his death in 2013. During his rule, he changed the structure of the politics, economy and the government. Owing to his aspiration to create equality for all and the initiatives he undertook to that end, he became a very charismatic leader among the people in a very short time.

The dream of Chavez to replace capitalism with twenty-first century socialism was the focus of the Chavez administration, and his governments focused on meeting the needs of the lower and middle classes. To this end, started by changing the name of the country to the Bolivarian Republic of Venezuela, he gradually made reforms (Briceño-Ruiz, 2019). The most important elements of the Bolivarian Revolution—which is another name Chavismo uses for the twenty-first century socialism—were the consolidation of power by removing the lines between the party and the government, and the nationalisation of the most important segments of the economy such as oil and electricity companies. These helped Chavez to fight poverty by funding several social programmes, which were named as 'missions to save people' and focused on the distribution of essential goods and services such as healthcare, education, food and social benefits like scholarships. With the social programmes funded by the nationalisation initiative, Chavez had quite a success in reducing poverty in Venezuela at the initial phase, wherein the poverty levels dropped from 54.4% in 2002 to 28.5% in 2009 (De la Torre, 2017; Gonzalez, 2019b). With this initiative, he also created a new sort of consumer that was mostly dependent on the government's sources of income, which was quite high until the government's poor economic decisions such as making the country's income contingent on the oil revenues. As long as the oil prices were high, this seemed like the most profitable way to create income rather than investing in other industries. This economic choice made Venezuela dependent on the imported goods in every field, and in the long run, these policy choices became the underlying reasons for the current economic issues of Venezuela (Gonzalez, 2019a).

Even though Chavismo had fulfilled its promise of reducing poverty in Venezuela, in doing so, it also created its own Bolivarian bourgeoisie. With its focus on the lower class of the population, government actions created a feeling of rejection among the upper and middle classes which in turn strengthened the opposition. In April 2002, the Workers Confederation of Venezuela (*Confederación de Trabajadores de Venezuela*, CTV) and the business federation *Fedecámaras* organised strikes and demonstrations supported by all branches of the media, opposition parties and some sections of the military to overthrow the Chavez government. The polarisation of the people of Venezuela became clear during this coup attempt (Cannon, 2004), which lasted for 2 days, and during which the president of the *Fedecámaras*, Pedro Carmona assumed the interim presidency until Chavez was restored to power by his supporters (Buxton, 2009).

After the events of April 2002, it was apparent that Chavez had the support of the people as well as the prominent members of the society. Especially with the help of his supporters in the military, he got through the coup attempt successfully and returned to power. With this experience, he also had the chance to identify the anti-Chavismos in the military and cleanse the army from them. Beginning from 2004, Chavismos (i.e.

the Chavists) began to take control of the State by politicising the military under the President's rule and restructuring *Tribunal Supremo de Justicia* (TSJ), and placing fellow Chavismos in these institutions (Briceño-Ruiz, 2019). Nationally, even though there were significant signs of authoritarianism and corruption, Chavez maintained the support of the people with his successful social initiatives. In the meanwhile, at the international level, Venezuela also had the support of like-minded countries such as Bolivia, Cuba, Dominica, Ecuador, Grenada, Nicaragua, Antigua and Barbuda, Saint Kitts and Nevis, Saint Lucia, Saint Vincent and the Grenadines. This led to the creation of the Bolivarian Alliance for the Peoples of Our America (*Alianza Bolivariana para Los Pueblos de Nuestra América*, ALBA) as a free trade agreement to encourage mutually productive cooperation as an anti-US alternative (Gonzalez, 2019a). At the end of Chavez's rule, corruption in the country was paramount. Yet, it was not until the drastic drop in the oil prices, which happened during the Maduro administration that this level of corruption was going to become disturbingly clear and destructive for the people of Venezuela.

Before his death, Chavez named Maduro as his successor. However, unlike Chavez who won the elections six months ago with a majority of 11%, Nicolas Maduro became President-elect in April 2013 with less than one per cent majority against his opponent. This was an encouraging result for the opposition. In the meantime, the oil prices started to drop leading to the stagnation of the market. Even though Venezuela had one of the largest oil reserves in the world, and oil was the only income of the country, the State had not invested in the development of the industry. Because of these ill-fated economic decisions made by the previous government, such a drop in the oil prices hit the Venezuelan economy hard and ignited the current economic and political crisis.

Starting off with a weak support from the public, Maduro inherited a dangerously fragile country in economic terms, which soon fell into a severe economic crisis. Taking advantage of the deteriorating situation, the opposition organised several protests in order to weaken Maduro's government. The first protest that resulted in excessive use of force by the government's security forces was suppressed quickly, but several human rights violations such as wrongful imprisonment, violent and disproportionate use of force by security forces, physical and sexual abuses and depriving the detainees of water, food or sleep were reported (Human

Rights Watch, 2014; Gonzalez, 2019b). Thus, adding to the deteriorating economic conditions in the country, the political turmoil that followed the protests put a spotlight on the Venezuelan crisis, raising many questions to answer.

Failure of the Venezuelan Government

Due to the economic contraction taking hold of the country, by 2014, the rising prices of basic goods and services had already undermined the Chavismo regime. Thus, when the opposition-led protests started again, even though the slogans were mainly anti-Chavismo, they quickly expanded to include the economic issues of the people and spread all over the country. Hence, their ramifications were much severe than before (Briceño-Ruiz, 2019; Gonzalez, 2019b). These protests were mostly aimed to disrupt the government's ability to provide basic services for the public in order to gain support to remove Maduro from power. It is noteworthy that these protests mostly focused on the middle-class neighbourhoods of the country rather than the poor (Gonzalez, 2019b). It can be argued that since the middle class were the main supporters and beneficiaries of Chavismo, they were also the ones most affected by the economic crisis the country was in, and therefore, they had a good reason to support the opposition. However, as the protests intensified and spread all over the country, human rights violations also increased.

After a brutal confrontation with the Maduro government during the 2014 protests, in December 2015, the opposition won two-thirds of the majority at the National Assembly elections, which led to a more authoritarian approach from Maduro since this result meant that the opposition now had the power to change and block his decisions (Briceño-Ruiz, 2019). The right-wing in the country now had the support of the middle and lower classes even though their leadership consisted of their own bourgeoisie who were determined to return power to those who had it before Chavez. Nevertheless, Maduro was determined not to surrender to the opposition. To maintain power, he appointed new TSJ judges while the National Assembly was not in session. Moreover, to change the majority in the National Assembly to his favour, he used his presidential powers in TSJ to declare null and void the proclamation of three deputies from the opposition on grounds of alleged electoral corruption. In January 2016, when the opposition swore those deputies in against its decision, the TSJ responded by declaring that the Assembly was in contempt and rendered the Assembly ineffective. After the continuing showdown between the TSJ and the Assembly in 2017, the TSJ took over the legislative powers thereby annulling the Assembly altogether. Using this to his advantage, Maduro decided to adopt a new constitution (Briceño-Ruiz, 2019).

In an environment of politics that transformed into a struggle for power between the Government and the Assembly, it became clear that the opposition also had no interest in the basic problems of the public such as scarcity and lack of security. Their only motivation was to remove Maduro from power regardless of the consequences for the people (Gonzalez, 2019b). Such turmoil along with the escalating economic problems led to a new wave of protests all over the country, which was again countered with a brutal wearing-down strategy by the government forces. By 2018, the protests were mostly worn down but still going on with a minimal effect. After postponing the elections that were to be held at the end of 2017, Maduro announced a surprise election in May 2018, which gave him an advantage against his opponents. The elections were held with an attendance rate of less than 50%, and Maduro won with a 67% majority. Given the controversial way, the elections were announced along with the low attendance rate, the legitimacy of Maduro's presidency was questioned by both the opposition and the international observers.

While the political and social unrest was growing, the economic crisis of Venezuela was deepening as well, creating a situation that would only get worse for the Venezuelan people. With the dramatic drop of oil prices in the world, combined with its old and underinvested technology, Venezuela's oil production became more costly than its price. This led to hyperinflation and the collapse of the economy (Kahn, 2017). 'In February 2019, the rate of inflation reached 2.30 million per cent' (ECR2P, n.d, Para. 3). The situation has rapidly culminated in a humanitarian crisis. There are shortages of water and power all over the country; people are water rationing, swap trading or using the black market to get basic needs such as medicine, bread or toilet paper; the government institutions like schools and hospitals are rendered mostly useless (Van Roekel & de Theije, 2020). As van Roekel and de Theije (2020, p. 8) stress, currently, 'in Venezuela almost everything is scarce or unaffordable'.

In the meantime, with no regard to the difficulties the Venezuelan people were facing, Maduro was determined to swear in for another term and continue his rule. However, on 5 January 2019, Juan Guaido, who was recently appointed as the president of the National Assembly, declared that Maduro was usurping the presidency and called for a mass protest after Maduro's swearing-in for another term on 10 January. On 25 January, protests started all over the country, and Guaido proclaimed himself as the interim president with the support of the Venezuelan public (Briceño-Ruiz, 2019). The TSJ did not recognise Guaido's proclamation and declared Maduro as the president-elect of the country. However, Guaido's claim found vast recognition from other States, which rendered Maduro as the usurper of the presidency in the eyes of most members of the international community.

The humanitarian implications of these political and economic struggles in Venezuela have been going on in an escalating manner since 2013. According to the Human Rights Watch World Report (2020) since 2014, in the protests and demonstrations, 15,000 people have been arrested, 840 of whom have been prosecuted in military courts in violation of international law and 400 remain as political prisoners. Moreover, since 2016, nearly 18,000 people have been killed in situations of alleged resistance to authority. However, these numbers do not include most of the deaths caused by the lack of basic goods and services in daily life (Human Rights Watch, 2020). Before he was fired in 2017, the Venezuelan Health Minister released official data indicating that during 2016, maternal mortality had increased by 65%, and infant mortality by 30% (Human Rights Watch, 2020). Due to lack of health care and unattainability of medicine, Venezuelan people have been dying from curable ancient diseases. Lack of food and security, starvation and fear of life are now part of people's daily lives and the reason that 'more than 4.5 million people have fled the country since 2014' (UNHCR, n.d.).

Despite questions of legitimacy over his presidency, Maduro remains in control of the vital institutions of the government, and by way of using presidential authority; he continues to violate the human rights of the Venezuelans. In the light of this, it can be concluded that the Venezuelan authorities are not only failing to uphold their responsibility to protect the population but they are also the perpetrators of these mass violations (GCR2P, 2020), which leads us to the question of the responsibility of the international community.

The International Community's Involvement in the Venezuelan Crisis

The escalation of the current humanitarian crisis in Venezuela partly owes to the international community's failure to react to the situation at the early stages of the situation. Following further escalation of the situation, we see a combination of Pillar Two and Three measures in action, wherein there were initiatives for peace talks on the one hand, and sanctions on the other.

After Maduro came to power, there were signs of forthcoming violent authoritarianism, yet the international community did not necessarily pay attention to the early warning signs. At the time, the United States (US) under the Obama administration was more concentrated on a regional solution effort. Hence, it promoted the Union of South American Nations (UNASUR) to seek a resolution to the crisis without considering the effectiveness of such path and the immediacy of the situation (Gonzalez, 2019a p. 47). In 2017, with the deepening of the economic crisis and the increased aggressiveness of the government against the Venezuelan people, the brutality and recklessness of Maduro became more visible, and hence, in search for a resolution, the international community encouraged peace talks between the government and the opposition. At Maduro's request, UNASUR became the mediator in these talks. 'Protests and civil unrest have proliferated amid Venezuela's collapsing economy and human rights violations. To quell the violence, both Maduro and the opposition then led by Henrique Capriles initiated dialogues overseen by UNASUR' (Rendon et al., 2019, p. 2), but this had no positive outcome since the Maduro government made no concessions. Nevertheless, by participating in these peace talks long enough, Maduro managed to soften the reaction of the international community to turn the tables (Gonzalez, 2019a).

By 2015, there has been a shift in power and a rise in centre-right wing governments in the Latin American region. This change in the region also affected the events in Venezuela since it caused Maduro to lose some of his supporters. The exacerbated humanitarian implications of the economic and political problems in Venezuela led to the creation of the Lima Group in 2017. 'The original Lima Group countries were Argentina, Brazil, Canada, Chile, Colombia, Costa Rica, Guatemala, Honduras, Mexico, Panama, Paraguay and Peru. Guyana and Saint Lucia joined later' (Gonzalez, 2019a, p. 55). The Group's objective was to assist Venezuela in resolving its crisis. It was established to help prevent the human rights violations in the country by calling for free elections, offering humanitarian aid and trying to facilitate the release of political prisoners. Meanwhile, following a change in policy under the Trump Administration, the US started to pursue a hostile approach towards Venezuela. It imposed economic sanctions, as well as individual sanctions on prominent political actors of the country, while the Lima Group was in charge of the regional response to the Maduro government (Gonzalez, 2019a).

It was not until after the 2018 elections that the international community started to take more tangible actions regarding Venezuela, but it was too little, too late. With Maduro swearing in for another term and Guaido's self-proclamation as the interim president, the international community reacted rather swiftly in terms of choosing sides. The first country to recognise Guaido's proclamation was the US. The Lima Group followed suit by rejecting the result of the elections and declared that they recognised Guaido's proclamation as interim president. The European Union (EU) opted for asking Maduro to call for a new election first, and when Maduro refused to do so, it recognised Guaido's claim. With the support of most of the Western States, as well as many of the regional States, Guaido became a substantial opponent to Maduro, who had the support of States such as China, Russia, Cuba and Turkey (Briceño-Ruiz, 2019).

As for international organisations, the UN released several reports regarding human rights violations in the country. The UN Office of the High Commissioner for Human Rights (OHCHR) published a report in June 2018 on the basis of the information they obtained through remote monitoring since they were not allowed in the country. The report detailed the human rights violations and specific crimes taking place since 2017 and proposed solutions for both the members of the UNHRC and the Venezuelan government (OHCHR, 2018).

Under Pillar Two, there were also other initiatives that were carried out with the help of third parties such as the Lima Group, the EU, Canada, Norway and the United Kingdom (UK). In April 2019, an initiative comprising of eight EU Member States and four Latin American States presented proposals for peace talks to both Maduro and Guaido in Caracas, and both sides agreed to send delegates to Oslo upon the invitation of Norway (Vasquez & Rosati, 2019). Following the meeting, a new wave of protests initiated by the opposition turned into a failed uprising.

On 30 April 2019, 'Interim President Guaidó and his supporters launched "Operation Liberty", a nationwide protest that called for members of the military to defect from the regime' (Rendon et al., 2019). This attempt to spark change was not successful and had devastating effects on the opposition as it caused divisions, which then led to the emergence of smaller opposition parties of today's Venezuela. This allowed Maduro to keep his power by dividing and conquering the opposition (Briceño-Ruiz, 2020).

Maduro and Guaidó decided to continue the peace talks regardless of the events of 30 April. Norway called for the delegates of both sides for another round of peace talks. Same as before, Guaido's response to the invitation was contingent upon the answer of the Maduro government. The call for the second round of the peace talks was accepted by both sides, yet it became another failure since the parties did not meet face to face, instead they communicated through mediators in the form of formal meetings within the framework of the negotiations (Vasquez & Rosati, 2019). Cooperative attitudes and the engagement of both sides in the second meeting after the events of 30 April led to another meeting in Oslo. Although both sides agreed to meet, this did not mean that they were ready to trust each other enough to make concessions (Gibbs, 2019). No final agreements were achieved at the end of the peace talks led by Norway, but this led to another round of meetings for the same objective.

The aforementioned efforts of the international community that pertain to Pillar Two proved insufficient to deliver the needed protection for the Venezuelan population and were undermined by the unilateral actions of international actors. In other words, the lack of unity and/or harmony within the international community disabled any kind of preventive measure from making a real difference. This is why along with the measures under Pillar Two, peaceful measures under Pillar Three were pursued by concerned regional actors as opposed to the US which opted for coercive means. The first of the regional attempts took place through the International Criminal Court (ICC). 'On 26 September 2018, Argentina, Canada, Chile, Colombia, Paraguay and Peru forwarded the reports of crimes against humanity to the ICC prosecutor' (ECR2P, n.d., Para. 9), which made it clear that the international community was not going to sit still when Venezuela was committing mass human rights violations. This case is currently at phase 3 of the preliminary examination (ICC, n.d.).[1]

In a similar vein, following the fourth round of the peace talks that started in Barbados in July 2019, on 23 September, 16 governments across the Americas initiated a legal process in order to capture, pursue and extradite Venezuelan officials involved in international crimes invoking the provisions of the Rio Treaty, which have not been invoked since the 9/11 attacks (Jakes, 2019).

Coercive Measures and the Deepening of the Crisis

The US has been an influential actor in the South American region for a very long time. Since the Chavez Government, the relations between the US and Venezuela have been shaped by their ideological differences and with Guaido's appearance in the Venezuelan politics, the impact of this political power struggle created a more intense confrontation between them. Yet, it was not until the Trump Administration in 2017 that the US policies towards Venezuela became more assertive. Not long after Trump was elected, the US started to increase the pressure they put on the Venezuelan government by enforcing individual and economic sanctions on prominent figures of Chavismo. Following the broad economic sanctions imposed by the US, the trade between the two countries was prohibited at many levels, and the US chapter of the *Petróleos de Venezuela, S.A.* (PDVSA), oil and natural gas corporation owned by the Bolivarian Republic of Venezuela, has been blocked from sending money to the government. The US sanctions combined with the continuing drop of the oil prices made the country's economy even more fragile and contributed to the ongoing humanitarian crisis (Gonzalez, 2019a).

After the controversial elections of 2018, the US was the first to recognise Guaido's proclamation of interim presidency and to declare Maduro as a usurper. One of the most excessive outcomes of the internationalisation of this conflict for the Venezuelan people has been the sanctions imposed by the US. In the second half of 2019, the US broadened

[1] As a matter of fact, on 13 February 2020 Venezuela referred a case in its own territory to the ICC bringing allegations against the US. In its referral, 'the Government of Venezuela states that crimes against humanity are committed as a result of the application of unlawful coercive measures adopted unilaterally by the government of the United States of America against Venezuela, at least since the year 2014' (ICC, 2020, para. 1).

its assertive strategy by threatening with sanctions foreign companies and/or governments who had dealings with the Maduro government. The Trump administration had the majority's support in the Congress regarding the sanctions against Venezuela due to the violations of human rights. The US treasury has imposed financial sanctions on 98 Venezuelans along with the other broad economic sanctions as of 1 June 2020. While only seven of these individual sanctions belonged to the Obama administration, after assuming office, the Trump administration imposed sanctions through executive orders on 91 individuals including Maduro and anyone related to him or his administration including the members of the supreme court, the army, the central bank, etc. These sanctions included the freezing of individuals' accounts, forbidding transactions, confiscation of assets, arms embargoes and travel bans (Broughtan & Tokar, 2019; Seelke, 2020).

Along with the US, the EU has imposed sanctions on Venezuela in the hopes of removing Maduro from power and ending the humanitarian crisis. In the second half of 2018, the EU announced an aid package to provide emergency supplies for the people of Venezuela and to assist the neighbouring countries hosting Venezuelan immigrants. After the events of January 2019, the EU imposed sanctions against Venezuela, especially on arms with a view to preventing their use on the Venezuelan people by the security forces (ECR2P, n.d.).

From an R2P point of view, the sanctions imposed on Venezuela would be considered as coercive measures under Pillar Three, which were applied at the same time with the peaceful measures adopted by regional and international actors in the form of peace talks. Nevertheless, it is noteworthy that these initiatives were undermined by the unilateral actions of international actors. For instance, on 26 January 2019, the United Nations Security Council (UNSC) held a meeting at the request of the US in order to discuss the situation in Venezuela. This was followed by a briefing a month later. After this briefing, on 28 February 2019, two draft resolutions on the situation in Venezuela were presented in the Security Council. The one presented by Russia in support of Maduro failed to get enough votes from the Council, whereas the one presented by the US in support of Guaido was vetoed by Russia and China. The divide between the Permanent Members of the Council (P5) made the UNSC an ineffective actor on the subject. After this meeting where the great powers made their sides clear, in April 2019, the UNSC held another meeting at the request of the US regarding the humanitarian implications of the conundrum in Venezuela. Delivering the US statement at the meeting, Vice President of the US Mike Pence made it clear that Venezuela needed a regime change, and the Trump Administration was prepared to take all the necessary actions in order to achieve that objective. He also announced additional sanctions on Venezuela on their part (UNSC, 2019). Following this, Maduro decided to drop the peace talks, since his only demand was the removal of the US sanctions in all seven rounds.

Besides their negative implications on the ongoing peace talks, the unilateral sanctions also had controversial effects by exacerbating the economic crisis in the country. The problem with these sanctions was that they were not tailored to deal with the humanitarian crisis but were targeted at regime change. In this regard, the historical aspects of the US–Venezuela relations along with the ideological differences and the hostile attitudes of the political figures against one another raises the question of the genuine intent behind these sanctions, which ended up undermining the objectives of R2P.

Conclusion

The humanitarian crisis in Venezuela has been underway for so long now, wherein the international community has failed to collect the early warning signs of an authoritarian and assertive regime, which paved the way for mass human rights violations. As the 2020 UNHRC (2020) Report has also clearly established the crisis in Venezuela as a case where mass atrocity crimes in the form of crimes against humanity are committed, this chapter has examined the case of Venezuela from the perspective of the R2P norm and through a pillar-by-pillar analysis.

As the fact-finding mission's report has revealed, the '[d]eaths caused by security forces, political assassinations, lack of basic needs, arbitrary detentions, torture and degrading treatments against detainees, government security forces' excess use of power during protests, and the state's failure to provide basic human rights and needs' (UNHRC, 2020) show that the Venezuelan government is not only unable to fulfil its responsibility to protect the Venezuelan population, but also the perpetrator of most of these human rights violations. Hence, after establishing the failure of the State authorities, this chapter studied the international responses to the situation in Venezuela through the lenses of Pillars Two and Three.

It can be observed that the international community has sought for a peaceful resolution addressing the political crisis between the government and the opposition. When we look at these initiatives through the lenses of R2P, one may argue that the Oslo and Barbados Talks were carried out in a manner consistent with the objectives of Pillar Two. However, the timing of the implementation was problematic, and it was too late for these preventive measures to work. Thus, the initiatives directed at preventing further human rights violations proved to be a failure on the part of the international community.

After the failed attempts towards a peaceful solution to the crisis and further escalation of the political power struggle in Venezuela, the international community had become more involved in the crisis than it was before. By taking sides in the political stalemate of the country and imposing sanctions against Venezuela and the Maduro government, certain international actors, especially the US, have resorted to coercive measures which can be interpreted as a form of implementation under Pillar Three of R2P. However, sanctions that were imposed on the government as a coercive action also proved to be ineffective since the Maduro government has endured these sanctions for more than three years now and still has control over the country. A further result of these sanctions was that they were not only unable to prevent or stop the violations of human rights in Venezuela, but also they further deepened the crisis. As we have seen in the US sanctions, the main motive behind these sanctions were to force Maduro to step down. Hence, rather than proving fruitful in terms of the protection of the Venezuelan population, they had a negative impact on the situation by instigating reluctance on the Maduro administration to reach a peaceful solution and providing a foundation for Maduro to claim that the country was being victimised by an imperialist conspiracy (Ciurlizza, 2016). We can also argue that the US-led economic sanctions on Venezuela have contributed to the exacerbation of the humanitarian crisis in the country as well. These sanctions have created a situation where Venezuela's inability to export has led to the lack of foreign exchange, which is needed to obtain essential goods, along with the loss of personnel in essential professions such as in health care due to migration, which thus created another problem for Venezuelan people as they had difficulty to attain health care.

Consequences of this deepening economic situation have made access to basic goods like food, water and especially medicine more challenging for the Venezuelans indirectly contributing to an increase in poverty and death rates (Weisbrot & Sachs, 2019). Moreover, there are also concerns about the implications of the sanctions on the financial abilities of humanitarian-aid organisations, which essentially makes it hard for them to operate in Venezuela, especially during the COVID-19 pandemic (Broughtan & Tokar, 2019; Seelke, 2020). Therefore, as the analysis of the case at hand makes it evident, external intervention through coercive measures, such as unilateral sanctions not tailored to the necessities of the case and not carried out with an R2P intent and mindset might escalate the crisis, let alone contributing to its resolution.

Regarding the humanitarian aspect of the Venezuelan crisis, it is not fair to blame just one actor for the plight that emerged. The lack of basic human rights in Venezuela is the combined result of the policies and actions of the past administration, Maduro's decisions, US sanctions, as well as Guaido's actions and the inability of the international community to act in time. As for R2P in the case of Venezuela, both the government and the international community have failed. Furthermore, focusing on the political aspects of the crisis, coercive measures as sanctions have been imposed regardless of their implications for the population of Venezuela. The main problem with considering the sanctions as an attempt to end the humanitarian crisis, especially the ones imposed by the US—which proved to be the broadest and most effective sanctions in the case of Venezuela—is that the intentions behind those sanctions do not read the same as those of R2P.

It is a fact that the people of Venezuela have been failed on so many levels, but the question is, is it the actors or the R2P who failed them? As it was demonstrated in this chapter, there was no harmony between the members of the international community in responding to the crisis in Venezuela, and different actors followed their own agendas in terms of handling the political situation. In this regard, lack of an R2P intent coupled with the divide between the P5 culminated in the failure to protect the already suffering Venezuelan population. Overall, the self-interested motives of prominent actors at the individual, regional and international levels, as well as the incapability of the UNSC to carry out its R2P authority in an objective manner suggest imperfect conditions for the realisation of the responsibility to protect. Hence, it can be argued that '[a]s long as it remains dependent on the usual practices of the Security Council and the questionable commitment of its Member States, the responsibility to protect cannot achieve what was envisioned for it by the ICISS' (Gözen Ercan, 2016, p. 124). With the Permanent Members of the UNSC on different sides of the Venezuelan crisis, not only the implementation of R2P but any decision regarding the issue is most likely to be blocked without ever getting realised. In conclusion, when considered as an R2P case, even though we can consider the dire situation in Venezuela as a story of failure, it is not the idea behind the norm that failed in Venezuela but the priorities and policy choices of those who were to implement it.

References

Briceño-Ruiz, J. (2019). The crisis in Venezuela: A new chapter, or the final chapter? *Latin American Policy, 10*(1), 180–189.

Briceño-Ruiz, J. (2020). The Persistent Crisis in Venezuela. *Latin American Policy, 11*(1), 165–174.

Broughton, K., & Tokar, D. (2019, August 16). *Humanitarian Groups Face Banking Challenges as Venezuelan Sanctions Escalate*. https://www.wsj.com/articles/humanitarian-groups-face-banking-challenges-as-venezuelan-sanctions-escalate-11565990980. Accessed 10 December 2020.

Buxton, J. (2009). Venezuela: The political evolution of Bolivarianism. In G. Lievesley & S. Ludlam (Eds.), *Reclaiming Latin America: Experiments in radical social democracy* (pp. 57–74). Zed Books.

Cannon, B. (2004). Venezuela, April 2002: Coup or popular rebellion? The myth of a united Venezuela. *Bulletin of Latin American Research, 23*(3), 285–302.

Ciurlizza, J. (2016, October 12). *The Wrong Message: U.S. Sanctions on Venezuela*. https://www.crisisgroup.org/latin-america-caribbean/andes/venezuela/wrong-message-us-sanctions-venezuela. Accessed 11 December 2020.

De la Torre, C. (2017). Hugo Chávez and the diffusion of Bolivarianism. *Democratization, 24*(7), 1271–1288.

Duddy, P. (2015). *Political crisis in Venezuela. Council on foreign relations*. http://www.jstor.org/stable/resrep05688

European Center for the Responsibility to Protect (ECR2P). (n.d.). *Venezuela*. https://ecr2p.leeds.ac.uk/research-2/r2p-in-brief/venezuela/. Accessed 16 June 2020.

Gibbs, S. (2019). Oslo hosts a new round of Venezuela peace talks. *The Sunday Times*. https://www.thetimes.co.uk/article/oslo-hosts-new-round-of-venezuela-peace-talks-zk6p75hfr. Accessed 12 August 2021.

Global Center for the Responsibility to Protect (GCR2P). (2020). *Venezuela*. https://www.globalr2p.org/countries/venezuela/. Accessed 16 June 2020.

Global Center for the Responsibility to Protect (GCR2P). (2021). *Venezuela*. https://www.globalr2p.org/countries/venezuela/. Accessed 11 May 2021.

Gonzalez, J. S. (2019a). The Venezuelan Crisis and Salvador Allende's Glasses. *Prism, 8*(1), 40–55.

Gonzalez, M. (2019b). *Venezuela: In the Ebb of the Pink Tide*. Pluto Press.

Gözen Ercan, P. (2016). *Debating the Future of the "Responsibility to Protect": The Evolution of a Moral Norm*. Palgrave Macmillan.

Human Rights Watch. (2014). *Venezuela*. World Report 2014. https://www.hrw.org/world-report/2014. Accessed 11 December 2020.

Human Rights Watch. (2020). World Report 2020. Venezuela events of 2019. https://www.hrw.org/world-report/2020/country-chapters/venezuela. Accessed 5 December 2020.

International Criminal Court (ICC). (1998). *Rome Statute of the International Criminal Court*. https://www.icc-cpi.int/nr/rdonlyres/ea9aeff7-5752-4f84-be94-0a655eb30e16/0/rome_statute_english.pdf. Accessed 18 November 2020.

International Criminal Court (ICC). (2020, 19 February). *Venezuela II*. https://www.icc-cpi.int/venezuelaII. Accessed 18 November 2020.

International Criminal Court (ICC). (n.d.). *Venezuela I*. https://www.icc-cpi.int/venezuela. Accessed 12 June 2021.

Jakes, L. (2019, September 23). The U.S. Seeks More Sanctions on Venezuela's Leaders and Faults Europe's Inertia. *The New York Times*. https://www.nytimes.com/2019/09/23/world/americas/us-venezuela-europe-united-nations.html

Kahn, R. (2017). *Venezuela after the fall: Financing, debt relief and geopolitics*. Accessed 18 November 2020.

Rendon, M., Schneider, M. L., & Vázquez, J. (2019). Analyzing Obstacles to Venezuela's Future. *Center for Strategic & International Studies*. https://www.csis.org/analysis/analyzing-obstacles-venezuelas-future. Accessed 18 November 2020.

Seelke, C. R. (2020). Venezuela: Overview of US sanctions. *Current Politics and Economics of South and Central America, 13*(1), 21–27.

Stuenkel, O. (2017). How South America Let Venezuela Down. *Insight Turkey, 19*(4), 55–67.

UN Office of the High Commissioner for Human Rights (OHCHR), Human rights violations and abuses in the context of protests in the Bolivarian Republic of Venezuela from 1 April to 31 July 2017. https://www.ohchr.org/Documents/Countries/VE/HCReportVenezuela_1April-31July2017_EN.pdf. Accessed 6 June 2020

UN Office of the High Commissioner for Human Rights (OHCHR). (2018, June). *Human rights violations in the Bolivarian Republic of Venezuela: A downward spiral with no end in sight*. https://www.ohchr.org/Documents/Countries/VE/VenezuelaReport2018_EN.pdf. Accessed 6 June 2020.

United Nations Human Rights Council (UNHRC). (2020, 15 September). *Detailed findings of the independent international fact-finding mission on the Bolivarian Republic of Venezuela* (A/HRC/45/CRP.11).

United Nations Security Council (UNSC). (2019, April 10). *8506th Meeting, S/PV.8506.*

Van Roekel, E., & de Theije, M. (2020). Hunger in the land of plenty: The complex humanitarian crisis in Venezuela. *Anthropology Today, 36*(2), 8–12.

Vasquez, A., & Rosati, A. (2019). *Venezuela Talks in Oslo Hinge on Maduro Accepting a New Vote* (1). Bloomberg. https://www.bloomberg.com/news/articles/2019-05-23/venezuela-talks-in-oslo-hinge-on-maduro-accepting-new-elections. Accessed 6 June 2020.

Weisbrot, M., & Sachs, J. (2019). Economic sanctions as collective Punishment: The case of Venezuela. *Center for Economic and Policy Research*, 1–25.

CHAPTER 14

R2P at Twenty: A Shared Responsibility?

Pınar Gözen Ercan

It was twenty years ago that the International Commission on Intervention and State Sovereignty (ICISS) coined the term 'Responsibility to Protect' (R2P) for the first time. Four years later the Member States of the United Nations (UN) adopted with consensus the 2005 World Summit Outcome Document (WSOD), which under Paragraphs 138 and 139 established the States' and the international community's responsibility to protect. This was a watershed moment in the early years of R2P's evolution as a norm, which was celebrated by its proponents (Evans, 2006).

A lot has happened since then in terms of R2P's institutionalisation under the roof of the UN. While inconsistent implementations of the norm triggered discussions on the reform of the UN and specifically UN Security Council (UNSC), initiatives such as 'Responsibility while Protecting', 'Code of Good Conduct' and 'Rights up Front' put forth ways to enhance R2P practice and encouraged responsible protection. Meanwhile, the discussions concerning the norm's implementation have been continuing under the auspices of the UN General Assembly

P. Gözen Ercan (✉)
Department of International Relations, Hacettepe University, Ankara, Turkey

P. Gözen Ercan (ed.), *The Responsibility to Protect Twenty Years On*,
https://doi.org/10.1007/978-3-030-90731-0_14

(UNGA) since the UN Secretary-General's first detailed report on R2P dated 2009. In the last four years with the support of a majority of Member States, R2P has thrice found a place in the formal agenda of the UNGA. To date, R2P has been discussed four times in the UNGA formal debates and eight times in interactive dialogues that convened as a follow-up to the Secretary-General's annual R2P reports. While there was no R2P related discussion in the UNGA in 2020 due to the COVID-19 pandemic, most recently—with 115 votes in favour, 28 abstentions and 15 voting against (UNGA, 2021b)—the UNGA adopted Resolution 75/277, which decided to formally include R2P as an item in the Assembly's annual agenda, and also requested 'the Secretary-General to report annually to the General Assembly on the responsibility to protect and the prevention of genocide, war crimes, ethnic cleansing and crimes against humanity' (UNGA, 2021a). This was another watershed moment in R2P's two-decade history, the results of which we are yet to see. Meanwhile, (based on Resolution 44/14, which it adopted on 24 July 2020), on 11 May 2021 the Human Rights Council (UNHRC) convened in an intersessional discussion to commemorate R2P's fifteenth anniversary. This was the first time that the UNHRC adopted a thematic resolution on R2P 'to raise awareness and to reflect on achievements, best practices and challenges, at the national, regional and international levels, with regard to' R2P (UNGA, 2020).

While the UN Secretaries-General (as well as their Special Advisers on Genocide and R2P) have been the principal driving force behind the institutionalisation of R2P, most of these developments also owed to the efforts of the Member States mainly organised under the framework of 'the Group of Friends of the Responsibility to Protect' (GoF), which proactively endorses R2P and supports the UN Secretary-General in his efforts to improve the norm's implementation. Over the years, it is not only the number of the members of the Group of Friends of R2P that has increased, but also the number of the R2P Focal Points appointed. Currently, 61 States in addition to the European Union (EU) and the Organization of American States (OAS) have R2P Focal Points (GCR2P, n.d.).

Notwithstanding these positive developments and the growing verbal support for R2P among the Member States for the norm's continued inclusion in the UNGA's agenda, in different parts of the world human-made disasters continue to take place. Currently, there are situations in more than 30 countries which constitute an R2P concern (GCR2P,

2021). Hence, as the former and current UN Secretaries-General Ban Ki-moon and António Guterres have expressed on various occasions, there still exists a gap between words and practice. Rich in its geographical scope, through a study of representative cases, this book has attempted to address this very issue, and asked 'has R2P become a shared responsibility over the last two decades'? Therefore, it is important to understand the underlying reasons for the failure to protect vulnerable populations and identify the existing gaps.

Mindset, Rhetoric and Implementation: Identifying the Gaps

Over the last decade, scholarly discussions on R2P and its effectiveness have centred on the 'failures of R2P'. The much debated military intervention carried out at the early stages of the crisis unfolding in Libya and the controversial lack of response in Syria despite the gravity of the situation have culminated in a rather critical literature on R2P. While some contend that the Libyan case marked the beginning of the end of R2P (Brockmeier et al., 2016; Dalal, 2013, p. 208; Kuperman, 2013; Powers, 2015), others reiterate such contention arguing that Syria became the last nail in the coffin (Nuruzzaman, 2013). Meanwhile, the controversies arising from the 'sharp end of Pillar Three' due to the use of military force in Libya, which did not render a very positive result, led others to focus more on the peaceful measures of the norm following the course of the discussions in the UNGA (Zifcak, 2012; Thakur, 2013; Stuenkel, 2014; Welsh, 2016).

As Bellamy (Chapter 2) suggests, 'translating R2P into consistent practice has proven difficult, and the practical record is mixed. That is primarily because R2P does not sit apart from world politics, but is a part of it', and that is why 'a more differentiated account—comprising intent, practices and outcomes—might be a better way of evaluating R2P'. This is why through varied lenses focusing on the depth of R2P's toolkit, we have explored numerous cases from the larger perspective of the three-pillar implementation strategy and the measures implemented as a whole, and sought for components of success and failure in practice rather than labelling each case as a success or failure of R2P per se.

Prevention Prioritisation vs. Intention

When we compare the main themes of and the arguments presented in the UNGA discussions on R2P with the practices of the UNSC and the Member States, it becomes possible to identify the very first gap, that is between prioritisation of mass atrocity prevention and the actual intent driving the practice. Following the 2005 consensus on R2P, and especially since the first Secretary-General Report on R2P in 2009, there has been growing emphasis on the prevention of mass atrocity crimes, which has received vast support from the Member States (Gözen Ercan, 2019). Correspondingly, most of the Secretary-General reports on R2P have been focused on prevention through Pillar Two as well as Pillar One. Nevertheless, when we look at the cases studied in this book, or situations of R2P concern in general, we see only exceptional examples of successful prevention, which are the cases of Kenya and Guinea. As Koç (Chapter 4) underlines, both Kenya and Guinea as situations of peacetime atrocities are of great significance in terms of the roles direct/operational and structural/root cause prevention play in the realisation of the responsibility to protect. In both cases, Pillars Two and Three were implemented in an intertwined manner to address the root causes and to develop immediate responses to enable escalation prevention. The active engagement of regional arrangements/organisations with actual intent of protecting the vulnerable populations yielded successful prevention.

In some cases, there were no assertive preventive efforts early into the crises, such as in the cases of Gaza, Xinjiang, Myanmar and Venezuela. For instance, as Arslan (Chapter 13) observes, in the case of the latter, the regional attention directed towards preventing human rights violations in Venezuela and delivering humanitarian aid was divided by the political discord between the Permanent Members of the UNSC (P5). While the United States (US) supported Guaido (followed by the Lima Group and the EU) and pursued a policy based on sanctions, China and Russia sided with Maduro. Such split, as well as lack of a common international strategy helped only to exacerbate the internal situation at the expense of the Venezuelan population. Similarly, in the case of Myanmar, China's adherence to the principle of non-intervention—as did ASEAN—resulted in continued suffering of the Rohingya. Hence, in both cases it was the absence of an R2P intent and/or a prevention concern of the actors responding to the situations that resulted in a failure to prevent.

In some other cases (such as Côte d'Ivoire, Darfur, Nigeria and Yemen), the efforts of the national authorities and/or the international community fell short of providing protection to the vulnerable populations at an early stage. A prominent reason for such failure has arguably been the absence of action carried out in the light of the R2P mindset even in cases where it was not the State authorities but non-state armed groups (NSAGs) who were mainly responsible for the mass atrocity crimes. In the case of Nigeria, for instance, the main motive of the national authorities and supporting States has been countering Boko Haram. Likewise, in Yemen, despite their use of the R2P language in invoking military action, the incumbent government and the Saudi-led coalition were driven by their self-interested motives regarding their sovereign powers rather than a concern for protecting the Yemeni population from the actions of the Houthi armed rebels.

When we look at the post-intervention period in Afghanistan, we see that a lot has been done by various international actors as well as the national authorities to improve the capacity and resilience of the Afghan State, which were in line with Pillars One and Two of R2P. Nevertheless, the Afghan case has never been viewed from an R2P lens, and the international efforts that have mainly concentrated on the counterterrorism agenda failed to provide a sustainable protection for the population in the long-term despite the heavy international engagement in the country.

In the case of Libya, wherein the international focus quickly shifted towards Pillar Three, we see neither the use of the R2P language in the justifications for the coercive actions nor a serious consideration of exhausting preventive measures prior to the decision to militarily intervene. As Murray (2013) argues,

> Libya was by far the best opportunity for R2P to be used both in principle and in action because it posed absolutely no genuine strategic military threat to an intervening force and very few world leaders would lament the loss of Gaddafi's hold on power. ... However, members of the P5, the UN more broadly and NATO ended up doing almost everything in their power not to mention or invoke R2P in their justifications for a mission into Libya.

Accordingly, as Kul (Chapter 7) notes, the conclusion of the military operation with the toppling of Gaddafi not only fuelled the criticisms that the intervention was aimed for regime change, but also resulted in a second cycle of civil war in Libya and a failure to prevent reescalation. Different States fighting wars in Syria in pursuit of their own interests with disregard for the protection of the Syrian population also resulted in a failure to prevent further escalation of the situation. While components of failure have been quite obvious in both cases in terms of the implementation at the level of the home States due to lack of genuine R2P intent, from the perspective of the protection of refugees the record has been mixed. At the level of Pillar One, it is possible to talk about a genuine intent to protect refugees on the part of the host States that welcomed people fleeing the conflict zones in Libya and Syria. While they have been carrying out their responsibility to the best of their ability, it is questionable if we can say the same for the efforts of the international community. Although there have been numerous initiatives to assist the host States to cope with the mass influx of refugees and to build their capacity to provide better conditions for the refugees, some States have done so mainly to keep the refugees outside their borders. Hence, once again there remains not only a question of genuine intent, but also, as Kul argues, a failure to prevent further crises that may result from secondary movements.

Case-By-Case Implementation vs. Selectivity

The issue of the lack of genuine intent on the part of individual States brings us to the question of selectivity in R2P's implementation. As set out in Paragraph 139 of the WSOD, and later reiterated in the Secretary-General reports, R2P is to be implemented 'on a case-by-case basis' (UNGA, 2005). As Ban Ki-moon clarifies, such wording suggests a response 'tailored to the circumstances of the situation' (UNGA, 2009, p. 22), not a 'choice' as to whether or not to implement R2P in a specific humanitarian crisis. Nevertheless, once again there remains a gap between what is envisioned and what the practice has been. We see the benefits of a tailored approach in the cases of Kenya, Guinea and Côte d'Ivoire wherein responses pertaining to Pillars Two and/or Three have yielded positive outcomes at least in the short-term. Yet, as for the case of Côte d'Ivoire and why implementation arguably succeeded at the level of Pillar Three but not earlier, France's selectivity at the early stages of the situation is noteworthy. As Savaş Cazala (Chapter 6) shows, France was reluctant to get involved in the situation of its ex-colony and preferred to restrain its unilateral actions so as not to be subjected to criticisms as it was in the cases of Chad and Zaire.

In some other humanitarian crises, which have been an immediate R2P concern, we have seen no fruitful action. For instance, Gaza and Xinjiang have been highly politicised cases wherein the adoption of an R2P approach by the UNSC—or any approach at all—has been out of question. As Eskiduman (Chapter 8) demonstrates, in the case of the former it has been the US as one of the P5 that has blocked any decision that would be to the detriment of Israel and prevented the potential of any sort of R2P response. Usurping its great power status to support its good old ally, the US has even threatened the International Criminal Court (ICC) to block it from opening an investigation into the situation in Palestine. On the other hand, in the case of the latter, as Karamık (Chapter 12) contends, it has been the stronghold of another member of the P5, China, that has prevented the consideration of the situation within the framework of R2P under the UN. While there have been numerous efforts to address the issue in different platforms such as the UNHRC and the UNSC, China did not allow Member States to bring allegations against it and easily succeeded in blocking investigations and/or further action. Such deadlock in terms of implementation also has to do with the prevalent state-centric approach to R2P practices despite the variety of the actors mentioned in the Secretary-General reports.

Multiplicity of Actors vs. State-Centric Focus on R2P

A primary reason why we can enumerate a much smaller number of components of success compared to that of failure in the cases we have covered in this book is the state-centric focus to R2P crises. While there have been attempts to prevent the escalation of the situation in various cases (such as those of Afghanistan, Côte d'Ivoire, Darfur, Nigeria, Yemen and Venezuela), these efforts have failed also because the multiplicity of actors that could trigger/undertake R2P action and/or commit mass atrocity crimes has been disregarded in implementation. As Açıkyıldız (Chapter 5), Wan Rosli (Chapter 9) and Balkan-Şahin (Chapter 10) observe, in the cases of Nigeria and Yemen—and similarly in Afghanistan—the NSAGs being the perpetrators posed a challenge because the actors involved tried to cope with the crises through traditional security approaches. Hence, we can argue that a tailored R2P approach was missing, and even though regional actors were involved, their actions were concentrated on the counterterrorism agenda rather than devising a response that aimed for the protection of populations and root cause prevention. In some other cases, the international response was constrained either by adherence to State sovereignty—as Afewerky (Chapter 3) notes for the case of Darfur—and/or lack of political will in the UNSC, such as in the examples of Gaza, Syria, Venezuela and Xinjiang. All these failures to prevent the humanitarian crises and/or absence of implementation due to constraints by national security concerns or strategic alliances hint at the prevalent state-centric approach in R2P's implementation.

If R2P is to reach its full potential, we first need to acknowledge that we do not always depend on the States and the UNSC to implement R2P. For instance, besides the positive examples of Kenya and Guinea wherein eminent individuals and regional organisations have heavily contributed to the resolution of the two crises, in the case of Myanmar, we see the role played by international courts as well as individuals' initiatives. As Kapucu (Chapter 11) demonstrates, though we are yet to see the actual outcomes of the three separate judicial processes concerning Myanmar, the actions undertaken through the international justice system, besides raising international awareness about the case, increased the prospects for the Rohingya's access to protection and justice by holding the perpetrators accountable for their crimes. Similarly, in the highly politicised case of Gaza which has been at a deadlock in the UNSC, the ICC investigation creates the possibility of holding all three authorities—namely the Palestinian Authority, Hamas and Israel—accountable for the mass atrocity crimes in Gaza from 13 June 2014 onwards.

Conclusion: Towards Sustainable Protection

In the first two decades of R2P, the world has witnessed numerous humanitarian crises where there was compelling evidence of mass atrocity crimes. Right after the 2005 consensus, as the earliest case of concern in R2P history, Darfur became the first and the last case where the UNSC referred to Paragraphs 138 and 139 of the WSOD in a country specific resolution. After 2006, the Council did not make any references to Paragraph 139 although it recalled the responsibility of national authorities in different cases including that of Libya. While in a majority of cases R2P mindset has been missing in action, such change in language evinced the political dynamics driving R2P practice and the desire of the Member

States to avoid a collective duty to protect populations (Gözen Ercan, 2016, pp. 63–65). As Bellamy (Chapter 2) reminds, 'R2P does not outside world politics. It is a product of world politics and, to the extent that it is impactful, achieves things by operating through world politics'. This is a major reason why R2P has had a mixed record so far and has not yet turned into a shared responsibility.

In this vein, to better understand what is required for achieving sustainable protection, with the holistic approach we adopted in this book, we have tried to identify the components of success and failure. Though R2P is far from being a shared practice at the current state of affairs, diverging from the dark picture that critics paint for R2P, we have found that there are a lot of grey zones in the assessment of what has been achieved through R2P. For instance, Murray (2013, p. 227) posits that 'what has become evident since 2001 is that states and international institutions do not see R2P as the framework through which to approach human insecurity'. Nevertheless, States have not yet totally dismissed R2P. While it is true that some States just pay lip service without any intent to internalise R2P or to reflect it in their actions, the norm's consideration under the auspices of the UNGA continue in a more compelling manner as R2P is now placed as an item in the formal agenda of the Assembly. It is also important to remind that the UNGA suggested the Secretary-General to continue to deliver annual reports on R2P. Such support from the UNGA is very important, because as Bellamy (Chapter 2) observes, politics not only constrains R2P's implementation but also enables it. This is also a significant point to consider because not enough attention is paid to these reports (and the depth of R2P's toolkit as presented in these reports) in the scholarly assessments of R2P. That is why, if we wish to achieve sustainable protection of populations and break the cycle of impunity, we need to focus more on the measures of R2P in depth, incline towards tailored approaches, aim for root cause prevention and move beyond the purely state-centric conceptions/assessments of the responsibility to protect.

To this end, we need to focus on upstream implementation of R2P through civil society and private sector actors, as well as regional and non-governmental organisations. All these actors may prove very helpful in terms of the assessment of the early warning signs, devising tailored approaches to the needs of each situation, as well as root cause prevention. Furthermore, we need to raise awareness on individual responsibility, which helps to build resilience in the mid- to long-term as well as to end impunity. At the end of the day, the mass atrocity crimes that define the scope of R2P are committed by individuals, and also can be prevented by individuals. Hence, there is a dual role played by individuals, and that is why prevention starts within societies, not States. As Karen Smith (2020) remarks:

> Viewing R2P from the perspective of the global South, including the southern African notion of *ubuntu*, the Latin American idea of *sumak kawsay*, or Daoist understandings of relationality, allows us to conceive of responsibility towards others in a slightly different way. Despite their differences, all of these worldviews emphasise that, as humans, we are all inextricably connected to one another, and according to some, also to nature. As individuals, and as states (which, arguably, are an extension of the individual), we therefore do not merely have a responsibility towards others due to a sense of obligation or duty, but rather because we are all intimately related.

In general terms, shifting the focus on to the non-state actors as well as regional arrangements is not to suggest that States and the UN should be dismissed as agents of R2P. We need to recognise that there is more to R2P than unwilling States and incapable international community that are not fulfilling their obligations. Moreover, I contend that it is not R2P that fails to protect populations but the States and the international community that do not uphold their responsibilities. Given the political constraints surrounding it, perceiving or presenting R2P as a panacea to all human-made disasters does not do justice to the norm in terms of what we can expect from it. At the end of the day, R2P provides us with a framework based on the existing international law and obligations, as well as a toolkit to tackle humanitarian challenges. As Welsh (2018, p. 357) asserts, 'R2P was designed by its advocates to serve as a means of enhancing compliance with existing bodies of law that aim to protect civilian populations, but also, more broadly, of fostering greater political will and institutional capacity to prevent and respond to atrocity crimes'.

Accordingly, what R2P puts on the table is already an inherent part of the UN system. In this vein, it is also important to recognise the link between R2P and the 2030 Sustainable Development Agenda, especially Goal 16, which aims to '[p]romote peaceful and inclusive societies for sustainable development, provide access to justice for all and build effective, accountable and inclusive institutions at all levels' (UN-DoESA, 2021). Achieving the targets of Goal 16 at the individual and the State levels gets us one step closer to the achievement of R2P objectives as it also helps to eliminate the root causes of internal conflict. As we have seen in previous chapters, a problem common to all the cases that we have studied in this book hints at the absence of sustainable protection. Even in situations where success was achieved in terms of preventing and/or halting the atrocity crimes, today there still remains the potential of reescalation. This owes mainly to the failure to address to the root causes with short-termed policies and/or ignoring the importance of the discarded element of R2P, namely the responsibility to rebuild. In this regard, in relevance with Goal 16, building resilience as well as the capacity of the States, and ensuring justice and accountability are of vital importance at all stages of R2P's implementation.

Last but not least, we need to recognise the shortcomings of the UN as the world organisation, and call for reform. As Annan (cited in Hooper, 2009) asserts: 'The current architecture of managing global affairs is broken and needs to be fixed. [...] We cannot continue to run the world based on countries that won a war 60 years ago'. Hence, recognising the political and practical constraints that surround R2P, I would like to conclude arguing that although it has not become a shared responsibility in its first two decades, R2P remains a relevant and viable norm in terms of approaching human (in)security. Yet, we also need to acknowledge that there are major political challenges we need to address to enable R2P's effective and consistent implementation to provide the necessary sustainable protection to population.

References

Brockmeier, S., Stuenkel, O., & Tourinho, M. (2016). The Impact of the Libya intervention debates on norms of protection. *Global Society, 30*(1), 113–133.

Dalal, N. E. (2013). The R2P is dead. Long live the R2P: Libya, Syria, and the responsibility to protect. *Law School Student Scholarship, 208*, 1–31.

Evans, G. (2006, March 31). *From humanitarian intervention to the responsibility to protect*. http://www.crisisgroup.org/home/index.cfm?id=4060&l=1. Accessed 24 April 2018.

Global Centre for the Responsibility to Protect (GCR2P). (n.d.). *Global network of R2P focal points*. https://www.globalr2p.org/the-global-network-of-r2p-focal-points/. Accessed 1 August 2021.

Global Centre for the Responsibility to Protect (GCR2P). (2021). *Populations at risk*. https://www.globalr2p.org/populations-at-risk/. Accessed 1 August 2021.

Gözen Ercan, P. (2016). *Debating the future of the 'responsibility to protect': The evolution of a moral norm*. Palgrave Macmillan.
Gözen Ercan, P. (2019). UN general assembly dialogues on the responsibility to protect and the use of force for humanitarian purposes. *Global Responsibility to Protect, 11*(3), 313–332.
Hooper, S. (2009). *Annan: World faces "crisis of governance"*. CNN. http://edition.cnn.com/2009/BUSINESS/01/28/davos.wef.annan/index.html?eref=rss_. Accessed 21 June 2021.
Kuperman, A. (2013). A model humanitarian intervention? Reassessing NATO's Libya campaign. *International Security, 38*(1), 105–136.
Murray, R. W. (2013). Conclusion: The responsibility to protect after Libya. In A. Hehir & R. Murray (Eds.), *Libya, the responsibility to protect and the future of humanitarian intervention* (222–228). Palgrave Macmillan.
Nuruzzaman, M. (2013). The 'responsibility to protect' doctrine: Revived in Libya Buried in Syria. *Insight Turkey, 15*(2), 57–66.
Powers, M. (2015). Responsibility to protect: Dead, dying, or thriving? *The International Journal of Human Rights, 19*(8), 1257–1278.
Smith, K. (2020, August 17). *A reflection on the responsibility to protect in 2020*. https://www.globalr2p.org/publications/a-reflection-on-the-responsibility-to-protect-in-2020/. Accessed 15 August 2021.
Stuenkel, O. (2014). The BRICS and future of R2P: Was Syria or Libya the exception? *Global Responsibility to Protect, 6*, 3–28.
Thakur, R. (2013). R2P after Libya and Syria: Engaging emerging powers. *The Washington Quarterly, 36*, 61–76.
United Nations Department of Economic and Social Affairs (UN-DoESA). (2021). Sustainable Development. https://sdgs.un.org/goals/goal16. Accessed 21 June 2021.
United Nations General Assembly (UNGA). (2005, October 24). *Resolution adopted by the General Assembly on 16 September 2005*. 60/1. 2005 World Summit Outcome, A/Res/60/1.
United Nations General Assembly (UNGA). (2009, January 12). *Implementing the responsibility to protect*. Report of the Secretary-General, A/63/677.
United Nations General Assembly (UNGA). (2020, July 24). Resolution adopted by the Human Rights Council on 17 July 2020. 44/14. Fifteenth anniversary of the responsibility to protect populations from genocide, war crimes, ethnic cleansing and crimes against humanity, as enshrined in the 2005 World Summit Outcome. A/HRC/RES/44/14.
United Nations General Assembly (UNGA). (2021a). *Resolution adopted by the General Assembly on 18 May 2021*. A/RES/75/277.
United Nations General Assembly (UNGA). (2021b). *Resolutions of the 75th session*. https://www.un.org/en/ga/75/resolutions.shtml. Accessed 22 August 2021.

Welsh, J. M. (2016). The responsibility to protect after Libya & Syria. *The Journal of the American Academy of Arts & Sciences, 145*(4), 75–87.

Welsh, J. M. (2018). The responsibility to protect and non-state armed groups. In M. Lattimer & P. Sands (Eds.), *The grey zone: Civilian protection between human rights and the laws of war* (pp. 357–376). Hart Publishing.

Zifcak, S. (2012). The responsibility to protect after Libya and Syria. *Melbourne Journal of International Law, 13*(1), 59–93.

Index

A

Accountability, 7, 9, 31, 61, 64, 83, 93, 127, 163, 190, 191, 208, 222, 231, 233, 236–238, 299
  accountability mechanism, 189, 190
Afghanistan, 7, 163, 197–216, 293, 295
  Afghanistan National Development Strategy (ANDS), 202, 203, 212
  Afghanistan Reconstruction Trust Fund (ARTF), 209
African Commission on Human and Peoples' Rights (ACHPR), 64
African Union (AU), 40, 41, 59–64, 66–71, 93, 96
  African Union Mission in Sudan (AMIS), 33, 40–42, 47
Al-Qaida, 201, 250, 252
Annan, Kofi, 13–15, 22, 27, 31, 55, 59–62, 70, 71, 145, 182, 299
Anti-corruption, 211
Arab League, 18
Arab uprisings, 133, 134, 137, 174, 179
Arakan Rohingya Salvation Army (ARSA), 225, 234
Asian Development Bank (ADB), 209
Association of Southeast Asian Nations (ASEAN), 229, 230, 261, 292
Asylum seeker, 138–140, 143, 146
Atrocity crimes, 1, 3–7, 9, 15–23, 27–30, 36, 47, 56, 59, 61, 63–65, 72, 81, 95, 97, 98, 108, 118, 120, 126, 133, 134, 137, 144, 145, 153, 154, 161, 164, 166, 167, 171, 172, 176–185, 187–190, 198, 205, 207, 214, 215, 223, 231–234, 238, 246, 255, 265, 271, 283, 292, 293, 295, 296, 298, 299
Atrocity prevention, 4, 20–22, 24, 55, 57, 73, 203, 214–216

B

Brazil, 18, 31, 278

P. Gözen Ercan (ed.), *The Responsibility to Protect Twenty Years On*, https://doi.org/10.1007/978-3-030-90731-0

C
Capacity-building, 8, 62, 64, 67, 68, 90, 95, 116, 143, 146, 197, 207, 214, 215, 229, 256
Case-by-case implementation, 165, 294
Central Intelligence Agency (CIA), 199, 206
Chávez, Hugo, 272–275
China, 9, 14, 16, 17, 31, 36, 38, 39, 122, 136, 137, 165, 186, 230, 233, 235, 245, 246, 248–264, 279, 282, 292, 295
  China Cables, 255
Chinese Communist Party, 248, 252
Civilian Joint Task Force (CJTF), 85
Clearance operations, 225, 230
Commission of Inquiry into Post-Election Violence (CIPEV), 61
Commonwealth Observer Group (COG), 58
Compliance, 2, 17, 18, 20, 21, 46, 85, 95, 120, 141, 298
  compliance pull, 19
  non-compliance, 18, 19
Comprehensive Peace Agreement (CPA), 37
Concerned Citizens for Peace (CCP), 71
Contestation, 30, 227
Counter-narcotics, 212
Crimes against humanity, 1, 7, 16–18, 58, 61, 63, 67, 69, 89, 94, 96, 111, 119, 121, 127, 137, 145, 154, 158, 160, 163, 166, 176, 202, 205, 206, 225, 226, 232, 233, 254, 255, 260, 280, 281, 283, 290
Cultural Revolution, 245, 248–250

D
Darfur Liberation Front (DLF), 36
Dual responsibility, 15, 178
Duty of conduct, 30

E
East Turkestan, 245, 252
  East Turkistan Republic (ETR), 247, 249
Economic Community of West African States (ECOWAS), 62–64, 66, 68–71, 85, 112–114, 116, 118
Election related violence, 116, 125, 127
Electoral Commission of Kenya (ECK), 58
Escalation prevention, 59, 64, 292
Ethnic cleansing, 1, 16, 17, 46, 59, 145, 176, 202, 222, 225, 226, 230, 231, 260, 290
Ethnic division, 66
European Union (EU)
  European Observation Mission (EUOM), 58
  European Union Police Mission to Afghanistan (EUPOL), 210, 211

F
Fact-finding commissions, 66, 71
Focal points, 87, 290
Formal agenda, 290, 297
Formal debates, 166, 290
France, 28, 62, 64, 71, 111–116, 120, 122, 123, 126, 136, 155, 294

G
Genocide, 1, 3, 14–17, 28, 33–35, 37–39, 42, 43, 45, 47, 48, 94,

145, 176, 202, 205, 222, 225, 226, 230, 232, 234, 235, 254, 260, 263, 290
Genocide Convention, 233, 234
Global Center for the Responsibility to Protect (GCR2P), 61, 62, 64, 65, 125, 137, 204, 205, 233, 254, 272, 277, 290
Global north, 95, 141, 166
Global south, 18, 141, 298
Global War on Terror, 251
Great Leap Forward, 248
Great Proletariat Cultural Revolution, 249
Group of Friends of the Responsibility to Protect (GoF), 290
Guaido, Juan, 276, 277, 279–282, 285, 292
Gulf Cooperation Council (GCC), 174, 175, 177–181
Guterres, António, 55, 93, 139, 231, 232, 291

H

Han Chinese, 245, 248, 249
Human rights, 6, 9, 18, 27, 61, 64, 67, 82, 88, 91, 95, 96, 98, 153, 157–159, 167, 174, 176, 185, 198, 201–204, 206, 210, 212, 213, 215, 216, 222, 225–228, 230, 232, 233, 235, 246, 250, 251, 253, 255–258, 261, 263–265, 271, 274, 275, 277–280, 282–285, 292
Human Rights Council (HRC), 63, 64, 228
Human Rights up Front, 289
Human security, 83, 98

I

Ili National Army (INA), 247
India, 18, 31, 121, 199, 230
Individual responsibility, 73, 145, 226, 297
Interactive dialogues, 290
Inter-Afghan peace, 210, 211
Internally displaced persons (IDPs), 40, 42, 44, 45, 60, 134, 160, 201, 207
International Commission on Intervention and State Sovereignty (ICISS), 1, 15, 16, 34, 46, 47, 178, 182, 190, 255, 285, 289
International community, 3–10, 17, 19, 20, 26, 27, 30, 33–38, 40, 42–48, 62–66, 68, 70, 72, 73, 83–87, 90, 92–98, 108, 112, 116–120, 122, 126, 127, 135, 141–146, 154, 158, 160–162, 164, 166, 167, 171, 172, 176, 178–181, 183, 185–191, 197–199, 201, 202, 207, 209–211, 213–216, 228–232, 237, 246, 250, 253, 255, 256, 259, 260, 262–265, 272, 277–280, 283–285, 289, 293, 294, 298
International Contact Group on Guinea (ICG-G), 71
International Court of Justice (ICJ), 8, 182, 183, 189, 232–238
International Criminal Court (ICC), 8, 39, 41, 45, 46, 61, 63–65, 67, 72, 73, 85, 89, 93–96, 125, 135, 159, 162–164, 167, 205, 206, 232–234, 236–238, 254, 260, 262, 280, 281, 295, 296
International criminal law, 97, 233
International Humanitarian Law (IHL), 91, 188, 189, 208, 231, 233

International Human Rights Law (IHRL), 91, 189
International justice system, 8, 9, 221–223, 226, 231, 233, 236–238, 296
International responsibility, 17, 68, 143, 145, 146, 154, 172, 182
International Security Assistance Force (ISAF), 203, 208, 210, 211, 215
International tribunals, 205, 222, 236
Intervention by Invitation (IvI), 7, 172, 181, 189
Invited interveners, 181, 187–189
Islamic State
  Islamic State-Khurasan Province (ISKP), 204
  Islamic State of Iraq and Levant (ISIL), 92, 137
  Islamic State of Iraq and the Levant (ISIS), 86
  Islamic State West Africa Province (ISWAP), 86, 87
Israel, 6, 153, 155–160, 162–166, 295, 296
Israeli Defence Forces (IDF), 157, 159, 160, 164

J
Judicial settlement, 8, 67, 222, 232
Justice, 8, 9, 16, 39, 46, 48, 67, 96, 124, 159, 203, 204, 208, 210, 211, 222, 231–234, 236–238, 296, 298, 299
Justice and Equality Movement (JEM), 36, 42

K
Kenyan National Dialogue and Reconciliation (KNDR), 60
Kenyans for Peace with Truth and Justice (KPTJ), 58
Khartoum, 35, 36, 38–41, 47, 48
Ki-moon, Ban, 55, 56, 59, 64, 71, 95, 97, 135, 156, 176, 182, 215, 291, 294
Kosovo, 13, 14

L
Lake Chad Basin Commission (LCBC), 93
Law enforcement, 19, 89, 202, 210, 214
Libya, 2, 5, 6, 26, 31, 57, 107, 108, 120, 123, 125, 126, 133–139, 141, 143–145, 165, 172, 185, 188–190, 291, 293, 294, 296
Linas-Marcoussis Agreement, 113–116, 126

M
Maduro, Nicolás, 271, 274–285, 292
Mass atrocities, 3, 8, 14–17, 23, 30, 31, 35, 37–39, 47, 48, 56, 57, 59, 60, 62, 65–67, 89, 119, 127, 144, 145, 161, 166, 197, 198, 214, 229
Mass atrocity prevention, 19, 57, 67, 127, 292
Mediation, 17, 22, 59, 60, 62, 63, 65, 66, 69–72, 178, 179, 189
Multinational Joint Task (MNJTF), 96

N
Nigerian Security Forces (NSF), 85, 87–89, 95
Non-coercive measures, 120, 221, 222, 226, 231, 260
Non-governmental organisations (NGOs), 38, 71, 94, 142, 211, 214, 297

Non-International Armed Conflicts (NIACs), 98, 182
Non-state armed groups (NSAGs), 4, 81, 97, 293
North Atlantic Treaty Organization (NATO), 13, 14, 26, 31, 136, 138, 197, 203, 205, 207, 211–213, 215, 293
North-South War, 37

O

Office of the High Commissioner for Human Rights, 59, 92, 93, 137, 223, 279
Office of the Prosecutor (OTP), 85, 93, 94, 97, 205
Operation Cast Lead, 6, 154, 156, 157
Operation Decisive Storm, 175, 181, 185, 187–189
Operation Protective Edge, 6, 154, 156–158, 160
Operation Renewal of Hope, 187
Orange Democratic Movement (ODM), 58, 60
Organization for Economic Cooperation and Development (OECD), 209

P

Palestinian Authority (PA), 6, 156–159, 162, 163, 165, 296
Palestinian Liberation Organization (PLO), 156
Pandemic, 23, 142, 204, 285, 290
  COVID-19, 23, 142, 204, 285, 290
Parameters on the use of force, 172, 182
Party of National Unity (PNU), 58
Peaceful measures, 8, 17, 56, 65, 69, 72, 90, 162, 222, 231, 232, 237, 238, 280, 282, 291
Peacetime atrocities, 4, 57, 292
People Liberation Army (PLA), 250
Political will, 3, 5, 20, 38, 45, 48, 68, 70, 92, 126, 162, 227, 235, 296, 298
Prevention, 4, 15, 20, 22–27, 30, 31, 34, 46, 55–57, 60, 61, 65, 67–70, 72, 73, 90, 94, 126, 162, 165, 176, 198, 212, 216, 229–231, 238, 255, 259, 265, 290, 292, 298
  direct prevention, 4, 60, 61, 63, 65, 68
  operational prevention, 57, 60
Provincial Reconstruction Teams (PRT), 210, 211

Q

Qing dynasty, 247

R

Rakhine State, 223–225, 230, 232
Recurrence prevention, 61, 72
Re-education camps, 246, 253
Referendum, 25, 34, 124
Reform, 17, 22, 23, 61, 62, 64, 65, 67, 68, 109, 123, 167, 202, 203, 210, 211, 272, 289, 299
  UN reform, 265
  UNSC reform, 123, 289
Refugee, 5, 6, 34, 40, 42, 44, 45, 134, 135, 138–146, 155, 163, 198–201, 203, 207, 222, 232, 294
  refugee flow, 97, 144, 201
  refugee protection crisis, 6, 139, 141
Resistance, 37, 199, 251, 257, 277

Responsibility to prevent, 38, 57, 63, 73, 126, 256
Responsibility to react, 34, 48, 55, 56, 126, 127, 161
Responsibility to rebuild, 3, 34, 35, 43, 46–48, 127, 299
Responsibility while Protecting (RwP), 289
Right to intervene, 31
Root cause prevention, 57
Root causes, 2–5, 47, 60, 61, 65–67, 72, 93, 107, 124, 203, 222, 272, 292, 299
Rural development, 210
Russia, 14, 16, 20, 21, 31, 36, 38, 39, 121, 122, 136, 137, 186, 199, 233, 235, 246, 247, 262, 279, 282, 292
Rwanda, 14, 22, 23, 40, 112, 127, 234

S
Sanctions, 10, 28, 36, 39, 63, 65, 66, 69, 71, 91, 95, 98, 118, 121, 125, 162, 163, 260–264, 278, 279, 281–285, 292
Saudi-led coalition, 7, 172, 176, 181, 182, 184, 185, 187, 188, 293
Selectivity, 30, 153, 165, 294
Self-determination, 9, 245, 265
Shanghai Five, 251, 261, 262
South Africa, 18, 31, 122
South Sudan Independence War, 37
Sovereignty, 6, 13–15, 20, 24, 30, 34, 38, 40, 48, 81, 95, 137, 141, 157, 158, 166, 177, 183–185, 189, 190, 226, 233, 254, 256, 265, 296
Spark Alliance, 250
Special Adviser on the Responsibility to Protect, 118, 141
State-centric, 4, 73, 81, 97, 295–297
Statelessness, 8, 226–228
Strike Hard (*Yanda*) Campaign, 251–253
Structural causes, 292
Structural prevention, 56, 57, 60, 61, 64, 65, 67, 72
  root cause prevention, 4, 9, 292, 296, 297
Sudan, 35–39, 43, 46, 47
Sudanese Liberation Movement (SLM), 36, 42
Sustainable Development Goals
  Goal 16, 298, 299
Sustainable prevention, 34, 67, 68, 72, 73
Sustainable protection, 3–5, 8–10, 46, 48, 98, 108, 127, 135, 138, 141, 146, 223, 238, 293, 297, 299

T
Taliban, 198, 201–213
Tatmadaw, 223, 225, 228, 232, 236, 237
Three-pillar implementation strategy, 2, 7, 43, 68, 84, 97, 98, 108, 126, 138, 145, 189, 213, 246, 255, 272, 291
Tiananmen Square Protests, 250
Tribunal Supremo de Justicia (TSJ), 274–277
Troika, 37
Truth, Justice and Reconciliation Commission (TJRC), 59, 61, 66
Turkestan Islamic Party (TIP), 250
Turkic Muslims, 248
Turkish Islamic Republic of Eastern Turkistan (TIRET), 247

U
Unión de Naciones Suramericanas (UNASUR), 278

United Kingdom (UK), 37, 71, 90, 122, 136, 143, 186, 207, 258, 263, 279
United Nations–African Union Mission in Darfur (UNAMID), 42–44
United Nations Development Program (UNDP), 88, 209
United Nations General Assembly (UNGA), 14–18, 26, 31, 55, 56, 63–68, 87, 90, 95, 97, 98, 114, 116, 154, 155, 157–161, 166, 176, 183, 190, 205, 207, 208, 212, 226–232, 235, 238, 260, 261, 263, 289–292, 294, 297
United Nations Human Rights Council (UNHRC), 167, 182–184, 186–189, 257, 258, 261, 271, 279, 283, 290, 295
United Nations Mission in Afghanistan (UNAMA), 198, 204–206, 208, 209
United Nations Operation in Côte d'Ivoire (UNOCI), 108, 114–124, 126, 127
United Nations Security Council (UNSC), 2, 5, 7, 9, 14–19, 21–23, 26, 31, 34, 36–40, 45, 47, 57, 62–64, 66, 69, 71, 72, 87, 91–94, 96, 97, 107–110, 113–127, 135–137, 154, 161–166, 172, 174–177, 179–183, 185–187, 189, 190, 203, 207, 208, 214, 215, 228, 232, 233, 235, 257, 260–264, 282, 285, 286, 292, 295, 296
United States (US), 19, 21, 36–38, 59, 60, 62–64, 70, 71, 86, 90, 94, 118, 136, 137, 159, 161–166, 181, 197–202, 204, 206, 207, 209, 251, 252, 257, 258, 262, 263, 278, 280–285, 292, 295
Universal jurisdiction, 8, 233, 236
Use of force, 5, 7, 14, 27, 34, 63, 64, 66, 88, 95, 96, 107, 108, 119–122, 126, 137, 145, 165, 172, 173, 181, 183–186, 189–191, 225, 231, 274

V

Vocational Education and Training Centres, 252

W

War crimes, 1, 7, 16–18, 39, 85, 86, 89, 94, 96, 111, 121, 127, 145, 154, 157–160, 162, 163, 166, 176, 188, 189, 202, 204–206, 232, 260, 290
War on terror, 86, 201, 206, 207, 212, 246, 251, 252, 263
Welsh, Jennifer, 24, 27, 29, 30, 56, 81, 82, 96–98, 141, 206, 213, 291, 298
Women empowerment, 210
World Summit Outcome Document (WSOD), 17, 34, 47, 65, 94, 120, 161, 176, 181, 190, 226, 227, 255, 256, 260, 289, 294, 296

X

Xinjiang, 165, 246–261, 264, 265, 292, 295, 296
  Xinjiang Uyghur Autonomous Region (XUAR), 9, 245, 248, 252, 255, 258, 264

Y

Yemen, 7, 171–191, 258, 293, 295
Yugoslavia, 23

The manufacturer's authorised representative in the EU is Springer Nature Customer Service Centre GmbH, Europaplatz 3, 69115 Heidelberg, Germany. If you have any concerns regarding our products, please contact ProductSafety@springernature.com

Printed and bound by CPI Group (UK) Ltd, Croydon, CR0 4YY
30/09/2026
02225461-0014